THE ONE SHOW

*Judged To Be Advertising's Best Print, Radio, TV. Volume 14
A Presentation of The One Club for Art & Copy*

THE ONE CLUB
FOR ART & COPY

ROBERT REITZFELD
President

MARY WARLICK
Executive Director

WENDY BECKER
One Show Manager

ROBERT REITZFELD
Designer

RYUICHI MINAKAWA
Art Director

NAOMI MINAKAWA
Layout & Production

MARY WARLICK
Editor

JOHN L. MIMS
KRISTIN OVERSON
Assistant Editors

PUBLISHED AND DISTRIBUTED BY
RotoVision S.A.
Route Suisse 9
CH-1295 Mies
Switzerland
Telephone: 22-755-30-55
Fax: 22-755-40-72

IN ASSOCIATION WITH
The One Club for Art & Copy
3 West 18th Street
New York, NY 10011

Printed and bound in Singapore by
Tien Wah Press, Ltd.

CONTENTS

ROBERT REITZFELD

PRESIDENT'S MESSAGE

This is my third and last year as president of the Board of Directors of The One Club. And, as is customary at this time of year, I have to write a president's message for The One Show annual. Well after the first two go-rounds I wondered what I could possibly write about this time. After all, we'd had another world class group of judges. We'd stayed at the incredible Arizona Biltmore yet again, and I'd written about both before. As I sat pondering my predicament time passed, as time usually does, and before I knew it The One Show happened.

All of a sudden it became clear to me. Sure the judges worked their tushes off, and sure The Biltmore was spectacular, but it all comes down to this: *the work.* THE WORK. That's what this show is and always has been about, *the work.* And the work in this year's show is magnificent. It is sharp. It is focused. It is clear. Like tapping on a piece of fine crystal, it rings true. The work is what makes The One Show the one show. There may be others, but there is no other. There is truly only one. As I've said before, The One Show is advertising's best, choosing advertising's best. If there was any one piece of advice I could give to my successor, it would be this: *Keep up the good work.*

I want to thank Mary and the Board and everyone at the Club for three years of hard work, and for making this an exciting and successful term.

Enjoy the book.

Study the work.

Try and beat it next year.

The Judges

RALPH AMMIRATI
Ammirati & Puris

BOB BARRIE
Fallon McElligott

ALLAN BEAVER

CATHIE CAMPBELL
Ogilvy & Mather

EARL CAVANAH
Scali McCabe Sloves

MARTY COOKE
Chiat/Day/Mojo

MIKE DRAZEN
*Earle Palmer Brown
& Spiro*

JIM DURFEE
*Della Femina
McNamee WCRS*

DAVID FOWLER
Fox Broadcasting

STEVE FRANKFURT
*Frankfurt Gips
Balkind*

BILL HAMILTON
Ogilvy & Mather

HARRY JACOBS
The Martin Agency

ROCHELLE KLEIN
Hal Riney & Partners

BOB KUPERMAN
Chiat/Day/Mojo

MIKE LESCARBEAU
Fallon McElligott

KEN MANDELBAUM
*Mandelbaum
Mooney Ashley*

TOM MESSNER
*Messner Vetere
Berger Carey
Schmetterer*

TOM MONAHAN
*Leonard Monahan Lubars
& Kelly*

CATHI MOONEY
*Mandelbaum
Mooney Ashley*

NANCY RICE
Rice & Rice

DEAN STEFANIDES
Scali McCabe Sloves

MARTY WEISS
*Weiss Whitten
Carroll Stagliano*

Lisa Garrone

Katherine Gates-Keeley

Daniel Geller

Dean Gemmell

Maria Giachino

Dona Gibbs

Frank Ginsberg

Marc Giragossian

Mark A. Girand

Nicole Gladner

Robert Gloddy

Charles Goldman

Bruce Goldstein

Mark Goldstein

Milt Gossett

Bob Gouveia

Kerry Graham

John Greenberg

Debra Greene

Rosalind Greene

Audrey Greenfield

Brian Greenhalgh

Jeff Griffith

Paul B. Groman

Roland Grybauskas

Albert Guerra

Amy Haddad

David T. Halberstadt

Matthew Hallock

Trace Hallowell

Ari Halper

Bryan Hammond

Dean Hanson

Sally Harley

Cabell Harris

Jay Harris

Karen E. Hawkins

Barry Hedge

Bill Heinrich

Kathleen Hennicke

Roy Herbert

Steven Michael Herman

Madelyn Herschorn

Jennifer Hertslet

Dawn Hibbard

Peter Hirsch

Debra Hirschorn

Geoffrey D. Hoffman

Keith Hollander

Jenine Holmes

Julia Hopkins

Laurence Horvitz

Hugh Hough

David Hubbert

Dion Hughes

Mike Hughes

Neal Hughlett

Lisa Hurwitz

Jon Iafeliece

Patrick Ireland

George Jaccoma

Dick Jackson

Harry M. Jacobs, Jr.

Corrin Jacobsen

Mark Jacobson

Suzanne Jaffe

Steven Jamilla

John Jarvis

Mark Jensen

Anthony Johnson

Patrick Johnson

Raymond Johnson

Robert Johnson

Sharla Kahan

Charles Kane

Christina Kane

Meg Kannin

Barbara Ann Kaplan

Woody Kay

Phillip L. Kellogg

Jeffrey Kerrin

Kyu Kim

Eric King

Jon King

Richard Kirshenbaum

Richard Klauber

Stephanie Klein

Joe Knezic

Andrew Knipe

Kathleen Knox

Julian Koenig

Robin S. Konieczny

Ronni Korn

Renee Korus

Jennifer Kosarin

Jean Kostelich

Elias Kotsias

Felice A. Kramer

Kimberly Krause

Ken Krimstein

Helmut Krone

Stewart Krull

Paul Krumenacker

Mike LaMonica

Roberto LaVita

Galina Lachman

Larry Laiken

Christopher J. Landi

Robin G. Landis

Andy Langer

Anthony LaPetri

Peter M. Laurie

Mary Wells Lawrence

Bruce Lee

Dylan Lee

Ruth Lee

Mitchell Lemus

Dany Lee Lennon

David Lentini

Margaret M. Leonard

Mike Lescarbeau

Sharon Lesser

Diane Letulle

Robert Levenson

Susan Levine

Peter Leviten

Alexander Lezhen

Marc Lichtenstein

Ann-Marie Light

David Lindberg

Lisa Lipkin

Katherine H. Lipsitz

Wallace Littman

Margaret Livingston

Roger Livingston

George Lois

Eric J. Lontok

Jessamyn C. Lowy

Margaret Lubalin

Peter Lubalin

David Lubars

Lisa Lurie

Tony Macchia

Murray Macpherson

Maureen Madigan

Laurie Magee

Joel MaHarry

Jamie Mambro

Sara B. Mandel

Frank Mangano

Michael Mangano

Amy Mangel

Bradley Manier

Craig Jarlath Mannion

Howard Margulies

Louis Marino

Richard Marino

John Mariucci

Kenneth J. Markey

Gayle Marshall

Rodd Martin

Ann Mathis

Elizabeth Mauldin

Scott McAfee

Ed McCabe

Kevin McCabe

Clem McCarthy

Lisa McCarthy

Ruth McCarthy

Kevin McCaul

David McCoy

Kit McCracken

Matthew P. McCutchin

Tom McDonnell

Tom McElligott

Laura McFarland-Taylor

Robin McIver

William B. McKenna

Raymond McKinney

Paul McKittrick

Gordon McNenney

Rob McPherson

Mark Mendelis

Ari Merkin

Mario G. Messina

Tom Messner

Lyle Metzdorf

Greg Meyers

Karen Micciantuono

Scott Michelson

Dennis Mickaelian

Michael Migliozzi II

Mark Millar

Don Miller

Josh Miller

Lawrence Miller

John Lane Mims

Jonathan L. Mindell

Marise Mizrahi

Thomas J. Monahan

Deborah Morrison

Regina Morrone

Dina Morrongiello

John Frank Morton

Gregory Motylenski

Jim Mountjoy

William Munch, Jr.

Thomas Muratore, Jr.

Michael Myers

Thomas Nathan

Nelson Nazario

Ted Nelson

Thomas Nelson

David S. Newton

Elizabeth Nice

Steve Nicholas

Jennifer Noble

Dick O'Brien

Vincent O'Dowd

Joe O'Neill

David Oakley

Rip Odell

David Ogilvy

Vicky Oliver

Peter Oravetz

Seymon Ostilly	Mark Rothenberg	Virgil Shutze	Tom Thomas	David Wojdyla
Richard Ostroff	Carolyn A. Rothseid	Fred Siegel	Elsebeth Thomsen	Stefen Wojnarowski
Cele Otnes	Steve Rotterdam	Mark Silveira	Kevin Tiernan	Mark G. Wolf
Maxine Paetro	Michelle Rusgo	Kate Silverberg	Sean Tierney	Paul Wolfe
Elaine Paque	John Russo	Leonard Sirowitz	Todd Tilford	Alan L. Wolk
Azita Panahpour	Nat Russo	Melissa Sison	Maureen Tobin	David Wong
Jeff Pappalardo	Steven Russo	Noelle Sisti	Garrett Tom	James Woo
Jon Parkinson	Mel Rustom	Carolyn Slapikas	Guy Tom	Adrienne T. Wright
Joanne Pateman	Susan Ryan	Mike Slosberg	Daniel Tomaselli	Liani Wunderlich
Michael Pavone	Mike Rylander	Robert Slosberg	Bill Tomlinson	H. Scott Wyatt
Michael Paxton	Paul Safsel	Anne Smith	Lori Travis	Elizabeth Wynn
Andrew Payton	Steve Sage	Linda Leigh Smith	Wendy W. Tripp	Kaori Yamane
Ron Pellegrino	Nelson Salis	Matt Smith	Lynn Troncone	John Young
Steven Penchina	Kenneth Sandbank	Richard Solomon	William Troncone	Timi Young
Tina Perez	Jon Sandhaus	Dennis Soohoo	Michael Tubis	Gerard Young, Jr.
Ellen Perless	Bret Sanford-Chung	John A. Sowinski	Rebecca Tudor-Foley	W. Scott Zacaroli
Christopher Perone	Jon Saunders	Larry Spector	Michael D. Tuggle	Michelle Zadlock
David Piatkowski	Joanne Scannello	Mark Spector	Dion A. Tulloch	Joe Zagorski
Gina Picone	Phil Schatz	Helayne Spivak	Anne Tum Suden	Robert Zaslow
Darlene Pike	Michael Scheiner	Paige Elizabeth St. John	Carol Turturro	Lynette Zator
Donna Pilch	Kimberly Scheremeta	Joseph Staluppi	Ben Urman	Rainer Zierer
Chris Pollock	Glenn Scheuer	Pamela A. Stansel	Victor Valadez	Mark Zukor
Shirley Polykoff	Mark Schimmel	Todd Stanton	Kerri Valentino	
Jill Powers	Scott Schindler	Scott Stefan	Paul Venables	
Tony Pucca	Sy Schreckinger	Dean Stefanides	Matthew Vescovo	
James Pyle	Ruth Schubert	Karl H. Steinbrenner	Thomas Vogel	
Elissa Querze	Michael Schwabenland	Dan Stern	Ronald Wachino	
Brian Quinn	Robert B. Schwartz	Joe Stutts	Nina Wachsman	
G. Ashley Reese	Paul Scolaro	Christine Sullivan	Elaine Wagner	
Robert Reitzfeld	Adam Seifer	E. Ski Sullivan	Judy Wald	
Bill Replogle	Tod Seisser	Luke Sullivan	Marvin Waldman	
Nancy Rice	Sherrie Shamoon	Pamela Sullivan	Allison M. Warren	
Hope Rich	David Shane	James Robert Sullivan, Jr.	Karen Wasserman	
Allen Richardson	Ari Z. Shapiro	Dale Sutphen	Mary Webb	
Anthony Rivello	Gary A. Shaw	Robert Swartz	Les Weiner	
Tim Roan	Gillian C. Shaw	Joe Sweet	Bill Westbrook	
Phyllis Robinson	Steven Shearin	Leslie Sweet	Tom White	
Manny Rodriguez	Michael Shetler	John Sweney	Wendy White	
Courtney Rohan	Brett Shevack	Noriko Takabishi	Connie Whittington	
Gad Romann	Matt Shevin	Arty Tan	Scott Wild	
Ron Rosenfeld	Edward Shieh	Norman Tanen	Richard Wilde	
Elizabeth Rosenthal	Bob Shiffrar	Craig Tanimoto	Steve Williams	
Robert G. Rosenthal	Kelvin L. Shiver	Jay Taub	Emil Wilson	
Steven Rosenthal	Constantine Shoukas	Mike Tesch	Wayne Winfield	
Stuart Rosenwasser	Dean Shoukas	Alfred Tessier	Jennifer Winn	

Gold, Silver & Bronze Awards

021257

The One Show

GOLD, SILVER, & BRONZE AWARDS

CONSUMER NEWSPAPER
OVER 600 LINES: SINGLE

1 GOLD
ART DIRECTOR
Tom Lichtenheld
WRITER
John Stingley
PHOTOGRAPHERS
Paul Miller
Dave Jordano
CLIENT
Jim Beam Brands
AGENCY
Fallon McElligott/
Minneapolis

2 SILVER
ART DIRECTOR
Tom Lichtenheld
WRITER
John Stingley
PHOTOGRAPHERS
Craig Perman
Dave Jordano
CLIENT
Jim Beam Brands
AGENCY
Fallon McElligott/
Minneapolis

Fortunately, every day comes with an evening.

1 GOLD

Fortunately, every day comes with an evening.

GOLD, SILVER, & BRONZE AWARDS

CONSUMER NEWSPAPER OVER 600 LINES: SINGLE

3 BRONZE
ART DIRECTOR
Paul Shearer
WRITER
Rob Jack
CLIENT
Windsor Healthcare
AGENCY
Butterfield Day Devito Hockney/London

4 BRONZE
ART DIRECTOR
Mark Johnson
WRITER
John Stingley
PHOTOGRAPHER
Jeff Zwart
CLIENT
Porsche Cars North America
AGENCY
Fallon McElligott/ Minneapolis

IF YOUR SKIN WAS THIS NEWSPAPER, THE SUN'S RAYS WOULD HAVE REACHED THE SPORTS PAGE.

Don't underestimate the power of the sun's UVA rays. Unlike UVB which burns, UVA passes right through the outer layers of your skin into the deeper living tissue.

The collagen (which gives the skin its elasticity) breaks down, eventually causing it to sag, wrinkle and age.

Help is at hand. Uvistat suncreams and lotions filter out a wider range of harmful UV rays than most other products on the market. The protection starts at Factor 6 and goes up to Factor 30 Ultrablock. (There's also an aftersun and lipscreen.) Naturally, we care for all skin types.

Uvistat is hypo-allergenic, lanolin free and non-greasy.

So the good news is you can let through some of the rays that help you tan and stop the ageing rays at page one.

If you'd like to know more, send the coupon to Uvistat, Windsor Healthcare Ltd, Bracknell, Berks. RG12 4YS.

Name

Address

Postcode

UVISTAT
THE GENTLE ART OF SUN CONTROL.

3 BRONZE

It would seem, in the last year or two, that some astounding things are happening. And while we wouldn't presume to place our new Tiptronic automatic transmission on the same level of import as the crumbling of the Berlin Wall, the news does seem to leave people somewhat stunned.

An automatic in the world's classic performance sports car?

The simple fact is, automatics have always been a good idea. After all, if you don't have to let up on the power, and depress another pedal, you should be able to drive even harder and with greater concentration, right? Professor Porsche has long believed this, and has long led the search for a true high performance version of this concept.

That was the idea when our Type 962 racing car teams developed a clutchless transmission they could shift with a simple flick of a lever. The result was a flurry of championships.

Still, the race drivers had to shift. The car couldn't sense what they wanted to do. For our sports cars, we solved that by combining the gearbox with a sophisticated computer. The result was the Tiptronic; a transmission that lets the driver choose between clutchless manual shifting like the racing 962, or a full automatic that actually "thinks."

In automatic mode, while you watch the road, the Tiptronic watches you. Electronic sensors monitor forward and lateral acceleration;

engine speed; vehicle speed; even the way you are working the throttle. The car determines how aggressively you wish to drive, then chooses the proper shifting style from among five different "maps," adjusting every 30 to 100 milliseconds.

Go into a hard turn with a typical automatic and let off the throttle, and the car will up-shift, reducing your control. The Tiptronic reads the aggressive cornering forces and prevents such an upshift. The same choice you would make if you were shifting.

When you want to take over, slip the shifter through a channel to the manual side. Then just "tip," the shifter forward for upshifts and backward for downshifts. You needn't pause or let off power. In fact, 8 of 10 of our Porsche test-drivers had faster laps with the Tiptronic in manual mode than they had with a straight stick.

A test-drive is so convincing that over 40% of all Carrera 2 Cabriolets now being bought are Tiptronics. Of course, only your own test-drive at an authorized Porsche dealer can actually prove to you how stunning this new concept is. Suffice it to say that Automobile Magazine named it Technology of the Year, saying, "Of all the good ideas that have popped up recently...Tiptronic...will have the most profound effect on future cars."

A Porsche having a profound effect on the future. Well, at least you know some things aren't going to change.

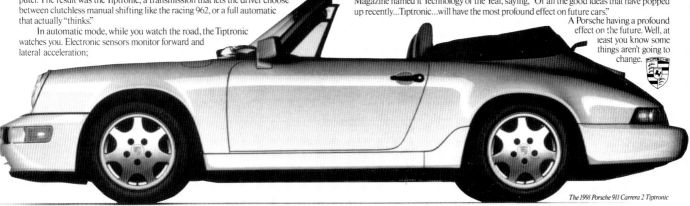

The 1991 Porsche 911 Carrera 2 Tiptronic

The fall of Communism?
Broccoli banned in the White House?
A Porsche 911 with an automatic?

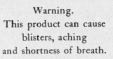

Warning.
This product can cause blisters, aching and shortness of breath.

The damp morning air wheezes in and out of your healthy lungs as if each breath might be your last. The hill you've been climbing seems to get steeper with every step. Was that a twig snapping? Or was it your knee creaking?

Congratulations.

You are enjoying the countryside with the help of an Ordnance Survey map.

Enjoying? Don't we really mean to say enduring? The truth is, with our maps you'll be able to do more than your share of each.

You see, at Ordnance Survey we believe when it comes to travelling through the wilds of Great Britain, the best route to take isn't always the easiest one.

That's why maps like our Landranger Series will not only show you quiet country roads, but also very quiet country pathways.

They'll help you to discover many little known public rights of way, which often lead to some even lesser known picnic spots.

And they'll point out the hill that's over

With Ordnance Survey maps, you can not only find yourself a quiet picnic spot, you can also choose which kind of trees you'd like to be sitting under. You'll discover three different kinds of wood listed in the key of your Ordnance Survey map; coniferous, non-coniferous and mixed. The solid light green here indicates a wood of mixed species.

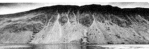

the hill, and has a better view of the lake.

All of which might induce you to expend a little more energy. But is sure to be well worth the effort.

Fair Quiet have I found thee here, and Innocence, thy sister dear,

Mistaken long, I sought you then, in busy companies of men.

Your sacred plants, if here below, only among the plants will grow.

Society is all but rude, to this delicious solitude. - Andrew Marvell

Each weekend, thousands of people escape the crowded, noisy cities of Britain only in order to meet up with each other a few hours away at crowded, noisy tourist spots. [So much for finding delicious solitude].

The problem, of course, is that everybody seems to go to the same few places.

Well, in addition to all the things an Ordnance Survey map can help you find, there are also some things it can help you avoid. Like other people.

With more details on your map, you'll have more places to choose from for a day away. Including many that aren't overrun with your fellow travellers.

Moreover, wherever you decide to go, you can always trust those details will be the most accurate available.

After all, at Ordnance Survey we've had exactly 200 years practice making maps.

The first Ordnance Survey maps were

commissioned in the late 18th century for one reason. To map the South Coast in case of attack from Napoleon.

Naturally, the job had to be done to an exacting standard. And we still create maps today as if someone's life might depend on them.

Although nowadays people use our maps to plan peaceful weekends, instead of battles.

You finally reach the crest of the hill and look up from your aching feet. Suddenly, you find yourself staring out in utter awe across thirty miles of folding hills and valleys.

If you need an incentive to keep yourself striding boldly up a challenging hillside, nothing can beat the views you are bound to encounter when you go out rambling with an Ordnance Survey map. You can gaze down upon ancient stone monuments. Spy way off in the distance what might be the site of King Arthur's first court. Or perch high up above famous medieval battlefields, [seeing them from a safe distance, just as the generals did].

But even if the vista has no known historical significance, you will still be able to enjoy something the road-bound traveller rarely experiences. Nature.

Or what William Wordsworth called 'The anchor of my purest thoughts, the nurse, the guide, the guardian of my heart, and the soul of all my moral being'.

In Wordsworth's Lake District alone, Ordnance Survey maps can guide you to well over a hundred waterfalls, dozens of ancient earthworks and countless historic houses.

One of these houses, in fact, was lived in by a Mrs Heelis, a prosperous lady sheep farmer whose hobby was writing and illustrating stories under her maiden name, *Beatrix Potter*.

It seems Beatrix Potter Heelis enjoyed a quiet walk in the country as much, if not more, than sitting in her Lake District home and writing some of the world's most famous tales for children.

'I loved to wander the Troutbeck Fell,' said the much admired author in a 1942 interview. 'Sometimes I had with me an old sheepdog, more often, I went alone. But I was never lonely. There was company of gentle sheep, and wild flowers, and singing waters.'

Meanwhile, Beatrix had written in a letter to her publisher, 'These d____d little books... I am utterly tired of doing them, and my eyes are wearing out'.

Still, she did do them, and you can see the study she toiled in even today, as long as you know where to look.

You look down one last time at the green and yellow quilt of fields below, and stand to start your descent. This time, you're glad for the extra weight around your middle. Gravity will be doing most of the work.

There are three kinds of walking maps made by Ordnance Survey, and you can get one to cover every field, every wood, every lake and every stream in Britain.

In the more popular touring regions of the countryside, one of our Outdoor Leisure maps will help you know your way around as well as the locals, maybe even better.

If you're planning to travel to other areas, we suggest the Landranger Series or the larger scale Pathfinder Series maps.

Each has dozens of helpful symbols in its key that point out important features you won't find on other maps.

For instance, you'll find three different symbols used just for marking churches, with tower, with spire, without tower or spire.

Are we going overboard? Does anyone really need this much detail in a map?

The Wasdale Head area is often said to be the home of England's highest mountain, deepest lake, smallest church and biggest liar. The latter is almost certainly true, since nearby Santon Bridge hosts an annual 'Biggest Liar in the World' contest, during which about all you can believe is the Ordnance Survey map that shows you the way there.

Well, considering that most of our customers are on foot, yes, we think they do.

Ramblers don't have motorway signs to go by, and need landmarks to find their way.

Landmarks that are mapped accurately, since getting lost on the moors is somewhat more unsettling than getting lost on the M6.

So if you're going to venture out to those places where there might not be anyone to ask for directions, we strongly suggest that

From this distance, it might appear to be a perfect hill for climbing, but a quick look at your Ordnance Survey map will make you think twice. This hillside is marked as being 'scree', which indicates that you'd be in for a nearly impossible slog through deep, loose gravel and dangerous falling rock. Don't worry, we can show you a far better way.

you take along a map from Ordnance Survey.

Because we wouldn't want you to suffer from any more blisters, aching and shortness of breath than you absolutely have to.

Ordnance Survey.
The most detailed maps in the land.

Whose countryside
would you rather see?
Thomas Hardy's?
Or John McAdam's?

Can you imagine curling up with a novel entitled 'Tess of the M4'?

Or how about 'Far from the Madding Service Station'?

Perhaps 'The Mayor of Motorbridge' would have you digging into your wallet next time you're in the bookshop in eager anticipation of a thundering good read? No? We thought not.

Yet sadly, these titles are probably an accurate reflection of the way most of us experience the landscapes that Nature so generously gave our great writers, composers and painters for inspiration.

Why is this? Why do more and more people seem content to limit their enjoyment

of our wondrously beautiful countryside to a sort of high-speed slide show, conveniently framed by a car window?

A show where no sounds are allowed. They might, after all, clash with the pop music coming from the hi-tech dash board.

A show devoid of smells. Own up. Don't your own children turn up their noses at the unusual scents and pungent aromas which characterise the countryside?

Yet this sorry state of affairs needn't exist. The glorious, undulating landscape described in Thomas Hardy's books is there still. And it is waiting for you to discover it in the very same way he did.

Not at 70 miles per hour. Not cushioned in velour. Not protected from the sounds of the first cuckoo and the smell of newly-mown hay by shatterproof glass.

But by leisurely strolling or cycling along the lanes and by-ways of the Dorset countryside he loved.

The only difference between you and Thomas Hardy is that while he knew the area well, you might have to call on the services of an experienced and trusted guide. *Ordnance Survey.*

The subject of our Touring Map and Guide number 15, for example, is ***Wessex***, the Anglo-Saxon kingdom used as a backcloth to Hardy's lyrical stories of rural intrigue.

Like all Ordnance Survey maps, this particular guide is both friend and tutor.

Do you need a telephone? A picnic spot? A camp site? Allow us to give you their precise location.

Are you interested in old battlesites? Historic houses? Or what about those caves you've heard tell are in the area?

Once again, an Ordnance Survey map can show you the way. [We will even furnish you with the date that battle took place].

And though our maps are invaluable in assisting you in getting from the proverbial A to B, they can also greatly enrich the journey.

On the reverse side of most Ordnance Survey Touring Maps is a heading: Where to go and what to see.

This masterpiece of English understatement conceals deep and expert knowledge of

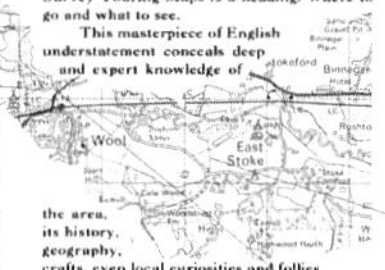

the area, its history, geography, crafts, even local curiosities and follies.

Map 15, for instance, will direct you to the smallest pub in Britain. Or to a monument shaped as a pyramid in honour of a horse that saved its owner's life.

It reveals the whereabouts of the local vineyard that is open to the public. Pin-points the lesser-known Elizabethan manor which has interesting additions by John Nash and gardens landscaped by Capability Brown.

It will also take you on a guided tour of Thomas Hardy's old haunts. The church where Tess was married. The cottage where he wrote Far from the Madding Crowd. The graveyard which, rather gruesomely, contains the author's heart. [*His ashes are interred at Westminster Abbey*].

You will also learn which particular roads Hardy liked to travel and why.

But how, you may be wondering, does Ordnance Survey unearth these little nuggets of information? What drives us to leave no stone, cobble or pebble unturned to bring you these insights into our countryside and its famous inhabitants?

It's quite simple. This year is our two hundredth anniversary.

We drew our first map at the end of the eighteenth century when Britain was faced with invasion by Napoleon. The British Army desperately needed accurate maps of the South Coast and this was duly carried out by the Board of Ordnance.

And while Napoleon failed to show up, the age of the map certainly arrived.

So you see, map-making has been in our blood for a very long time.

To the extent that Ordnance Survey originated practically all the maps of Britain that are around today.

[Indeed most of the maps with other brand names on were originally drawn by us. But don't tell them we told you].

Of course, nowadays our maps are used less for the defence of the realm and more by those people who wish to appreciate it.

If you like going for regular jaunts into the countryside, you might like to take one of our Landranger maps with you next time you head off.

Usually more detailed than our Touring Maps, a Landranger will show you what kind of trees populate your local forests or woodlands, point out particular rock formations in the region and, perhaps most important of all when you're walking in the countryside, where to find a public convenience.

If Landranger maps are for people who like a little information on their rambles, our Pathfinder Series is for those who like a little rambling with their information.

Thomas Hardy enthusiasts following our Pathfinder 1318, for instance, will be able to amble around the outskirts of his beloved Dorchester certain in the knowledge that they are walking on the remains of an old Roman road, that ahead lies ground covered in bracken and that half a mile in front of them there's a natural spring still burbling away.

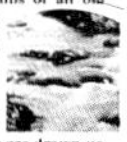

Coming into the main part of town, the same narrow streets Hardy meandered along are drawn up in such detail that even houses and their boundaries are clearly marked.

Do we really need to provide you with this degree of accuracy? We think so.

Every day the face of our towns, villages and countryside changes. Sometimes it is imperceptible. At other times, when property boundaries are moved or roads are added, the changes actually reshape our country.

The better your knowledge of these changes, the greater your appreciation will be of what the British countryside in its many guises has to offer.

Then, who knows? Perhaps one day, with the guidance of Ordnance Survey, you may get to know Wessex almost as well as Thomas Hardy did.

Even see it through his eyes. Feel what he felt when he wrote '*Wessex Heights*'.

'There are some heights in Wessex, shaped as if by kindly hand

For thinking, dreaming, dying on, and at crises when I stand,

Say, on Ingpen Beacon eastward, or on Wylls-Neck westwardly,

I seem where I was before my birth, and after death may be."

Now, isn't that the kind of countryside you want to see?

Ordnance Survey.

The most detailed maps in the land.

Ever heard of Cull-peppers
Dish, Turners Puddle,
Throop, or Yearlings Bottom?
No? Good.

The door of the tiny disused church at *Turners Puddle* lies ajar, offering an invitation that hasn't been taken up for years.

Inside, thick walls that have patiently absorbed every sermon since early in the 12th century, stoically fulfil their one remaining duty: that of hotel to scores of barn owls, swallows and swifts.

Outside, the shimmering new foliage advances mercilessly on the exhausted, old edifice, led by that silent strangler, ivy.

Further along the way, the village of *Throop*, nestled in slanting meadows, goes quietly about its business. Which, in this part of the world, is no business of yours, thank you very much.

A short distance ahead, *Yearlings Bottom* lays out a welcoming carpet of blue bells to any person who inadvertantly stumbles upon its whereabouts.

While over at *Cull-peppers Dish*, Alice-in-Wonderland trees, gnarled and haughty, reach upwards seeking the light.

Where are all these magical-sounding places? Do they actually exist? Or are they just figments of a romantic imagination?

Yes, they certainly do exist. They're huddled together in the east of Dorset, not that many miles off the beaten track.

That you haven't heard of these places shouldn't really surprise you. Rather, your ignorance of these evocative names should persuade you that there are indeed some backwaters left to discover in these crowded islands.

But before you set off in search of lonely churches, unassuming villages and untrodden woodland, it might be wise to seek directions.

And who better to guide you on your travels than Ordnance Survey?

After all, our intrepid surveyors have measured and recorded detailed descriptions of every yard of Britain.

A rare diligence that has found its reward in the reputation our maps enjoy not only with serious ramblers but with the many people who just like going for a walk, usually after Sunday lunch.

And while there is always a certain excitement in wandering through uncharted territory, so to speak, following a map brings other joys.

Cast an eye over our Landranger map 194, for example. It's like reading a detailed history of the Dorchester and Weymouth area of Dorset.

Cold, eerie castles dating back to the Iron Age await your inspection. Sturdy Norman bridges sit astride tumbling rivers. Even the dismantled railway track, untended but still bursting with life, has a story to tell. Map 194 will have you striding confidently towards them all.

Still not tired? Cardio-vascular muscle still pumping? Then, we'll keep going. The very same map will soon have you

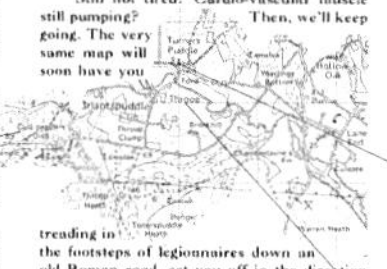

treading in the footsteps of legionnaires down an old Roman road, set you off in the direction of one of Dorset's only remaining windmills and, as you've been so good about taking exercise, it will even identify a public house where you can rest for a while and enjoy a picturesque view.

And as you saunter along, you will undoubtedly come across other unfamiliar, slightly odd names.

Nettlecombe Tout. Moots Copse. Droop. Well Bottom Down. Each place conjures up a history worthy of investigation.

When were they named? Who named them? Romans in the 1st century? Saxons in the 7th? Was it the Normans? Or simply local farmers with a mischievous way with words?

Your imagination suitably stirred, you might well decide to plough on, and enter Puddletown Forest to see what it has to offer.

Again, you will find Landranger map 194 a useful and entertaining companion.

Employing easy-to-read symbols, it indicates nature trails, a meandering forest walk and the actual path the Romans took along the south of the forest.

It points out two car parks, gives you two picnic sites to choose from, directs you to Thomas Hardy's birthplace and even tells you which types of tree you are likely to pass along the way.

Of course, there are many people who don't require this degree of detail in order to appreciate the countryside.

For them, Ordnance Survey produces many Touring Maps and Guides which often include useful information and interesting historical notes about the area on the reverse side of the map.

Touring Map 15, for example, allows the bicyclist or car driver to plot a course through *Wessex*, the ancient Saxon kingdom, which took in much of Dorset, Hampshire and a large part of Wiltshire.

With it, you can plan fascinating trips to go on like 'The Ancient World Tour'. This journey of some 88 miles connects some of the most ancient and mysterious sites in Great Britain.

And, like any self-respecting guide, it explains the history and significance of the place you're visiting.

How many years did it take to construct Stonehenge? Who carved the first White Horse into the chalk slopes of Bratton Hill? Why should those with a superstitious nature stay well away from West Kennet Long Barrow on Midsummers Day? Touring Map 15 will enlighten you on these subjects and, indeed, many others.

You will also receive guided tours of Bath and Salisbury, be treated to delicious snippets of information about the traditional food and drink available in the region, and even directed towards an inn built in 1397 that still serves the local fare.

To our surveyors, intimate knowledge of facts such as these is all part of a day's work. Or, to be absolutely accurate [and we absolutely have to be] it's all part of two hundred years' work.

For 1991 is the two hundredth anniversary of our very first map.

It was drawn in 1791 for the British Army who believed that Napoleon was about to cross the Channel.

The top brass decided our soldiers might put up more of a show if they all knew precisely where they were and, should they need to move their position, how long it might take them to get from one place to another.

In the event, this major advance in military thinking went untested as Napoleon and his army stayed at home.

Nevertheless, highly-detailed maps of the South Coast were drawn up by the Board of Ordnance [*later to become Ordnance Survey*] and the rest, as they say, is cartography.

The next time you are thinking of embarking on a journey to the countryside, perhaps you should stop by your local bookstore and purchase one of our maps or guides before you set off.

Hopefully, you will then be able to appreciate the unknown landscapes, villages and historic buildings that are just sitting patiently awaiting your visit.

And while you may not know any of them, at least you now have someone who can effect an introduction: Ordnance Survey.

Ordnance Survey.

The most detailed maps in the land.

5 GOLD

IF YOU'RE PAYING OVER $100 FOR A DRESS SHIRT, MAY WE SUGGEST A JACKET TO GO WITH IT?

With men's and women's designer clothes selling at 40-70% off everyday, you'd be crazy to shop anywhere else. Elizabeth, East Hanover, Paramus, Wayne & New York City.

DAFFY'S
CLOTHES THAT WILL MAKE YOU, NOT BREAK YOU.

6 SILVER

IF HE HAD SPENT LESS ON THE SUIT, HE COULD HAVE SPENT MORE ON THE HAT.

Come into Daffy's this weekend and find something Columbus never could. 40-80% off designer clothes. Elizabeth, East Hanover, Paramus, Wayne & New York City.

DAFFY'S
CLOTHES THAT WILL MAKE YOU, NOT BREAK YOU.

GOLD, SILVER, & BRONZE
AWARDS

CONSUMER NEWSPAPER
OVER 600 LINES:
CAMPAIGN

7 BRONZE
ART DIRECTOR
Simon Bowden
WRITER
Ed McCabe
ILLUSTRATORS
Milton Glaser
Dayal
CLIENT
Coleman Natural Meats
AGENCY
McCabe & Company/
New York

REMEMBER HOW GREAT
BEEF USED TO TASTE?

No you don't.

Way back, before man came along and started messing with it, all beef had a taste as clean, pure and natural as the Coleman brand. But that was a long, long time ago.

That was back before hormones were used to accelerate the growth and fattening of beef cattle. Before the administering of antibiotics became frequent and commonplace. Before any scientific or technological "breakthroughs" could come between you and the taste of beef at its most basic, natural and delicious.

Today, the only thing standing between your family and that natural beef taste is a few more cents per pound. A small price to pay for a trip back in time to a taste you'll never forget.

Coleman Natural Meats, Inc., 1-800-442-8666. 5140 Race Court, Denver, Colorado 80216.

WHERE TO BUY
COLEMAN NATURAL BEEF

★ Purity Supreme ★
Heartland ★ Cape Ann Markets
Angelos ★ Shubes Markets ★

RAISED WITHOUT HORMONES OR ANTIBIOTICS

100% PURE AND NATURAL

COLEMAN
NATURAL BEEF

MEL COLEMAN, PROP.

RAISED AT THE HEAD OF THE CREEK

MAN HASN'T MESSED WITH IT.

They grazed these special cattle up high in the mountains, way up at the head of the creek, where the water is clean and pure. They fed them on rangeland untainted by pesticides or chemical fertilizers, kept them off drugs

remark on how "clean" it tastes. Others have described the experience as not unlike quitting a lifelong smoking habit and only then truly tasting something for the first time.

Mel Coleman finds all the

beef, in its pure and natural form, is one of the most nutritionally perfect foods there is.

Coleman Natural Beef is high in protein and, in sensibly-sized servings, surprisingly low in fat. And even if you've reduced the amount of beef you eat, all the more reason to give Coleman Natural Beef a try. If you've made beef into an occasional treat, why not treat yourself to the best?

GOOD NEWS, BAD NEWS. First the good. You shouldn't have to search high and low to find Coleman Natural Meat. Many quality-conscious supermarkets have started to carry Coleman in addition to their

cattle put on as much as 3½ lbs. per day, a large proportion of which is fat you don't want anyway. Coleman beef is always *naturally* lean and tender.

If you're ever out near

"WE'RE SO SURE YOU'LL THINK
OUR BEEF IS BETTER
WE BET THE RANCH ON IT."

— The Coleman Family

Since back before Colorado gained its statehood, the Colemans have had their boots in stirrups and their minds on meat. Cattlemen, head to toe, since 1875.

For close on a century, the Coleman family sold calves to cattle feeders who'd take Coleman's calves, fatten 'em up as fast as they could and rush them to market.

As science and technology "advanced," so did the artificial nature of beef production. Growth hormones, not unlike the steroids employed by athletes, came into common use. Cattle were given antibiotics just to prevent illness, rather than treat it. And even their feed was laced with antibiotics.

The Colemans never cottoned to these new-fangled notions. They set aside a few head, and raised them their own way. The way their collective conscience told them was best.

EATING LESS MEAT? With many families cutting down on their consumption of red meat, it may strike you as an odd time for the Coleman family to be promoting their beef. Not at all. The Colemans believe that

find it, you'll have to pay more for it. That's because it costs more to raise pure beef than the adulterated kind. In their final months of feeding, for example, Coleman cattle gain only 2¾ lbs. per day. Chemical

who bet the whole family's future on your finding it worth every extra penny you pay.

Coleman Natural Meats, Inc. General Offices: 5140 Race Court, Denver, Colorado 80216 1-800-442-8666

LESS FAT, MORE FLAVOR. In just a few years, Coleman Natural Beef has become the largest-selling brand of beef in natural food stores. People who care deeply about the wholesomeness of the food they eat have been attracted to a product that's totally free of chemical additives and has up to 25% less fat than conventionally raised beef.

Mostly, though, they've been won over by the taste. Folks trying Coleman beef for the first time invariably

MAN HASN'T MESSED WITH IT.

TASTE THE BEEF THAT
ESCAPED THE MEDDLESOME
HAND OF MAN.

Once upon a time, all beef tasted pure and natural like the Coleman Natural brand. But that was a long time ago, back before science and technology reared their heads.

That was back when beef was untouched by humans who, being human, don't know how to leave well enough alone.

Today, most beef cattle are raised with man's unflinching eye turned more toward profit than palatability. From birth,

many are shot with hormones to speed their growth. It is common practice to give cattle regular doses of antibiotics to ward off disease.

There is no clinical proof that eating

Mel Coleman, head of the Coleman clan and the man who pioneered natural beef

this kind of beef is bad for you. But plain common sense should tell you that, at the very least, it ain't natural.

Now we know "natural" is the most overused and near meaningless word in advertising lingo today.

But when it comes to the Coleman family and the beef we raise, "natural" isn't a word, it's a mission. We Colemans have been involved in the rearing of natural beef since 1875. That's a long-term commitment.

In recent years, we've grown into a totally integrated beef producer that controls every aspect of product quality from conception to consumption, enforcing rigorous standards every step of the way.

No Coleman cattle are given hormone or steroid implants ever.

No Coleman cattle are treated with antibiotics, either by injection or through feeding, ever.

All feeds are regularly tested for chemical

residues and rejected if any traces are found.

All Coleman beef cuts are trimmed of fat to tighter standards than conventional beef. Some cuts are as much as 40% lower in fat.

One of the results of this total dedication: Coleman has surged to become the largest selling brand of beef in America's natural food stores, where customers are fanatically finicky about the wholesomeness of the food they eat.

Another result is the taste of the beef itself.

Coleman beef is lean without any loss of tenderness, never stringy. It's juicy without tasting fatty.

In fact, it's so clean, unadulterated and honest-tasting that once you've tried it, there will be no going back to anything less.

Good beef isn't bad for you

Especially if your family is eating less beef than it used to. When it's Coleman, less is more.

For more information write to: Coleman Natural Meats, Inc., 5140 Race Court, Denver, Colorado 80216.

MAN HASN'T MESSED WITH IT.

CONSUMER NEWSPAPER 600 LINES OR LESS: SINGLE

8 GOLD
ART DIRECTOR
Tom Lichtenheld
WRITER
John Stingley
PHOTOGRAPHERS
Ave Bonar
Dave Jordano
CLIENT
Jim Beam Brands
AGENCY
Fallon McElligott/
Minneapolis

9 SILVER
ART DIRECTOR
Bob Barrie
WRITER
Luke Sullivan
PHOTOGRAPHER
Jim Arndt
CLIENT
Porsche Cars North America
AGENCY
Fallon McElligott/
Minneapolis

10 BRONZE
ART DIRECTOR
Michael Kadin
WRITER
Jim Garaventi
CLIENT
The Narragansett
AGENCY
Leonard Monahan Lubars &
Kelly/Providence

Fortunately, every day comes with an evening.

WINDSOR CANADIAN

8 GOLD

Costs an arm ~~and a leg.~~

Because of a special factory incentive program designed to reduce your tax burden, the Porsche 928 is now available at substantial savings from your participating New York area Porsche dealer. But for a limited time only. So shake a leg and come in for a test drive.

PORSCHE

WE WROTE THE
BOOK ON FASHION.
UNFORTUNATELY,
IT ENDS WITH
CHAPTER 11.

At our going out of business sale you'll save
80% on European fashions. Au-revoir and Arrivederci.

the narragansett

SAVE UP TO 80% DURING OUR GOING OUT OF BUSINESS SALE.

(Oh sure, now you'll come in.)

The narragansett

AT 50-80% OFF
THE ONLY THING
YOU CAN'T SAVE
IS OUR STORE.

The dresses are going. The skirts are going.
The fixtures are going. Shouldn't you be going too?

the narragansett

WE WROTE THE
BOOK ON FASHION.
UNFORTUNATELY,
IT ENDS WITH
CHAPTER 11.

At our going out of business sale you'll save
80% on European fashions. Au-revoir and Arrivederci.

the narragansett

This is the spoiler.

This is not.

Special terms until March 31st.

We've just added one more feature to the Porsche Carrera to make it go faster: special rates. Thanks to new low lease and financing rates from Chase Manhattan you can now drive a new Carrera for less than you ever imagined. Call 1-800-843-3748 for the dealer nearest you. True, there are lease offers out there on other cars. But once you drive a Porsche, it'll spoil you for anything else. **PORSCHE**

Now the only thing between you and a Porsche is a very well engineered door.

Special terms until May 31st.

If you've ever dreamed of a new Porsche, opportunity is knocking very loud. Thanks to very special lease and finance rates through Chase Manhattan, combined with our traditionally high resale value,* the cost of driving a new Porsche Carrera may never be lower. For details, call 1-800-843-3748 for the dealer nearest you.

But act soon, because this very well engineered window of opportunity is closing on May 31st. **PORSCHE**®

Everyone has leases. But no one else has Porsches.

Special terms until March 31st.

Thanks to special lease and financing rates from Chase Manhattan, you can now drive a genuine Porsche Carrera for less than many mere cars. So the classic high performance sportscar you've always dreamed of could well become reality. Call 1-800-843-3748 for the dealer nearest you. You may find other attractive rates. But you certainly won't find a more attractive car. **PORSCHE**®

GOLD, SILVER, & BRONZE AWARDS

CONSUMER NEWSPAPER 600 LINES OR LESS: CAMPAIGN

13 BRONZE
ART DIRECTOR
Jeff Hopfer
WRITER
Todd Tilford
PHOTOGRAPHER
Richard Reens
CLIENT
Tabu Lingerie
AGENCY
The Richards Group/Dallas

REMEMBER, MEDICAL EXPERTS
RECOMMEND INCREASING YOUR HEARTRATE
AT LEAST THREE TIMES A WEEK.

Crossroads Center, 183 & Burnet, 452-TABU

LINGERIE

ACTUALLY, THERE IS ONE
KNOWN CURE FOR SNORING.

JUST FOR THE RECORD, BASEBALL
ISN'T AMERICA'S FAVORITE PASTIME.

Crossroads Center, 183 & Burnet, 452-TABU

LINGERIE

Crossroads Center, 183 & Burnet, 452-TABU

TABU
LINGERIE

GOLD, SILVER, & BRONZE AWARDS

**CONSUMER MAGAZINE B/W
1 PAGE OR SPREAD: SINGLE**

14 GOLD
ART DIRECTOR
Gary Goldsmith
WRITER
Ty Montague
PHOTOGRAPHER
Steve Hellerstein
CLIENT
Everlast
AGENCY
Goldsmith/Jeffrey, New York

15 SILVER
ART DIRECTOR
Bob Brihn
WRITER
Bruce Bildsten
PHOTOGRAPHER
Hal Crocker
CLIENT
Porsche Cars North America
AGENCY
*Fallon McElligott/
Minneapolis*

16 BRONZE
ART DIRECTORS
Cheryl Heller
Nick Kaldenbaugh
WRITER
Bill Weithas
PHOTOGRAPHER
Pamela Hanson
CLIENT
Loehmann's
AGENCY
*Wells Rich Greene BDDP/
New York*

**TRADE B/W 1 PAGE OR
SPREAD: SINGLE**

14 GOLD
ART DIRECTOR
Gary Goldsmith
WRITER
Ty Montague
PHOTOGRAPHER
Steve Hellerstein
CLIENT
Everlast
AGENCY
Goldsmith/Jeffrey, New York

This is not one of those scented ads. Good thing.

1968 Porsche First

1970 Porsche First

1971 Porsche First

1973 Porsche First

1975 Porsche First

1977 Porsche First

1978 Porsche First

1979 Porsche First

1980 Porsche First

1981 Porsche First

1982 Porsche First

1983 Porsche First

1984 Porsche First

1985 Porsche First

1986 Porsche First

1987 Porsche First

1989 Porsche First

1991 Porsche First

Like clockwork, for 18 out of the last 23 years, a Porsche has emerged victorious at the 24 Hours of Daytona IMSA Camel GT endurance race. In fact, this year, with record-breaking drivers like Hurley Haywood piloting the winning Joest Blaupunkt Porsche 962C, we took three of the first five places.

True, over the years the drivers have changed, and the cars have evolved, but in the world's toughest endurance races no car has endured like Porsche. Our perseverence has earned us 286 IMSA victories—twice as many as any other manufacturer. As well as 17 overall victories at the 12 Hours of Sebring, 12 overall victories at LeMans, and 27 World Championships.

And unlike so many other carmakers, we put the same technology we develop for our race cars into our passenger cars. Our first car to win at LeMans in 1951 was based on our 356 street car. Just as today the engine in our winning car at Daytona is based on the same flat six configuration we use in our new 911 Carreras.

You see, at Porsche—as at Daytona—the important things never really change. Just the decals.

PORSCHE

For 23 years about the only thing that's changed at Daytona are the decals.

"A fashion victim is someone who pays retail."

Pity those who have yet to learn, Loehmann's has the latest styles, incredible fashions, designer designs, and career clothes at the guaranteed lowest prices in town. But then again, their ignorance is your bliss. Returns for store credit. MasterCard, Visa, and Discover accepted.

Loehmann's
The most of the best for the least.

Bronx: Riverdale-Kingsbridge · Brooklyn · Queens · Long Island · Westchester · Connecticut · New Jersey · For information call (212) 409-4721.

GOLD, SILVER, & BRONZE AWARDS

CONSUMER MAGAZINE COLOR 1 PAGE OR SPREAD: SINGLE

17 GOLD
ART DIRECTOR
Gary Goldsmith
WRITER
Ty Montague
PHOTOGRAPHER
Steve Hellerstein
CLIENT
Everlast
AGENCY
Goldsmith/Jeffrey, New York

18 SILVER
ART DIRECTOR
Tom Lichtenheld
WRITER
John Stingley
PHOTOGRAPHERS
Jim Arndt
Dave Jordano
CLIENT
Jim Beam Brands
AGENCY
Fallon McElligott/ Minneapolis

19 BRONZE
ART DIRECTOR
Tom Lichtenheld
WRITER
John Stingley
PHOTOGRAPHERS
Craig Perman
Dave Jordano
CLIENT
Jim Beam Brands
AGENCY
Fallon McElligott/ Minneapolis

TRADE COLOR 1 PAGE OR SPREAD: SINGLE

17 BRONZE
ART DIRECTOR
Gary Goldsmith
WRITER
Ty Montague
PHOTOGRAPHER
Steve Hellerstein
CLIENT
Everlast
AGENCY
Goldsmith/Jeffrey, New York

Made under license by U.S.A. Classic, Inc. from trademark owner "Everlast."

This is not one of those scented ads. Good thing.

Fortunately, every day comes with an evening.

Fortunately, every day comes with an evening.

The 30-minute workout that reduces your heart rate instead of raising it.

Imagine a workout that psyches you up without tiring you out. Imagine that instead of pushing and pulling your muscles, you gently stretch them out. Then you use our breathing and meditation techniques to fill yourself with energy and to focus your mind. This can help you be prepared to effectively handle the stress you feel every day.

For classes or instructional materials, just call The American Yoga Association at (800) 226-5859, or write 513 South Orange Avenue, Sarasota, Florida 34236.

Find out how 30 minutes of Yoga each day can help you feel better about life.

AMERICAN
YOGA
ASSOCIATION

A free introductory course in *Yoga*.

(*1. Breathe in.*)

(*2. Breathe out.*)

There. Feeling better already? You see, Yoga is about relaxing. There are many Yoga breathing exercises to help you cope with stress, feel refreshed and increase your energy.

And breathing techniques are just the beginning. Through stretching exercises and relaxing meditation, you can learn to slow down and feel more in control of your everyday stresses.

The American Yoga Association, a non-profit, educational organization, takes 5,000-year-old, proven relaxation methods and applies them to our modern, fast-paced world. In some very practical ways.

Find out what Yoga can do for you.

Contact us for information on classes, literature or audio and video materials. Call (216) 371-0078 or write 3130 Mayfield Road, Cleveland, Ohio 44118.

Then sit back. Take a deep breath. And see how good it will feel to know how to handle the stresses in your life.

AMERICAN
YOGA
ASSOCIATION

One of the typically bizarre positions you'll find yourself in when you practice *Yoga*.

If you don't find yourself in a relaxed position very often, try Yoga. Contrary to what you might think, Yoga isn't about tying yourself up in bizarre pretzel shapes. It's about relaxing.

There are simple breathing techniques, stretching exercises and a relaxing meditation you can do at home or even at the office to prepare you to deal with the stresses you face.

The American Yoga Association, a non-profit, educational organization, takes 5,000-year-old, proven relaxation methods and applies them to our modern, fast-paced world.

Find out what Yoga can do for you. Contact us for information on classes, literature or audio and video materials. Call (216) 371-0078 or write 3130 Mayfield Road, Cleveland, Ohio 44118.

The word Yoga actually means to join together. So if you've ever been pulled in a dozen directions at once, try Yoga. It could put you in a better position.

AMERICAN
YOGA
ASSOCIATION

GOLD, SILVER, & BRONZE AWARDS

CONSUMER MAGAZINE COLOR 1 PAGE OR SPREAD: CAMPAIGN

21 GOLD
ART DIRECTOR
Tom Lichtenheld
WRITER
Bruce Bildsten
PHOTOGRAPHERS
Andreas Burz
Daniel Jouanneau
Shawn Michienzi
CLIENT
Porsche Cars A.G.
AGENCY
*Fallon McElligott/
Minneapolis*

Product benefits:

Too fast.
Doesn't blend in.
People will talk.

PORSCHE

You may not have one
in your garage, but
you probably have one
parked in your mind.

©1991 PORSCHE A.G.

PORSCHE

Old cars go to scrap yards.
Old Porsches go to museums.

OUR FIRST PORSCHE: 1948 TYPE 356 ROADSTER.

PORSCHE

Fortunately, every day comes with an evening.

Fortunately, every day comes with an evening.

Fortunately, every day comes with an evening.

GOLD, SILVER, & BRONZE AWARDS

CONSUMER MAGAZINE COLOR 1 PAGE OR SPREAD: CAMPAIGN

23 BRONZE
ART DIRECTOR
Dean Hanson
WRITER
Phil Hanft
PHOTOGRAPHERS
Mark Coppos
Shawn Michienzi
CLIENT
Ralston Purina/
Nature's Course
AGENCY
Fallon McElligott/
Minneapolis

Too many artificial colors in your dog's food?

There are no artificial colors in our new, natural dog food.
No artificial flavors.
No artificial preservatives.
No meat by-products.

None of that stuff. Only real chicken and real beef. And whole grains certified grown without chemical pesticides. And the natural sweetness

of molasses. All the good things. Nature's Course Brand Dog Food. Natural ingredients plus essential vitamins and minerals.

Too many pesticides in your dog's food?

Our new, natural dog food uses whole grains certified grown without chemical pesticides. And only real chicken and real beef. And only the natural sweetness of molasses. All the good things.

No artificial preservatives. No artificial flavors. No artificial colors. No meat by-products.

None of that stuff. Nature's Course Brand Dog Food. Natural ingredients plus essential vitamins and minerals.

Too many pesticides in your dog's food?

Our new, natural dog food uses whole grains certified grown without chemical pesticides. And only real chicken and real beef. And only the natural sweetness of molasses. All the good things.

No artificial preservatives. No artificial flavors. No artificial colors. No meat by-products.

None of that stuff. Nature's Course Brand Dog Food. Natural ingredients plus essential vitamins and minerals.

GOLD, SILVER, & BRONZE AWARDS

THOUSANDS STILL IN STOCK.
We carry the most popular campaign buttons in history. And then some. **POLITICAL AMERICANA**

25 SILVER

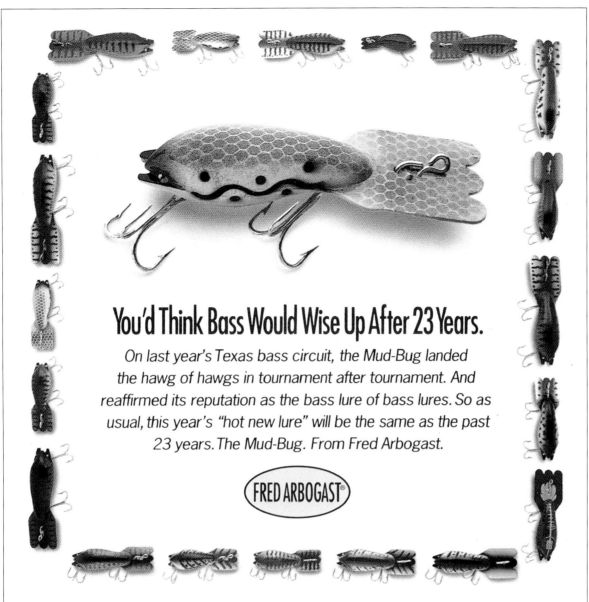

You'd Think Bass Would Wise Up After 23 Years.

On last year's Texas bass circuit, the Mud-Bug landed the hawg of hawgs in tournament after tournament. And reaffirmed its reputation as the bass lure of bass lures. So as usual, this year's "hot new lure" will be the same as the past 23 years. The Mud-Bug. From Fred Arbogast.

FRED ARBOGAST®

ACTUALLY WORN BY PRESIDENT FORD.

We sell authentic campaign buttons at prices that won't dent your wallet. **POLITICAL AMERICANA**

THOUSANDS STILL IN STOCK.

We carry the most popular campaign buttons in history. And then some. **POLITICAL AMERICANA**

Gold, Silver, & Bronze Awards

Outdoor: Single

29 GOLD
ART DIRECTOR
Nick Cohen
WRITER
Ty Montague
PHOTOGRAPHER
Ilan Rubin
CLIENT
Tiny Mythic Theatre Company
AGENCY
Mad Dogs & Englishmen/ New York

30 SILVER
ART DIRECTOR
Cabell Harris
WRITER
Dion Hughes
PHOTOGRAPHER
Rick Dublin
CLIENT
NYNEX Information Resources
AGENCY
Chiat/Day/Mojo, New York

Frankenstein. The Musical. Feb 22-Mar 10. Ohio Theatre.

TINY MYTHIC THEATRE COMPANY PRESENTS A MUSICAL ADAPTATION OF MARY SHELLEY'S CLASSIC · FRANKENSTEIN: THE MODERN PROMETHEUS OHIO THEATRE 66 WOOSTER ST SOHO NYC FEB 22 - MAR 10 8PM $10 ($6 STUDENTS/SNRS) RES: (212) 274 9807

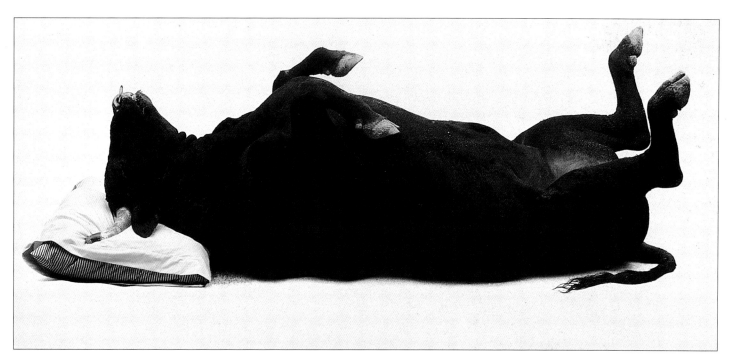

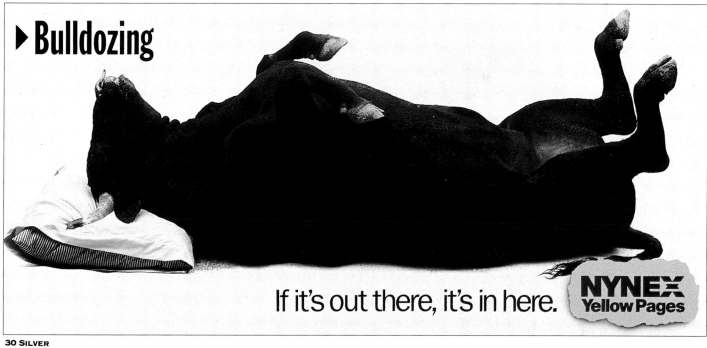

▶ Bulldozing

If it's out there, it's in here. **NYNEX Yellow Pages**

GOLD, SILVER, & BRONZE AWARDS

OUTDOOR: SINGLE

31 BRONZE
ART DIRECTOR
Cabell Harris
WRITER
Dion Hughes
PHOTOGRAPHER
Rick Dublin
CLIENT
NYNEX Information Resources
AGENCY
Chiat/Day/Mojo, New York

▶Steel Wool

If it's out there, it's in here.

**GOLD, SILVER, & BRONZE
AWARDS**

OUTDOOR: CAMPAIGN

32 GOLD
ART DIRECTOR
Cabell Harris
WRITER
Dion Hughes
PHOTOGRAPHER
Rick Dublin
CLIENT
*NYNEX Information
Resources*
AGENCY
Chiat/Day/Mojo, New York

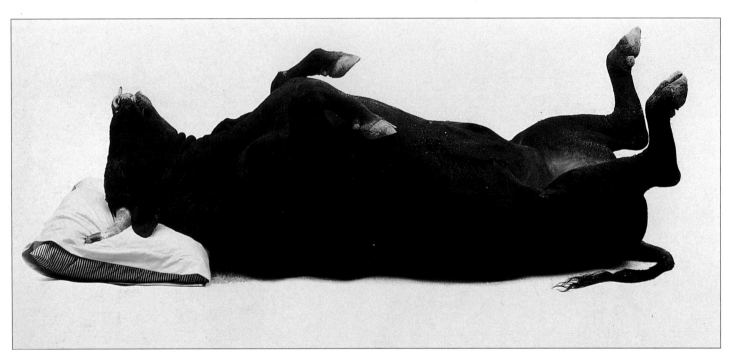

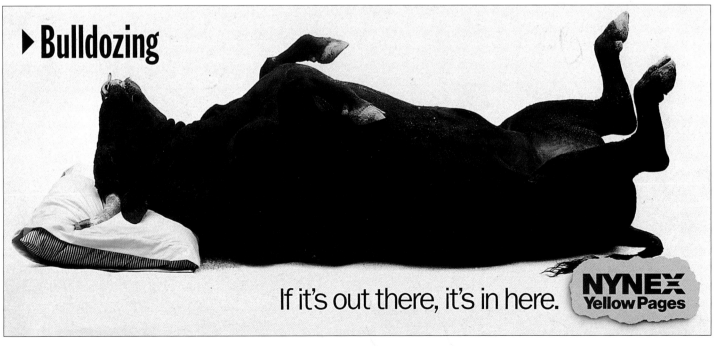

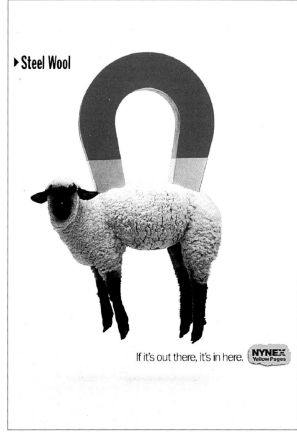

▶ **Steel Wool**

If it's out there, it's in here. **NYNEX** Yellow Pages

▶ **Hair Tinting**

If it's out there, it's in here. **NYNEX** Yellow Pages

OUTDOOR: CAMPAIGN

33 SILVER
ART DIRECTOR
Michael Wilde
WRITER
Jim Noble
CLIENT
The Red and White Fleet
AGENCY
*Goldberg Moser O'Neill/
San Francisco*

EVERY AMUSEMENT PARK HAS A THEME, OURS JUST HAPPENS TO BE CORRUPTION, BRUTALITY AND MURDER.

ALCATRAZ
The Red And White Fleet Departs Hourly From Pier 41

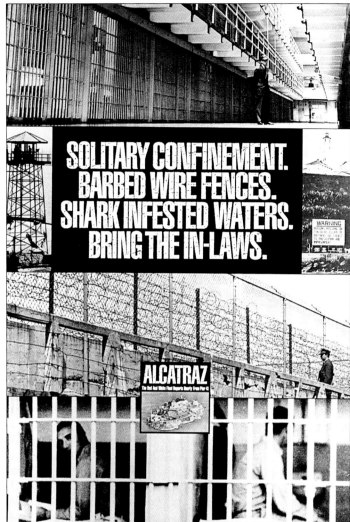

SOLITARY CONFINEMENT. BARBED WIRE FENCES. SHARK INFESTED WATERS. BRING THE IN-LAWS.

ALCATRAZ
The Red And White Fleet Departs Hourly From Pier 41

OUTDOOR: CAMPAIGN

34 BRONZE
ART DIRECTOR
Cabell Harris
WRITER
Dion Hughes
PHOTOGRAPHER
Rick Dublin
CLIENT
NYNEX Information Resources
AGENCY
Chiat/Day/Mojo, New York

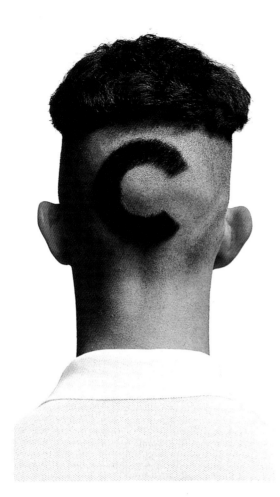
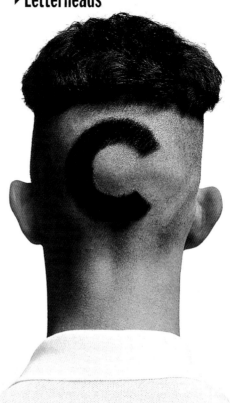

If it's out there, it's in here. NYNEX Yellow Pages

▶ Honeycomb

If it's out there, it's in here. NYNEX Yellow Pages

GOLD, SILVER, & BRONZE AWARDS

TRADE B/W 1 PAGE OR
SPREAD: SINGLE

35 SILVER
ART DIRECTOR
Bob Brihn
WRITER
Doug de Grood
PHOTOGRAPHER
Joe Lampe
CLIENT
Fallon McElligott
AGENCY
*Fallon McElligott/
Minneapolis*

36 SILVER
ART DIRECTOR
Joe Shands
WRITERS
*Mark Waggoner
Jim Carey*
PHOTOGRAPHER
Doug Petty
CLIENT
The Oregonian
AGENCY
Cole & Weber/Portland

We might not make as much as those New York creatives, but look what we get for the money.

PAT BURNHAM'S HOUSE
$59,900

PHIL HANFT'S HOUSE
$43,700

DEAN HANSON'S HOUSE
$51,900

BOB BARRIE'S HOUSE
$39,500

SUSAN GRIAK'S HOUSE
$49,900

JARL OLSEN'S HOUSE
$28,900

MARK JOHNSON'S HOUSE
$46,000

BRUCE BILDSTEN'S HOUSE
$45,900

TOM LICHTENHELD'S HOUSE
$58,500

LUKE SULLIVAN'S HOUSE
$42,000

JOHN STINGLEY'S HOUSE
$50,200

CAROL HENDERSON'S HOUSE
$38,900

MIKE GIBBS' HOUSE
$36,800

ARTY TAN'S HOUSE
$48,300

MIKE FAZENDE'S HOUSE
$23,400

BILL MILLER'S HOUSE
$53,700

FALLON McELLIGOTT

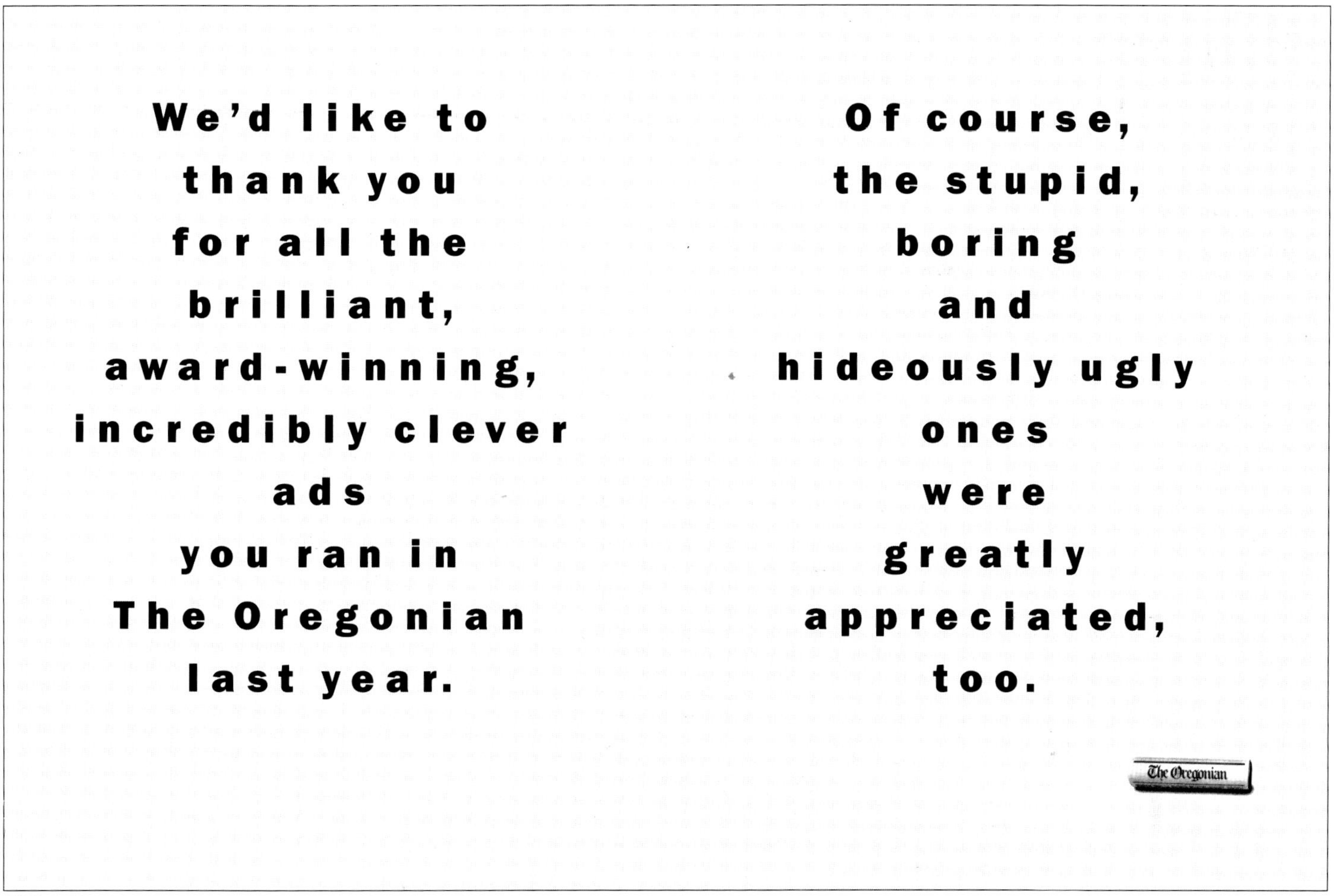

We'd like to
thank you
for all the
brilliant,
award-winning,
incredibly clever
ads
you ran in
The Oregonian
last year.

Of course,
the stupid,
boring
and
hideously ugly
ones
were
greatly
appreciated,
too.

The Oregonian

Sam Wosmek, 1956.

Sam Wosmek, 1991.

35 years of retouching experience.
332-4696

22% Of Our Subscribers Can Afford To Buy Crain's. (The Company, Not The Magazine.)

Our readers must be getting a lot out of Crain's because almost a quarter of our subscribers are millionaires. However, we can't be bought. (Unless, of course, you're talking about ad space.) Call 312-649-5370 for a sales representative.

TRADE COLOR 1 PAGE OR SPREAD: SINGLE

39 SILVER
ART DIRECTOR
Arty Tan
WRITER
Luke Sullivan
PHOTOGRAPHER
Shawn Michienzi
CLIENT
The Lee Company
AGENCY
Fallon McElligott/ Minneapolis

TRADE LESS THAN A PAGE B/W OR COLOR: SINGLE

40 SILVER
ART DIRECTOR
Bob Barrie
WRITER
Jarl Olsen
PHOTOGRAPHER
Kerry Peterson
CLIENT
Hush Puppies Shoes
AGENCY
Fallon McElligott/ Minneapolis

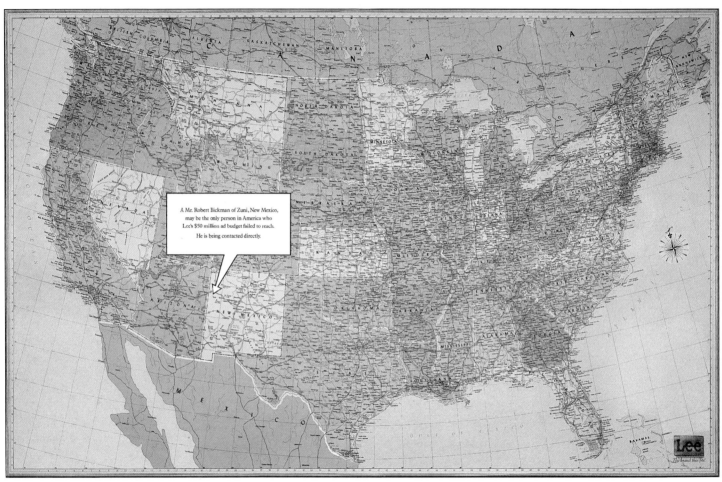

39 SILVER

Our new washable shoes.
(They're under there, somewhere.)

If a kid gets these specially treated suede and canvas shoes dirty, you can throw them right in the washer. The shoes, that is. In five durable styles for spring and fall.

Hush Puppies® BRAND SHOES
for Kids

40 Silver

GOLD, SILVER, & BRONZE AWARDS

**TRADE LESS THAN A PAGE
B/W OR COLOR: SINGLE**

41 SILVER
ART DIRECTOR
Brian Burke
WRITER
Chris Wigert
PHOTOGRAPHER
Steve Umland
CLIENT
Fred Arbogast Company
AGENCY
*TBWA Kerlick Switzer/
St. Louis*

42 BRONZE
ART DIRECTORS
*Joe Shands
Bill Karow*
WRITER
Mark Waggoner
ILLUSTRATOR
Jeff Foster
PHOTOGRAPHER
Doug Petty
CLIENT
The Oregonian
AGENCY
Cole & Weber/Portland

You'd Think Bass Would Wise Up After 23 Years.

On last year's Texas bass circuit, the Mud-Bug landed the hawg of hawgs in tournament after tournament. And reaffirmed its reputation as the bass lure of bass lures. So as usual, this year's "hot new lure" will be the same as the past 23 years. The Mud-Bug. From Fred Arbogast.

FRED ARBOGAST®

When was the last time you clipped a coupon off the TV?

Probably about the same time you turned on the radio to hunt for a sale. Or to compare prices. Or to learn more about a product.

In other words: never. Which is yet another reason so many successful retailers make The Oregonian a part of their overall multi-media plan.

Consumers themselves call the newspaper the most helpful, believable and influential source of advertising information available.

And they want the information enough that they're willing to pay for it. Because, unlike TV and radio, newspaper gives you as much time to study an ad as you want—when you want, where you want, at the pace you want.

To learn more, call Brian Bounous here at The Oregonian: 221-8279. Of course, if you're busy right now, you can always call later. Just cut out this ad and save the number.

**GOLD, SILVER, & BRONZE
AWARDS**

**TRADE ANY SIZE B/W OR
COLOR: CAMPAIGN**

**43 GOLD
ART DIRECTOR**
Arty Tan
WRITER
Luke Sullivan
PHOTOGRAPHERS
*Jim Arndt
Rick Dublin
Shawn Michienzi*
CLIENT
The Lee Company
AGENCY
*Fallon McElligott/
Minneapolis*

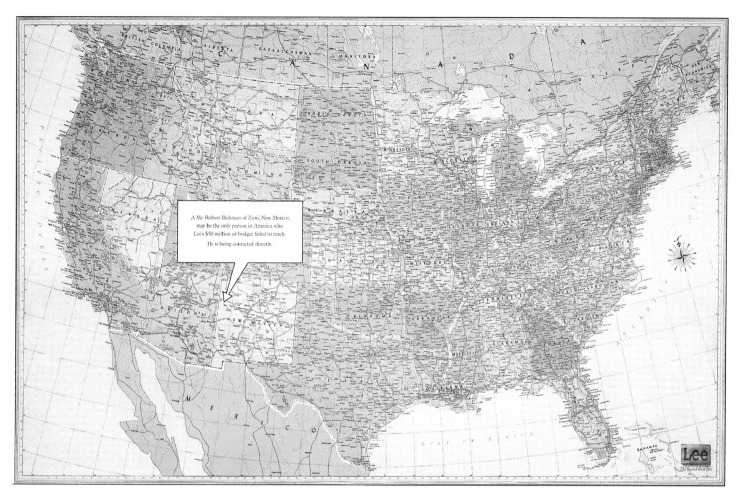

Our new price margins are the widest things we've offered since 1972.

We've lowered our wholesale prices on our entire line of Lee jeans. Which means, of course, more margin potential and more profit for you. We think it's something everyone in the retail establishment will dig, man.

GOLD, SILVER, & BRONZE AWARDS

TRADE ANY SIZE B/W OR COLOR: CAMPAIGN

44 SILVER
ART DIRECTOR
Gary Goldsmith
WRITER
Ty Montague
PHOTOGRAPHER
Steve Hellerstein
CLIENT
Everlast
AGENCY
Goldsmith/Jeffrey, New York

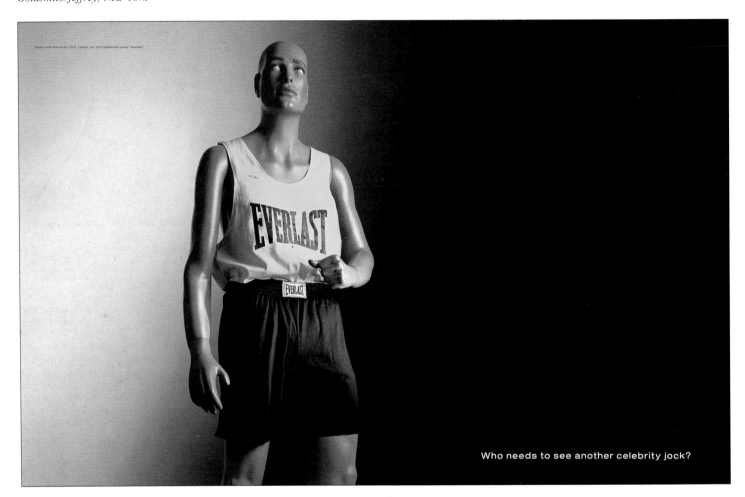

This is not one of those scented ads. Good thing.

You may never have the legs of a body builder. Great shorts, however, are readily available.

63.1% Of Our Subscribers Are In Top Management. 32.1% Are In Middle Management. The Other 4.8% Like The Pictures.

If you want to reach for the top you should know that 95.2% of our subscribers are in management positions. (When probed, they too admitted to liking the pictures.) Call 312-649-5370 for ad space.

22% Of Our Subscribers Can Afford To Buy Crain's.
(The Company, Not The Magazine.)

Our readers must be getting a lot out of Crain's because almost a quarter of our subscribers are millionaires. However, we can't be bought. (Unless, of course, you're talking about ad space.) Call 312-649-5370 for a sales representative.

A Recent Subscriber To Crain's Reported An Annual Salary Of $157,000.
(There Go Our Demographics.)

Our subscribers have an average household income of $162,500. (Of course that was before the slug earning 157 grand came along.) Call 312-649-5370 for a sales representative.

BOAT SHOES SHOULD BE JUDGED BY HOW THEY GO WITH A BLACK SKY. NOT A BLUE BLAZER.

Don't get us wrong. If you want to use our new boat shoes with the Interactive Grip System to fox-trot across the yacht club dance floor, that's your choice. We guarantee you and your blazer will look good, and we promise to accept your money.

Just be aware that we engineered these shoes so you could dance on a very different surface. The storm-blackened foredeck of a boat that's bucking like a rodeo bull.

On so wet and treacherous a playing field, one slip of the foot could be one slip too many. Preventing it is what the

INTERACTIVE GRIP SYSTEM

Quadrant cut sole has 50% more leading edges than standard wave cut soles.

Quadrant cut exceeds wave cut for traction, providing 360° of grip.

Internal Fit System keeps foot in correct position for comfort, balance and grip.

Interactive Grip System is all about.

As its name implies, the System starts where the foot interacts with the boat. At the sole. Our new design gives you such a profusion of siping (razor cuts for traction) that the number of leading edges exceeds the traction capacity of traditional boat soles by a good 50%. What's more, the edges are clustered in an exclusive quadrant cut pattern. (Competitors beware.

The Timberland® quadrant cut sole so outgrips standard wave cut soles it may cause mutiny at the yacht club.)

Part Two of the Interactive Grip System makes sure that your foot stays in the right place so the quadrant cut sole can do its work. Your foot is secured for proper balance and energy distribution by an Internal Fit System, a contoured sleeve that keeps your toes from jamming when the boat makes a violent lurch.

These brand new benchmarks for marine footwear aren't just

high-tech, but true high performance for the 1990's. A new definition of authenticity that puts our imitators in an embarrassing place.

Overboard.

BOOTS. SHOES. CLOTHING.
WIND, WATER, EARTH AND SKY.

FOOT SLIPS SINK SHIPS.

Loose lips sink ships.

That's how the saying goes when it's war on the high seas.

But we're talking about a special kind of war on the high seas. A cup race. And then the danger doesn't come from your lips, but from your slips. The valuable

seconds you lose (or worse) when your feet can't properly grip a slippery deck in a rollercoaster sea. If you're experienced enough to be in such

a race the problem isn't likely to be your feet, but your outdated boat shoes. Chances are that the shoes you use now have a sole design that's one to three decades old.

Let Timberland bring you into the 1990's with a new class of shoes and a new technology, the Interactive Grip System. So named for its ability to maximize slip resistance through the inter-action of a radically advanced sole design with the hazardous surface of a storm-tossed deck.

Part one affects the siping (razor cuts for traction) found on all boat shoe soles. On our new soles there's such a

profusion of siping that the number of leading edges exceeds the traction capacity of traditional soles by a good 50%. And while traditional soles have the old-style wave cut, ours have an exclusive quadrant cut pattern, far supe-rior to any wave cut in gripping power and efficiency.

Part two of the Interactive Grip System makes sure that your foot stays in the right place so the quadrant cut sole can do its work. Your foot is secured by an Internal Fit System, a contoured sleeve that keeps your toes from jam-ming when the boat makes a violent lurch.

Now that the Interactive Grip System has made your old-style boat shoes obsolete, is there any place left for you to use them?

Certainly. The yacht club dance floor.

BOOTS, SHOES, CLOTHING, WIND, WATER, EARTH AND SKY.

WHAT TO HAVE ON YOUR FEET WHEN THE ONLY THING DRY IS THE HEAVES.

number of leading edges exceeds the traction capacity of traditional soles by a good 50 per-cent. What's more, the edges are clustered in a special quadrant cut pattern, a Timberland exclusive. This new cut so amplifies grip that any comparison with the traditional wave cut (a design almost three decades old) becomes a lopsided contest. Wave cuts are obsolete, period.

Part Two of the Inter-active Grip System makes sure that your foot stays in the right place so the quadrant cut sole can do its work. Your foot is secured by an Inter-nal Fit System, a contoured sleeve that keeps your toes from jamming when the boat makes a violent lurch.

All of which may leave only one place for your old boat shoes.

Dry land.

If you know the sea, you know there are those days when nothing will stay down.

Not breakfast. Not lunch. Not even a rum and tonic. And certainly not the boat, which the ocean seems to be trying to upchuck.

On such days the waves look like bile. They look the way your intestinal tract feels. No wonder they call it "blowing like stink."

In turbulence so extreme, there may not be a boat shoe on the face of the earth that can give the experienced sailor all the protection, agility and traction he deserves.

We'd like to introduce the one possible exception. A new class of per-formance boat shoes from Timberland. Shoes that are proving so superior to anything else in competitive trials we urge you to check them out.

What drives these shoes is a proprietary technol-ogy called the Interactive Grip System. So named for its ability to maximize slip resistance through the inter-action of a radically advanced sole design with the hazardous surface of a storm-tossed deck.

Let us explain, starting with the sole. It has such a profusion of siping (razor cuts for traction) that the

BOOTS, SHOES, CLOTHING, WIND, WATER, EARTH AND SKY.

**GOLD, SILVER, & BRONZE
AWARDS**

**COLLATERAL BROCHURES
OTHER THAN BY MAIL**

47 GOLD
ART DIRECTOR
Kathy Delaney
WRITER
Greg Di Noto
PHOTOGRAPHER
Earl Culberson
CLIENT
The Waldorf Astoria
AGENCY
Bartleby/New York

48 SILVER
ART DIRECTORS
Warren Johnson
David Carter
WRITER
Kerry Casey
PHOTOGRAPHER
Ron Crofoot
CLIENT
Carmichael Lynch
AGENCY
*Carmichael Lynch/
Minneapolis*

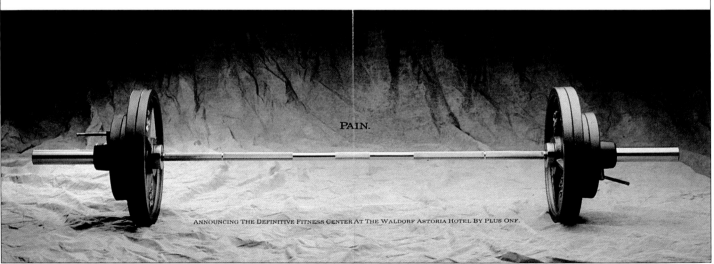

AFTER ACHIEVING NEAR PERFECTION
IN THE ART OF GIVING PLEASURE, THERE WAS ONLY
ONE THING LEFT FOR THE WALDORF TO OFFER.

PAIN.

ANNOUNCING THE DEFINITIVE FITNESS CENTER AT THE WALDORF ASTORIA HOTEL BY PLUS ONE.

47 GOLD

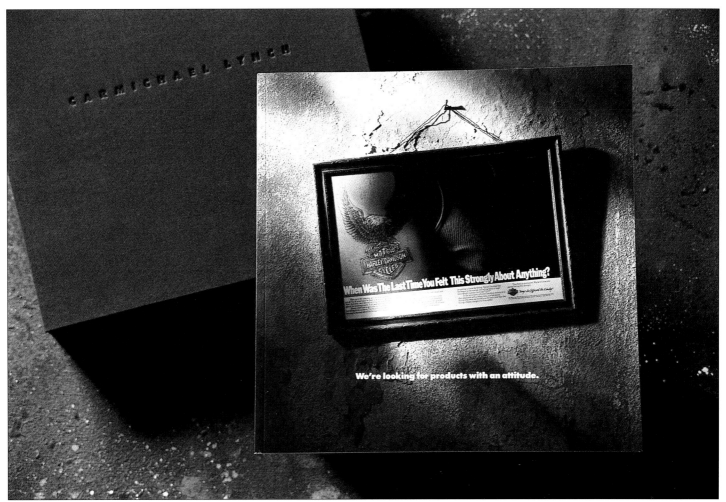

Gold, Silver, & Bronze Awards

Collateral Brochures Other Than By Mail

49 BRONZE
ART DIRECTORS
Paul Marciano
Samantha Gibson
WRITER
Emily Corey
PHOTOGRAPHER
Various
CLIENT
Guess?
AGENCY
Guess?/Los Angeles

Collateral Sales Kits

50 SILVER
ART DIRECTOR
Bob Barrie
WRITER
Jarl Olsen
PHOTOGRAPHERS
Rick Dublin
Kerry Peterson
CLIENT
Jim Beam Brands
AGENCY
Fallon McElligott/
Minneapolis

COLLATERAL SALES KITS

51 BRONZE
ART DIRECTOR
Bob Barrie
WRITER
Jarl Olsen
PHOTOGRAPHERS
Rick Dublin
Kerry Peterson
CLIENT
Jim Beam Brands
AGENCY
Fallon McElligott/
Minneapolis

52 BRONZE
ART DIRECTORS
Andrew Pogson
Peter Rae
Stefan Sagmeister
Mike Chan
WRITER
Stefan Sagmeister
ILLUSTRATORS
Andrew Pogson
Jimmy Law
CLIENT
Leo Burnett/Hong Kong
AGENCY
Leo Burnett Design Group/
Hong Kong

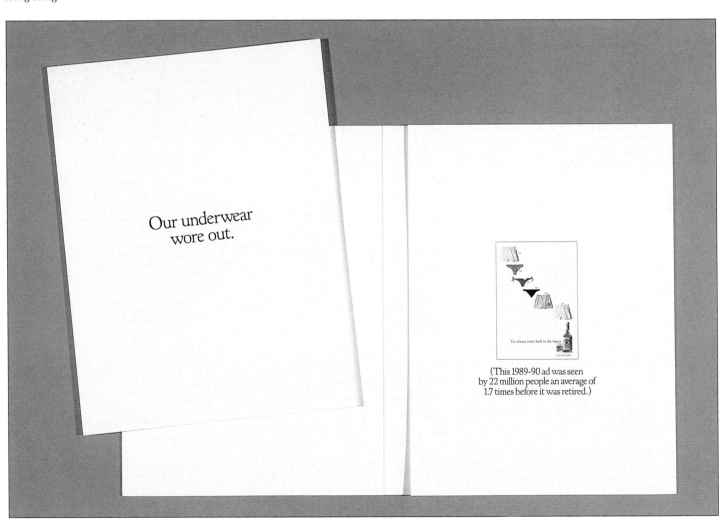

Our underwear
wore out.

(This 1989-90 ad was seen
by 22 million people an average of
1.7 times before it was retired.)

51 BRONZE

GOLD, SILVER, & BRONZE AWARDS

COLLATERAL DIRECT MAIL: SINGLE

53 GOLD
ART DIRECTOR
Bob Barrie
WRITER
Doug de Grood
CLIENT
Art Directors/Copywriters Club of Minnesota
AGENCY
Fallon McElligott/ Minneapolis

54 SILVER
ART DIRECTOR
Tom Routson
WRITER
Steve Skibba
CLIENT
Christian Biker Association
AGENCY
Mothra/Charlotte

Yikes! Have you noticed that a lot of ads lately start out with really big type which gets progressively smaller as you work your way down the page? Good agencies are doing it. Mediocre agencies are doing it. Even really lame agencies are doing it. Why? Some might call it a trend. Others, a breakthrough. Whatever. Love it. Hate it. The truth is, it can and has been done well. Most notably by the creator of the Nature Company ads, Tracy Wong, who (all these types of ads come to a point eventually) will be speaking to the Art Directors/Copywriters Club, Thursday, November 14. Tracy, for those of you who think "CA" stands for "California," is an art director at Goodby, Berlin & Silverstein in San Francisco. Oh, and he's not a girl, as his name might suggest. Although he does have a ponytail. This type is getting really squinty now, so we'll wrap it up: Azur Restaurant. 5:30 Cocktails. 6, dinner. 7, Tracy. 20 bucks for non-members. Members free. RSVP by Nov. 12, 339-1990. Futura Extra-Bold Condensed lives!

Tracy Wong at the Art Directors/Copywriters Club, Nov. 14.

Type: TSES/Letterman   Printing: Franklin Press   Concept: Bob & Doug

53 GOLD

RAISE HECK.

In the Christian Biker Association we're born again, not born to be wild. But having a good time is something we also believe in. If you love to ride, and would like to meet other people who do too, write P.O. Box 896, Pineville, NC, 28296. And join us on our annual run. It'll be a heck of a good time for everyone. We swear.

CHRISTIAN BIKER ASSOCIATION ANNUAL RUN.

**GOLD, SILVER, & BRONZE
AWARDS**

**COLLATERAL DIRECT
MAIL: SINGLE**

55 BRONZE
ART DIRECTOR
Paul Norwood
WRITER
Court Crandall
CLIENT
Atlantic Exterminating
AGENCY
*Admen Against Big Logos/
El Segundo*

56 BRONZE
ART DIRECTOR
Jeannine Caesar
WRITER
Nancy Wellinger
CLIENT
August Productions
AGENCY
*Caesar/Wellinger Group,
Farmington Hills, MI*

55 BRONZE

THANKS FOR
HELPING US CLEAR
UP A FEW THINGS.
THIS WATER,
FOR EXAMPLE.

This water was taken from the Rouge River, one of several dumping sites under investigation for carcinogenic toxins and other harmful pollutants. To help stem the tide, a donation has been made in your honor to FRGIM, a non-profit organization that's helping to clear up Michigan's troubled waters.

Here's to a clean outlook for the New Year.

AUGUST
PRODUCTIONS

GOLD, SILVER, & BRONZE AWARDS

COLLATERAL DIRECT MAIL: CAMPAIGN

57 GOLD
ART DIRECTOR
Jeff Hopfer
WRITER
Todd Tilford
PHOTOGRAPHER
Richard Reens
CLIENT
Tabu Lingerie
AGENCY
The Richards Group/Dallas

REMEMBER, MEDICAL EXPERTS
RECOMMEND INCREASING YOUR HEARTRATE
AT LEAST THREE TIMES A WEEK.

TABU
LINGERIE

ACTUALLY, THERE IS ONE
KNOWN CURE FOR SNORING.

TABU
LINGERIE

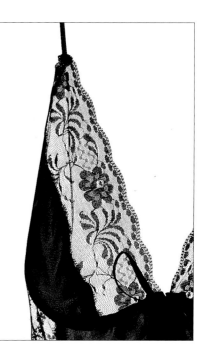

JUST FOR THE RECORD, BASEBALL
ISN'T AMERICA'S FAVORITE PASTIME.

TABU
LINGERIE

GOLD, SILVER, & BRONZE AWARDS

COLLATERAL DIRECT MAIL: CAMPAIGN

58 SILVER
ART DIRECTOR
Chris Robb
WRITER
Joe Nagy
PHOTOGRAPHER
John Bateman
CLIENT
Cheryl Robb
AGENCY
*Carmichael Lynch/
Minneapolis*

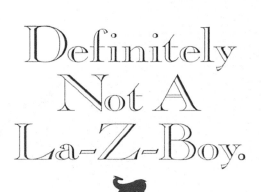

Definitely Not A La-Z-Boy.

Hand-Painted

the armchair, hand-painted by cheryl robb, one at a time, one of a kind.

It Won't Just Sit There.

Hand-Painted

the "matisse" chair, hand-painted by cheryl robb, one at a time, one of a kind.

What Has Four Legs And Stands Alone?

Hand-Painted

the table, hand-painted by cheryl robb, one at a time, one of a kind.

Gold, Silver, & Bronze Awards

Collateral Direct Mail: Campaign

59 BRONZE
ART DIRECTOR
Tom Simons
PHOTOGRAPHER
Harry De Zitter
CLIENT
Harry De Zitter
AGENCY
PARTNERS & Simons/Boston

· Harry DE ZITTER ·

BLACK *and* WHITE
Pictures

■

· *Harry* DE ZITTER ·

BLACK *and* WHITE
Pictures

·

· *Harry* DE ZITTER ·

BLACK *and* WHITE
Pictures

·

EVERY AMUSEMENT PARK HAS A THEME, OURS JUST HAPPENS TO BE CORRUPTION, BRUTALITY AND MURDER.

ALCATRAZ
The Red And White Fleet Departs Hourly From Pier 41

60 GOLD

(Actual Size)   (Almost Actual Sound)

Introducing Micro Sonic Air Conditioners. Quite Possibly The Smallest, Quietest Air Conditioners Ever Made. **MICRO SONIC**

61 Silver

SAVE UP TO 80% DURING OUR GOING OUT OF BUSINESS SALE.

(Oh sure, now you'll come in.)

the narragansett

62 BRONZE

SHE'D HAVE A BETTER CHANCE OF GETTING 3 SQUARE MEALS A DAY IF SHE WERE A CONVICTED MURDERER.

In New York, thousands of homebound elderly have to worry about where their next meal will come from.

Or when.

Simply because they're too frail to go to the supermarket or too weak to even cook.

Unfortunately, government money only provides meals Monday through Friday. So, for the past 10 years, Citymeals-on-Wheels has been supplying the homebound elderly with meals on weekends and holidays, times when they would otherwise go without.

But what about those who are still on the waiting list for the government's weekday meal program? Or who are only able to receive one weekend meal?

With your contribution, we'll be able to hand-deliver Emergency Food Packages of twelve complete meals to those who desperately need it.

100% of your contribution will go directly to feeding the homebound elderly.

Consider it justice for people whose only crime is growing old.

Yes, I want to help!

☐ $55 for one Emergency Food Package.
☐ $220 for four Emergency Food Packages.
☐ $_____ for #_____ Emergency Food Packages.

$_____ is my contribution to help in any way I can.

Name_____

Address_____

City_____ State_____ Zip_____

Simply fill out this coupon and send your tax-deductible contribution made payable to: CITYMEALS-ON-WHEELS, 280 Broadway, Room 213E, New York, NY 10007.

CITYMEALS-ON-WHEELS is a public-private partnership with the New York City Department for the Aging. This ad is a gift from friends.

GOLD, SILVER, & BRONZE AWARDS

PUBLIC SERVICE NEWSPAPER OR MAGAZINE: SINGLE

64 SILVER
ART DIRECTOR
Brian Stewart
WRITER
Barry Delaney
CLIENT
Supporters of Salman Rushdie
AGENCY
Delaney Fletcher Slaymaker Delaney & Bozell/London

65 BRONZE
ART DIRECTORS
Paul Asao
Lynne Scrimgeour
WRITERS
Dean Buckhorn
Sharyn Panagides
PHOTOGRAPHER
Claude Vasquez
CLIENT
Goodwill
AGENCY
Earle Palmer Brown/ Bethesda

On the 14th February 1989 sentence of death was pronounced on a British citizen, living in this country.

It was not handed down by a British Court of Law. Nor did it have the authority of the British parliament.

It was decreed by a foreign government — the government of Iran.

The "crime" which they deemed worthy of the ultimate penalty was the writing of a book.

On November 11th 1991 the author of the book, Salman Rushdie, will have lived under this threat to his life for one thousand days.

There is no dispute that the book is controversial. Many people have admired it and it has won literary prizes in Britain, Italy and Germany.

On the other hand certain passages have offended some (but not all) Muslims.

In this country however, people are not killed for writing controversial books.

IN 1989 THE DEATH PENALTY WAS RE-INTRODUCED IN BRITAIN. NOT FOR TERRORISM. NOT FOR MURDER. BUT FOR WRITING A BOOK.

To millions of people this threat to the life of an innocent man is deeply offensive.

It is important that such people make their feelings known.

Not by issuing violent threats, but by the free, legal and democratic expression of their views.

Each one of us is free to write to a member of parliament or the British Foreign Secretary, Douglas Hurd.

We can ensure that Salman Rushdie's plight is not allowed to be forgotten.

We can demand that the desire of governments to secure lucrative overseas contracts is not allowed to take precedence over the removal of an unlawful threat to the life of a British citizen.

And we can remind Douglas Hurd that if threats of this kind are seen to prevail, it will not be long before the very democracy that elected him to office is also threatened.

WRITE TO THE RT. HON. DOUGLAS HURD CBE. MP., FOREIGN & COMMONWEALTH OFFICE, KING CHARLES STREET, LONDON SW1A 2AH.

JOIN THE 24 HOUR SHOW OF SUPPORT, FROM 11A.M. ON THE 11TH NOVEMBER, THE 1000TH DAY, AT WESTMINSTER CENTRAL HALL, 1 CENTRAL BUILDINGS, STOREYS GATE, LONDON SW1H 9NH.

THIS ADVERTISEMENT WAS PRODUCED & PLACED BY THE SUPPORTERS OF SALMAN RUSHDIE.

They say you have to walk before you can run. How ironic. We trained a guy with no legs to run a whole company.

We're Goodwill Industries. And contrary to popular belief, the most important commodity we produce isn't recycled clothes. It's rehabilitated workers.

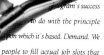

Edgar Helms
Founder

The fact is, Goodwill is America's largest non-profit provider of vocational training for the physically and mentally disabled. We have 179 facilities throughout the U.S. and Canada, all of them linked by a common goal. To see that people get well-trained. Not welfare.

It's not a new idea. Edgar Helms came up with it back in 1890. Imagine. A Methodist minister from the South End of Boston who believed poverty should be fought, not with charity, but with trade skills. If he only knew how powerful his concept would be when applied to disabled and disadvantaged citizens over 100 years later. Goodwill is proof that self-help is a system that works.

In fact, it's working harder than ever. Last year, Goodwill

our Projects With Industry program. Today, they're holding down real jobs with companies like IBM, Control Data, and Texas Instuments. Of course, the program's success has a lot to do with the principle upon which it's based. Demand. We train people to fill actual job slots that are already available in the community. Even the slots that many employers find difficult to fill.

It's true. Goodwill graduates wash windows. They also handle micrographics, data entry, state-of-the-art software systems, mechanical assembly and electrical engineering. And they do it on a full- or part-time basis.

Just ask the Ford Motor Company. Or Coca-Cola. They'll tell you how Goodwill's Contract Services program can solve long-term line requirements, last-minute production problems, and temporary assignments in almost any field.

HOW DOES A MAN WITH NO LEGS GET HIS FOOT IN THE DOOR?

graduates earned $126 million in salaries and wages. That's 40 million dollars straight to Uncle Sam. It's also 17,000 tax payers who used to be tax recipients. Pretty good for people who never expected to work a day in their lives.

Still, for those of you who find it difficult to see how a blind woman finds her way into the business world, or how a paralytic moves up the corporate ladder, consider how they got there.

Last year, over 15,000 people learned new skills through

But good references don't get jobs. People do. Our suggestion then, is that you interview a Goodwill graduate. With them, hard work, company loyalty and sweat of the brow is the norm, not the exception.

Think about it. You could talk to a woman right now who's learned to type over 50 words a minute in our Vocational Rehabilitation program. She's got a bubbly personality. Plenty of initiative. The only thing she's missing is her arms. Proof that you don't need a hand to give one. So if you're looking for good employees, contact Goodwill. It's a chance for thousands of people with disabilities to achieve something they never thought possible. Jobs.

GOODWILL JOB TRAINING

WE TRAIN THE BEST WORKERS IN AMERICA.

He was a carpenter one minute. A paraplegic the next. In one brief moment his life was blown to pieces right along with his arms.

But here's the truly shattering part. People think because he can't hold a hammer, he can't swing a job. That's the perception.

These are the facts.

Losing a limb does not lower your IQ. It will not diminish your drive. Or dampen your desire. It simply channels your energy in other directions.

179 of them to be exact. Wherever Goodwill Industries operates.

That's right, Goodwill. The same organization that's known for recycling clothing and furniture also restores something a lot more valuable. Hope.

Think about it. A good worker who sets a good example for the rest of your staff. It's just like hiring an employee that comes with his own benefits. One who's also available on a project basis. Which presents a viable solution to your short-term requirements in areas such as electrical and automotive assembly, food service, custodial maintenance, data entry, plus printing and mailing, just to name a few.

EMPLOYEE HANDBOOK

But before you hire a Goodwill graduate, there's something you should know. They're not your average employees. They work a little harder. They care a little more. And they show up on time. It's the first time they have somewhere to go besides downhill.

AFTER HE LOST HIS ARMS, WE TAUGHT HIM TO POUND NAILS WITH HIS HEAD.

Goodwill Industries is America's largest network of vocational training facilities for the disabled and disadvantaged. Last year, we taught new skills to over 100,000 people. We turned carpenters into computer experts. Bus drivers into bookkeepers. Plumbers into printers.

Pretty impressive. Especially when you consider they

Edgar Helms
Founder

landed real jobs at companies like IBM, Hewlett-Packard, Coca-Cola, Marriott and General Motors.

Now you may be wondering how a person with no arms opens so many doors. In a word, training. Hours of intensive instruction at a Goodwill facility. Or at the actual job site, where we provide up to six months of follow-up services free of charge. But that's not all that's free. There's also the feeling you'll get from putting something back into a community that's given so much to you and your business.

It was a Methodist minister in the South End of Boston who gave Goodwill its start way back in 1902. Edgar Helms believed poverty could be fought with trade skills, *and over the years he proved it.*

Today, the concept of self help has been expanded to include the disabled and disadvantaged. And from the look of things, it's working. Even for you.

So if you're looking for someone who will give you an honest day's work, get in touch with Goodwill. The person we send may be missing an arm. But rest assured, they can stand on their own two feet.

GOODWILL JOB TRAINING

WE TRAIN THE BEST WORKERS IN AMERICA.

GOLD, SILVER, & BRONZE AWARDS

PUBLIC SERVICE NEWSPAPER OR MAGAZINE: CAMPAIGN

67 SILVER
ART DIRECTOR
Kevin Kearns
WRITER
Jay Nelson
PHOTOGRAPHER
Marcus Halevi
CLIENT
Free Romania Foundation
AGENCY
Arnold Fortuna Lane/Boston

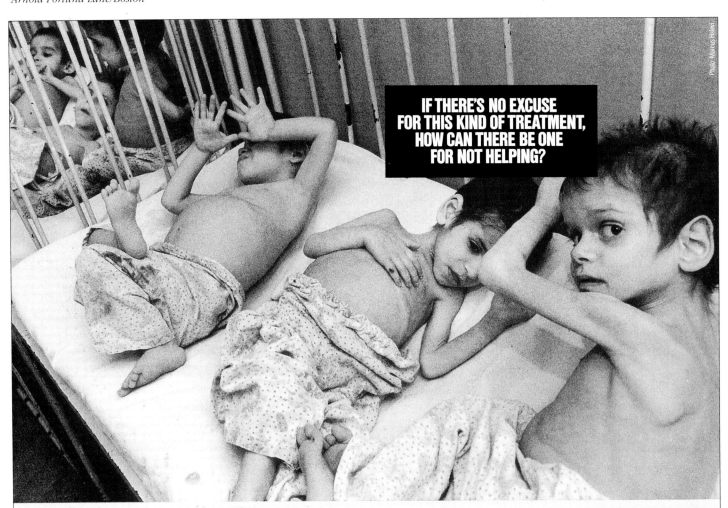

IF THERE'S NO EXCUSE FOR THIS KIND OF TREATMENT, HOW CAN THERE BE ONE FOR NOT HELPING?

How do you explain handicapped children who are strapped to their beds lying in their own urine? Or sickness that goes untreated? Or malnutrition? But that's the very treatment given to handicapped children in Romania. Thousands who have been labeled "non-recoverable," many for handicaps as treatable as a club foot, are condemned to grossly understaffed, unsanitary institutions for as long as they live. There is no medical care, no therapy, and little chance to survive. Unless something is done. That's why the Free Romania Foundation needs your help. You can donate. Or you can adopt, like many Americans already have. You can also volunteer. We need special education teachers, pediatric doctors, physical therapists and nurses. To help, call 617-876-3378. These children need help, not excuses.

FREE ROMANIA FOUNDATION
725 Concord Ave., Box 12, Cambridge, MA 02138

THE MOST DISTURBING THING ABOUT THIS PICTURE IS HOW MANY PEOPLE WILL IGNORE IT.

Would you ignore a child who cried out in pain? Or in hunger? Or simply because they needed a diaper changed? That's the kind of neglect handicapped children in Romania live with every day. Thousands of children have been labeled "non-recoverable," many for handicaps as minor as a hairlip. They are condemned to grossly understaffed, unsanitary institutions. Many are tied to their beds and lie in their own urine for weeks. Others suffer from malnutrition. There is no medical care, no therapy, and little chance for survival. Unless we help. Supporting the Free Romania Foundation will help these children get the care they need. You can donate. Or you can adopt, like many Americans already have. You can also volunteer. We need special education teachers, pediatric doctors, physical therapists, nutritionists, and nurses. Anything you can do would make a big difference in these children's lives. Call 617-876-3378 to help. These children have been ignored long enough. **FREE ROMANIA FOUNDATION**

725 Concord Ave., Box 12, Cambridge, MA 02138

IN THE UNITED STATES THIS WOULD BE A CRIME. IN ROMANIA, IT'S DAY CARE.

The treatment of handicapped children in Romania is alarming. Their needs are neglected. Sickness goes untreated. Many suffer from malnutrition. Others are strapped to their beds and lie in their own urine for weeks. Thousands of these children have been labeled "non-recoverable," many for handicaps as treatable as a hairlip. And are condemned to understaffed, unsanitary institutions for as long as they live. Without any laws to protect them. That's why the Free Romania Foundation needs your help. You can donate. Or you can adopt, like many Americans already have. You can also volunteer. We need special education teachers, pediatric doctors, physical therapists, and nurses. Anything you can do would make a big difference in these children's lives. To help, call 617-876-3378. There are no laws to help them. Only us. **FREE ROMANIA FOUNDATION**

725 Concord Ave., Box 12, Cambridge, MA 02138

The next time you're at your favorite restaurant, about to order one of the

House Specialties

consider that, for the price of a
Broiled Seafood Platter
we could provide a week's worth of foster care for a newborn awaiting adoption.

For the price of an
8 oz. Top Sirloin
we could offer three children swimming lessons and water safety training.

For the price of an
Oven Roasted Chicken
we could provide a half dozen homeless people with a sandwich and

a bowl of our own
Soup Du Jour

And, even the nominal amount you'd pay for a
Fresh Garden Salad
would provide a complete meal for a homebound elderly or disabled person.

We want you to
Enjoy Your Meal
but please remember, your contribution to United Way can provide physical and emotional nourishment for many. Just some food for thought.

United Way
of South Hampton Roads

GOLD, SILVER, & BRONZE AWARDS

PUBLIC SERVICE:
OUTDOOR

69 GOLD
ART DIRECTOR
Mike Bevil
WRITERS
Tim Bauer
Brian Brooker
Daniel Russ
CLIENT
American Civil Liberties
Union San Francisco
AGENCY
GSD&M/Austin

70 SILVER
ART DIRECTOR
Carol Henderson
WRITER
Bill Miller
CLIENT
Violence Against Women
Coalition
AGENCY
Fallon McElligott/
Minneapolis

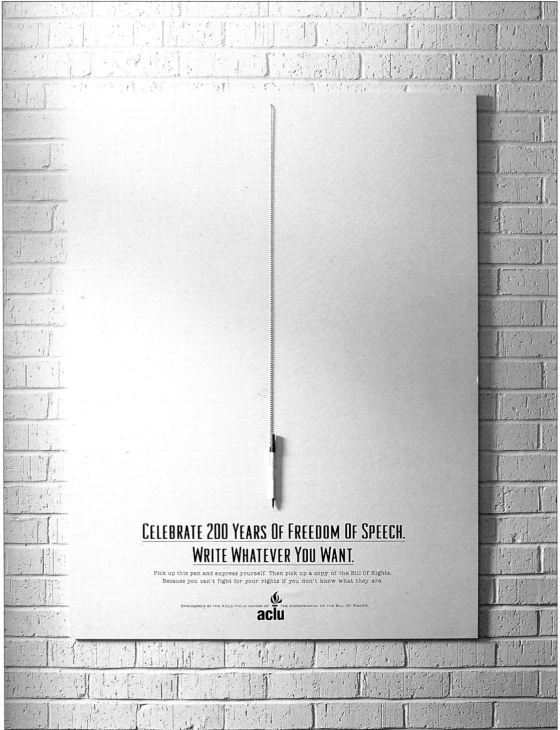

69 GOLD

1 IN 4 WOMEN WILL BE RAPED IN HER LIFETIME.

WILL IT BE YOUR MOTHER, YOUR SISTER, YOUR DAUGHTER OR YOUR WIFE?

The statistics won't improve if you pretend they aren't true.
Help stop the violence. Call 920-4642 for information.

The Violence Against Women Coalition

The Violence Against Women Coalition is a project of the JLM Junior League Minneapolis, 3033 Excelsior Boulevard, Minneapolis, MN 55416.

GOLD, SILVER, & BRONZE AWARDS

PUBLIC SERVICE:
OUTDOOR

71 BRONZE
ART DIRECTOR
Jerry Torchia
WRITER
Tripp Westbrook
PHOTOGRAPH
Historic Archives
CLIENT
Amnesty International
AGENCY
*The Martin Agency/
Richmond*

PUBLIC SERVICE RADIO:
SINGLE

72 SILVER
WRITER
Jef Loeb
AGENCY PRODUCER
Andrea Sanchez
PRODUCTION COMPANY
Jim Kirby & Company
CLIENT
*Bay Area Suicide &
Crisis Hotline*
AGENCY
*Katsin/Loeb Advertising,
San Francisco*

73 BRONZE
WRITERS
Terry Bremer
Gary Bingner
AGENCY PRODUCER
Gary Bingner
CLIENT
National Easter Seal Society
AGENCY
*Campbell-Mithun-Esty/
Minneapolis*

MOST STATES WOULD HAVE PUT THESE KIDS IN REFORM SCHOOL. VIRGINIA PUT THEM TO DEATH.

Clem Cive and Bill James are just two of the 29 children who have been executed in Virginia. Let's change the laws that allow this to happen. Call Amnesty International USA if you'd like to know how to help. **AMNESTY INTERNATIONAL USA, 1-800-55AMNESTY**

72

VETERAN: Hello, hello . . . you still there?

OPERATOR: I'm here.

VETERAN: Well, I don't know . . . don't know
    if it's worth it.

OPERATOR: Can you tell me where you're staying?

VETERAN: We go over there, drag our . . . in the mud,
    nobody listens . . .

OPERATOR: I'm here.

VETERAN: Been 20 years, now.

OPERATOR: Do you have a friend you could call . . .
    to be with you?

VETERAN: Ain't got no friends.

OPERATOR: Would you like us to send some help?

VETERAN: No cops, don't want no cops.

ANNCR: It's been 20 years since the war in Vietnam . . .
    but America has yet to hear the last shot. Every year
    more Vietnam veterans commit suicide. Just like
    teens, the elderly, the desperately ill. Call the Bay
    Area Suicide and Crisis Hotlines. If you aren't there
    for us, we can't be there for them. Send help.
    Don't let them die.

VETERAN: You know, I kept my gun.

(SFX: BREATHING)

73

MAN: Hello, my name is Peggy and I am deaf. Because
    of my hearing loss, I find it difficult to speak clearly.
    So as a little girl, I learned American sign language.
    Thanks to Easter Seals, my friend, Dave, also learned
    sign language. Now, Dave and I communicate more
    easily, and when I want to talk to others, Dave can
    read my signing, and speak for me. Just like he's
    doing now. Thank you, Dave. (LAUGHS) You can
    stop now.

ANNCR: Support Easter Seals. And give the power
    to overcome.

**PUBLIC SERVICE
TELEVISION: SINGLE**

74 GOLD
ART DIRECTOR
Carol Henderson
WRITER
Bill Miller
AGENCY PRODUCER
Vicki Oachs
CLIENT
*Violence Against
Women Coalition*
AGENCY
*Fallon McElligott/
Minneapolis*

75 SILVER
ART DIRECTOR
Paul Asao
WRITER
Dean Buckhorn
AGENCY PRODUCER
Robin Sherman
PRODUCTION COMPANY
Van Dusen Films
DIRECTOR
Don Petrie
CLIENT
Goodwill Job Training
AGENCY
*Earle Palmer Brown/
Bethesda*

76 SILVER
ART DIRECTOR
Eric Glickman
WRITER
Steve Hersh
AGENCY PRODUCER
Sande Breakstone
PRODUCTION COMPANY
*Lovinger/Grasso/
Cohn & Associates*
DIRECTOR
Jeff Lovinger
CLIENT
*United Negro College Fund/
Ad Council*
AGENCY
Young & Rubicam/New York

77 BRONZE
ART DIRECTOR
Randy Hughes
WRITER
Bill Johnson
AGENCY PRODUCER
Arlene Kulis
PRODUCTION COMPANY
Lotter, Inc.
DIRECTOR
Jim Lotter
CLIENT
*Minnesota Department of
Public Safety*
AGENCY
*Chuck Ruhr Advertising/
Minneapolis*

74
SUPER: TED BUNDY. 18 HOURS BEFORE
HIS EXECUTION.
TED BUNDY: . . . And what scares and appalls me,
Dr. Dobson is when I see on cable TV, some of the
violence in the movies . . .
SUPER: RAPED AND MURDERED OVER 30 WOMEN.
TED BUNDY: That stuff is, I'm telling you from personal
experience, that is graphic violence on screen . . .
it's scary . . .
ANNCR: Isn't it ironic that Ted Bundy was probably
more concerned about the violence on television
than you are? Help stop the violence.
Call 920-4642.
SUPER: THE VIOLENCE AGAINST WOMEN COALITION.
CALL 920-4642 FOR MORE INFORMATION.

75
(MUSIC: PROUD, EMOTIONAL)
SUPER: CHRISTINA GAISER, DYSLEXIC.
SUPER: SHAD BLACKWELL, PARAPLEGIC.
SUPER: MICHELLE VIDRA, TRIPALEGIC.
ANNCR: The reason we're showing you these people is
not because they need your help.
SUPER: LOU DIPILLA, RETARDED.
ANNCR: We thought you might need theirs.
SUPER: DARRYL LEWIS, DEAF.
ANNCR: Goodwill Job Training. We train the best
workers in America.

76

PRINCIPAL: . . . That you will always have a friend here at Carver High. Congratulations.

(SFX: APPLAUSE)

MICHAEL: Hey, how you doin' Mrs. F?

MRS. F: Fine. What are you going to do after graduation, Michael?

MICHAEL: I'm going to go home and make a sandwich.

(LAUGHS)

MR. D: Michael.

MICHAEL: Hey, how you doin' Mr. D?

MR. D: Congratulations. What are you doing after graduation?

MICHAEL: I don't know. I'm thinking about going home and brushing the teeth and combin' the hair. . . . Hey, what's up girl? You made it.

GIRL: I couldn't have gotten through physics without you.

MICHAEL: Yeah, well, you're on your own at college.

GIRL: It's not fair.

MICHAEL: It's all right. I'm going to get a job. You know start working. I'll save. I'll be in college in another year or two.

WOMAN: So what'd you have planned, Mike?

MICHAEL: I'm going to go home . . . make a sandwich . . .

ANNCR: Support the United Negro College Fund. A mind is a terrible thing to waste.

77

(MUSIC: OMINOUS)

ANNCR: In a 60 mph collision, your car will hit you like it was dropped on you from 120 feet. Your automatic shoulder belts and lap belts are the only things that will keep you from being crushed. Think about that the next time you're tempted to disconnect them.

(SFX: WHAM)

SUPER: SHOULDER BELTS + LAP BELTS. TOGETHER THEY SAVE LIVES.

CONSUMER RADIO:
SINGLE

78 GOLD
WRITER
Mark Fenske
AGENCY PRODUCER
Mark Fenske
PRODUCTION COMPANY
The Bomb Factory
CLIENT
Wolfgang Puck Food Company
AGENCY
The Bomb Factory/ Los Angeles

79 SILVER
WRITER
Dean Hacohen
AGENCY PRODUCER
Dean Hacohen
CLIENT
Crain's New York Business
AGENCY
Goldsmith/Jeffrey, New York

80 BRONZE
WRITER
Dion Hughes
AGENCY PRODUCER
Lisa Horowitz
PRODUCTION COMPANY
John Crawford Radio
CLIENT
NYNEX Information Resources
AGENCY
Chiat/Day/Mojo, New York

78

ANNCR: Sometimes I wake up in the morning and I look out at the sun coming up and I think to myself what's the big deal I seen this before so I turn on the TV and there's a horse talking in a human voice and I think I seen this before and so I get in the shower and the shampoo and conditioner are together in the same bottle and I think I seen this before so I go to work and the boss says you're on a plane to Paris tomorrow and I think I done this before and so I turn on the radio and there's a woman singing falsetto Portuguese while accompanying herself on the zither and I think I heard this before and so I go home and there's my wife lying on the couch in a sheer black body stocking with candles lit and I think I done this before so I go look in the freezer and there's a Wolfgang Puck Frozen Pizza with fontina and goat cheese cilantro and pesto sauce and it's ready in fifteen minutes in the oven and I think to myself you have not eaten Wolfgang Puck Frozen Pizza with goat cheese before so I thought back to the first time the wife and I tried the body stocking and I decided I'd give the pizza a try.

79

ANNCR: A few years back, Frank Sinatra released his colossal hit, "New York, New York." The lyrics of which include the much repeated and ballyhooed line, "If I can make it there, I can make it anywhere." And who can forget, "I want to be A-Number-1, King of the Hill, Top of the Heap." What troubles us, is that nowhere in this song does Mr. Sinatra mention the necessity for a subscription to Crain's New York Business. Perhaps it was an oversight. Maybe he just forgot. Frankly, we are as surprised as you are. And sincerely hope Mr. Sinatra will consider re-recording these lyrics in the interest of making them more accurate.

80

MIKE: It's absolutely true, you can find anything and everything in your NYNEX Yellow Pages, and today under "Dentists," I found Dr. Joseph Tam of The Dental Discounters. Joe, I see from your ad that you stock off-the-rack dentures.

JOE: Thith ith correct, Michael. We manufacture them thmall, medium, largthe, and metric.

MIKE: And is that an example of your work?

JOE: You're referring to my dentureth?

MIKE: Yes, they, um, they don't seem to fit very well.

JOE: What you thacrifithe in thithe, you more than make up in convenienthe and prithing.

MIKE: Now, do people really buy these things?

JOE: Thure. Many people keep them ath a thecond pair.

MIKE: You mean spares?

JOE: Well, back upths, yeah. Thome clienth buy many pairth. Mikth and match. It'th a very original and inekthpenthive fashion statement. Aaaayee . . .

MIKE: What's the matter, Dr.?

JOE: My teeth, they're locked, Michael.

MIKE: Oh no, does this happen often?

JOE: M. Everytime you thay an "m" you run the danger of them locking.

MIKE: Can I help you?

JOE: Do you have a ball point pen I could borrow?

MIKE: No, not really. Well, there you have it. Further proof that if it's out there, it's in your NYNEX Yellow Pages.

JOE: Ith thith the model with the withdom teeth or without?

MIKE: Looks like some wisdom teeth back there.

JOE: Oh, even worth.

MIKE: Why would anyone need another?

Gold, Silver, & Bronze Awards

Consumer Radio: Campaign

81 GOLD
WRITER
Dion Hughes
AGENCY PRODUCER
Lisa Horowitz
CLIENT
NYNEX Information Resources
AGENCY
Chiat/Day/Mojo, New York

Consumer Radio: Campaign

82 SILVER
WRITERS
Thomas Hripko
Brian Nadurak
Tom Bodett
AGENCY PRODUCER
Harvey Lewis
CLIENT
Motel 6
AGENCY
The Richards Group/Dallas

83 BRONZE
WRITER
Jerry Williams
AGENCY PRODUCERS
Jerry Williams
Jim Paddock
CLIENT
Peasant Restaurants
AGENCY
Fitzgerald & Company/Atlanta

84 BRONZE
WRITER
Jay Williams
AGENCY PRODUCERS
Laurie Hughes
Kelly Pauling
CLIENT
Staples
AGENCY
Hill Holliday Connors Cosmopulos/Boston

81 I

MIKE: It's absolutely true, you can find anything and everything in your NYNEX Yellow Pages, and today under "Dentists," I found Dr. Joseph Tam of The Dental Discounters. Joe, I see from your ad that you stock off-the-rack dentures.

JOE: Thith ith correct, Michael. We manufacture them thmall, medium, largthe, and metric.

MIKE: And is that an example of your work?

JOE: You're referring to my dentureth?

MIKE: Yes, they, um, they don't seem to fit very well.

JOE: What you thacrifithe in thithe, you more than make up in convenienthe and prithing.

MIKE: Now, do people really buy these things?

JOE: Thure. Many people keep them ath a thecond pair.

MIKE: You mean spares?

JOE: Well, back upths, yeah. Thome clienth buy many pairth. Mikth and match. It'th a very original and inekthpenthive fashion statement. Aaaayee . . .

MIKE: What's the matter, Dr.?

JOE: My teeth, they're locked, Michael.

MIKE: Oh no, does this happen often?

JOE: M. Everytime you thay an "m" you run the danger of them locking.

MIKE: Can I help you?

JOE: Do you have a ball point pen I could borrow?

MIKE: No, not really. Well, there you have it. Further proof that if it's out there, it's in your NYNEX Yellow Pages.

JOE: Ith thith the model with the withdom teeth or without?

MIKE: Looks like some wisdom teeth back there.

JOE: Oh, even worth.

MIKE: Why would anyone need another?

81 II

MIKE: You know, it really is true you can find anything in the NYNEX Yellow Pages. For instance, today under "Entertainers," I found The Amazing Mr. Andy, and your ad says you're a man of a thousand voices.

ANDY (WEIRD VOICE): That's right, Michael.

MIKE: Hey, that's really funny. Who's it supposed to be?

ANDY: Whaddya mean? This is my real voice.

MIKE: Oh . . . uhhh . . . I'm sorry. I just thought . . .

ANDY: You find this amusing, pencil neck? You think I'm a clown.

MIKE: No, really, I ahhh . . .

ANDY (NORMAL VOICE): Just kidding, that was my big tough guy voice. Had you going though, didn't I?

MIKE: I, well, uh, what other voices do you do?

ANDY: Listen to this.

(SFX: THROAT CLEARING)

ANDY (BROOKLYN VOICE): Morning Andy. Can I borrow your hedge clippers?

MIKE: Gee, I can't seem to place that one.

ANDY: That's Jacky, my next door neighbor. You don't know Jacky?

MIKE: No.

ANDY: Aw, that's a shame. Sounds exactly like him.

MIKE: Oh, I bet it does.

ANDY: Okay, get this.

(SFX: THROAT CLEARING)

ANDY (SOUNDING LIKE MIKE): They say you can find anything in the NYNEX Yellow Pages.

MIKE: Now that would be . . .

ANDY: That's you, Mike. Yeah, even called your girlfriend this morning and proposed to her. I used your voice.

MIKE: What?

ANDY (AS MIKE): Well, there it is, more proof that if it's out there, it's in your NYNEX Yellow Pages.

MIKE: Boy, you have an awesome power, Andy. I hope you use it responsibly.

ANDY (AS MIKE): Why would anyone need another?

MIKE: Oooh, spooky.

81 III

(SFX: HISSING AND WHEEZING OF LEAKY FURNITURE)

MIKE: You know how they say you can find just about anything in the NYNEX Yellow Pages? Today, I found the Inflatable Furniture Warehouse and with me is sales manager Rick Slovitt.

RICK: Mike, welcome to the largest inventory of inflatable home furnishings on the eastern seaboard.

MIKE: So, I'm curious, why would anyone want an inflatable file cabinet?

RICK: Well, Mike, inflatable means deflatable. So if you ever get a surprise IRS audit you just pull the plug here. It deflates into a briefcase and you're out the back door.

MIKE: That's clever. Okay. This table looks kind of lopsided.

RICK: That's a pressure thing that's easily fixed.

(SFX: HAND PUMP)

RICK: There we go. Part of our Louis XIV collection. Hand-painted vinyl.

MIKE: Are leaks a problem?

RICK: No, we offer a one year warranty provided you don't own cats or knit.

MIKE: Right, yeah.

RICK: You can't beat our inflatables for comfort. Ever experience an inflatable chaise lounge, Mike?

MIKE: Not that I know of.

RICK: Sit down here.

MIKE: Well, you sink right in.

RICK: Floating on air. Hey, that isn't a pin, uh?

(SFX: BALLOON BURST AND RAPID DEFLATING)

MIKE: Whooooaaaahhhh.

RICK: Hold on, Mike, we'll have you down in no time.

MIKE: Well, there you have it. If it's out there, it's in your NYNEX Yellow Pages.

RICK: I'll get some air into this ladder.

(SFX: HAND PUMP)

MIKE: Why would anyone need another?

RICK: If you're going to fall, fall onto the inflatable coffee table, okay?

82

TOM: Hi. Tom Bodett for Motel 6 with good news for the traveler. Well it's time for the biannual trip to see Aunt Josephine. She's a wonderful lady, but the only problem is her cats. It never fails, the moment you step in the door, the big black one, Muffie, starts that curling thing around your leg and for the rest of your stay, you're doomed to be the object of Muffie's desire. It makes it hard to concentrate on Aunt Josephine's story about Mildred's cousin's husband's neighbor, who just had their goiter worked on. But maybe I got a way to get you off the hook with Muffie. Motel 6. We'll give you a clean, comfortable room for the lowest prices of any national chain. Around 25 bucks in most places. A lot less in some, a little more in others, but always a heck of a deal. And at Motel 6, you'll never wake up to find Muffie flipping her tail in your face. And personally, that's worth the price of the room right there. I'm Tom Bodett for Motel 6 and we'll leave the light on for you.

83

WOMAN 1: How many immigrants have passed through Ellis Island?

ANSWER MAN: 5,235,457. Next question.

WOMAN 2: Does my bologna have a first name?

ANSWER MAN: Yes, Oscar. Next question.

MAN 1: What makes people subscribe to sports magazines?

ANSWER MAN: Sneaker telephones. Next question.

MAN 2: Are shoe sizes different than sock sizes for a reason?

ANSWER MAN: Yes. Next question.

MAN 3: Who crafted the Missouri Compromise?

ANSWER MAN: Henry Clay. Next question.

WOMAN 3: Are Morey Amsterdam and Buddy Hackett the same guy?

ANSWER MAN: Yes. Next question.

MAN 4: How many megawatts could be generated by reclaiming the petroleum content of MC Hammer's clothing?

ANSWER MAN: 57. Next question.

WOMAN 4: What's Don King's favorite snack?

ANSWER MAN: Sausage wieners. Next question.

MAN 5: What's the best restaurant in Atlanta?

ANSWER MAN: Any Peasant Restaurant. Including The Pleasant Peasant, The Peasant Uptown, The Peasant Restaurant and Bar, The Country Place, Dailey's, Winfields' or The Public House. Next question.

MAN 6: What was the biggest factor in German reunification?

ANSWER MAN: Fahrvergnugen.

84

(MUSIC: STIRRING THROUGHOUT)

ANNCR: To succeed in business, you don't need to be big. All you need is a dream. Just a dream and the passion to pursue it. And the dedication to see it through. And the talent to build it on. And the opportunity to use your talent. And a little luck. And some pencils. And pens. Maybe some typewriter ribbon and correction fluid. And some of those little yellow note pads with the sticky stuff on the back. And some computer paper. And some laser printers to put it in. And some desks to put the printers on. And a fax machine. And some of those #10 envelopes with the little windows in them so you can send out bills. And you can save a bundle on all of these things at Staples, The Office Superstore. Because Staples offers guaranteed lowest prices on over 5,000 basic business necessities. With such incredibly low prices, you can take all that money you save and put it into your dream, instead.

Staples, The Office Superstore. Conveniently located in Cincinnati and Springdale or call for delivery at 1-800-333-3330. Dreams sold separately.

85
(MUSIC: LATHAM THEME)
BOUGH: That's a nice rug, sir . . .
LATHAM: That's not a rug, Bough, it is a Bedouin birthing blanket. Tradition has it, a powerful aid to fertility.
BOUGH: Great! I'll get me mum one.
LATHAM: A Barclaycard? Put it away, Bough. The Tuareg are an ancient people, they respect only hard cash and hard bargaining.
Al ahra achakaraha.
TRADER (ARABIC DIALECT): What are you on about?
LATHAM: Ah! Shamali daktak!
TRADER (ARABIC DIALECT): What? Are you potty?
LATHAM: Bouwa, bouwa.
BOUGH: You sound fluent, sir!
LATHAM: We are both fluent, Bough. Sadly, in different languages. How much is the rug?
So! Where did your Barclaycard get you?
BOUGH: Well, it got me rug insured for the next three months.
LATHAM: Insurance, Bough? I think I can handle a rug. Ah, smell those Tuareg campfires . . . unmistakable.
(MUSIC: LATHAM THEME)
LATHAM: Look, shoo! Push off . . .
SUPER: BARCLAYCARD. IT DOES MORE THAN YOU'D CREDIT.

86
(MUSIC: PIANO THROUGHOUT)
SUPER: THERE IS NO FINISH LINE.
SUPER: NIKE 180 AIR.
SUPER: JUST DO IT.

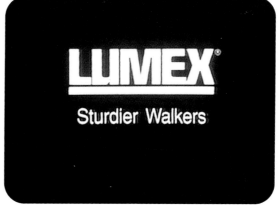

87

SUPER: AIR. BY BO JACKSON.
ANNCR: A-one . . . two, three, four!
(MUSIC: UP)
CHORUS: Huhhh!
BO: Aaaaiiiii!
CHORUS: *Bo knows it's got the . . . air thing!*
BO (SINGING): *Nice shoes!*
CHORUS: *Bo knows it works!*
BO (SINGING): *Bo knows it's got the . . . air thing!*
CHORUS: *Bo knows they . . .*
(MUSIC: STOPS)
BO: Stop! This is ridiculous. I'm an athlete not an
actor. Let me out of this thing. I've got rehab to do.
GUY: Bo?
BO: Gimme those shoes.
GUY: Bo?
BO: Excuse me.
KID: Nice . . . shoes!
BO: You watch too much TV, kid.
(MUSIC: UP)
CHORUS: *Bo knows it's got . . . the air thing!*
BO: Hey! Where's that music coming from?
CHORUS: *Bo knows it's . . .*
(SFX: NEEDLE DRAGGING ACROSS RECORD)
(MUSIC: STOPS)
BO: You know I don't have time for this!
GEORGE: But I do! Hit it!
CHORUS: *George knows it's got the air thing!*
GEORGE (SINGING): *George knows . . .*
(MUSIC: FADE OUT)

88

(MUSIC: JAZZY SAXOPHONE THROUGHOUT)
ANNCR: Just because you're 75, doesn't mean you have
to feel as if you're 105.
SUPER: LUMEX. STURDIER WALKERS.

GOLD, SILVER, & BRONZE AWARDS

CONSUMER TELEVISION OVER :30 (:45/ :60/ :90) CAMPAIGN

89 GOLD
ART DIRECTOR
Fraser Adamson
WRITER
Jon Matthews
AGENCY PRODUCER
Sarah Pollitt
PRODUCTION COMPANY
Limelight Productions
DIRECTOR
John Lloyd
CLIENT
Barclaycard
AGENCY
BMP DDB Needham Worldwide/London

90 SILVER
ART DIRECTOR
Richard Crispo
WRITER
Jeanette Tyson
AGENCY PRODUCERS
Gary Streiner
Lesley Crews
PRODUCTION COMPANIES
RSA/USA
Dektor/Higgins & Associates
DIRECTORS
Willi Patterson
Leslie Dektor
CLIENT
Saturn Corporation
AGENCY
Hal Riney & Partners/ San Francisco

89 I

(MUSIC: LATHAM THEME)

LATHAM: Thank you, ladies and gentlemen. A very impressive turnout. In fact, the only person I can't see here is the ambassador.
Ah, that's better.

AMBASSADOR: What the devil do you think you're playing at, Latham?

LATHAM: I was about to ask you the same question, Ambassador! Yesterday, you collected rather a lot of money from this man. And today, we hear you are to meet a courier in this very embassy. That, ambassador, is the behavior pattern of a mole!

AMBASSADOR: It is the behavior pattern of a man who's lost his Barclaycard. First they send emergency cash, then a replacement card.

LATHAM: Oh, come on, Mr. Moley!

BOUGH: Sir!

LATHAM: Yes Bough, let him in, the more the merrier. A Barclaycard? To Moscow? And how do they do that, pray? By motorcycle messenger?
Thank you, Sir Wilfred, for taking part in our training exercise. Realism is obviously of paramount importance. C'mon Bough, untie Sir Wilfred.

(MUSIC: LATHAM THEME)

SUPER: BARCLAYCARD. IT DOES MORE THAN YOU'D CREDIT.

89 II

(MUSIC: LATHAM THEME)

BOUGH: That's a nice rug, sir . . .

LATHAM: That's not a rug, Bough, it is a Bedouin birthing blanket. Tradition has it, a powerful aid to fertility.

BOUGH: Great! I'll get me mum one.

LATHAM: A Barclaycard? Put it away, Bough. The Tuareg are an ancient people, they respect only hard cash and hard bargaining.
Al ahra achakaraha.

TRADER (ARABIC DIALECT): What are you on about?

LATHAM: Ah! Shamali daktak!

TRADER (ARABIC DIALECT): What? Are you potty?

LATHAM: Bouwa, bouwa.

BOUGH: You sound fluent, sir!

LATHAM: We are both fluent, Bough. Sadly, in different languages. How much is the rug?
So! Where did your Barclaycard get you?

BOUGH: Well, it got me rug insured for the next three months.

LATHAM: Insurance, Bough? I think I can handle a rug. Ah, smell those Tuareg campfires . . . unmistakable.

(MUSIC: LATHAM THEME)

LATHAM: Look, shoo! Push off . . .

SUPER: BARCLAYCARD. IT DOES MORE THAN YOU'D CREDIT.

89 III

(MUSIC: LATHAM THEME)

TINKERBELL: Latham?

LATHAM: Hello, Tinkerbell.

TINKERBELL: Division told me you were back in the field. Know what you need?

LATHAM: Yes! Thirty yards of dental floss garotte wire, a twelve-bore pump-action stapler and a five pound bag of your finest stun-potatoes. Oh, and the scuba trousers. Black. High cut.

TINKERBELL: You've been away a long time, Latham. Here . . . your 4929

LATHAM: Ingenious. What is it?

TINKERBELL: It's a Barclaycard, Latham.

LATHAM: Ye-es! . . . And? Ho!

TINKERBELL: Over here.

LATAM: Ah! The mission.

TINKERBELL: No, no. The places that take Barclaycard. Sign here.

LATHAM: A Barclaycard?

TINKERBELL: It's all you need, Latham.
 Sorry, old stock. Back way out, please.

(MUSIC: LATHAM THEME)

SUPER: BARCLAYCARD. IT DOES MORE THAN YOU'D CREDIT.

90

ANNCR: Who knew what to expect. I'd never been to Alaska before. I had no idea it was so, well, so far away. But coming from Tennessee, it's up there, and Petersburg, it's even farther. Of course, I wasn't going to have a good time. I was going to check on a car, and fix a little problem we had with our seat recliner. It was something you'd normally just bring into the retailer. But Robin Millage, she'd ordered her Saturn sight unseen and had it shipped 2500 miles. Well, Robin couldn't very well bring her car to us, so we went to her. And, it didn't take long to make things right. Just a few minutes. And I was on my way home. I tell folks Alaska's a great place. People go out of their way to make you feel comfortable. But I'd recommend staying more than a day.

SUPER: DIFFERENT KIND OF COMPANY.

SUPER: DIFFERENT KIND OF CAR.

SUPER: SATURN.

GOLD, SILVER, & BRONZE AWARDS

CONSUMER TELEVISION OVER :30 (:45/ :60/ :90) CAMPAIGN

91 BRONZE
ART DIRECTOR
Chris Dewey
WRITER
Jeff Glover
AGENCY PRODUCER
Norman Zuppicich
PRODUCTION COMPANY
Window Productions
CLIENT
Pacific Access
AGENCY
George Patterson/Melbourne

CONSUMER TELEVISION :30/ :25 SINGLE

92 GOLD
ART DIRECTOR
Steve Sweitzer
WRITERS
Dick Sittig
Bob Rice
AGENCY PRODUCER
Kathi Calef
PRODUCTION COMPANIES
Lucas Films
Industrial Light & Magic
DIRECTOR
Barry Sonnenfeld
CLIENT
Reebok
AGENCY
Chiat/Day/Mojo, New York

93 SILVER
ART DIRECTOR
Rick Carpenter
WRITER
Mark Monteiro
AGENCY PRODUCER
Connie Myck
PRODUCTION COMPANIES
Story Piccolo Guliner
Crossroads Films
CLIENT
GTE
AGENCY
DDB Needham/Los Angeles

94 SILVER
ART DIRECTOR
Dean Hanson
WRITER
Bruce Bildsten
AGENCY PRODUCER
Judy Brink
PRODUCTION COMPANY
Sedelmaier Film Productions
DIRECTOR
Joe Sedelmaier
CLIENT
Timex Corporation
AGENCY
Fallon McElligott/ Minneapolis

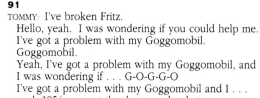

91
TOMMY: I've broken Fritz.
  Hello, yeah. I was wondering if you could help me. I've got a problem with my Goggomobil. Goggomobil.
  Yeah, I've got a problem with my Goggomobil, and I was wondering if . . . G-O-G-G-O
  I've got a problem with my Goggomobil and I . . . yeah 1954, no, not the dart, not the dart.
  They always think it's the dart. It's a wee ripper. I tell ya.
SUPER: YELLOW PAGES.

92
(SFX: TENNIS BALL MACHINE)
BOSSBALL: Listen Smith, you want to make it in this corporation you gotta give up your weekends, you gotta push . . .
(SFX: THWAP)
POLICEMANBALL: Alright missy, pull it over. It's people like you that give lady . . .
(SFX: THWAP)
DOGBALL: Yap yap yap yap yap . . .
(SFX: THWAP)
LOUNGE LIZARD: Hey baby, are you gonna hog the court forever?
PLAYER: Just one more.
LOUNGE LIZARD BALL: Hey baby, are you gonna hog the court forever?
(SFX: THWAP)
SUPER: LIFE IS SHORT.
SUPER: PLAY HARD.
SUPER: REEBOK.

93

MOTHER: One time she stuck a green bean in her ear.
  Had to go to the hospital.
  Well, she's always had a thing about her weight.
  You know for her first Halloween, she was a bunny.
  She looked so cute.
GIRL: Mom, is that Grandma?
MOTHER: No some boy named Jason from your school.
(GIRL SCREAMS)
MOTHER: She'll have to call you back.
ANNCR: With Smart Ring from GTE your phone can tell
  you who a call is for before you pick it up. One
  ring for you.
(SFX: RING)
ANNCR: And another for the kids.
(SFX: RING, RING)
SUPER: SMART RING. 1-800-SMART-91. GTE.
  THE POWER IS ON.

94

(MUSIC: LIGHT PIANO)
(SFX: GLASS SHATTERING)
ANNCR (JOHN CAMERON SWAYZE): Timex. It takes a licking
  and keeps on ticking.

GOLD, SILVER, & BRONZE AWARDS

CONSUMER TELEVISION :30/ :25 SINGLE

95 BRONZE
ART DIRECTOR
Amy Nicholson
WRITERS
Glen Porter
Jeff Watzman
Andrew Spade
AGENCY PRODUCER
Amy Saunders
PRODUCTION COMPANY
Crossroads Films
DIRECTOR
Mark Pellington
CLIENT
Multimedia Entertainment
AGENCY
Kirshenbaum & Bond/New York

CONSUMER TELEVISION :30/ :25 CAMPAIGN

96 GOLD
ART DIRECTORS
Darryl McDonald
Susan Hoffman
Michael Prieve
WRITERS
Jim Riswold
Geoff McGann
Bob Moore
AGENCY PRODUCERS
Derek Ruddy
Trish Reeves
DIRECTORS
Joe Pytka
Dominic Sena
CLIENT
Nike
AGENCY
Wieden & Kennedy/Portland

95
WOMAN: I like to humiliate myself in public. I like to wear strange wigs and hang out at rodeos. Small children laugh at the sight of me. I play with wild and dangerous animals. I have a nose . . . that squirts.
SUPER: THINGS A CLOWN MIGHT SAY.
ANNCR: The $100,000 Pyramid. Get a clue.

96 I
(SFX: THROUGHOUT)
SUPER: AIR. BY ANDRE AGASSI.
JULIA CHILD: The one exception is the artichoke . . .
SUPER: JUST DO IT.
SUPER: NIKE AIR.

96 II

SUPER: AIR. BY BO JACKSON.
ANNCR: A-one . . . two, three, four!
(MUSIC: UP)
CHORUS: Huhhh!
BO: Aaaaiiiii!
CHORUS: *Bo knows it's got the air thing!*
BO (SINGING): *Nice shoes!*
CHORUS: *Bo knows they . . .*
(MUSIC: STOPS)
BO: Stop! This is ridiculous. I'm an athlete not
   an actor.
(MUSIC: UP)
CHORUS: *Bo knows it's got the air thing!*
BO: Hey! Where's that music coming from?
CHORUS: *Bo knows it's . . .*
(SFX: NEEDLE DRAGGING ACROSS RECORD)
(MUSIC: STOPS)
BO: You know I don't have time for this!
GEORGE: But I do! Hit it!
(MUSIC: UP)
CHORUS: *George knows it's got the air thing!*
(MUSIC: FADE OUT)

96 III

SUPER: AIR. BY CHARLES BARKLEY.
BARKLEY 1: Any knucklehead can score.
BARKLEY 2: Who said that?
BARKLEY 1: You did.
BARKLEY 2: Oh yeah.
BARKLEY 1: As I was saying, any knucklehead can score.
   But rebounding takes brains.
BARKLEY 2: And wit!
BARKLEY 1: And good looks.
BARKLEY 2: And charm!
BARKLEY 1: And a nice haircut.
BARKLEY 2: And a warm heart.
BARKLEY 1: And big shoes!
   And a kind disposition . . . and a beautiful smile . . .
   and a certain savoir-faire. Don't you agree? ·
BARKLEY 2: Most certainly.
ANNCR BARKLEY: And a catchy slogan . . .
   and a nice logo.

Gold, Silver, & Bronze Awards

97 GOLD
ART DIRECTOR
Tracy Wong
WRITER
Steve Simpson
AGENCY PRODUCER
Betsy Flynn
PRODUCTION COMPANY
In-House
DIRECTORS
Tracy Wong
Steve Simpson
CLIENT
Chevys Mexican Restaurants
AGENCY
*Goodby Berlin & Silverstein/
San Francisco*

98 SILVER
ART DIRECTORS
Ian Potter
Steve Sweitzer
Jerry Gentile
WRITERS
April Winchell
Ian Potter
Bob Rice
Rob Feakins
AGENCY PRODUCER
Kelly Waltos
PRODUCTION COMPANY
Coppos Films
Johns + Gorman Films
DIRECTORS
Brent Thomas
Gary Johns
CLIENT
Eveready Battery
AGENCY
Chiat/Day/Mojo, Venice

99 BRONZE
ART DIRECTOR
Amy Nicholson
WRITERS
Glen Porter
Jeff Watzman
Andrew Spade
AGENCY PRODUCER
Amy Saunders
PRODUCTION COMPANY
Crossroads Films
DIRECTOR
Mark Pellington
CLIENT
Multimedia Entertainment
AGENCY
*Kirshenbaum & Bond/
New York*

97
(MUSIC: THROUGHOUT)
SUPER: THIS COMMERCIAL WAS MADE TODAY.
STEVE: Ladies! Can you tell me the date today? Okay, here's a hint. It's Wednesday. Can you read the weather? Morning low clouds . . .
SUPER: FRESH TV.
ANNCR: We made this commercial today. We call this "Fresh TV."
SUPER: FRESH MEX.
ANNCR: At Chevys, we make our food fresh every day. Using 100 percent real cheese. We call this "Fresh Mex." Real cheese from real cows. Cows outstanding in their field. Sure, we could pay more for our puns, but we pass the savings on to you.
SUPER: CHEVYS FRESH MEX.
STEVE: Did you hear "thirtysomething" was cancelled?
COW: Mooo . . .
STEVE: What a bummer, huh?

98
ANNCR: Spanning the globe to bring you the constant variety of sports. The thrill of victory. And the agony of defeat . . .
(SFX: BOOM, BOOM, BOOM . . .)
ENERGIZER ANNCR: Still going. Nothing outlasts the Energizer. They keep going and going and going . . .

99
BIKER: I have to go to the baffroom. Someone stole my little brown truck. Can I have a puppy? I got a boo-boo. I don't like that new baby sitter. Where's my mommy . . . I want my mommy now!
SUPER: WHAT A CHILD SAYS.
ANNCR: The $100,000 Pyramid. Get a clue.

**CONSUMER TELEVISION
:20 AND UNDER SINGLE**

100 GOLD
ART DIRECTOR
David Angelo
WRITER
Paul Spencer
AGENCY PRODUCER
Eric Herrmann
PRODUCTION COMPANY
Coppos Films
DIRECTOR
Brent Thomas
CLIENT
New York State Lottery
AGENCY
*DDB Needham Worldwide/
New York*

101 GOLD
ART DIRECTOR
Raul Pina
WRITER
Margaret Elman
AGENCY PRODUCER
David Kinyon
PRODUCTION COMPANIES
*Big Picture
Phantom Audio*
CLIENT
*Dribeck Importers/
Beck's Beer*
AGENCY
*Della Femina McNamee/
New York*

102 GOLD
ART DIRECTOR
Dean Hanson
WRITER
Phil Hanft
AGENCY PRODUCER
Char Loving
PRODUCTION COMPANY
Coppos Films
DIRECTOR
Mark Coppos
CLIENT
*Ralston Purina/
Nature's Course*
AGENCY
*Fallon McElligott/
Minneapolis*

103 SILVER
ART DIRECTOR
Jerry Gentile
WRITER
Rob Feakins
AGENCY PRODUCER
Kelly Waltos
PRODUCTION COMPANY
Johns + Gorman Films
DIRECTOR
Gary Johns
CLIENT
Eveready Battery
AGENCY
Chiat/Day/Mojo, Venice

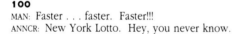

100
MAN: Faster . . . faster. Faster!!!
ANNCR: New York Lotto. Hey, you never know.

101
(MUSIC: CLASSICAL)
ANNCR 1: The Germans gave us the greatest of the great
  German beers. And we gave them . . .
(MUSIC: CHIA PET THEME)
ANNCR 2: Chia Pet. The pottery that grows.
ANNCR 1: Who do you think made out? Beck's.
  The number one imported German beer.

102

(SFX: BUZZING)

ANNCR: Too many pesticides in your dog's food? There are no pesticides in new Nature's Course.

103

ANNCR: Tonight on The Adventure Channel, join explorer Marceau Surlamer as he unlocks the mystery of the Great Barrier . . .

(SFX: BOOM, BOOM, BOOM . . .)

ENERGIZER ANNCR: Still going. Nothing outlasts the Energizer. They keep going and going and going . . .

GOLD, SILVER, & BRONZE AWARDS

CONSUMER TELEVISION :20 AND UNDER SINGLE

104 BRONZE
ART DIRECTOR
Dean Hanson
WRITER
Phil Hanft
AGENCY PRODUCER
Char Loving
PRODUCTION COMPANY
Coppos Films
DIRECTOR
Mark Coppos
CLIENT
*Ralston Purina/
Nature's Course*
AGENCY
*Fallon McElligott/
Minneapolis*

CONSUMER TELEVISION :20 AND UNDER CAMPAIGN

105 GOLD
ART DIRECTORS
Ian Potter
Jerry Gentile
WRITERS
April Winchell
Ian Potter
Rob Feakins
AGENCY PRODUCER
Kelly Waltos
PRODUCTION COMPANIES
Coppos Films
Johns + Gorman Films
DIRECTORS
Brent Thomas
Gary Johns
CLIENT
Eveready Battery
AGENCY
Chiat/Day/Mojo, Venice

104
(SFX: VACUUM)
ANNCR: Too many artificial preservatives in your dog's food? There are no artificial preservatives in new Nature's Course.

105 I
ANNCR: Tonight on The Adventure Channel, join explorer Marceau Surlamer as he unlocks the mystery of the Great Barrier . . .
(SFX: BOOM, BOOM, BOOM . . .)
ENERGIZER ANNCR: Still going. Nothing outlasts the Energizer. They keep going and going and going . . .

105 II

(MUSIC: "ALFRED HITCHCOCK PRESENTS" THEME)

(SFX: BOOM, BOOM, BOOM . . .)

ENERGIZER ANNCR: Still going. Nothing outlasts the Energizer. They keep going and going and going . . .

105 III

ANNCR: Not just white . . .

WOMAN: Really White!

ANNCR: Not just white . . .

WOMAN: Really White!

ANNCR: When you want whiter whites, you want . . .

(SFX: BOOM, BOOM, BOOM . . .)

ENERGIZER ANNCR: Still going. Nothing outlasts the Energizer. They keep going and going and going . . .

CONSUMER TELEVISION :20 AND UNDER CAMPAIGN

106 SILVER
ART DIRECTOR
Dean Hanson
WRITER
Phil Hanft
AGENCY PRODUCER
Char Loving
PRODUCTION COMPANY
Coppos Films
DIRECTOR
Mark Coppos
CLIENT
*Ralston Purina/
Nature's Course*
AGENCY
*Fallon McElligott/
Minneapolis*

CONSUMER TELEVISION UNDER $50,000 BUDGET

107 GOLD
ART DIRECTOR
Guy Lowe
WRITER
Guy Lowe
AGENCY PRODUCER
Joan Karpeles
PRODUCTION COMPANY
Crawford
CLIENT
Opti-World
AGENCY
*Fitzgerald & Company/
Atlanta*

108 SILVER
ART DIRECTOR
Kevin Donovan
WRITERS
*Todd Godwin
Marian Godwin*
AGENCY PRODUCER
Camie Taylor
PRODUCTION COMPANY
Crossroads Films
DIRECTOR
Steve Eshelman
CLIENT
Luis Gomez
AGENCY
LHS and Used to B/New York

109 BRONZE
ART DIRECTORS
*Charlie McQuilkin
Lynda Chalmers*
WRITERS
*Charlie McQuilkin
Neal Howard*
AGENCY PRODUCER
Julie Burmeister
PRODUCTION COMPANY
Gary Noren Productions
DIRECTOR
Gary Noren
CLIENT
Shoney's
AGENCY
Ogilvy & Mather/Atlanta

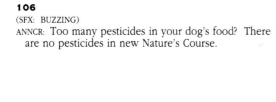

106
(SFX: BUZZING)
ANNCR: Too many pesticides in your dog's food? There are no pesticides in new Nature's Course.

107
ANNCR: Franklin Roosevelt wore glasses. The question is, was he wearing them when he married Eleanor? Harry Truman wore glasses. But was he wearing them when he married Bess? John Kennedy, however, didn't wear glasses. Whoops! L.B.J. wore glasses, but was he wearing them when he married Lady Bird? Indeed, was she wearing her glasses when she married him? Before you get married, or before you vote, please, get an eye exam at Opti-World.

SHONEY'S
Hot Fudge Cake.
The Plump.

108

WOMAN: Now Skippy, be good while I'm gone.
(SFX: DOOR CLOSES)
(MUSIC: THROUGHOUT)
(SFX: APARTMENT BEING DESTROYED)
ANNCR: Just a reminder, 90 percent of all accidents occur in the home.
SUPER: LUIS GOMEZ, MASTER DOG TRAINER, 212-866-7836.

109

(SFX: WHOOSH, WHOOSH)
TOM: Have you seen these shoes with the gizmo to make them tighter? Well, Shoney's has a gizmo to make everything you wear tighter.
Shoney's hot fudge cake. Just eat it.
SUPER: SHONEY'S. HOT FUDGE CAKE. THE PLUMP.
(SFX: WHOOSH, WHOOSH, WHOOSH)

GOLD, SILVER, & BRONZE AWARDS

NON-BROADCAST: CINEMA/VIDEO

110 GOLD
ART DIRECTOR
John Pallant
WRITER
Matt Ryan
PHOTOGRAPHER
Chris Duffy
AGENCY PRODUCER
Mark Hanrahan
PRODUCTION COMPANY
Paul Weiland Film Company
DIRECTOR
Frank Budgen
CLIENT
British Airways
AGENCY
Saatchi & Saatchi/London

111 SILVER
ART DIRECTORS
Eric Anderson
Seiji Kishi
WRITER
Bob Gerke
PHOTOGRAPH
Stock
AGENCY PRODUCER
Laura Kelley
DIRECTORS
Eric Anderson
Bob Gerke
CLIENT
Earth Communications Office
AGENCY
BBDO/Los Angeles

112 BRONZE
ART DIRECTOR
John Morrison
WRITER
Jean Rhode
ANIMATOR
Chel White
AGENCY PRODUCERS
Jean Rhode
Chel White
CLIENT
Memorial Blood Center of Minneapolis
AGENCY
McElligott Wright Morrison White/Minneapolis

110
(MUSIC: ROMANTIC)
ANNCR: This weekend, love is in the air. British Airways Holidays can offer you weekend breaks in 41 romantic destinations. Like Paris. From just £129 per person including flights and hotel.
MICHELLE: I don't believe it . . . it can't be. Oh my god . . . it is.
MICHELLE (TO NEIGHBORING CINEMA-GOERS): That's my boyfriend. Nigel! Psst . . . Nigel! . . . oi, Nigel . . . NIGEL BAXTER!
NIGEL: Michelle?
AMANDA: Michelle?
MICHELLE: Hello Nigel.
NIGEL: Ah, Michelle. Er, hi. What a surprise.
MICHELLE: I'll bet. Having a nice time?
AMANDA: Nigel . . .
NIGEL: Er, yes . . . I mean no . . . I mean . . .
MICHELLE: I thought you said you were away on business?
NIGEL: Yes well . . .
MICHELLE: And I suppose this is your business colleague?
AMANDA: Nigel who is this?
NIGEL: Well this is Michelle, Amanda . . . Amanda, Michelle.
AMANDA: Nigel, who is she?
NIGEL: Well, she's a friend . . .
MICHELLE: Girlfriend, Nigel, girlfriend . . . I'm his girlfriend.

AMANDA: Well, what a coincidence.
NIGEL: Look I can explain . . .
AMANDA AND MICHELLE: Yes?
NIGEL: Well . . . er . . . er . . .
AMANDA: We're waiting . . .
MICHELLE: We're all waiting Nigel.
NIGEL: Er . . .
AMANDA: Well, it seems he's been stringing us both along, Michelle.
NIGEL: Oh, c'mon . . .
MICHELLE: I think so, Amanda. Goodbye Nigel!
NIGEL: Michelle!
AMANDA: Goodbye Nigel!
NIGEL: Amanda!
ANNCR: Er, well, why not surprise your loved one with a British Airways Holidays City Break this weekend. From British Airways, the world's favorite airline.

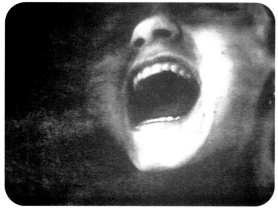

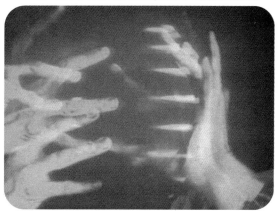

111

(MUSIC: "WONDERFUL WORLD" AS SUNG BY WILLIE NELSON)
SUPER: LAST YEAR, BY RECYCLING PAPER, YOU
 SAVED 600 MILLION TREES. 22% OF YOU CAR
 POOLED, KEEPING MILLIONS OF TONS OF
 POLLUTANTS OUT OF THE AIR. YOU RECYCLED
 50% OF ALL THE ALUMINUM CANS PRODUCED,
 SAVING ENERGY AND LAND. AND, BY BUYING
 DOLPHIN-SAFE TUNA, YOU SAVED 50,000
 DOLPHINS. KEEP AT IT. YOU'RE MAKING
 A WORLD OF DIFFERENCE.
 EARTH COMMUNICATIONS OFFICE.

112

SUPER: MEDICAL TECHNOLOGY CAN COPY JUST
 ABOUT ANYTHING.
SUPER: EXCEPT BLOOD.
SUPER: MEMORIAL BLOOD CENTER OF MINNEAPOLIS.
SUPER: GIVE BLOOD.

GOLD, SILVER, & BRONZE AWARDS

NON-BROADCAST: OUT-OF-HOME

113 GOLD
ART DIRECTOR
Noam Murro
WRITER
Dean Hacohen
AGENCY PRODUCERS
Dean Hacohen
Noam Murro
DIRECTOR
Tim Beiber
CLIENT
Lumex
AGENCY
Goldsmith/Jeffrey, New York

114 SILVER
ART DIRECTOR
Marty Weiss
WRITER
Nat Whitten
PRODUCTION COMPANY
Perry Pictures
DIRECTOR
Laura Belsey
CLIENT
Weiss Whitten Carroll Stagliano
AGENCY
Weiss Whitten Carroll Stagliano/New York

115 BRONZE
ART DIRECTOR
Michael Fazende
WRITER
Bill Miller
AGENCY PRODUCER
Vicki Oachs
CLIENT
Aveda Corporation
AGENCY
Fallon McElligott/ Minneapolis

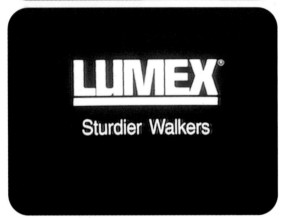

113
(MUSIC: JAZZY SAXOPHONE THROUGHOUT)
ANNCR: Just because you're 75, doesn't mean you have to feel as if you're 105.
SUPER: LUMEX. STURDIER WALKERS.

114
MILTON: I'm Milton Haynes. I'm a psychotherapist in practice in New York City, and Nat Whitten has been my client for half a dozen years.
(MUSIC: "HAPPY DAYS ARE HERE AGAIN")
HELEN: I am Helen Weiss.
BERNIE: And I am Bernie Weiss. We are the parents of Martin Weiss.
BENJAMIN: I'm Benjamin Whitten.
JANE: And I'm Jane Whitten.
BETTY: I'm Betty Carroll, and I am Tom Carroll's mother.
AGNES: I'm Agnes Harbison, and I am Tommy Carroll's grandmother.
ANTHONY: I am Anthony J. Stagliano Sr., I'm Adam's father.
MILTON: They're all very, very different people, with different areas of interest and expertise, and things to bring to the party. That's really gonna generate a lot of energy.
ANTHONY: A very precocious child, everybody was concerned and interested in him, and would love to ask him questions because he gave very intelligent answers.
WRESTLING COACH: Adam wrestled 127 pounds and 133 pounds, and he was very aware of what other people thought of him, and his performance against other teams, and wanted to make a good impression all the time.
BETTY: Tom is the, the talking, right? Tom's got a gift . . .
AGNES: Gift of gab.

(MUSIC: "WE'RE IN THE MONEY")
BETTY: He walked into the first ad agency and he said,
"I have to have a job." and the story . . .
AGNES: They had no job.
BETTY: They didn't have a job and . . .
AGNES: He said, "I gotta have a job."
JANE: From the moment he was born, I knew Nat was
filled with creative ability.
BENJAMIN: He used to write lyrics for his confounded
rock band.
KATHY: It's gotten worse, I think, since we've gotten
married, but he used to be very funny.
BERNIE: I always was hoping that he'll be a
professional, a lawyer, or a doctor, and be able to
support the family in his future.
DRY CLEANER: I couldn't stop myself from asking him,
and he told me he was a, art director.
INTERVIEWER: Those must be all his trophies there, right?
BERNIE: No they are not. They are his younger
brother's trophies. But we do have some items
which he doesn't let us throw out he made in grade
school, and we have to keep it.
INTERVIEWER: What is that?
BERNIE: I don't know what it is.
DRY CLEANER: If you do some business or politics or
some art without achieving yourself, make yourself
man first, you can't achieve anything.
MILTON: Breaking new ground is, either for a client in
advertising or in psychotherapy, very frightening. It
means crossing some forbidden territory.
WRESTLING COACH: The only people that knew a work
ethic, and knew to get results you had to work hard,
were wrestlers. And I wouldn't trust anybody else
with my business other than wrestlers.
BETTY: Now wait a minute, it's a mouthful. Weiss,
Whitman, Carroll and Stagliano. Is it Whitman?
HELEN: Whitney. Whitney?
ANTHONY: Weiss, Wheaton . . . Carroll and Stagliano.
BENJAMIN: Call Weiss, Whitten. . . . What was their
name again?

115
(MUSIC: "LADYSMITH BLACK MAMBAZO" THROUGHOUT)
SUPER: THIS ENVIRONMENTAL MESSAGE IS BROUGHT
TO YOU BY AVEDA.
SUPER: OUR PRODUCTS ARE MANUFACTURED IN
PLANTS ALL OVER THE WORLD.
SUPER: AVEDA.

Gold, Silver, & Bronze Awards

Consumer Television: Foreign Language

116 GOLD
ART DIRECTORS
Bente Amundsen
Johan Gulbranson
WRITERS
Lisbeth Amundsen
Stein Leikanger
PRODUCTION COMPANY
Leo Film
DIRECTOR
Johan Gulbranson
CLIENT
Sparebankkort
AGENCY
Nordskar & Thorkildsen
Leo Burnett/Oslo

117 SILVER
ART DIRECTORS
Bente Amundsen
Johan Gulbranson
WRITER
Lisbeth Amundsen
PRODUCTION COMPANY
Leo Film
DIRECTOR
Johan Gulbranson
CLIENT
Ernst G. Mortensens Forlag
AGENCY
Nordskar & Thorkildsen
Leo Burnett/Oslo

116
(MUSIC: ACCORDIAN THROUGHOUT)
(After having his beard shaven off, the client hands his Visa-Card to the barber who compares the photo on the back of the card with his client. After everyone has scrutinized the photo and the newly shaven man, the barber refuses to accept the card.)
SUPER: THE NEW VISA-CARD HAS GOT YOUR
  PICTURE ON IT.

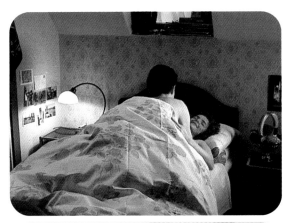

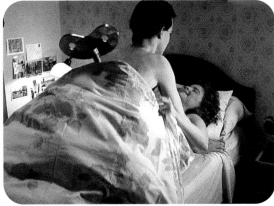

117
(MUSIC: "MAD PASSIONATE LOVE")
SUPER: THE MAGAZINE FOR GIRLS WHO MAKE THEIR
   OWN DECISIONS.

COLLEGE COMPETITION

118 GOLD
ART DIRECTOR
Steve Taylor
WRITERS
Bob Rickert
Greg Collins
COLLEGE
Portfolio Center/Atlanta

119 SILVER
ART DIRECTOR
David J. Dickey
WRITERS
Matthew Elhardt
Ryan Ebner
COLLEGE
University of Minnesota/ Minneapolis

120 BRONZE
ART DIRECTOR
Melissa Sison
WRITER
David Lentini
COLLEGE
School of Visual Arts/ New York

CLBRTNG R 50TH BRTHDY.

Bill Karow, Art Director

Do Squat This Summer.

George Brumis, Copywriter

Jannie Matheson, Copywriter

HALF OFF SPECIALS 365 DAYS A YEAR.

PT'S TOPLESS BAR

Larry Jarvis, Art Director

The first jeans designed for fish.

Raymond McKinney, Copywriter

A WOMAN IS OFTEN MEASURED ... STATISTICS LIE

Charlotte Moore, Art Director

GET A BUTT LIKE CHER.
Women's tattoos a specialty.
BERNIE'S TATTOOING

Jelly Helm, Art Director

Another Salesman That Won't Shut Up.

⊗TDK 3
ENDLESS CASSETTE

Pat Harris, Art Director

It's The Only Upward Mobility Some Women Ever Achieve.

Working Opportunities For Women 647-9900.

David Fox, Art Director

Michael Wilde, Art Director

PORTFOLIO CENTER GRADUATES ARE MORE INFLUENTIAL THAN HARVARD'S.

Every year hundreds of highway workers hit the streets.

Robyn Dunn, Art Director
J. Paige Ruddle, Copywriter

Bill Pullum, Art Director

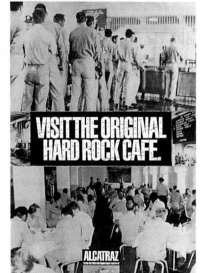

VISIT THE ORIGINAL HARD ROCK CAFE.

ALCATRAZ

Chances are you've already been influenced by our school and you don't even know it. In addition to what you see here, our graduates are creating ads for Reebok, Budweiser, United Airlines and Kodak, just to name a few.

They learned from professionals with expertise in copywriting, art direction, photography, illustration and graphic design. It's a learning environment many consider the best of it's kind for putting together a great portfolio.

Which means if you enroll now, you're only eight quarters away from influencing people with your own ads. And getting paid for it.

1-800-255-3169

 PORTFOLIO CENTER

Who but *Subaru* would sign up for a *torturous* seven month long *race* and enter their *mid-priced family sedan?*

Fifty-five thousand students aren't here for the weather.

While the winters here aren't exactly cozy, you'll find our academic curriculum a warm welcome compared to other universities. Not only do we offer over 60 undergraduate majors in everything from Architecture to Zoology, but our graduate programs are some of the best in the nation. Another attraction is the Minneapolis-St. Paul metropolitan area, which adds a cultural dimension to any education.

So as application deadlines near, don't leave the University of Minnesota out in the cold. For more information on the University, and to learn about admissions, call toll-free 1-800-752-1000. And remember, our weather builds character. Isn't that what college is all about?

UNIVERSITY OF MINNESOTA
TWIN   CITIES   CAMPUS

SCHOOL OF
VISUAL ARTS
DOESN'T PROVIDE
FACULTY
WITH OFFICES.
THEY HAVE THEIR
OWN.

WHERE THE MOST CREATIVE MINDS IN ADVERTISING DO LUNCH.

(MUSIC: ROMANTIC)

ANNCR: This weekend, love is in the air. British Airways Holidays can offer you weekend breaks in 41 romantic destinations. Like Paris. From just £12 per person including flights and hotel.

MICHELLE: I don't believe it . . . it can't be. Oh my god . . . it is.

MICHELLE (TO NEIGHBORING CINEMA-GOERS): That's my boyfriend. Nigel! Psst . . . Nigel! . . . oi, Nigel . . . NIGEL BAXTER!

NIGEL: Michelle?

AMANDA: Michelle?

MICHELLE: Hello Nigel.

NIGEL: Ah, Michelle. Er, hi. What a surprise.

MICHELLE: I'll bet. Having a nice time?

AMANDA: Nigel . . .

NIGEL: Er, yes . . . I mean no . . . I mean . . .

MICHELLE: I thought you said you were away on business?

NIGEL: Yes well . . .

MICHELLE: And I suppose this is your business colleague?

AMANDA: Nigel who is this?

NIGEL: Well this is Michelle, Amanda . . . Amanda, Michelle.

AMANDA: Nigel, who is she?

NIGEL: Well, she's a friend . . .

MICHELLE: Girlfriend, Nigel, girlfriend . . . I'm his girlfriend.

AMANDA: Well, what a coincidence.

NIGEL: Look I can explain . . .

AMANDA AND MICHELLE: Yes?

NIGEL: Well . . . er . . . er . . .

AMANDA: We're waiting . . .

MICHELLE: We're all waiting Nigel.

NIGEL: Er . . .

AMANDA: Well, it seems he's been stringing us both along, Michelle.

NIGEL: Oh, c'mon . . .

MICHELLE: I think so, Amanda. Goodbye Nigel!

NIGEL: Michelle!

AMANDA: Goodbye Nigel!

NIGEL: Amanda!

ANNCR: Er, well, why not surprise your loved one with a British Airways Holidays City Break this weekend. From British Airways, the world's favorite airline.

Best Of Show

ART DIRECTOR
John Pallant
WRITER
Matt Ryan
PHOTOGRAPHER
Chris Duffy
AGENCY PRODUCER
Mark Hanrahan
PRODUCTION COMPANY
Paul Weiland Film Company
DIRECTOR
Frank Budgen
CLIENT
British Airways
AGENCY
Saatchi & Saatchi/London

Gold Award Winners
On The
Gold Award Winners

**CONSUMER NEWSPAPER
OVER 600 LINES: SINGLE**

AGENCY
Fallon McElligott
CLIENT
Jim Beam Brands

At most agencies, two One Show golds for a large packaged goods client would mean a huge bonus and raise, equity in the agency and a company Porsche. At Fallon McElligott, it means you get to keep your job. Thank you for allowing our families to eat for another year.

*TOM LICHTENHELD
JOHN STINGLEY*

1

**CONSUMER NEWSPAPER
600 LINES OR LESS: CAMPAIGN**

AGENCY
Leonard Monahan Lubars & Kelly/Providence
CLIENT
The Narragansett

The client did in fact go out of business. So who says award winning ads don't work?

*MICHAEL KADIN
JIM GARAVENTI*

11

**CONSUMER NEWSPAPER
UNDER 600 LINES: CAMPAIGN**

AGENCY
Fallon McElligott
CLIENT
Jim Beam Brands

Response from our client when we called to tell him that his campaign had won two golds, three silvers and a bronze in The One Show: "Is that good?"

*JOHN STINGLEY
TOM LICHTENHELD*

8

**CONSUMER MAGAZINE
COLOR 1 PAGE OR SPREAD:
SINGLE**

**CONSUMER MAGAZINE B/W
1 PAGE OR SPREAD: SINGLE**

**TRADE B/W
1 PAGE OR SPREAD: SINGLE**

AGENCY
Goldsmith/Jeffrey, New York
CLIENT
Everlast

Clichèd response #1:
Winning a gold pencil makes all the sweat worthwhile.
(SFX: SNARE DRUM)

Clichèd response #2:
A great product. A great client. A great budget. How could we have done an ad that stunk?
(SFX: SNARE DRUM)

Clichèd response #3:
We'd like to thank the judges. Without their keen sense of smell, this would never have been possible.
(SFX: SNARE DRUM, CYMBAL)

*GARY GOLDSMITH
TY MONTAGUE*

14

CONSUMER MAGAZINE
COLOR 1 PAGE OR SPREAD: CAMPAIGN

AGENCY
Fallon McElligott
CLIENT
Porsche Cars A.G.

To come up with this campaign, we sat in a room for two weeks and imagined what it would be like if we had listened to a head hunter and could actually afford one of these things.

BRUCE BILDSTEN
TOM LICHTENHELD

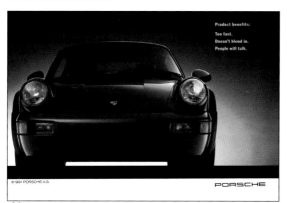

21

OUTDOOR: SINGLE

AGENCY
Mad Dogs & Englishmen/New York
CLIENT
Tiny Mythic Theatre Company

Frankenstein. The Musical?? What else could you do?

NICK COHEN
TY MONTAGUE

29

OUTDOOR: CAMPAIGN

AGENCY
Chiat/Day/Mojo, New York
CLIENT
NYNEX Information Resources

When we started workng on the NYNEX account in January '91, we inherited a lot of old baggage:
    A TV campaign that illustrated yellow pages' headings with visual puns.
    A format where the viewer had to guess the heading before it was actually revealed.
    An endline.
    A white background.
Somehow, we managed to make it work on outdoor.

DION HUGHES
CABELL HARRIS

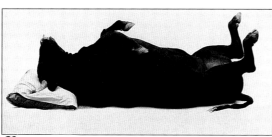

32

TRADE COLOR
1 PAGE OR SPREAD: SINGLE

AGENCY
Gordon/Gier, Chicago
CLIENT
Crain's Chicago Business

With all the interdepartmental strife, the committees, the layers of approval and the political backstabbing within our worldwide conglomerate it was a wonder we got this ad out the door.

George Gier, Senior Group Executive Grand Imperial Chancellor of Creative Operations in the Southern Hemisphere.

Mitch Gordon, Senior Group Executive Grand Imperial Chancellor of Creative Operations in the Northern Hemisphere.

GEORGE GIER
MITCH GORDON

38

**THE GOLD AWARD
WINNERS ON
THE GOLD AWARD
WINNERS**

AGENCY
Fallon McElligott
CLIENT
The Lee Company

We tried to do ads that didn't look like other ads.
Or even look like ads at all. (Okay, that one
"bellbottoms" ad looks like an ad, but Arty did that
one.)

As for the grammatical error in the "map" ad, that's
Arty's fault, too.

Also, we share credit with a great client that trusts its
agency enough to run an ad without a headline or
even a logo, as they allowed us to do with the
"changing booth" ad. (Arty said it needed a long,
explanatory headline and a big logo, but I told him
to shut up.)

*LUKE SULLIVAN
ARTY TAN*

43

AGENCY
Fallon McElligott
CLIENT
Art Directors/Copywriters Club of Minnesota

We would like to present the copy from this mailer
as a public service to all those who have gone blind
trying to read ads reprinted in show books:

Yikes! Have you noticed lately that a lot of ads start
out with really big type that gets progressively
smaller as you work your way down the page?
Good agencies are doing it. Mediocre agencies are
doing it. Even really lame agencies are doing it.
Why? Some might call it a trend. Others, a
breakthrough. Whatever. Love it. Hate it. The
truth is, it can and has been done well. Most
notably by the creator of the Nature Company ads,
Tracy Wong, who (all these types of ads come to a
point eventually) will be speaking to the Art
Directors/Copywriters Club, Thursday, November
14. Tracy, for those of you who think "CA" stands
for "California," is an art director at Goodby, Berlin
& Silverstein in San Francisco. Oh, and he's not a
girl, as his name might suggest. Although he does
have a ponytail. This type is getting really squinty
now, so we'll wrap it up. Azur Restaurant. 5:30,
cocktails. 6, dinner. 7, Tracy. 20 bucks for non-
members. Members free. RSVP by Nov. 12, 339-
1590. Futura Extra-Bold Condensed lives!

*BOB BARRIE
DOUG DE GROOD*

AGENCY
Bartleby/New York
CLIENT
Waldorf Astoria

Once there lived a giant who regularly terrorized the
children of a woodland village. Whenever they
played at river's edge, the giant would burst from
the forest and the children would flee screaming in
horror. Then one day one of the children, a little
girl, stopped in the path of the stampeding giant
and so surprised him that he nearly stumbled.
"Please, Mr. Giant," she implored, "have mercy. We
are only poor children from the village." As she
finished her entreaty, the young girl held forth a
small flower. The giant took the flower in his hand,
his lip began to tremble, and a tear came to his eye.
He was so grateful to the young girl, that he lifted
her into his arms to thank her and crushed her to death.

*GREG DI NOTO
KATHY DELANEY*

47

Yikes! Have you noticed that a lot of ads lately start

out with really big type which gets progressively smaller as you

work your way down the page? Good agencies

are doing it. Mediocre agencies are doing it. Even

really lame agencies are doing it. Why? Some might call it a trend.

Others, a breakthrough. Whatever. Love it. Hate it. The truth is, it can and

has been done well. Most notably by the creator of the Nature Company ads, Tracy Wong, who (all these

types of ads come to a point eventually) will be speaking to the Art Directors/Copywriters Club, Thursday, November 14.

Tracy, for those of you who think "CA" stands for "California," is an art director at Goodby, Berlin & Silverstein in San Francisco. Oh, and he's not a girl, as his name might

53

COLLATERAL DIRECT MAIL: CAMPAIGN

AGENCY
The Richards Group/Dallas
CLIENT
Tabu Lingerie

I pulled a lot of all-nighters coming up with the ideas for this campaign. (Thanks, Tammy, for such heavenly inspiration.)

TODD TILFORD

I finally get a chance to do a photo shoot with a bunch of beautiful, scantily-clad women. And I blow it.

JEFF HOPFER

57

PUBLIC SERVICE NEWSPAPER OR MAGAZINE: SINGLE

AGENCY
Della Femina McNamee/New York
CLIENT
City Meals On Wheels

Ironically, we came up with this ad over lunch.

LARRY SILBERFEIN
DAVID LEINWOHL

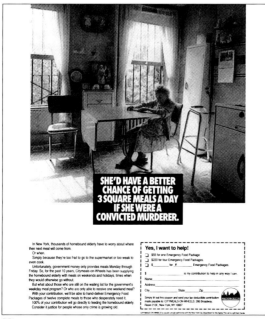

63

COLLATERAL P.O.P.

AGENCY
Goldberg Moser O'Neill/San Francisco
CLIENT
The Red and White Fleet

One Show Gold and no raise?
Obviously, crime doesn't pay.

JIM NOBLE
MICHAEL WILDE

60

PUBLIC SERVICE NEWSPAPER OR MAGAZINE: CAMPAIGN

AGENCY
Earle Palmer Brown/Bethesda
CLIENT
Goodwill

Studies show that disabled workers get to work earlier, stay later, and work harder than average employees. (Good thing we didn't tell them about all the glamorous, high-paying jobs in advertising, or we'd all be out on the street.)

PAUL ASAO
DEAN BUCKHORN
SHARYN PANAGIDES
LYNNE SCRIMGEOUR

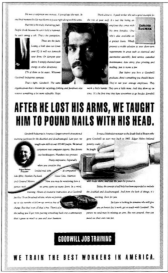

66

**PUBLIC SERVICE:
OUTDOOR**

AGENCY
GSD&M/Austin
CLIENT
American Civil Liberties Union/San Francisco

Three writers and one art director sat around in a room pounding ideas out. After a few hours, the art director just said, "Look, it's 10:30. I've got a wife and kids at home. You guys write whatever you want," and left. So we did.

Screw him.

*BRIAN BROOKER
TIM BAUER
DANIEL RUSS
MIKE BEVIL*

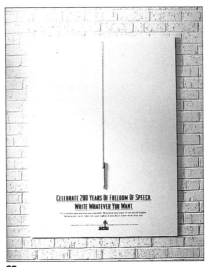

69

**PUBLIC SERVICE TELEVISION:
SINGLE**

AGENCY
Fallon McElligott
CLIENT
The Violence Against Women Coalition

Isn't it ironic that a lot of television stations refused to run this commercial?

*BILL MILLER
CAROL HENDERSON*

In memory of Mary Foley.

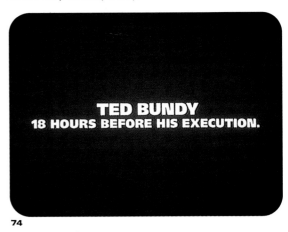

74

**CONSUMER RADIO:
SINGLE**

AGENCY
The Bomb Factory/Los Angeles
CLIENT
Wolfgang Puck Food Company

It was pretty classy of Jane McCann and the people at Propaganda Films to go along with the idea of me doing radio for someone who came to them asking for a TV spot and I hope by now they've forgotten about how much money this may have cost them.

MARK FENSKE

CONSUMER RADIO:
CAMPAIGN

AGENCY
Chiat/Day/Mojo, New York
CLIENT
NYNEX Information Resources

To create effective, award-winning advertising requires an almost inhuman level of commitment. Success can only be achieved through great hardship and personal sacrifice. For example, I missed out on the company picnic to write these NYNEX spots.

DION HUGHES

CONSUMER TELEVISION
OVER :30 (:45/:60/:90) CAMPAIGN

AGENCY
BMP DDB Needham Worldwide/London
CLIENT
Barclaycard

Most ads begin life with a blank piece of paper, a blank copywriter and a blank art director.

This time, the director and actor were there at the birth.

Story lines got suggested, rejected, revived and remodeled. Dialogue got turned upside down. So did one of the cast.

In the end, it looked like the scripts just tripped off the typewriter. Dream on.

JON MATTHEWS
FRASER ADAMSON
JOHN LLOYD

89

CONSUMER TELEVISION
:30/:25 SINGLE

AGENCY
Chiat/Day/Mojo, New York
CLIENT
Reebok

We'd like to dedicate this award to Yoda, the brave Mexican hairless chihuahua who made the ultimate sacrifice so that we can all enjoy four seconds of pretty cool film.

DICK SITTIG
STEVE SWEITZER
BOB RICE

92

CONSUMER TELEVISION
:30/ :25 CAMPAIGN

AGENCY
Goodby Berlin & Silverstein/San Francisco
CLIENT
Chevys Mexican Restaurant

3:30 AM: Wake Up.
4:30 AM: Meet at agency.
4:30-5:30 AM: Have pre-pro, donuts.
5:30-7:00 AM: Shoot.
7:00-9:30 AM: Edit.
10:00 AM: Show to client.
10:15 AM: Dub. Send to stations.
10:30 AM: Go to work.

You try it sometime.

TRACY WONG
STEVE SIMPSON

97

The Gold Award Winners on The Gold Award Winners

Agency
DDB Needham Worldwide/New York
Client
The New York State Lottery

This spot was meant to focus attention on a very sad and serious subject: the plight of lottery-winning nerds. Judging from the laughter we heard at the awards ceremony, it's obvious most of you would rather dismiss it as one big joke. You should all be ashamed of yourselves.

PAUL SPENCER
DAVID ANGELO

100

Agency
Fallon McElligott
Client
Nature's Course

Thanks to Mark Coppos, the most difficult challenge on this shoot was keeping the crew from eating the dog trainer's supply of Oscar Mayer hot dogs.

DEAN HANSON
PHIL HANFT

102

Agency
Della Femina McNamee/New York
Client
Dribeck Importer/Beck's Beer

We could talk about some great strategy, or account management's incredible insight into the client's business, or even Jerry and Louise's personal collection of Chia Pets. But it happened a little more like this:

We had a 5:00 PM flight to Miami to meet wth another client. At 4:00 PM , Jim Durfee walked into our office and said, "We need a Beck's campaign that reaches a much younger target." We said, "Great, when do you need it?" He looked at his watch. We asked, "What's the budget?" and he just laughed. And laughed. We thought about it on the way to the airport. Talked a little at the gate. But the fear of flying outweighed the fear of not producing, and the Valium kicked in right on time before take-off. All we can say is when we landed in Miami, we were well-rested and had a nice idea for a campagin.

MARGARET ELMAN
RAUL PINA

101

**CONSUMER TELEVISION
:20 AND UNDER CAMPAIGN**

AGENCY
Chiat/Day/Mojo, Venice
CLIENT
Eveready Battery

The best thing about flying to Grand Cayman for a week to shoot the bunny underwater? We cut the account executive's air hose.

*ROB FEAKINS
JERRY GENTILE*

105

**CONSUMER TELEVISION
UNDER $50,000 BUDGET**

AGENCY
Fitzgerald & Company/Atlanta
CLIENT
Opti-World

Strange as it seems, I've always sort of preferred doing low-budget TV to doing big-budget stuff. Money corrupts—not only politicians and televangelists, but advertising ideas. Ideas don't need dollars. (Writers, however, do.) Don't get me wrong, I also like a decent sized budget now and again. In fact, a project I did not long ago, actually had enough money in it to buy the creatives lunch. Spam, the whole works.

GUY LOWE

107

**BEST OF SHOW
NON-BROADCAST:
CINEMA/VIDEO**

AGENCY
Saatchi & Saatchi/London
CLIENT
British Airways

This idea was actually conceived in New York where to our surprise, as reserved Englishmen, we witnessed a cinema audience shouting abuse at the characters in the film on the screen. Wouldn't it be funny, we thought, if the characters on the screen started shouting back?

As well as the cinema audience, we also have to thank our Creative Director, Paul Arden and Managing Director, David Kershaw; Account Executives, Annette Edwards, Julie Hart, David de Maestri and Michael Moszynski; TV Producer, Mark Hanrahan and PA Andrea Turner; the Paul Weiland Film Company, particularly Director Frank Budgen and Producer Paul Rothwell and, of course, our client.

Without their help and enthusiasm, an idea like this would never have got off the ground.

The commercial was surprisingly inexpensive to produce and generated TV, radio and press coverage that amounted to six times the media spend.

*JOHN PALLANT
MATT RYAN*

110

**NON-BROADCAST:
OUT-OF-HOME**

AGENCY
Goldsmith/Jeffrey, New York
CLIENT
Lumex

The category here is Out-Of-Home.

Considering that this spot illustrates how a walker can help the elderly and disabled get out and do things, it seems especially significant.

*NOAM MURRO
DEAN HACOHEN*

**CONSUMER TELEVISION
FOREIGN LANGUAGE**

AGENCY
Nordskar & Thorkildsen Leo Burnett/Oslo
CLIENT
Sparebankkort

The hardest part of creating this commercial was not coming up with the idea. That proved to be a painless and not too time-consuming process. The hardest part was to convince the client, after shooting the commercial, that the audience would have no difficulties in understanding the idea. He should be convinced by now.

*JOHAN GULBRANSON
BENTE AMUNDSEN
LISBETH AMUNDSEN*

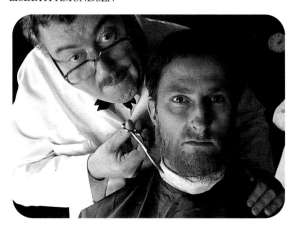

SCHOOL
Portfolio Center/Atlanta
ASSIGNMENT
Print ad promoting your college.

We're currently working on the sequel: "Portfolio Center Graduates Are More Employable Than Harvard's." Your help in this matter would be greatly appreciated.

GREG COLLINS (404) 609-9310
BOB RICKERT (503) 649-1095
STEVE TAYLOR (813) 238-3702

P.S. Eleven borrowed ideas in one ad. Isn't that some sort of record?

Print Finalists

121
ART DIRECTOR
Ron Brown
WRITER
David Abbott
TYPOGRAPHER
Joe Hoza
CLIENT
The Economist
AGENCY
Abbott Mead Vickers. BBDO/
London

122
ART DIRECTOR
John Horton
WRITER
Richard Foster
PHOTOGRAPHER
Graham Ford
CLIENT
Volvo
AGENCY
Abbott Mead Vickers. BBDO/
London

123
ART DIRECTOR
John Horton
WRITER
Richard Foster
TYPOGRAPHER
Joe Hoza
CLIENT
The Economist
AGENCY
Abbott Mead Vickers. BBDO/
London

124
ART DIRECTOR
Paul Blade
WRITER
Tom Thomas
PHOTOGRAPHER
Vic Huber
CLIENT
Saab Cars USA
AGENCY
Angotti Thomas Hedge/
New York

125
ART DIRECTOR
Norman Alcuri
WRITER
Jim Aitchison
PHOTOGRAPHER
Alex Kaikeong
CLIENT
UTA French Airlines
AGENCY
The Ball Partnership/
Singapore

"Send cash, grain and a subscription to The Economist."

Boris.

121

INSTEAD OF A COAT OF PAINT, WE GIVE IT A SUIT OF ARMOUR.

122

The Economist

123

THE SPORTS SEDAN FOR PEOPLE WHO INHERITED BRAINS INSTEAD OF WEALTH.

There are two ways to approach the purchase of a sports sedan. You can spend your way into one, or you can think your way there.

For those who'd rather think than spend, there's the Saab 9000S.

The 9000S is the sports sedan that brings something rare to the category: a complete car.

First, it's a driver's car, engineered for those who take driving seriously

> *The Saab 900 Series From $18,295 to $33,295.*
> *The Saab 9000 Series From $22,895 to $33,995.*
> *For more information, call 1-800-582-SAAB*

and do it well. It's propelled by the largest engine Saab ever built and a highly tactile steering system.

But unlike some driver's cars, the 9000S doesn't shortchange passengers. It's the only import roomy enough to be rated a "Large" car by the EPA.

Nor does it yield to a station wagon in its practicality. Fold down the split rear seats, and there's enough

space (56.5 cu. ft.) for a six-foot sofa, with a hatchback for easy loading.

In fact, you could buy a 9000S for its utility alone, but then you'd have to ignore its full complement of amenities. Including leather upholstery, electric sunroof, heated seats, a driver's-side air bag and anti-lock brakes.

All this in a car that, according to studies by the Highway Loss Data Institute (HLDI), ranks among the safest in its class. And is backed by

one of the longest warranties in its class: 6 years or 80,000 miles.**

No other $26,995* sports sedan can offer all that. So if you've in fact inherited brains instead of wealth, the best place to spend that inheritance is at your Saab dealer, where the 9000S awaits your test drive.

SAAB
WE DON'T MAKE COMPROMISES. WE MAKE SAABS.

124

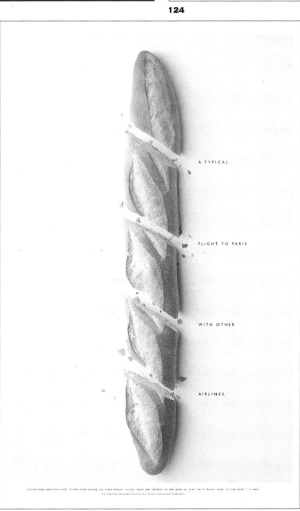

A TYPICAL

FLIGHT TO PARIS

WITH OTHER

AIRLINES.

125

126

127

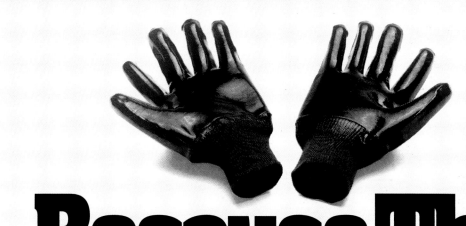

Because The Flesh Is Weak.

You can't be too careful these days. You need protection. You need our rubber work gloves for the low price of just $6.97. And with a pair of these, you should be able to get your hands on just about anything. *True Value* **The Hardware Store.**

555 Railroad Drive, Elk River, 241-0282

"Dad. What was Granny like?"

There's a lot of talk in the camcorder world about 'features.'

'Auto zoom magnifications,' 'low illumination' capabilities, 'amorphous pro heads' and so on.

But make no mistake. This isn't really what owning a camcorder is about at all.

Owning a camcorder is actually about children. And about wives.

About friends. And parents.

It's about the people with whom you share your life. About what she said. What he did. What they wore. How she walked.

About the song they sang.

How she laughed and laughed until she almost couldn't laugh any more.

How you ate too much: drank too much.

How they were when they were three feet tall.

The new Panasonic NV G2 is strong on the features. **VHSC**

8x magnification autozoom lens. Digitial autofocus. The ability to shoot in very low light. Detachable automatic light to keep you shooting when it really *would* otherwise be too dark.

It has 'long play,' allowing you up to ninety minutes shooting. Digital superimposing so you can add titles. It uses tapes you can play back on your VHS recorder, and it can be operated either manually or automatically.

But, for all of this, the reason to buy an NVG2 is not because you care about specifications.

It's because you care about people.

Panasonic
THE STATE OF THE ART

Camcorder NV G2

See the NVG2 at your nearest Panasonic Specialist Dealer listed in Yellow Pages or Thomson Directories. Panasonic Consumer Electronics UK, Willoughby Road, Bracknell, Berks RG12 4FP. (Telephone. 0344 852943)

Your children don't stop growing up just because you're dithering about which camcorder to buy.

How long is it, now, that you've been dithering about buying a camcorder? And for how much longer do you plan to carry on? Another few years, maybe?

After all, it's only your next three or four summer holidays and your child's next three or four birthday parties (eight parties with two kids, twelve if you've got three), that you're going to miss, isn't it?

(And a few first smiles, first words, first footsteps, family Christmases and school plays and prize-givings, too, of course.)

But, considering that you could go out today and buy yourself the Panasonic NV G2, what is it, exactly, that you are dithering *about?*

The NV G2 gives you outstanding picture quality, and it couldn't be simpler to use. **VHSC**

It has an 8x power zoom lens, and full-range 'digital' autofocus. It can shoot in low illumination, and it has a detachable light which automatically comes on to keep you shooting even when it *would* otherwise be too dark.

'Long play' gives you up to ninety minutes shooting per tape, and digital superimposing lets you add titles. On top of all that, the tapes play back on your VHS recorder.

Don't dither a second longer. Your kids only grow up once. You mustn't miss another moment of it.

Panasonic
THE STATE OF THE ART

Camcorder NV G2

See the NV G2 at your nearest Panasonic Specialist Dealer listed in Yellow Pages or Thomsons Directories. Panasonic Consumer Electronics UK, Willoughby Road, Bracknell, Berks RG12 4FP. (Tel. 0344 853943)

131

132

There are feet that don't care what a Bentley Turbo is going for these days. There are feet that could care less what the Nasdaq is doing. There are feet that wouldn't know an espresso machine if they tripped over one. Dunham. They get the job done.

133

There are feet that have never seen a David Hockney. There are feet that have never walked the streets of Cannes. There are feet unfamiliar with beluga at midnight. Dunham. They get the job done.

134

There are feet that will never meet the gas pedal of a Range Rover. There are feet that will never see a condo in Aspen. There are feet that will never winter in Palm Springs or Palm Beach or Palm anywhere. Dunham. They get the job done.

135

There are feet that have never gotten the corner office. There are feet that have never sat through a shareholder's meeting. There are feet that have never had sushi for lunch. There are feet that have never seen the inside of an Italian loafer. Dunham. They get the job done.

136

GO 15 M.P.H. BECAUSE YOU WANT TO.

Whoever first proclaimed that getting there is half the fun couldn't have been all there —or at least not sitting in rush-hour traffic.

Because for most of us, five straight days of life in the fast lane often makes us wonder if we're getting anywhere at all.

You'll have your head in the clouds too, once you see the purple mountain majesties of Western Maryland.

Fortunately though, it's nothing a weekend mini-vacation can't cure.

But not just anywhere, mind you. To a place where the living is easy and the pace is stop-and-smell-the-roses relaxingly slow.

One that's off the beaten track, far from the maddening

Ever travel back through time? Try the National Capital Trolley Museum in Wheaton or the Streetcar Museum in Baltimore.

crowd but not too far away from home.

And no, it's not somewhere over the rainbow but a place

On the Eastern Shore of the Chesapeake Bay, tiny ferries have aided the mingling of Marylanders since the 1600s.

that actually exists. It's a land called Maryland.

Where the mountains stand tall, the rivers run deep and the ocean goes on as far as the eye can see.

Where you can sail, kayak, windsurf, canoe, ride a trolley, boogie-board, hot-air-balloon, bike, snow-ski or water-ski, all in the course of a weekend. The modes of transport here are many. The traffic jams are few.

You see, Maryland is a place where you can leave the office at the office and exercise your inalienable right to pursue happiness. In a million-and-one different ways. Even if it is only for a couple of days.

To find out what's happening in Maryland 52 weekends a year, call for a free "More Than You Can Imagine" Travel Kit at 1-800-232-2820.

By land, by water or by sea, getting around Maryland can be a lot more than half the fun.

And remember, no matter where you choose to spend a weekend here, it's just a short drive away from home. But a million miles away from Monday morning.

Maryland
Live for the weekend.

137

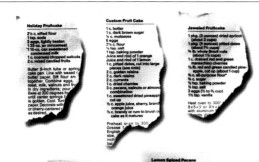

JUST THIS ONCE, WE'LL COVER MORE NUTS AND FRUITCAKES THAN THE TABLOIDS.

This holiday season, look for plenty of irresistible recipes, menus and helpful tips on entertaining in the Star Tribune. Pound for pound, it may be your best guide to the holidays.

Star Tribune
The Newspaper of the Twin Cities.

IT'S AS CRAZY AS THE TABLOIDS. ONLY TRUE.

Here again is proof positive that life is stranger than fiction. This quirky catalog of irony and irregular humor appears, appropriately, irregularly on Thursdays. News of the Weird. Look for it (but not too hard) in the Variety section.

Star Tribune
The Newspaper of the Twin Cities.

MEN AREN'T REALLY A DIME A DOZEN. BUT IT'S CLOSE.

For the price of the Star Tribune, you can meet all kinds of men. And you can get an even cheaper date by running an ad of your own. Call 673-9015 for details today.

"Get Acquainted" in the **Star Tribune**

SEE WHAT THE PEOPLE WITH PONYTAILS WILL BE DOING THIS WEEKEND.

Every Thursday, Weekend Alert tells you what the "cognoscenti" of the Twin Cities arts and entertainment community will be doing. Valuable information, whether you want to avoid them or join them. Theater, comedy, art, music, restaurants, tv, even movie rentals.

StarTribune
The Newspaper of the Twin Cities.

141

There is a car which resides in the Porsche museum in Stuttgart which is matter-of-factly referred to as "Number 1." Implying, simply, the first in a series.

In fact it was this very car, which, throughout the cold winter of 1948, Professor F. Porsche and his small company labored over. Laying down basic principles and design philosophies. Setting the extreme standards of handcrafted detail and technological leadership that Porsche has religiously adhered to since.

The body panels were of hand-hammered aluminum. (A material of which other sports cars are just beginning to take advantage.) The engine was meticulously built by hand at a bench. Each individual piece of the car was hand-fitted.

Over four decades later, the 1991 Porsche 928 shows just how unswervingly the concepts established on Porsche Number 1 have been maintained and advanced.

Joining together a myriad of alloys, aluminum, steel and polymers, the 928 broke new ground in exploiting such a mix for weight saving and tensile properties. This makes for awe-inspiring performance and handling, including a top speed of 171 mph for the 5-speed. It also makes for a construction process which, even by Porsche standards, is painstaking.

Welding alone requires 23 working

hours. Consistent with Porsche's racing heritage, welds are used for strength where other cars make do with bolts or rivets. Over 6,000 spot welds are performed before all is said and done.

The body is built up from hot-dip galvanized steel and aluminum panels to obtain the optimum balance of light weight and strength, while preventing corrosion. (When we pioneered zinc galvanizing in 1976 we had to develop our own electron-beam welding system to go through these sheets.)

The 26 step painting process finds white-gloved inspectors using special lights to find and correct virtually imperceptible blemishes. The finish is so flawless that all panels, be they aluminum, steel or polymer, flow fluidly together as one.

A team of eight bench-builds the aluminum engine by hand. It is then test-run for at least 30 minutes, taken all the way to redline, carefully checked for output and entirely re-torqued before being nestled in the car.

And it goes on and on. So how long does all this take? From the moment it is begun, to the moment it is deemed worthy to roll out the door, the average needed to bring a 928 into the world is no less than 3 weeks.

Still, no matter how impressive the process, you cannot begin to appreciate why we do all this until you experience a test-drive at your authorized Porsche dealer. If you decide that this obsessively conceived and executed automobile fits your lifestyle, however, don't wait long to get back to your dealer. Because, while after driving a 928 you may well make your decision overnight, we simply don't create them that way.

The 1991 Porsche 928 GT.

It takes us three working days just to weld the darned thing.

142

Look at it this way, it's either an expensive sportscar or a very reasonable racecar.

The new generation Porsche 911 Turbo is not an automobile built to the standards of a mere street car, but to the impossibly high standards of a race car.

From its immensely-powerful 315-horsepower turbocharged Porsche boxer six engine, to its massive ABS-fortified four-piston disc brakes, it is not just the world's ultimate sportscar. It is the ultimate Porsche.

The result? An automobile capable of accelerating from zero to sixty in a mere 4.25 seconds, and able to stop shorter than any production car in the world. Which is why a showroom stock version of the new 911 Turbo so handily defeated the world's reigning supercars to win the inaugural IMSA Bridgestone Potenza Supercar Championship.

True, that extra ten percent that separates the truly exceptional in this world from the merely good doesn't come easily. Or cheaply. But after one test drive, we're confident you'll agree, it's worth every penny.

The Porsche 911 Turbo.

The ultimate Porsche. (Isn't that redundant?)

Let us put it even more directly: The Porsche 911 Turbo is the Porsche of Porsches. An automobile that exemplifies everything we stand for and everything we've ever believed in. A sportscar built not to the standards of a sportscar, but to the impossibly high standards of a race car.

Statistically it is mind-boggling: 315 thoroughbred horses, 332 foot pounds of torque, and massive ABS-fortified brakes combine to not only propel it from 0 to 60 in a mere 4.25 seconds, but also to stop it faster than any production car in the world.

(Not surprisingly, a showroom stock version of the new 911 Turbo effortlessly crushed the likes of the Corvette ZR-1 and Lotus Turbo Esprit to win the inaugural IMSA Bridgestone Potenza Supercar Championship.)

Yet match that brawn to the dramatically-improved new transmission, steering, suspension, and creature comforts of the new generation of Carrera, and you have a beast that is remarkably well-mannered.

But enough adjectives. We are becoming redundant. Test drive the new generation of 911 Turbo and you will agree it is not just the world's ultimate sportscar. It is the ultimate Porsche.

The Porsche 911 Turbo.

Find the 1956 Porsche in this picture.

145

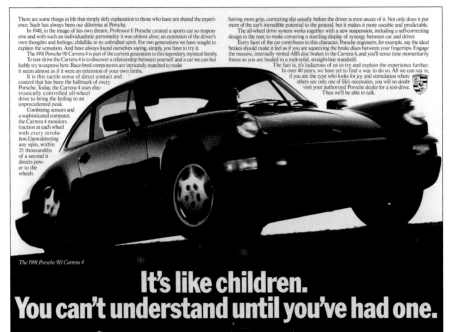

If you're one of those who thought you'd see an automatic in the 911 "when pigs fly," may we suggest you duck?

146

It's like children.
You can't understand until you've had one.

147

148

149

New York's Great Parisian Steakhouse
51st Street at 6th Avenue, Manhattan. 212-956-7100

Cité

155

THE RECESSION IS HAVING AN EFFECT ON A LOT OF STORES. INCLUDING OURS.

bloomingdale's
Closed two stores.

Saks Fifth Avenue
Closed one store.

BONWIT TELLER
Closed eleven stores.

jordan marsh
Closed two stores.

B. Altman & Co
Closed entire chain.

DAFFY'S
Opened new store, August 5th at the
Wayne Towne Center in Wayne, NJ.

While other stores are announcing their going-out-of-business sales, Daffy's is happy to announce the opening of yet another store. This one in the Wayne Towne Center in Wayne, New Jersey. And with men's, women's and children's designer clothing selling at all our stores for 40-80% off the suggested retail price, we expect to be in business for a while.

156

IF YOU'RE PAYING OVER $100 FOR A DRESS SHIRT, MAY WE SUGGEST A JACKET TO GO WITH IT?

With men's and women's designer clothes selling at 40-70% off everyday, you'd be crazy to shop anywhere else. Elizabeth, East Hanover, Paramus, Wayne & New York City.

DAFFY'S
CLOTHES THAT WILL MAKE YOU, NOT BREAK YOU.

NU Riflery Team

Name_____

Address_____

Class_____ Phone_____

Experience_____

C/O THE ATHLETIC DEPARTMENT, ANDREWS HALL, NORTHFIELD, VT 05663

Fill in this coupon today and in 3 months you'll be able to cut it out from 100 feet.

Do you have what it takes to be a true marksman? If you think you might, then the Riflery team's for you. Because we'll not only help you hone your skills, we'll give you the chance to show them off in collegiate and national competition. So tear out this coupon today and who knows, **Norwich University Riflery Team** in a few months you could well cut it out from 100 feet. C/O THE ATHLETIC DEPARTMENT, ANDREWS HALL, NORTHFIELD, VT 05663

In a typical personals ad, even Hemingway would have trouble sounding interesting.

I like to fish. I like to drink. I like to fish and drink. I am looking for a friend. Someone who likes to fish. Who likes to drink. Someone who likes to fish and drink.

With new Personal Calls from The Press-Enterprise you not only place a written personals ad, you also record a message in your own voice over the phone. That way when people see your ad in the paper, they can dial your code, hear your message and leave a message of their own. You can call, day or night, to get your messages. It's fast, it's easy and it helps people find out more about each other. Look in today's classifieds or call your local Press-Enterprise office and ask about our introductory offer. You might find a friend who **Personal Calls** likes to fish. Who likes to drink. Who likes to fish and drink. **The more Personal Personals**

CONSUMER NEWSPAPER
OVER 600 LINES: SINGLE

160
ART DIRECTOR
Steve Dunn
WRITER
Tim Delaney
PHOTOGRAPHER
John Claridge
CLIENT
Harrods
AGENCY
Leagas Delaney/London

161
ART DIRECTOR
Christine Jones
WRITER
Giles Montgomery
PHOTOGRAPHER
John Claridge
CLIENT
Timberland
AGENCY
Leagas Delaney/London

162
ART DIRECTOR
Christine Jones
WRITER
Giles Montgomery
PHOTOGRAPHER
John Claridge
CLIENT
Timberland
AGENCY
Leagas Delaney/London

163
ART DIRECTOR
Steve Dunn
WRITER
Tim Delaney
CLIENT
The Guardian
AGENCY
Leagas Delaney/London

164
ART DIRECTOR
Mark Oakley
WRITERS
David Lubars
Phil Calvit
PHOTOGRAPHER
Jack Richmond
CLIENT
*NYNEX Mobile
Communications*
AGENCY
*Leonard Monahan Lubars &
Kelly/Providence*

160

161

JUST WHAT YOU NEED WHEN IT'S POURING WITH RAIN. A JACKET FULL OF HOLES.

Timberland jackets are lined with Gore-Tex, a man-made material that contains 9 billion holes per square inch. They allow perspiration out but stop water getting in. So if you want to stay dry, make sure your jacket's got holes in it.

Timberland 🌲

162

I s the mistrust of our European partners bigotry? Party politics? Or historically justified? And what effect will it have on our ability to negotiate a beneficial deal in Maastricht? Every day next week, the Guardian reports on events leading up to the summit and analyses the stance of key politicians, while Guardian Europe this Friday will bring you comment and opinion on the issue from all of Europe's leading newspapers.

The **Newspaper of the year.** *The* **Guardian**

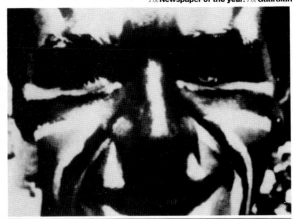

Britain has nothing against Europe. It's just the Italians, Germans and French we don't like.

163

BUY ONE, GET ONE FREE.

(Sorry, cars not included.)

Alas, we're not giving away any sleek foreign automobiles (but we did manage to get your undivided attention now, didn't we?). What we are giving away is the most valuable accessory any car can have: namely, a state-of-the-art 832-series cellular telephone from NYNEX Mobile Communications. Here's the deal: now through March 31st, 1991, when you buy one mobile telephone for its normal price of $395, we'll toss in an identical one absolutely free—nothing, gratis, nada—including standard installation. And with pricing plans as low as $19 a month ($14.25 if you pre-pay one year in advance), a NYNEX Mobile telephone remains inexpensive long after it's been installed. Add it all up and it's quite clear that, for mobile communications, the answer is NYNEX.

NYNEX
Mobile Communications Ⓐ

164

165

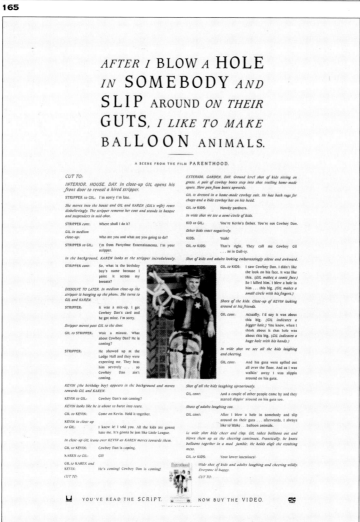

166

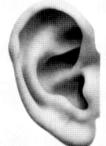

They're odd shaped, quirky looking things.

But they do give you great stereo sound.

They're odd shaped, quirky looking things.

But they do give you great stereo sound.

Supposing a pair of ears came up for review in a hi-fi magazine. Just what would the reviewer say?

No doubt there'd be references to their 'startlingly accurate frequency response.'

Praise would be heaped on the 'uncannily natural sound reproduction.'

And there'd certainly be a mention of 'the superb stereo effect wherever the listener is sitting.'

Well, there's a coincidence.

Because that's exactly the kind of thing that hi-fi reviewers have been saying about Canon's new S-50 loudspeakers.

The reason they've been saying it is a breakthrough called Wide Imaging Stereo technology.

No, that's not a marketing man's feeble attempt to deafen you with science.

It's a radically different method of creating stereo sound images.

And, as you'll observe, it's resulted in a radically different looking stereo speaker.

For a start, the enclosure is not the familiar box-shape, but domed.

And instead of pointing outwards, it's directed downwards onto a precisely angled 'acoustic mirror.'

This reflects sound out into the room, and in doing so achieves something quite remarkable.

A stereo 'hot spot' at least six times the size produced by conventional speakers.

Most impressive. But what does that mean in plain English?

It means simply that you can enjoy balanced stereo sound over a much larger area of your living room.

In other words, whether you're sitting on the left end of the sofa, or the right end, it'll still sound as though you're sitting exactly in the middle.

If you'd like to witness this remarkable phenomenon with your own ears, may we suggest you call in at your local Canon Audio outlet listed opposite.

On the other hand, to understand more about the technical story behind the S-50, we'd recommend a pair of scissors.

They're odd-shaped, quirky looking things. But they're great for cutting out coupons.

Canon WIDE IMAGING STEREO

Heathland under threat

Miles to go?

You are what you wear

Ancient hare of the dog revealed

Construction firm set to dig deep

It's a dog's life

Trend towards a healthier diet

The basic principle behind a Lloyds Bank savings account.

Leave your money in any Lloyds Bank savings account and you know exactly what to expect. More money.

But while the thinking behind them may be the same, the accounts themselves are not. Each offers a different combination of interest and access.

So you're free to choose the one that best suits your financial situation.

To find out more, phone 0800 444230,

or pop into your local branch for a chat with our staff. You'll find them all ears.

Lloyds Bank

THE THOROUGHBRED BANK.

"Wow! I Could've Had A V8!"

With new auto loans starting at just 9¾% APR* from National City Bank, you could save enough money to buy a more powerful engine or any number of other tasty options. To pre-qualify for your auto loan, simply call our Downtown Office at 340-3003 or our Southdale Office at 920-4910. Or see a Personal Banker.

*36-month rate. 20% down + tax & license. Monthly payments on a $10,000 loan are $321.59. Longer terms also available. Ask about our used car, boat and motor home financing, too. Rates effective June 3, 1991. Subject to change without notice.

9¾% APR

 NCB NATIONAL CITY BANK

Member FDIC—An Equal Opportunity Lender © 1991 National City Bank

CONSUMER NEWSPAPER
OVER 600 LINES: SINGLE

170
ART DIRECTOR
Cliff Sorah
WRITER
Joe Alexander
PHOTOGRAPHER
Jon Hood
CLIENT
Bank One Texas
AGENCY
*The Martin Agency/
Richmond*

171
ART DIRECTOR
Shari Hindman
WRITER
Joe Alexander
CLIENT
Signet Bank
AGENCY
*The Martin Agency/
Richmond*

172
ART DIRECTOR
Bob Meagher
WRITERS
John Mahoney
Kevin Grimsdale
PHOTOGRAPHER
Tony Sylvestro
CLIENT
Virginia Power
AGENCY
*The Martin Agency/
Richmond*

173
ART DIRECTOR
Bob Meagher
WRITER
Steve Bassett
PHOTOGRAPHER
Dean Hawthorne
CLIENT
Virginia Power
AGENCY
*The Martin Agency/
Richmond*

Wallpaper your entire house with one 8½x11 sheet.

If you need a home improvement loan fast, call 1-800-695-1111 anytime day or night and fill out this application over the phone. We'll give you an answer within 24 hours. Plus, we'll discount the published interest rate by one-half percent when you have your payments automatically deducted from your Bank One checking account. We'll even lock in your rate for 30 days. So call or stop in. And get some green paper for your walls in no time.

BANK≡ONE
Whatever it takes.

170

If money talks, this is the Larry King of savings accounts.

With low yields and no liquidity, the wrong savings plan could give your money a terminal case of laryngitis.

Which is why you should talk to us right away about the high yield, easy access Performance Savings account, just one part of Signeture Banking's Performance Option.℠

It offers consistently higher yields than other savings plans because it's tied to the BANK RATE MONITOR National Index,™ an average of money market rates paid by 100 of the largest banks and thrifts in the country.

You can earn 1% over the indexed rate when your collected balance reaches

$25,000. And unlike a CD, your money is liquid, meaning you can use it to speak on your behalf anytime.

You can write checks on your savings account and access your money at thousands of ATMs, 7 days a week, 24 hours a day.

The Performance Savings account is one part of the Signeture Banking Performance Option. In addition to a free interest checking account, you can design your banking package from a long list of options and services.

Like no annual fees on a Gold MasterCard® or VISA,® purchase protection, an ATM card that works like a check and special telephone banking privileges.

We could keep talking, but we think you get the picture.

Call 1-800-677-2150 for complete details or current rate information. Or talk to us today at a Signet office near you.

And before long, we'll not only be making your money talk. We'll be making it shout.

SIGNET®
One day we'll be your bank.

171

Batteries can do a lot more than run our radios and power our flash-lights. They can also contribute to our overflowing landfills.

Every year Americans throw away an estimated 2,700,000,000 batter-ies. That's eight batteries for every man, woman and child in the country.

Once discarded, they're taken to landfills and buried. If the land-

nating our drinking water supplies. What can you do?

Use rechargeable batteries. They're now available almost anywhere reg-ular batteries are sold.

While they aren't perfect (recharge-able batteries do contain some cad-mium and are not suitable for use in smoke detectors), they are ideal for use in toys, cameras and small electronics,

much less damage to the environment.

Why are we telling you all this?

We know you're concerned about environmental issues. So we'll be shar-ing more energy-saving ideas with

you in the coming weeks and months.

Because if we don't keep hazardous

The More You Know, The Better.™

substances out of our landfills, they'll keep going and going and going…

All These Batteries Are Long Lasting. They'll Do Damage for Decades.

fill hasn't been properly sealed (and many haven't), the hazardous sub-stances batteries contain can leak out and seep into the ground, contami-

and can be used over and over again.

Which means a lot fewer batter-ies going to the landfill.

Not to mention the potential for

Help Families In Need Add Some Extra Insulation To Their Homes This Winter.

This winter, your old sweaters can do a lot more than sit in the top of your closet, take up space in the attic, or clutter up your chest of drawers.

Your sweaters can help families all over Richmond who will be struggling to keep warm during the cold winter months ahead.

For those in our area who

are facing difficult times—families in crisis, people with limited resources, children, the elderly, the disabled—winter is especially difficult.

Too often, many rely on high-risk heating sources such as space heaters, ovens, and even open fires to keep warm. Sometimes with tragic results.

But your sweaters can go a long way in helping people in need stay warm and safe.

Virginia Power, in partnership with WWBT-TV12 and United Way Services, has set aside one day in September when you can make a difference. It's called the Sweater Recycling Project, and it's easy

to participate. Just bring your usable sweaters to any of the 22 area Ukrop's Super Markets on Saturday, September 28, between 9 a.m. and 4 p.m.

We need sweaters in all sizes for adults and children. So please, look through all your closets and bring whatever you can spare.

Volunteers from Virginia Power will be on hand to accept your sweaters and deliver them to the Richmond Area Association for Retarded Citizens.

From there, they'll be given to United Way affiliated agencies, other health and human service organizations, churches, synagogues, social service departments, and to schools for dis-tribution to people in need throughout the area.

So start gathering **VIRGINIA POWER**
The More You Know, The Better.™

your sweaters now. Then take them to your nearest Ukrop's on Saturday, September 28. It's something we can all feel a little warmer about this winter.

Consumer Newspaper
Over 600 Lines: Single

174
ART DIRECTORS
Taras Wayner
Nick Cohen
WRITER
Sharon Caplan
CLIENT
Village Voice
AGENCY
Mad Dogs & Englishmen/
New York

175
ART DIRECTORS
Taras Wayner
Nick Cohen
WRITER
Mikal Reich
CLIENT
Village Voice
AGENCY
Mad Dogs & Englishmen/
New York

176
ART DIRECTORS
Nick Cohen
Taras Wayner
WRITERS
Aimee Heller
Courtney Rohen
CLIENT
Village Voice
AGENCY
Mad Dogs & Englishmen/
New York

177
ART DIRECTORS
Taras Wayner
Nick Cohen
WRITER
Mikal Reich
CLIENT
Village Voice
AGENCY
Mad Dogs & Englishmen/
New York

178
ART DIRECTORS
Taras Wayner
Nick Cohen
WRITERS
Nick Cohen
Courtney Rohen
CLIENT
Village Voice
AGENCY
Mad Dogs & Englishmen/
New York

SITUATIONS WANTED

Tired of walking Fluffy but want to keep him around? Taxidermist. At home service. ☎ 3564

176

SITUATIONS WANTED

SOCIAL WORKER. If I don't get a job soon I'll kill myself. ☎ 2876

178

SITUATIONS WANTED

I, right now, am at the current time presently in the throes of, or should I just simply say, am "involved" with an endeavor which is new to me and is, coincidentally, my first attempt, am basically now actively looking for, and over the course of the last several weeks, which by the way seemed more like several months, have made extensive inquiries about and the type of inquiries where you spend more time on the phone than doing other types of things that you wished you were really doing rather than making inquiries on the phone, but unfortunately not, as I'd originally had hoped for, with as much luck as that I had from the start desired, an appropriate, and fitting, according to my background, a position, at a particular firm, and or, agency or agencies, suited, in a fashion, to my particular skills and strengths and talents. COPY EDITOR ☎ 8666

177

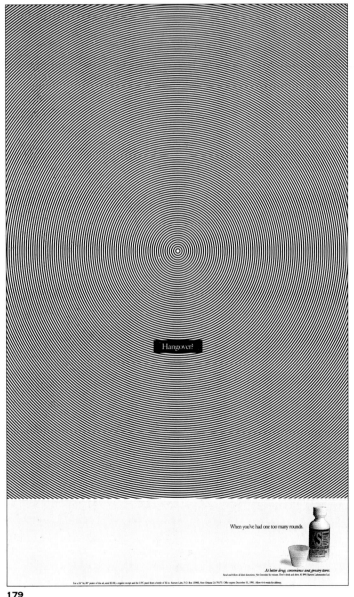

179

180

See How The Other Half Lives.

Considering that injuries on the passenger's side can be every bit as serious as those on the driver's side, it seems more than fair to ask: What's your car going to do about it?

Well, in addition to equipping every 1991 Acura Legend with shoulder harnesses, crumple zones and reinforced steel body and door panels, not to mention a driver's side airbag, we've equipped our Legend LS Sedan with something else. A passenger's side airbag as standard equipment.

However, what really makes each and every Legend unique isn't just the features that help you survive accidents. It's also the many other features that help you prevent them.

Such as Acura NSX-inspired steering and double wishbone suspension for improved accident avoidance. A longer and wider wheelbase for improved handling. And let's not forget every Legend offers anti-lock brakes.

But why take this ad's word for it? Visit your Southern California Acura Dealer. Because when you think about it, there are safe investments. And investments in safety. And an Acura Legend is undoubtedly both.

ⒶACURA
Southern California Dealers

181

182

183

184
ART DIRECTOR
Paul Blade
WRITER
Tom Thomas
PHOTOGRAPHER
Vic Huber
CLIENT
Saab Cars USA
AGENCY
*Angotti Thomas Hedge/
New York*

185
ART DIRECTOR
Jill Bohannan
WRITER
Barton Landsman
PHOTOGRAPH
Stock
CLIENT
Flashy Trash
AGENCY
*Bohannan Landsman and
a Fax Machine/
San Francisco*

THE SPORTS SEDAN FOR PEOPLE WHO INHERITED BRAINS INSTEAD OF WEALTH.

There are two ways to approach the purchase of a sports sedan. You can spend your way into one, or you can think your way there.

For those who'd rather think than spend, there's the Saab 9000S.

The 9000S is the sports sedan that brings something rare to the category: a complete car.

First, it's a driver's car, engineered for those who take driving seriously and do it well. It's propelled by the largest engine Saab ever built and a highly tactile steering system.

But unlike some driver's cars, the 9000S doesn't shortchange passengers. It's the only import roomy enough to be rated a "Large" car by the EPA.

Nor does it yield to a station wagon in its practicality. Fold down the split rear seats, and there's enough space (56.5 cu. ft.) for a six-foot sofa, with a hatchback for easy loading.

In fact, you could buy a 9000S for its utility alone, but then you'd have to ignore its full complement of amenities. Including leather upholstery, electric sunroof, heated seats, a driver's-side air bag and anti-lock brakes.

All this in a car that, according to studies by the Highway Loss Data Institute (HLDI), ranks among the safest in its class. And is backed by one of the longest warranties in its class: 6 years or 80,000 miles.

No other $26,995* sports sedan can offer all that. So if you've in fact inherited brains instead of wealth, the best place to spend that inheritance is at your Saab dealer, where the 9000S awaits your test drive.

The Saab 900 Series: From $18,295 to $33,395.
The Saab 9000 Series: From $22,895 to $33,995.
For more information, call 1-800-582-SAAB.

SAAB
WE DON'T MAKE COMPROMISES. WE MAKE SAABS.

THE ONLY CONVERTIBLE THAT'S ACCEPTABLE IN CERTAIN CIRCLES. SUCH AS THE ARCTIC.

In Northern Sweden, which lies within the icy clutches of the Arctic Circle, it snows 245 days a year. Temperatures sometimes plummet to a bone-chilling 40 degrees below zero.

So what is a convertible doing in such an inclement place? Since it's a Saab, just about anything it's asked to.

The natives there don't hibernate in the winter, so naturally convertibles can't afford to either. And a Saab is engineered accordingly.

Its suspension is tuned to roads that can be snow-covered eight months of the year. Its front-engined, front-wheel-drive design places a full 60% of the car's weight above the drive wheels for extra traction, letting drivers negotiate snow drifts that would keep conventional cars garage-bound.

Of course, traction is no less important when stopping. So Saab has a triple-circuit, anti-lock braking system to bring the car to a straight-line halt even in panic stops on slippery road surfaces.

Inside, the outside is banished altogether. A fully lined automatic roof encloses an eminently civilized passenger compartment, complete with leather-upholstered seating for four adults, a removable AM/FM stereo/cassette system and a driver's-side air bag. There's even a heated glass rear window and heated front seats.

Finally, a Saab convertible protects you not just from longer and harsher winters, but more of them. It's covered by a 6-year/80,000-mile warranty, one of the longest in the industry. And it's available with a sprightly 140-horsepower engine ($30,595) or an extremely sprightly 160-horsepower, turbocharged version ($35,345).

So for a ragtop that doesn't compromise your need for a full-time car, see a Saab dealer. And test-drive the land that raised winter (and convertibles) to an art form. Or, for more information, call 1-800-582-SAAB.

SAAB
WE DON'T MAKE COMPROMISES. WE MAKE SAABS.

WE BUILD CARS AS THOUGH WE WERE BUYING THEM, NOT SELLING THEM.

What if the people who built cars were the same people who bought them?

What if carmakers had to drive, and live with, the cars they made?

For one thing, cars would be safer. They'd have steel safety cages surrounded by collision-absorbing crumple zones, front and rear. They'd have air bags and anti-lock braking systems. Yet even then they'd be hard-pressed to equal the safety record of Saab, which has repeatedly been ranked among the best in its class.

Besides protecting people better, cars would protect themselves better. Warranties would be longer, like the 6-year/80,000-mile warranty all Saabs offer now. And cars would require less scheduled maintenance, less often, as all Saabs do now.

Cars would also be less boring. Engines would be spirited, suspensions surefooted, and steering systems would allow you to communicate with, rather than insulate you from, the road. Much like a Saab.

But cars would also be much more flexible. A performance car would also perform at shopping malls, in car pools, or wherever else work needs to be done—like the Saab 9000S. Fold down its split rear seats, and it will effortlessly carry home a six-foot sofa. Fill it with a family, and it will chauffeur them around in an interior larger than any other imported sedan.

Finally, if builders were also buyers, they'd be in no great hurry to overcharge themselves. So prices would be more Saab-like. (See the box on the left.)

In short, in this improbable scenario, all cars would be complete cars, compromising no one virtue for the sake of another.

We don't advise waiting for that to happen. Instead, we invite you to pay a visit to your nearest Saab dealer, where cars *are* built by people as though they were buying them—and are sold in precisely the same spirit.

The Saab 900 Series: From $19,395 to $35,345.
The Saab 9000 Series: From $24,845 to $38,695.
For more information, call 1-800-582-SAAB.

SAAB
WE DON'T MAKE COMPROMISES. WE MAKE SAABS.

We Don't Carry
Calvin Klein Or Bill Blass.
But We Do Have
Maury Noodlebaum.

Vintage Clothes & Jewelry • 3524 N. Halsted • 312/327-9800 • Open 7 Days At Noon

Flashy Trash

We Didn't Find
Our Fashions
In Paris.
We Found Them
In Mothballs.

Vintage Clothes & Jewelry • 3524 N. Halsted • 312/327-9800 • Open 7 Days At Noon

Flashy Trash

We Don't Know
What Happened To Bud
And His Car.
But We've Got His Clothes.

Vintage Clothes & Jewelry • 3524 N. Halsted • 312/327-9800 • Open 7 Days At Noon

Flashy Trash

**CONSUMER NEWSPAPER
OVER 600 LINES:
CAMPAIGN**

186
ART DIRECTOR
Peter Richards
WRITER
Gary Graf
ILLUSTRATOR
John Fretz
CLIENT
*Boeing Commercial
Airplanes*
AGENCY
Cole & Weber/Seattle

187
ART DIRECTOR
John Doyle
WRITER
Ernie Schenck
PHOTOGRAPHER
Nadav Kander
CLIENT
The Dunham Company
AGENCY
Doyle Advertising/Boston

Rarely Can An Overnight Letter Answer A Follow-up Question.

OVERNIGHT LETTERS ARE USEFUL, RELIABLE, INEXPENSIVE. BUT THERE ARE TIMES WHEN THE MESSENGER IS THE MESSAGE, WHEN THERE'S

just no substitute for being there. ✦✦ Certainly there's no better way to express your interest than in person. You can actually sit down face to face. Not fax to fax or letter to letter. It's an opportunity to communicate, not just correspond. It's the difference between issuing a statement and having a dialogue. ✦✦ In many cultures it's important that this dialogue be unhurried, even relaxed.

The idea is to first form human relationships, then build business relationships. ✦✦ There's more to it than cultural nicety. A dialogue can correct misunderstandings, solve problems, reveal opportunities. ✦✦ So the next time you consider sending an overnight letter to your customers, perhaps it should relay one very important message: that you plan to be there in person. Soon.

SOMETIMES THERE'S NO SUBSTITUTE FOR BEING THERE.

BOEING

There's A Reason You've Never Heard The Expression: "Let's Fax On It."

THE FAX MACHINE IS CERTAINLY A BOON TO BUSINESS. BUT THERE ARE TIMES WHEN THERE'S JUST NO SUBSTITUTE FOR BEING THERE. THAT'S

because there's a lot more to business than business machines. ✦✦ It's important to see the look in the eye as well as the words on the page. To interpret tone of voice as well as confirm facts and data. To discover subtle shades of thought and meaning that unfold during private, unhurried conversation. ✦✦ The value of doing business one-on-one increases with both time and distance. You just can't fax, phone or video-conference the warmth of a handshake in America. Or the dignity of a deep, formal bow in Japan. Or the trust and camaraderie of an embrace in Europe. ✦✦ Direct, human contact. It's the way business has been done since business began. It's something people everywhere understand and appreciate. Simply put, in this high-tech world, high-touch is more important than ever before.

SOMETIMES THERE'S NO SUBSTITUTE FOR BEING THERE.

BOEING

There Are Some Service Calls You Just Can't Make By Phone.

AN OIL RIG IN THE NORTH SEA. A ROBOTICS INSTALLATION IN JAPAN. A PIPELINE ON THE ALASKAN TUNDRA. THERE ARE CERTAIN THINGS

you just can't fix by phone; certain times when there's just no substitute for being there. ✦✦ To see firsthand the nature of the problem. To prevent a delay from becoming a disaster. To insure that it's indeed business as usual. ✦✦ For those whose job is taking care of business, customer service is more than fixing something that's gone wrong. It's making sure things keep going right. ✦✦ After all, who's likely to know more about how a product is performing in the field? About how it stacks up against the competition? About what customers want in refinement and development? ✦✦ In a day and age when companies fight for even the smallest of market shares, service people need to be on the road, not just on the phone. Because chances are if you're not out there seeing your customers, your competition is.

SOMETIMES THERE'S NO SUBSTITUTE FOR BEING THERE.

BOEING

There are feet that don't care what a Bentley Turbo is going for these days.
There are feet that could care less what the Nasdaq is doing. There are feet that
wouldn't know an espresso machine if they tripped over one.
Dunham. They get the job done.

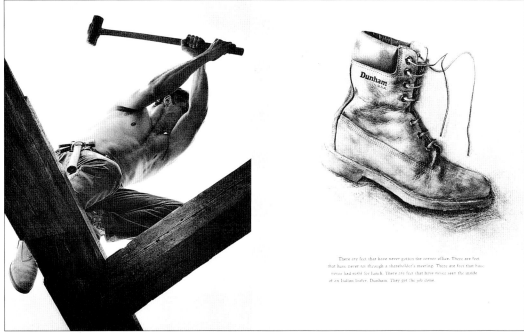

There are feet that have never gotten the corner office. There are feet
that have never sat through a shareholder's meeting. There are feet that have
never had sushi for lunch. There are feet that have never seen the inside
of an Italian loafer. Dunham. They get the job done.

There are feet that will never meet the gas pedal of a Range Rover.
There are feet that will never see a condo in Aspen. There are feet that will
never winter in Palm Springs or Palm Beach or Palm anywhere.
Dunham. They get the job done.

CONSUMER NEWSPAPER
OVER 600 LINES:
CAMPAIGN

188
ART DIRECTOR
Ty Harper
WRITER
Rob Schapiro
PHOTOGRAPHER
Pat Edwards
CLIENT
Reverend Frank Williams
AGENCY
*Earle Palmer Brown/
Richmond*

189
ART DIRECTOR
Andy Lewis
WRITER
Jeff McElhaney
ILLUSTRATORS
*Jeffrey Fisher
Whit Stillman*
CLIENT
Maryland Tourism
AGENCY
*Earle Palmer Brown/
Bethesda*

Holy Roller.

Reverend Frank Williams
Interior/Exterior Painting
353-5133

"Repaint, Ye Sinners."

Reverend Frank Williams
Interior/Exterior Painting
353-5133

A Man Of The Cloth.

Reverend Frank Williams
Interior/Exterior Painting
353-5133

JUST REMEMBER, THE WORKWEEK IS ONLY 40 HOURS. THE WEEKEND IS 48.

Just as all good things must come to an end, happily, so must the bad.

Or to put it another way, no matter how routine your days of 9-to-5, take heart. The weekend is close at hand.

And so is the perfect place to spend it.

Because just a short drive away, in a land called Maryland, lies a place where purple mountain majesties in the west and shining sea of the Eastern Shore are but a few hours apart.

A haven, of sorts, as far from the workaday as it

The Skipjack, a sailboat indigenous to Maryland and one of the many majestic vessels traveling our waters.

is from the everyday.

Where there are so many fun and unusual things to see and do in a weekend, you could almost forget you're so close to home.

Where the official state sport is jousting and the unofficial state pastime is just about anything you can do in or near the water.

And where a few Chesapeake Bay artisans can still carve a piece of wood to look so much like a duck, even a duck can't tell the difference.

You see, Maryland is a place where you can leave the office at the office and

Maryland may have good ol' Orioles baseball, but we also have jousting, lacrosse and kayaking.

See where Babe was just a babe, at the Babe Ruth Birthplace and Museum in Baltimore.

exercise your inalienable right to pursue happiness. In a million-and-one different ways. Even if it is only for a couple of days.

So to find out what's happening in Maryland 52 weekends a year, call for a free "More Than You Can Imagine" Travel Kit at 1-800-872-7467.

Because the way we look at it, life is much too short for all work and no play. Which makes the 48-hour weekend very precious indeed.

Is it a real duck or just a quack? Find out at the North American Wildfowl Art Museum in Salisbury.

Maryland
Live for the weekend.

GO 15 M.P.H. BECAUSE YOU WANT TO.

Whoever first proclaimed that getting there is half the fun couldn't have been all there —or at least not sitting in rush hour traffic.

Because for most of us, five straight days of life in the fast lane often makes us wonder if we're getting anywhere at all.

Fortunately though, it's nothing a weekend mini-vacation can't cure.

But not just anywhere, mind you. To a place where the living is easy and the pace is stop-and-smell-the-roses relaxingly slow.

One that's off the beaten track, far from the maddening

You'll have your head in the clouds too, once you see the purple mountain majesties of Western Maryland.

Ever travel back through time? Try the National Capital Trolley Museum in Wheaton or the Streetcar Museum in Baltimore.

crowd but not too far away from home.

And no, it's not somewhere over the rainbow but a place that actually exists. It's a land called Maryland.

Where the mountains stand tall, the rivers run deep and the ocean goes on as far as the eye can see.

Where you can sail, kayak, windsurf, canoe, ride a trolley, boogie-board, hot-air-balloon, bike, snow-ski or water-ski, all in the course of a weekend. The modes of transport here are many. The traffic jams are few.

On the Eastern Shore of the Chesapeake Bay, tiny ferries have aided the mingling of Marylanders since the 1600s.

You see, Maryland is a place where you can leave the office at the office and exercise your inalienable right to pursue happiness. In a million-and-one different ways. Even if it is only for a couple of days.

To find out what's happening in Maryland 52 weekends a year, call for a free "More Than You Can Imagine" Travel Kit at 1-800-232-2820.

And remember, no matter where you choose to spend a weekend here, it's just a short drive away from home. But a million miles away from Monday morning.

By land, by water or by sea, getting around Maryland can be a lot more than half the fun.

Maryland
Live for the weekend.

TAKE YOUR BODY WHERE YOUR MIND'S BEEN ALL WEEK.

The things we do to our bodies in the name of surviving Monday through Friday.

We overwork it, undersleep it, push it, rush it, work it out, overstuff it, underfeed it, only to turn around and caffeinate it so we can do it all longer.

Well, if your poor body hasn't told your mind already, time out.

Because this weekend, it's time to reward them both. With a two-day reprieve to a place where your body and soul will feel positively one again. Maryland.

A state where you can bike or hike along the 180-mile C&O Canal that stretches from Georgetown, DC to Cumberland in the

Are you tough enough to handle the world class white water of Savage River in Western Maryland? There's only one way to find out.

So you can't pan for gold in Maryland, but you can for prehistoric shark teeth at Calvert Cliffs.

Western part of Maryland.

Where you can white-water raft, kayak, sail, canoe, windsurf or paddle-boat. (There's plenty of ocean, bay, rivers and streams to go around, so pick your vessel.)

And where there's as much a flair for fun as for the funky. Like, when's the last time you saw a crab derby? Or a chicken clucking contest? Ever been to a Lotus Blossom Festival? Or hunted for prehistoric sharks' teeth?

You see, Maryland is a place where you can leave the office at the office and

Each June, a group of architects builds America's largest sandcastle in Ocean City - over 20 feet high and four blocks long!

exercise your inalienable right to pursue happiness. In a million-and-one different ways. Even if it is only for a couple of days.

So to find out what's happening in Maryland 52 weekends a year, call us for a complimentary "More Than You Can Imagine" Travel Kit at 1-800-543-4860.

While we can't promise you an out-of-body experience here, it's sure to be a reunion your mind and body have been looking forward to a long, long time.

Maryland's always been aglow about its collection of restored historical lighthouses - 25 in all.

Maryland
Live for the weekend.

HERE'S YOUR CHANCE TO WRITE FOR THE NEWSPAPER.

NOW'S YOUR CHANCE TO GET YOUR NAME IN THE PAPER.

THIS IS YOUR LIFE. JUST FILL IN THE BLANKS.

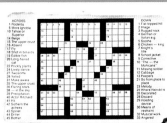

192
ART DIRECTOR
Bill Snitzer
WRITER
John Hage
CLIENT
The Riverside Press Enterprise
AGENCY
Larsen Colby/Los Angeles

193
ART DIRECTOR
Gary Marshall
WRITER
Paul Marshall
PHOTOGRAPHERS
The Douglas Brothers
CLIENT
Unipath
AGENCY
Leagas Delaney/London

**In a typical personals ad,
even Hemingway would have trouble
sounding interesting.**

With new Personal Calls from The Press-Enterprise you not only place a written personals ad, you also record a message in your own voice over the phone. That way when people see your ad in the paper, they can dial your code, hear your message and leave a message of their own. You can call, day or night, to get your messages. It's fast, it's easy and it helps people find out more about each other. Look in today's classifieds or call your local Press-Enterprise office and ask about our introductory offer. You might find a friend who likes to fish. Who likes to drink. Who likes to fish and drink. **Personal Calls**

**In a typical personals ad,
even Jackie Collins would have trouble
sounding romantic.**

With new Personal Calls from The Press-Enterprise you not only place a written personals ad, you also record a message in your own voice over the phone. That way when people see your ad in the paper, they can dial your code, hear your message and leave a message of their own. You can call, day or night, to get your messages. It's fast, it's easy and it helps people find out more about each other. Look in today's classifieds or call your local Press-Enterprise office and ask about our introductory offer. With the right man you could build your very own "Dynasty." (Oops. Wrong sister.) **Personal Calls**

**In a typical personals ad,
even Pavarotti would have trouble
sounding good.**

With new Personal Calls from The Press-Enterprise you not only place a written personals ad, you also record a message in your own voice over the phone. That way when people see your ad in the paper, they can dial your code, hear your message and leave a message of their own. You can call, day or night, to get your messages. It's fast, it's easy and it helps people find out more about each other. Look in today's classifieds or call your local Press-Enterprise office and ask about our introductory offer. You might just find someone to exchange phone numbers and lasagna recipes with. **Personal Calls**

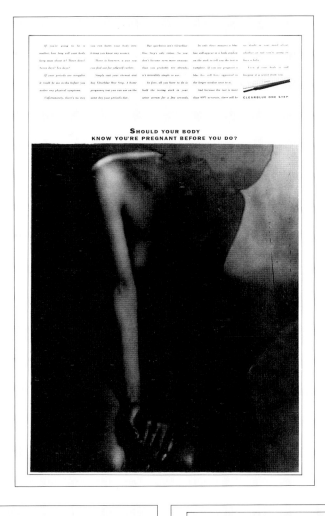

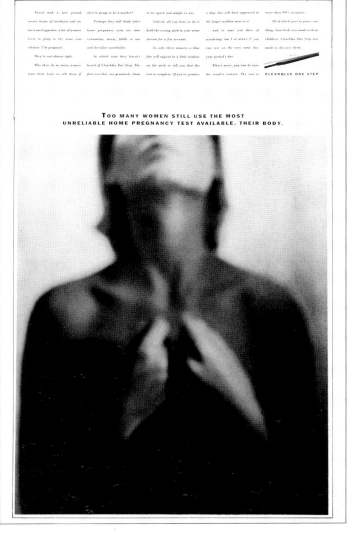

Consumer Newspaper Over 600 Lines: Campaign

194
ART DIRECTORS
Christine Jones
Steve Dunn
WRITERS
Giles Montgomery
Tim Delaney
PHOTOGRAPHER
John Claridge
CLIENT
Timberland
AGENCY
Leagas Delaney/London

195
ART DIRECTORS
Steve Dunn
Christine Jones
Gary Marshall
WRITERS
Tim Delaney
Paul Marshall
PHOTOGRAPHER
John Claridge
CLIENT
Harrods
AGENCY
Leagas Delaney/London

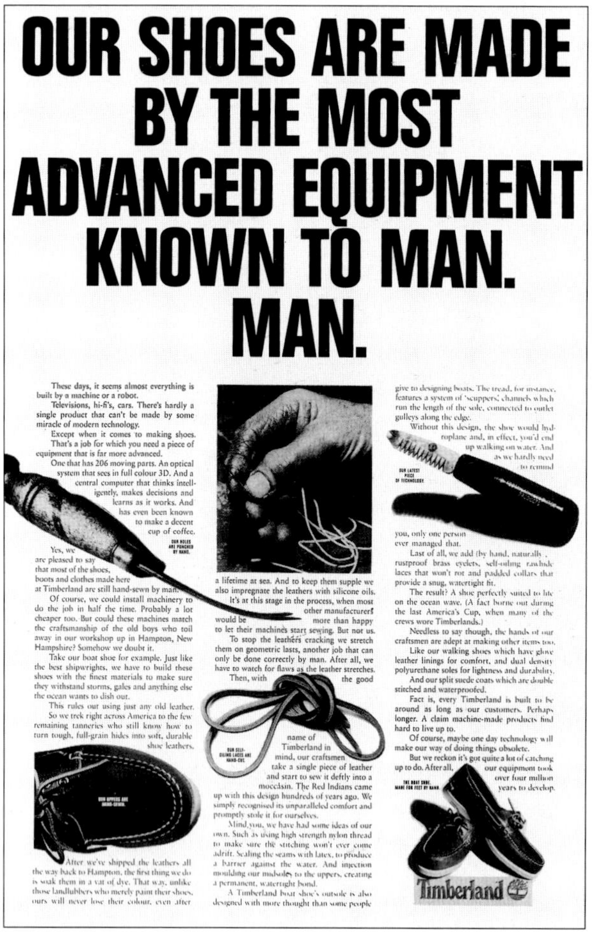
OUR SHOES ARE MADE BY THE MOST ADVANCED EQUIPMENT KNOWN TO MAN. MAN.
These days, it seems almost everything is built by a machine or a robot.
Televisions, hi-fi's, cars. There's hardly a single product that can't be made by some miracle of modern technology.
Except when it comes to making shoes. That's a job for which you need a piece of equipment that is far more advanced.
One that has 206 moving parts. An optical system that sees in full colour 3D. And a central computer that thinks intelligently, makes decisions and learns as it works. And has even been known to make a decent cup of coffee.
OUR HOLES ARE PUNCHED BY HAND.
Yes, we are pleased to say that most of the shoes, boots and clothes made here at Timberland are still hand-sewn by man.
Of course, we could install machinery to do the job in half the time. Probably a lot cheaper too. But could these machines match the craftsmanship of the old boys who toil away in our workshop up in Hampton, New Hampshire? Somehow we doubt it.
Take our boat shoe for example. Just like the best shipwrights, we have to build these shoes with the finest materials to make sure they withstand storms, gales and anything else the ocean wants to dish out.
This rules out using just any old leather. So we trek right across America to the few remaining tanneries who still know how to turn tough, full-grain hides into soft, durable shoe leathers.
After we've shipped the leathers all the way back to Hampton, the first thing we do is soak them in a vat of dye. That way, unlike those landlubbers who merely paint their shoes, ours will never lose their colour, even after a lifetime at sea. And to keep them supple we also impregnate the leathers with silicone oils.
It's at this stage in the process, when most other manufacturers would be more than happy to let their machines start sewing. But not us.
To stop the leathers cracking we stretch them on geometric lasts, another job that can only be done correctly by man. After all, we have to watch for flaws as the leather stretches.
Then, with the good name of Timberland in mind, our craftsmen take a single piece of leather and start to sew it deftly into a moccasin. The Red Indians came up with this design hundreds of years ago. We simply recognised its unparalleled comfort and promptly stole it for ourselves.
OUR SELF-OILING LACES ARE HAND-CUT.
Mind you, we have had some ideas of our own. Such as using high strength nylon thread to make sure the stitching won't ever come adrift. Sealing the seams with latex, to produce a barrier against the water. And injection moulding our midsoles to the uppers, creating a permanent, watertight bond.
A Timberland boat shoe's outsole is also designed with more thought than some people give to designing boats. The tread, for instance, features a system of 'scuppers', channels which run the length of the sole, connected to outlet gulleys along the edge.
Without this design, the shoe would hydroplane and, in effect, you'd end up walking on water. And as we hardly need to remind you, only one person ever managed that.
OUR LATEST PIECE OF TECHNOLOGY.
Last of all, we add (by hand, naturally), rustproof brass eyelets, self-oiling rawhide laces that won't rot and padded collars that provide a snug, watertight fit.
The result? A shoe perfectly suited to life on the ocean wave. (A fact borne out during the last America's Cup, when many of the crews wore Timberlands.)
Needless to say though, the hands of our craftsmen are adept at making other items too.
Like our walking shoes which have glove leather linings for comfort, and dual density polyurethane soles for lightness and durability.
And our split suede coats which are double stitched and waterproofed.
Fact is, every Timberland is built to be around as long as our customers. Perhaps longer. A claim machine-made products find hard to live up to.
Of course, maybe one day technology will make our way of doing things obsolete.
But we reckon it's got quite a lot of catching up to do. After all, our equipment took over four million years to develop.
THE BOAT SHOE. MADE FOR FEET BY HAND.
Timberland

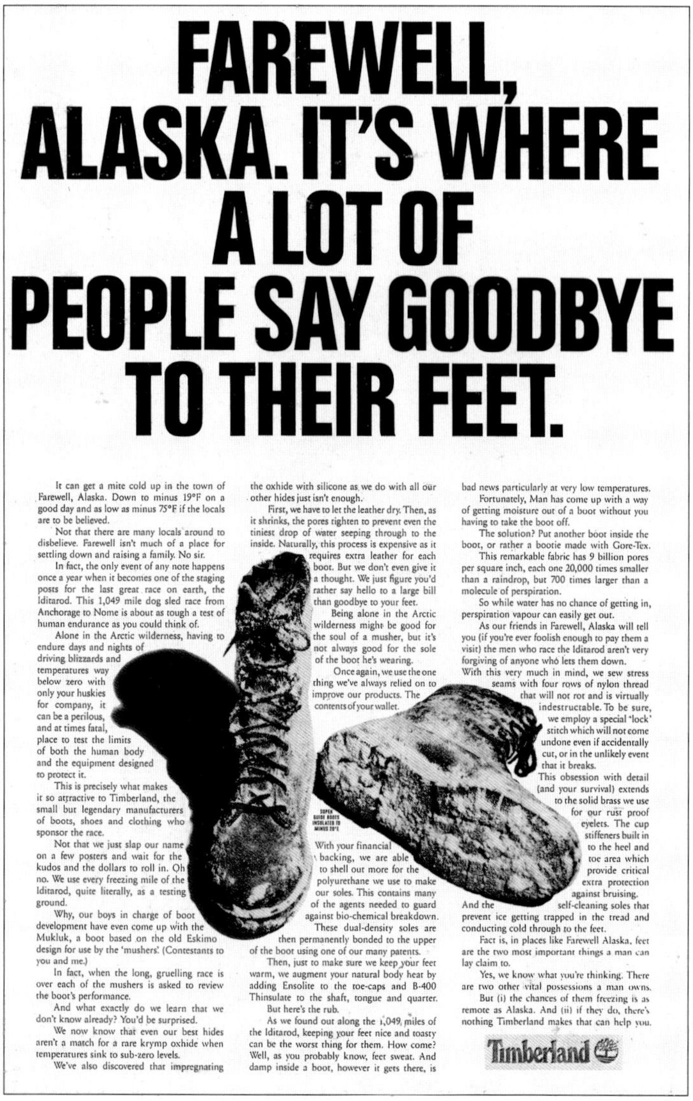
FAREWELL, ALASKA. IT'S WHERE A LOT OF PEOPLE SAY GOODBYE TO THEIR FEET.
It can get a mite cold up in the town of Farewell, Alaska. Down to minus 19°F on a good day and as low as minus 75°F if the locals are to be believed.
Not that there are many locals around to disbelieve. Farewell isn't much of a place for settling down and raising a family. No sir.
In fact, the only event of any note happens once a year when it becomes one of the staging posts for the last great race on earth, the Iditarod. This 1,049 mile dog sled race from Anchorage to Nome is about as tough a test of human endurance as you could think of.
Alone in the Arctic wilderness, having to endure days and nights of driving blizzards and temperatures way below zero with only your huskies for company, it can be a perilous, and at times fatal, place to test the limits of both the human body and the equipment designed to protect it.
This is precisely what makes it so attractive to Timberland, the small but legendary manufacturers of boots, shoes and clothing who sponsor the race.
Not that we just slap our name on a few posters and wait for the kudos and the dollars to roll in. Oh no. We use every freezing mile of the Iditarod, quite literally, as a testing ground.
Why, our boys in charge of boot development have even come up with the Mukluk, a boot based on the old Eskimo design for use by the 'mushers'. (Contestants to you and me.)
In fact, when the long, gruelling race is over each of the mushers is asked to review the boot's performance.
And what exactly do we learn that we don't know already? You'd be surprised.
We now know that even our best hides aren't a match for a rare krymp oxhide when temperatures sink to sub-zero levels.
We've also discovered that impregnating the oxhide with silicone as we do with all our other hides just isn't enough.
First, we have to let the leather dry. Then, as it shrinks, the pores tighten to prevent even the tiniest drop of water seeping through to the inside. Naturally, this process is expensive as it requires extra leather for each boot. But we don't even give it a thought. We just figure you'd rather say hello to a large bill than goodbye to your feet.
Being alone in the Arctic wilderness might be good for the soul of a musher, but it's not always good for the sole of the boot he's wearing.
Once again, we use the one thing we've always relied on to improve our products. The contents of your wallet.
SUPER GUIDE BOOTS INSULATED TO MINUS 20°F
With your financial backing, we are able to shell out more for the polyurethane we use to make our soles. This contains many of the agents needed to guard against bio-chemical breakdown.
These dual-density soles are then permanently bonded to the upper of the boot using one of our many patents.
Then, just to make sure we keep your feet warm, we augment your natural body heat by adding Ensolite to the toe-caps and B-400 Thinsulate to the shaft, tongue and quarter.
But here's the rub.
As we found out along the 1,049 miles of the Iditarod, keeping your feet nice and toasty can be the worst thing for them. How come? Well, as you probably know, feet sweat. And damp inside a boot, however it gets there, is bad news particularly at very low temperatures.
Fortunately, Man has come up with a way of getting moisture out of a boot without you having to take the boot off.
The solution? Put another boot inside the boot, or rather a bootie made with Gore-Tex.
This remarkable fabric has 9 billion pores per square inch, each one 20,000 times smaller than a raindrop, but 700 times larger than a molecule of perspiration.
So while water has no chance of getting in, perspiration vapour can easily get out.
As our friends in Farewell, Alaska will tell you (if you're ever foolish enough to pay them a visit) the men who race the Iditarod aren't very forgiving of anyone who lets them down.
With this very much in mind, we sew stress seams with four rows of nylon thread that will not rot and is virtually indestructable. To be sure, we employ a special 'lock' stitch which will not come undone even if accidentally cut, or in the unlikely event that it breaks.
This obsession with detail (and your survival) extends to the solid brass we use for our rust proof eyelets. The cup stiffeners built in to the heel and toe area which provide critical extra protection against bruising. And the self-cleaning soles that prevent ice getting trapped in the tread and conducting cold through to the feet.
Fact is, in places like Farewell Alaska, feet are the two most important things a man can lay claim to.
Yes, we know what you're thinking. There are two other vital possessions a man owns.
But (i) the chances of them freezing is as remote as Alaska. And (ii) if they do, there's nothing Timberland makes that can help you.
Timberland

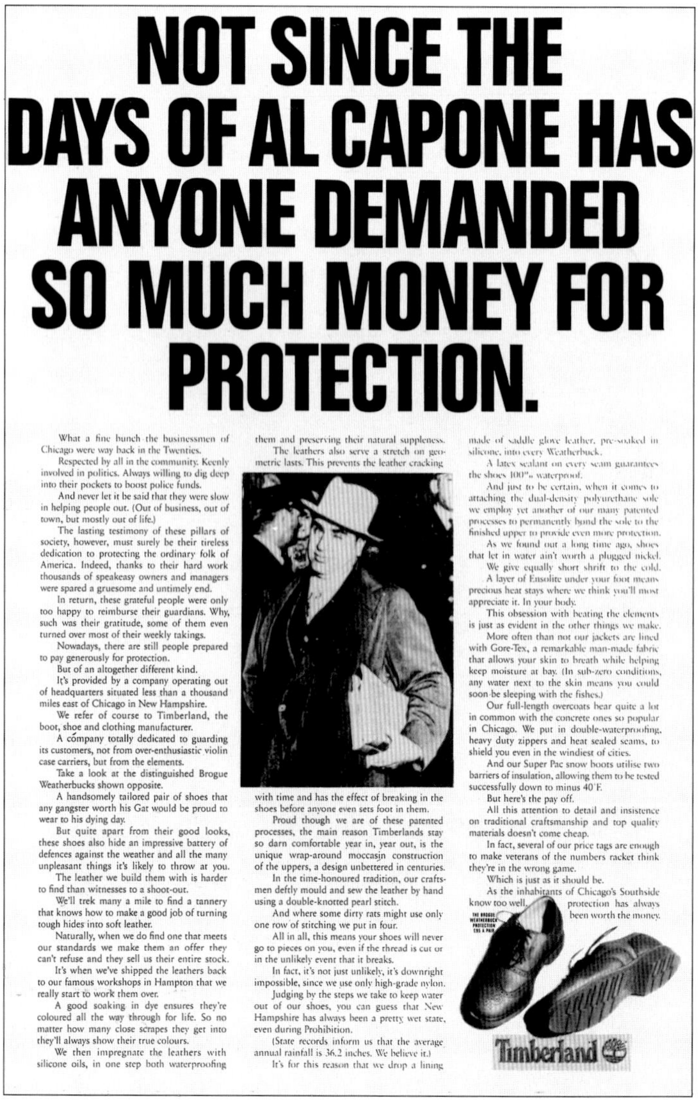
NOT SINCE THE DAYS OF AL CAPONE HAS ANYONE DEMANDED SO MUCH MONEY FOR PROTECTION.
What a fine bunch the businessmen of Chicago were way back in the Twenties.
Respected by all in the community. Keenly involved in politics. Always willing to dig deep into their pockets to boost police funds.
And never let it be said that they were slow in helping people out. (Out of business, out of town, but mostly out of life.)
The lasting testimony of these pillars of society, however, must surely be their tireless dedication to protecting the ordinary folk of America. Indeed, thanks to their hard work thousands of speakeasy owners and managers were spared a gruesome and untimely end.
In return, these grateful people were only too happy to reimburse their guardians. Why, such was their gratitude, some of them even turned over most of their weekly takings.
Nowadays, there are still people prepared to pay generously for protection.
But of an altogether different kind.
It's provided by a company operating out of headquarters situated less than a thousand miles east of Chicago in New Hampshire.
We refer of course to Timberland, the boot, shoe and clothing manufacturer.
A company totally dedicated to guarding its customers, not from over-enthusiastic violin case carriers, but from the elements.
Take a look at the distinguished Brogue Weatherbucks shown opposite.
A handsomely tailored pair of shoes that any gangster worth his Gat would be proud to wear to his dying day.
But quite apart from their good looks, these shoes also hide an impressive battery of defences against the weather and all the many unpleasant things it's likely to throw at you.
The leather we build them with is harder to find than witnesses to a shoot-out.
We'll trek many a mile to find a tannery that knows how to make a good job of turning tough hides into soft leather.
Naturally, when we do find one that meets our standards we make them an offer they can't refuse and they sell us their entire stock.
It's when we've shipped the leathers back to our famous workshops in Hampton that we really start to work them over.
A good soaking in dye ensures they're coloured all the way through for life. So no matter how many close scrapes they get into they'll always show their true colours.
We then impregnate the leathers with silicone oils, in one step both waterproofing them and preserving their natural suppleness.
The leathers also serve a stretch on geometric lasts. This prevents the leather cracking with time and has the effect of breaking in the shoes before anyone even sets foot in them.
Proud though we are of these patented processes, the main reason Timberlands stay so darn comfortable year in, year out, is the unique wrap-around moccasin construction of the uppers, a design unbettered in centuries.
In the time-honoured tradition, our craftsmen deftly mould and sew the leather by hand using a double-knotted pearl stitch.
And where some dirty rats might use only one row of stitching we put in four.
All in all, this means your shoes will never go to pieces on you, even if the thread is cut or in the unlikely event that it breaks.
In fact, it's not just unlikely, it's downright impossible, since we use only high-grade nylon.
Judging by the steps we take to keep water out of our shoes, you can guess that New Hampshire has always been a pretty wet state, even during Prohibition.
(State records inform us that the average annual rainfall is 36.2 inches. We believe it.)
It's for this reason that we drop a lining made of saddle glove leather, pre-soaked in silicone, into every Weatherbuck.
A latex sealant on every seam guarantees the shoes 100"." waterproof.
And just to be certain, when it comes to attaching the dual-density polyurethane sole we employ yet another of our many patented processes to permanently bond the sole to the finished upper to provide even more protection.
As we found out a long time ago, shoes that let in water ain't worth a plugged nickel.
We give equally short shrift to the cold.
A layer of Ensolite under your foot means precious heat stays where we think you'll most appreciate it. In your body.
This obsession with beating the elements is just as evident in the other things we make.
More often than not our jackets are lined with Gore-Tex, a remarkable man-made fabric that allows your skin to breath while helping keep moisture at bay. (In sub-zero conditions, any water next to the skin means you could soon be sleeping with the fishes.)
Our full-length overcoats bear quite a lot in common with the concrete ones so popular in Chicago. We put in double-waterproofing, heavy duty zippers and heat sealed seams, to shield you even in the windiest of cities.
And our Super Pac snow boots utilise two barriers of insulation, allowing them to be tested successfully down to minus 40°F.
But here's the pay off.
All this attention to detail and insistence on traditional craftsmanship and top quality materials doesn't come cheap.
In fact, several of our price tags are enough to make veterans of the numbers racket think they're in the wrong game.
Which is just as it should be.
As the inhabitants of Chicago's Southside know too well, protection has always been worth the money.
THE BROGUE WEATHERBUCK PROTECTION £95 A PAIR
Timberland

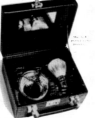

CONSUMER NEWSPAPER
OVER 600 LINES:
CAMPAIGN

196
ART DIRECTOR
Alan Fleming
WRITER
Phil Dearman
CLIENT
CIC Video
AGENCY
Lowe Howard-Spink/London

197
ART DIRECTORS
Nick Cohen
Taras Wayner
WRITERS
Nick Cohen
Sharon Caplan
Mikal Reich
Courtney Rohen
CLIENT
Village Voice
AGENCY
Mad Dogs & Englishmen/
New York

THERE'S SOME PSYCHO WOMAN OUT THERE KILLING GUYS.

A SCENE FROM THE FILM - SEA OF LOVE.

CUT TO:

INTERIOR. NEW YORK APARTMENT. NIGHT. *Camera pans up to a lighted apartment window. Dissolve through to dimly lit bedroom. In close-up a naked man is lying face down on his bed as if in the throes of sexual intercourse.*

NAKED MAN: So good . . . oh, so good.

In close-up the naked man turns to camera. He is crying.

NAKED MAN: Please. Don't. - -

Close-up of a hand-gun in the darkness. The naked man is shot in the back of the head.

CUT TO:

EXTERIOR. NEW YORK SUBURB. DAY. *A 35 year old woman opens her front door to reveal DETECTIVES FRANK KELLER and SHERMAN TOOHEY standing outside.*

KELLER to WOMAN: Good afternoon. I am Detective Frank Keller. This is Detective Sherman Toohey. Does a Raymond Brown live here?

MRS BROWN to KELLER: (Worried) What's the matter?

A little girl and boy have joined their mother. The little boy calls out to his father.

BOY to BROWN (his father): Dad! They're cops!

RAYMOND BROWN *joins his family at the door.*

BROWN: Hi, fellas. (To his wife) Just relax, honey.

CUT TO:

EXTERIOR. THE BROWN'S BACK GARDEN. DAY. *MRS BROWN is peering from behind her curtains. DETECTIVE TOOHEY is sitting at the table with BROWN. DETECTIVE KELLER stands beside them.*

BROWN to TOOHEY and KELLER: I want to tell you something. I love my family.

TOOHEY to BROWN: Hey, Raymond . . . no kidding, we don't give a shit. All we need are the names of the women you went out with and the letters you got back from the ladies.

BROWN in close-up: I don't have letters.

TOOHEY to BROWN in close-up: Raymond! There's some psycho woman out there killing guys.

BROWN in close-up. He's obviously lying

BROWN: I swear I didn't go out with any of them. I threw the letters

away. I didn't have the heart to go through with it.

Close-up panning shot of KELLER's face as he circles the table, bends down and talks directly into BROWN's face.

KELLER: You take the time to make up this beautiful poem about loneliness and silence. You spend $300 to put this ad in the magazine. You spend another $500 a month on some love nest in the Village. $50 for the post office box. (Angry now) And you're trying to tell us you never went out with any of them! Raymond! Please!

In a wide shot we see TOOHEY take his turn to pressurise BROWN.

TOOHEY: You know what the worst part of being a cop is?

As TOOHEY continues we see KELLER's face in close-up as he carefully watches BROWN's face for a reaction.

TOOHEY cont: Eight hours a day all you hear from people is lies. I didn't do it. I wasn't there. It was somebody else. Blah this. Blah that.

Close-up on BROWN's face.

BROWN to KELLER: I swear on the eyes of my children.

KELLER's face in close-up. He shakes his head slowly He obviously knows BROWN is lying

CUT TO:

INTERIOR. GREENWICH VILLAGE APARTMENT. NIGHT. *Close-up of curtains billowing in the wind from an open window In medium close-up we see RAYMOND BROWN lying naked, face down on a double bed. He is dead. He has been shot in the head. Off camera we hear DETECTIVE KELLER's voice.*

KELLER: I swear on the eyes of my children.

In a wide shot we see DETECTIVES KELLER and TOOHEY standing either side of the body on the bed.

KELLER: We should have tailed him.

Close-up of TOOHEY's face. He looks grim. KELLER in close-up. He looks tired.

KELLER: We screwed up.

Close-up on TOOHEY. He looks scornfully at the body.

TOOHEY: He screwed up.

Close-up of the dead man's head on the blood-stained pillow.

CUT TO: . . .

YOU'VE READ THE SCRIPT. NOW BUY THE VIDEO.

A MARTIN BREGMAN PRODUCTION · A HAROLD BECKER FILM · AL PACINO · ELLEN BARKIN · JOHN GOODMAN · "SEA OF LOVE" MUSIC BY TREVOR JONES · ASSOCIATE PRODUCER MICHAEL SCOTT BREGMAN
WRITTEN BY RICHARD PRICE · PRODUCED BY MARTIN BREGMAN AND LOUIS A. STROLLER · DIRECTED BY HAROLD BECKER · A UNIVERSAL PICTURE · © 1989 UNIVERSAL STUDIOS, INC./ALL RIGHTS RESERVED

AFTER I BLOW A HOLE IN SOMEBODY AND SLIP AROUND ON THEIR GUTS, I LIKE TO MAKE BALLOON ANIMALS.

A SCENE FROM THE FILM PARENTHOOD.

CUT TO:

INTERIOR. HOUSE. DAY. *In close-up GIL opens his front door to reveal a hired stripper.*

STRIPPER to GIL: I'm sorry I'm late.

She moves into the house and GIL and KAREN (GIL's wife) react disbelievingly. The stripper removes her coat and stands in basque and suspenders in mid-shot.

STRIPPER cont: . . . Where shall I do it?

GIL in medium close-up: Who are you and what are you going to do?

STRIPPER to GIL: I'm from Partytime Entertainments. I'm your stripper.

In the background, KAREN looks as the stripper incredulously.

STRIPPER cont: So, what is the birthday boy's name because . . . (GIL makes a comic face!) paint it across my breasts? -

DISSOLVE TO LATER. *In medium close-up the stripper is hanging up the phone. She turns to GIL and KAREN.*

STRIPPER: It was a mix-up. I got Cowboy Dan's card and . . . I got mine. I'm sorry.

Stripper moves past GIL to the door.

GIL to STRIPPER: Wait a minute. What about Cowboy Dan? He is coming?

STRIPPER: He showed up at the Lodge Hall and they were expecting me. They beat him severely so Cowboy Dan ain't coming.

KEVIN *(the birthday boy) appears in the background and moves towards GIL and KAREN.*

KEVIN to GIL: Cowboy Dan's not coming?

KEVIN looks like he is about to burst into tears.

GIL to KEVIN: Come on Kevin. Hold it together.

KEVIN in close up to GIL: I knew it! I told you. All the kids are gonna hate me. It's gonna be just like Little League.

In close-up GIL leans over KEVIN as KAREN moves towards them.

GIL to KEVIN: Cowboy Dan is coming.

KAREN to GIL: Gil!

GIL to KAREN and KEVIN: He's coming! Cowboy Dan is coming!

CUT TO:

EXTERIOR. GARDEN. DAY. *Ground level shot of kids sitting on grass. A pair of cowboy boots step into shot trailing home made spurs. Slow pan from boots upwards.*

GIL *is dressed in a home-made cowboy suit. He has both rags for chaps and a kids cowboy hat on his head.*

GIL to KIDS: Howdy pardoners.

In wide shot we see a semi circle of kids.

KID to GIL: You're Kevin's father. You're not Cowboy Dan.

Other kids react negatively.

KIDS: Yeah!

GIL to KIDS: That's right. They call me Cowboy Gil . . . as in Gull-ty.

Shot of kids and adults looking embarrassingly silent and awkward.

GIL to KIDS: I saw Cowboy Dan. I didn't like the look on his face. It was like this. (GIL makes a comic face.) So I killed him. I blew a hole in him . . . this big. (GIL makes a small circle with his fingers.)

Shots of the kids. Close up of KEVIN looking around at his friends.

GIL cont: Actually, I'd say it was about this big. (GIL indicates a bigger hole.) You know, when I think about it that hole was about this big. (GIL indicates a huge hole with his hands.)

In wide shot we see all the kids laughing and cheering.

GIL cont: And his guts went flailin' all over the floor. And as I was walkin' away I was slippin' around on his guts.

Shot of all the kids laughing uproariously.

GIL cont: And a couple of other people came by and they started slippin' around on his guts too.

Shots of adults laughing too.

GIL cont: After I blow a hole in somebody and slip around on their guts . . . afterwards, I always like to make . . . balloon animals.

In wide shot kids cheer and clap. GIL takes balloons out and blows them up as the cheering continues. Frantically, he knots balloons together in a mad jumble. He holds aloft the resulting mess.

Wide shot of kids and adults laughing and cheering wildly. Everyone is happy.

CUT TO:

YOU'VE READ THE SCRIPT. NOW BUY THE VIDEO.

YOU MADE THE RAIN BLACK. AND YOU SHOVED YOUR VALUES DOWN OUR THROATS.

A SCENE FROM THE FILM - BLACK RAIN.

CUT TO:

INTERIOR. SUGAI'S HOUSE IN A RICH SUBURB OF OSAKA. NIGHT.

In medium shot SUGAI stands by a large fireplace as his bodyguard SUMO lights a cigarette and places it in a cigarette holder for him.

SUGAI: You should be somewhere over the Pacific now, Conklin.

In medium shot DETECTIVE NICK CONKLIN looks at SUGAI. He says nothing.

SUGAI: We should be rid of you. Do you have any idea who I am?

Cut to CONKLIN who is looking at SUGAI closely.

CONKLIN: Yeah. I know who you are.

In medium shot, SUMO looks at SUGAI who laughs at CONKLIN.

SUGAI: No. If you did, you wouldn't have given me this.

SUGAI picks up a hundred dollar bill and waves it at CONKLIN.

Cut to CONKLIN who is still watching SUGAI.

CONKLIN: Good stuff.

Cut to medium shot of SUGAI holding up the money.

SUGAI: This is an old bill. A prototype.

In medium close up CONKLIN scrutinises SUGAI.

SUGAI: The new ones will be like everything we make. Perfect.

SUGAI crumples up the money and tosses it over his shoulder into the fireplace.

Cut to CONKLIN in medium close-up.

CONKLIN: Perfect, yeah. So who's gonna get the profits. You?

Cut to SUGAI being brought a drink by a tough-looking lackey.

Out of shot CONKLIN continues speaking.

CONKLIN: Or Sato?

Cut to CONKLIN in medium close up.

CONKLIN: See I know he's got the other plate.

In medium shot both SUGAI and his tough walk towards CONKLIN.

Out of shot CONKLIN continues speaking.

CONKLIN: That means you got nothing.

SUGAI: He might as well be an American. His kind respect just one thing Money.

Cut to a sceptical CONKLIN in medium close-up.

CONKLIN: So what are you in it for?

Cut to SUGAI in close-up.

Out of shot CONKLIN speaks.

CONKLIN: Love?

CONKLIN puts a cigarette in his mouth. The tough yanks it from his mouth and makes to hit CONKLIN.

Cut to SUGAI in medium close-up disciplining his lackey.

SUGAI: (Japanese order.)

The tough bows to SUGAI and retreats.

In close up SUGAI takes off his glasses and slowly leans towards CONKLIN.

SUGAI: I was ten when the B29's came. My family lived underground for three days.

When we came up, the city was gone.

In medium shot we see CONKLIN looking at SUGAI intently.

SUGAI: Then the heat brought rain. Black rain.

In medium close up SUGAI continues.

SUGAI: You made the rain black. And you shoved your values down our throats. We forgot who we were.

You created Sato and the thousands like him.

I'm paying you back.

SUGAI walks out of shot.

CUT TO: . . .

YOU'VE READ THE SCRIPT. NOW BUY THE VIDEO.

SITUATIONS WANTED

Ex-DMV clerical worker seeks position. But I'm in no hurry. ☎9876

SITUATIONS WANTED

SOCIAL WORKER. If I don't get a job soon I'll kill myself. ☎2876

SITUATIONS WANTED

He strainfully let go. It fell gently to the folded paper. A moist smack.
DOG WALKER/POET ☎3423

197

IF WE HAD BEEN AROUND BACK THEN, THEY MIGHT STILL BE AROUND TODAY.

Unfortunately, we're about 65 million years too late to save the dinosaurs. But when you come out to see our newest exhibition, The Wild Woods: From Dinos to Rhinos, it may seem as if they never left.

A forest full of 24 animated dinosaurs and prehistoric mammals created by Dinamation®, The Wild Woods is an astonishingly realistic tribute to these creatures. From the spiny-backed stegosaurus to the massive woolly mammoths, it's a journey to another time.

While you're here, take a look at some of the rare animals we're saving from extinction. Like Przewalski's wild horses and the northern white rhino.

And don't forget that by visiting the Wild Animal Park you help us continue to protect today's endangered animals. So they don't become tomorrow's dinosaurs.

DINOS TO RHINOS AT THE SAN DIEGO WILD ANIMAL PARK

CONSUMER NEWSPAPER OVER 600 LINES: CAMPAIGN

198
ART DIRECTOR
Bob Kwait
WRITERS
Cam Davis
Joe Lazo
ILLUSTRATOR
Daryl Milsap
CLIENT
San Diego Wild Animal Park
AGENCY
Phillips-Ramsey/San Diego

199
ART DIRECTORS
Louis Colletti
James Caporimo
WRITER
Margaret Lubalin
ILLUSTRATOR
Rick Meyerowitz
CLIENT
Home Ltd.
AGENCY
Waring & LaRosa/New York

THEY ROAMED THE EARTH FOR 150 MILLION YEARS. THIS TIME, THEY'LL ONLY BE HERE FOR A FEW MONTHS.

Maybe if there had been a Wild Animal Park about 65 million years ago, the dinosaurs might not be extinct. But when you visit us today, it'll seem as if they never left.

We've opened Wild Woods: From Dinos to Rhinos. A forest filled with lifelike dinosaurs and prehistoric mammals from Dinamation®.

Like the thundering Apatosaurus. The spine-tingling Stegosaurus. And the king of them all, Tyrannosaurus rex.

By observing these mysterious creatures of the past, you'll understand how important it is to protect and breed the thousands of rare animals at the Park today. Like the

northern white rhinos and Przewalski's wild horses. So they can continue to roam the earth for generations to come.

Dinos to Rhinos is featured at the Wild Animal Park for just a few short months. So come see the dinosaurs soon. Because there's no telling when they'll come back again.

DINOS TO RHINOS AT THE SAN DIEGO WILD ANIMAL PARK

198

ONCE AGAIN, THEIR DAYS ARE NUMBERED.

Like the dinosaurs and prehistoric mammals that once roamed the earth, the ones in our Wild Woods: From Dinos to Rhinos exhibit won't be around forever, either. In fact, they'll only be here 'til October 4th.

Tucked amidst the pines of our conifer forest are 23 dinosaurs and

prehistoric mammals created by Dinamation®. Besides looking incredibly realistic, they actually growl and snort and move their heads and tails.

Although we're about 65 million years too late to save any real dinosaurs, we've been able to rescue hundreds of rare and endan-

gered creatures from extinction. Many of which you can see when you visit.

And by coming to see the Wild Woods, you help us continue our work both here and abroad.

So that today's endangered species will be around for years to come.

**DINOS TO RHINOS AT THE SAN DIEGO WILD ANIMAL PARK
ENDS OCTOBER 4**

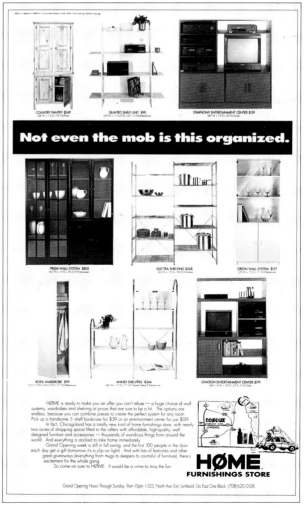

In Aspen, at the other end of the 911 lifeline, you'll find Saab 9000's. Which day in and day out, on shifts around the clock, must prove themselves as the official patrol cars of that city's police.

In fact, for 14 years the Saabs used by both the Aspen and Vail police have contributed to the kind of response times any precinct would be proud of.

Saab 9000's are well suited for careers in law enforcement. They come with spirited, yet reliable, 16-valve engines, road-hugging suspensions, plus such safety equipment as a driver's-side air bag and an anti-lock braking system. And, like all Saabs, 9000's feature a front-wheel-drive system that keeps even the Western Slope's legendary snowfalls from slowing the wheels of justice.

A reassuring notion if you happen to live in the Rockies. And food for thought when you're in the market for a new car, no matter where you live. See us for a test drive.

SAAB
**WE DON'T MAKE COMPROMISES.
WE MAKE SAABS.**

FOR A SAAB DEMONSTRATION IN ASPEN, DIAL 911.

200

Keep Your Blood From Circulating.

We've got prices on bug repellent that will make your heart beat faster. So get to us before they get to you. *True Value* **The Hardware Store.**
555 Railroad Drive, Elk River

201

If Our Glasses Got Any Sexier, They'd Steam Up All By Themselves.

Glasses, contacts, sunglasses, eye exams, frame selection assistance, quick adjustment and repairs. Moss Optical. Great selection and service at a great downtown location. Between Dayton's & Shinder's at 10 South 8th St. in Mpls. 332-7907. **MOSS OPTICAL**

Maybe These Glasses Aren't You. Maybe It Would Be Fun To Be Someone Else For A Change.

Glasses, contacts, sunglasses, eye exams, frame selection assistance, quick adjustment and repairs. Moss Optical. Great selection and service at a great downtown location. Between Dayton's & Shinder's at 10 South 8th St. in Mpls. 332-7907. **MOSS OPTICAL**

204

205

There's never been a better time to buy a new Porsche 928.

(Aren't recessions wonderful?)

Considering its 345-horsepower engine and the three weeks it takes to build, the Porsche 928 GTS is certainly no economy car. But thanks to the economy, it's now more affordable than it may ever be again. Seize the moment.

PORSCHE®

The good news is there's no room for all the kids.

Introducing the new Porsche America Roadster. A 911 Carrera 2 Cabriolet with the massive wheels, powerful brakes, tuned chassis, and flared fenders of the 911 Turbo. A minivan it is not.

PORSCHE®

Everyone has leases. But no one else has Porsches.

Special terms until March 31st.

Thanks to special lease and financing rates from Chase Manhattan, you can now drive a genuine Porsche Carrera for less than many mere cars. So the classic high performance sportscar you've always dreamed of could well become reality. Call 1-800-843-3748 for the dealer nearest you. You may find other attractive rates. But you certainly won't find a more attractive car. **PORSCHE**®

No clutch, but one heck of an accelerator.

Tiptronic® automatic transmission.

An automatic in a 911? Consider that the revolutionary new Porsche Tiptronic® transmission was developed from the technology found in our 962 race car. It allows both automatic and clutchless manual shifting for one heck of a leap forward in performance.

PORSCHE®

209

Let us describe the handling this way: rolling Velcro.®

Carrera 4

With its state-of-the-art all-wheel-drive system, the Porsche 911 Carrera 4 sticks to the road better than almost any automobile in the world. Come in for a test drive. You'll find it hard to tear yourself away from it.

PORSCHE®

210

Its 171 mph top speed may be irrelevant, but it certainly is inspiring, isn't it?

Unless you own a test track you'll never come close to seeing how fast the new 1993 Porsche 928 GTS really is. But isn't it nice to know those 345 horses are there? Come in for a highly inspirational test drive.

PORSCHE

214

Now the only thing between you and a Porsche is a very well engineered door.

Special terms until May 31st.

If you've ever dreamed of a new Porsche, opportunity is knocking very loud. Thanks to very special lease and finance rates through Chase Manhattan, combined with our traditionally high resale value,* the cost of driving a new Porsche Carrera may never be lower. For details, call 1-800-843-3748 for the dealer nearest you.
But act soon, because this very well engineered window of opportunity is closing on May 31st. **PORSCHE**

215

Don't get stuck paying the luxury tax.

Better yet, don't get stuck period.

Even though a Range Rover is considered the most luxurious sport utility vehicle in the world, it's excluded from the luxury tax.

Nevertheless, what makes a Range Rover so extraordinary is that unlike cars that come with the luxury tax, it comes with the ability to handle the absolute worst driving conditions no less luxuriously than the absolute best driving conditions.

So why not consider buying a Range Rover? Or, if you prefer, feel free to pay for the luxury of a much less capable car.

RANGE ROVER
1-800-FINE-4WD

Breathe easier underwater.

Relax.

A Range Rover is virtually dunk resistant. With its anti-lock braking system, and the added traction of permanent 4-wheel drive, a Range Rover can grip the kind of rain-soaked pavement that sends ordinary luxury cars slip-sliding away.

And what makes a Range Rover and its owner even more comfortable during torrential downpours, Nordic blizzards, or whatever else the sky has to offer, are its abundant amenities.

Why not come in for a test drive?

Even in the midst of a blinding typhoon, you'll be at the helm of a rather seaworthy vehicle.

One designed to relieve a little of that cabin pressure.

RANGE ROVER

There's no such thing as a sudden heart attack.
It requires years of preparation.

The heart is the hardest-working muscle in your body. However, it's often forced into an early retirement, given the way some people choose to live.

They smoke.

They eat foods high in saturated fats and cholesterol.

They don't exercise.

It can all lead to a heart attack. Slowly, but surely.

Every 32 seconds, in fact, someone dies of cardiovascular disease. The trouble often builds gradually. With atherosclerosis, for example, the most prevalent coronary disease, fat can start to harden arteries as early as childhood. And cause a heart attack 40 or 50 years later.

While news reports can leave people confused about how to reduce the risk of a heart attack, three factors have always played an important role.

Regular exercise.

A healthy diet, low in fat and cholesterol.

And no smoking.

So instead of waiting for the most common warning signal, a heart attack itself, call your doctor, or 1-800-MD-SINAI for a referral to one of ours.

It might mean you have to make some changes in your life. But your heart has to pump 2000 gallons of blood every day.

It really needs your full cooperation.

Mount Sinai.
Take good care of yourself.

A public health message from The Mount Sinai Medical Center.

**CONSUMER NEWSPAPER
600 LINES OR LESS:
SINGLE**

**219
ART DIRECTOR**
Steve Tom
WRITER
Mark Nardi
PHOTOGRAPHER
Roger Warner
CLIENT
Raynham
AGENCY
*Hill Holliday Connors
Cosmopulos/Boston*

**220
ART DIRECTOR**
Steve Tom
WRITER
Mark Nardi
CLIENT
Raynham
AGENCY
*Hill Holliday Connors
Cosmopulos/Boston*

**221
ART DIRECTOR**
John Lineweaver
WRITER
Eddie Van Bloem
CLIENT
Irish Tourist Board
AGENCY
*Hill Holliday Connors
Cosmopulos/New York*

**222
ART DIRECTOR**
John Shirley
WRITERS
*Bryan Behar
Harold Einstein*
CLIENT
*Acura Division of
American Honda*
AGENCY
*Ketchum Advertising/
Los Angeles*

**Lucky For Us,
Greyhounds Can't Read.**

Why pay an athlete millions of bucks when a can of puppy chow will do the trick? Find out on July third during the All-American Greyhound Triathalon Race. And don't forget our matinee and evening

**RAYNHAM/TAUNTON
GREYHOUND PARK**

performances on the 4th. If that's not enough, we have double-headers every day from June 27 to July 7. So come by—you could make lots of money. Just keep it to yourself, ok?

Racing every afternoon at 1:00 except Wed. Every night at 8:00 except Mon. and Tues. • Free general parking • Seniors free afternoons
Just off routes 495 (Exit 8) and 24 (Exit 16B) on 138. Raynham • Information. Reservations: (508) 824-4071.

219

**Experience The Thrill Of Victory.
The Agony Of Defeat.
The Smell Of Dog Breath.**

Welcome to the wide world of greyhound racing at Raynham/Taunton Greyhound Park. Where the air is filled with excitement, drama, and whatever

**RAYNHAM/TAUNTON
GREYHOUND PARK**

else happens to drift your way. Call 508-824-4071 for information. And get ready for some action that could leave you breathless. Really.

220

WHY THERE ARE PRENUPTIAL AGREEMENTS.

To many, it is considered to be the greatest exotic sports car ever built. The sculpted-aluminum, 270-horsepower, mid-engine Acura NSX. A sure guarantee that even if things don't happen to work out as planned, you're still going to be living happily ever after.

ACURA
PRECISION CRAFTED PERFORMANCE

(DEALER IMPRINT)

THE THINKING IS SO FRESH, WE WRAPPED IT IN ALUMINUM.

The Acura NSX doesn't only have the world's most advanced technology inside, but outside. Its 270-horsepower V-6 and four-wheel double-wishbone suspension are covered by an aluminum body that's both lighter and stronger than steel. Care to freshen up?

ACURA
PRECISION CRAFTED PERFORMANCE

(DEALER IMPRINT)

© 1991 Acura Division of American Honda Motor Co., Inc. Acura and NSX are registered trademarks of Honda Motor Co., Ltd.

223

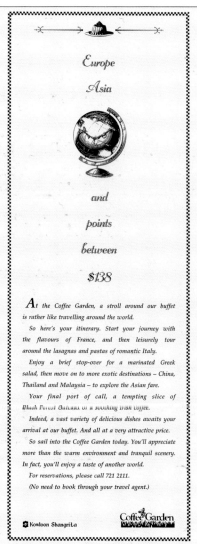

Europe

Asia

and

points

between

$138

At the Coffee Garden, a stroll around our buffet is rather like travelling around the world.

So here's your itinerary. Start your journey with the flavours of France, and then leisurely tour around the lasagnas and pastas of romantic Italy.

Enjoy a brief stop-over for a marinated Greek salad, then move on to more exotic destinations – China, Thailand and Malaysia – to explore the Asian fare.

Your final port of call, a tempting slice of Black Forest Gateau or a soothing Irish coffee.

Indeed, a vast variety of delicious dishes awaits your arrival at our buffet. And all at a very attractive price.

So sail into the Coffee Garden today. You'll appreciate more than the warm environment and tranquil scenery. In fact, you'll enjoy a taste of another world.

For reservations, please call 721 2111.

(No need to book through your travel agent.)

Kowloon Shangri-La   Coffee Garden

224

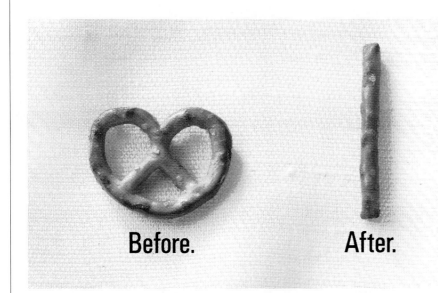

Before. **After.**

Look at it this way. Your back is the center of your whole body.

That's why when your back gets all twisted up, you seem to hurt all over. If you have chronic back problems, give me a call at (213) 749-6438 and we'll arrange an appointment.

Chiropractic is a proven, altogether safe technique. Which is why many insurance plans now cover it.

I think that after you see me, you'll feel a lot better than you did before.

Orlando Pardo D.C.
DOCTOR OF CHIROPRACTIC

225

AT 50-80% OFF THE ONLY THING YOU CAN'T SAVE IS OUR STORE.

The dresses are going. The skirts are going.
The fixtures are going. Shouldn't you be going too?

The narragansett

226

SAVE UP TO 80% DURING OUR GOING OUT OF BUSINESS SALE.

(Oh sure, now you'll come in.)

The narragansett

227

CONSUMER NEWSPAPER
600 LINES OR LESS:
SINGLE

228
ART DIRECTORS
Taras Wayner
Nick Cohen
WRITER
Sharon Caplan
CLIENT
Village Voice
AGENCY
Mad Dogs & Englishmen/
New York

229
ART DIRECTORS
Taras Wayner
Nick Cohen
WRITER
Mikal Reich
CLIENT
Village Voice
AGENCY
Mad Dogs & Englishmen/
New York

230
ART DIRECTORS
Taras Wayner
Nick Cohen
WRITERS
Shalom Auslander
Mikal Reich
CLIENT
Village Voice
AGENCY
Mad Dogs & Englishmen/
New York

231
ART DIRECTORS
Nick Cohen
Taras Wayner
WRITER
Aimee Heller
CLIENT
Village Voice
AGENCY
Mad Dogs & Englishmen/
New York

232
ART DIRECTOR
Sean Riley
WRITER
Raymond McKinney
PHOTOGRAPHER
Helen Hamilton Horsley
CLIENT
The Pet Gallery
AGENCY
The Martin Agency/
Richmond

SITUATIONS WANTED

He strainfully let go. It fell gently to the folded paper. A moist smack.
DOG WALKER/POET ☎ 3423

Place a **FREE** Situations Wanted ad for 4 weeks in our Help Wanted Classified Section. Someone out there is desperate to hire someone with your qualifications. To place an ad call 212-475-5555.

228

SITUATIONS WANTED

Hark! I beseech thee, fore not a beggar nor vagrant I, But art now, and not by choosing, without haven of a guild. I beg of you; grant respite within your good premises.
ACTOR SEEKS RESTAURANT POSITION. ☎ 5802

Place a **FREE** Situations Wanted ad for 4 weeks in our Help Wanted Classified Section. Someone out there is desperate to hire someone with your qualifications. To place an ad call 212-475-5555.

229

**No,**

I don't want to subscribe to the Village Voice. Who needs your crummy little radical, left-wing editorials, you Commie Pinkos, with your mud-slinging stories on politics and the government, why don't you just leave well enough alone? Quite frankly, I'm sick and tired of worrying about the homeless and corruption and injustice, why don't you stop stirring up trouble, anyway... hey, you know, this is America, love it or leave it... and your "scathing" reports on abortion and drugs and censorship and animal research, nothing's ever good enough for you is it, you, you, radical lunatic subversive radicals! ...Besides, you don't have any T.V. listings.

YES, I WANT TO BUY A ONE YEAR SUBSCRIPTION TO THE VILLAGE VOICE.

New York Metro Rate: $44.95 (NY, NJ & CT: Just 86c per copy)
National Rate: $47.95 (Just 92c per copy)

Name_____

Address_____

City/State/Zip_____

Amount enclosed $_____Bill me_____

Charge Me: AmEx_____ M/C_____ VISA_____

Credit Card Number_____Exp Date_____

Signature_____

To order, call toll-free 1-800-336-0686 or mail this coupon to: The Village Voice Subscriptions, P.O. Box 1905, Marion, OH 43302. Rates good in U.S. only. Canadian and foreign subscriptions $79.20 per year; must have payment with order. Please allow 4 to 6 weeks for delivery. For address changes, call 1-800-347-6969

SITUATIONS WANTED

CHOREOGRAPHER.

☏ 5 6 7 8

Place a **FREE** Situations Wanted ad for 4 weeks in our Help Wanted Classified Section. Someone out there is desperate to hire someone with your qualifications. To place an ad call 212-475-5555. **VOICE**

It won't wet the floor. Your mom might.

Our snakes make wonderful pets. And don't worry. Over time your mother will grow to love it.

The Pet Gallery

2403 S. Wrightsville Ave., Nags Head, 441-1852.

Which One We Use To Correct Your Heart Problem Is Up To You.

Did you know the word "lite" on a label doesn't always mean less fat or cholesterol? It may just mean a product weighs less. That's a taste of what our cardiac care program can teach you. For details call Judy at (603) 886-3211, x-2839. This one time, listen to your heart, not your gut.

NMH Nashua Memorial Hospital
Cardiac Rehab Center

233

Our idea of the perfect figure is 36-54-36.

We think pregnant women deserve to wear clothes that are every bit as beautiful as they are. Come see us for a complete selection of maternity dresses, tops and bottoms that, for once, measures up.

MATERNITY Rack
CLOTHING A MOTHER-TO-BE COULD LOVE.
Summerton Plaza, Rte 9 South, Manalapan, NJ 577-1514

234

We accept all your husband's major credit cards.

At Chelsea Boutique, we not only offer your favorite brands of clothes. We now offer your favorite methods of payment.

Chelsea Boutique. Featuring a wide range of designers from Anne Klein II to Tomatsu. Stop by and see us at 196 Birch Hill Road, Locust Valley.

Chelsea Boutique

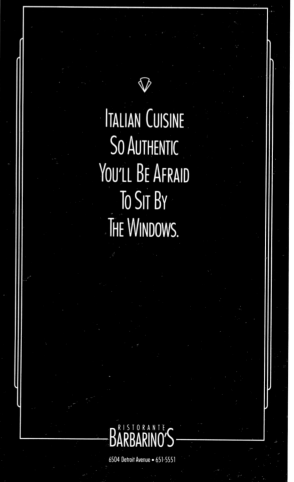

Shoplifters Will Be Prosecuted.

You can look. You can touch. Just don't forget to pay.

Marie Laveau's House of Voodoo

739 Bourbon St. and Riverwalk, New Orleans, La.

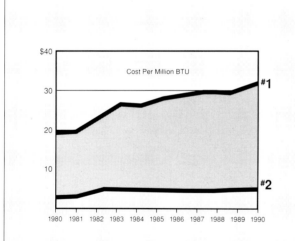

Line #1 is the cost of electricity.

Line #2 is the cost of natural gas.

The shaded area is that Hawaiian vacation you've been dreaming of.

Of course, you can spend the savings any way you choose. The point is that over the past five years, the cost of electricity in Northeast Ohio has steadily increased. While the cost of natural gas has actually decreased. The reason is that we at East Ohio Gas shop around for the best gas prices, then pass the savings on to you. So why spend more of your money on electricity, when you can spend more of your time on Maui?

THE EAST OHIO GAS COMPANY

ITALIAN CUISINE SO AUTHENTIC YOU'LL BE AFRAID TO SIT BY THE WINDOWS.

RISTORANTE BARBARINO'S

6504 Detroit Avenue • 651-5551

Consumer Newspaper 600 Lines or Less: Campaign

239
ART DIRECTOR
Paul Norwood
WRITER
Court Crandall
ILLUSTRATOR
Paul Norwood
CLIENT
Atlantic Exterminating
AGENCY
Admen Against Big Logos/ El Segundo

240
ART DIRECTOR
Bob Brihn
WRITER
Mike Lescarbeau
PHOTOGRAPHER
Joe Lampe
CLIENT
Star Tribune
AGENCY
Fallon McElligott/ Minneapolis

"HEY, CHECK OUT THE ADJECTIVES ON HER."

With our new voice mail system, the Star Tribune is making it easy to meet exactly the kind of people you'd like to. Call 673-9015 for sincere, honest, outgoing, friendly details today.

"Get Acquainted" in the **Star Tribune**

WHEN A GUY ANSWERS YOUR PERSONALS AD, AT LEAST YOU KNOW HE CAN READ.

Looking for a well read person? Advertise to the readers of the Star Tribune. With a readership of over one million, we'll help you reach the people who share your interests. And your vocabulary. Call 673-9015 for details today.

"Get Acquainted" in the **Star Tribune**

NEED A LAWYER?

With our new voice mail system, the Star Tribune is making it easy to meet exactly the kind of people you'd like to. Call 673-9015 for details today.

"Get Acquainted" in the **Star Tribune**

CONSUMER NEWSPAPER
600 LINES OR LESS:
CAMPAIGN

241
ART DIRECTOR
Bob Barrie
WRITER
Bruce Bildsten
PHOTOGRAPHER
Vic Huber
CLIENT
Porsche Cars North America
AGENCY
Fallon McElligott/
Minneapolis

242
ART DIRECTOR
Bob Barrie
WRITER
Bruce Bildsten
PHOTOGRAPHER
Vic Huber
CLIENT
Porsche Cars North America
AGENCY
Fallon McElligott/
Minneapolis

Didn't your doctor tell you to get more fresh air?

Compared to the cost of getting well these days, the therapeutic benefits of a Porsche 911 Carrera Cabriolet make it seem a downright bargain. Test drive one today. It will do you good.

PORSCHE®

It's not a statement. It's a hand gesture.

With an awe-inspiring 315-horsepower engine and a shape more akin to a rocket than an automobile, the Porsche 911 Turbo makes a very strong statement indeed. We now have this very rare automobile on hand.

PORSCHE®

The perfect four-wheel-drive vehicle for Los Angeles.

With the unsurpassed roadholding of all-wheel-drive, and a hand-fitted, power convertible top, the Porsche 911 Carrera 4 Cabriolet may just be the world's ultimate on-road vehicle.

PORSCHE®

CONSUMER NEWSPAPER
600 LINES OR LESS:
CAMPAIGN

243
ART DIRECTOR
Bob Barrie
WRITER
Bruce Bildsten
PHOTOGRAPHER
Vic Huber
CLIENT
Porsche Cars North America
AGENCY
*Fallon McElligott/
Minneapolis*

244
ART DIRECTOR
Bob Barrie
WRITER
Bruce Bildsten
PHOTOGRAPHER
Vic Huber
CLIENT
Porsche Cars North America
AGENCY
*Fallon McElligott/
Minneapolis*

What better way to announce to the world that you, too, are out of the recession?

If the improved economy has you leaning toward finally buying that Porsche you've always dreamed of, allow us to push you over the edge. Come test drive the new, improved Porsche: the remarkable new 968.

PORSCHE®

There's never been a better time to buy a new Porsche 928. (Aren't recessions wonderful?)

Considering its 345-horsepower engine and the three weeks it takes to build, the Porsche 928 GTS is certainly no economy car. But thanks to the economy, it's now more affordable than it may ever be again. Seize the moment.

PORSCHE®

Make the recession a tiny dot in your rearview mirror.

What better way to leave the recession far, far behind you? Considering the performance of our new 968, 928 GTS, and 911's, you'll forget the recession very quickly.

PORSCHE®

They've outlasted hippies, disco and yuppies.

Is it any wonder they hold their value so well?

Down the road, few things hold their value as well as the timeless Porsche 911 Carrera. Yet beneath those classic lines lies one of the world's most technologically-advanced automobiles. If only we all aged so gracefully.

PORSCHE®

Don't feel selfish. In a few decades you can pass it on to your children.

True, a sportscar may seem an indulgence. But with its timeless styling, remarkable durability, and exceptional resale value, a new Porsche 911 Carrera is virtually guilt-free.

PORSCHE®

It's already survived 10 Japanese model changes.

No sportscar is as timeless as the Porsche 911 Carrera. Yet, beneath those classic lines, constant evolution makes it one of the most advanced cars in the world. Come see the one car the Japanese have never been able to copy.

PORSCHE®

CONSUMER NEWSPAPER 600 LINES OR LESS: CAMPAIGN

245
ART DIRECTORS
John Shirley
Dennis Lim
WRITERS
Bryan Behar
Scott Aal
Harold Einstein
CLIENT
Acura Division of American Honda
AGENCY
Ketchum Advertising/ Los Angeles

246
ART DIRECTOR
Tom Routson
WRITER
Steve Skibba
PHOTOGRAPHER
Steve Knight
CLIENT
Political Americana
AGENCY
Loeffler Ketchum Mountjoy/ Charlotte

WHY THERE ARE PRENUPTIAL AGREEMENTS.

To many, it is considered to be the greatest exotic sports car ever built. The sculpted-aluminum, 270-horsepower, mid-engine Acura NSX. A sure guarantee that even if things don't happen to work out as planned, you're still going to be living happily ever after. **ACURA** PRECISION CRAFTED PERFORMANCE

(DEALER IMPRINT)

© 1991 Acura Division of American Honda Motor Co., Inc. Acura and NSX are registered trademarks of Honda Motor Co., Ltd.

THE THINKING IS SO FRESH, WE WRAPPED IT IN ALUMINUM.

The Acura NSX doesn't only have the world's most advanced technology inside, but outside. Its 270-horsepower V-6 and four-wheel double-wishbone suspension are covered by an aluminum body that's both lighter and stronger than steel. Care to freshen up? **ACURA** PRECISION CRAFTED PERFORMANCE

(DEALER IMPRINT)

LET THE KIDS WALK TO SCHOOL.

With its 270-horsepower, mid-engine, twin-cam, 24-valve V-6, the Acura NSX clearly wasn't designed for carpooling. Come in and see the sports car that many regard as the world's greatest. And as for the kids, don't worry. The walk will do them some good. **ACURA** PRECISION CRAFTED PERFORMANCE

(DEALER IMPRINT)

© 1991 Acura Division of American Honda Motor Co., Inc. Acura and NSX are registered trademarks of Honda Motor Co., Ltd.

BUY YOURSELF A POLITICIAN.

Get a prominent politician right where you want him: pinned on your lapel. **POLITICAL AMERICANA**

ACTUALLY WORN BY PRESIDENT FORD.

We sell authentic campaign buttons at prices that won't dent your wallet. **POLITICAL AMERICANA**

THOUSANDS STILL IN STOCK.

We carry the most popular campaign buttons in history. And then some. **POLITICAL AMERICANA**

Consumer Newspaper
600 Lines or Less:
Campaign

247
ART DIRECTORS
Nick Cohen
Taras Wayner
WRITERS
Shalom Auslander
Mikal Reich
CLIENT
Village Voice
AGENCY
Mad Dogs & Englishmen/
New York

248
ART DIRECTORS
Nick Cohen
Taras Wayner
WRITERS
Aimee Heller
Mikal Reich
CLIENT
Village Voice
AGENCY
Mad Dogs & Englishmen/
New York

☐ **No,** I don't want to take advantage of your special holiday subscription offer. What do you think I am, stupid or something? Yeah, sure..."Let's take a little cut off the regular price, and we'll get everyone to subscribe." I don't think so. You guys "offer" it for $34.95 a year, a measly 22% off the regular subscription price (or "ooooh", $25 year for an "additional gift subscription", a whopping 48% off), and now you want me to spread the word to other Voice readers that we'll "save time and money" by subscribing? Are you gonna pay me for this work? Huh? Nice try. What's next, maybe you'd like me to do your advertising for you also? Or perhaps I should just save everyone the trouble, quit my job, give up all my worldly possesions and work for you for free! Yeah, I got your "special offer" right here, pal.

☐ **YES,** I'LL TAKE ADVANTAGE OF YOUR SPECIAL HOLIDAY SUBSCRIPTION OFFER.

First subscription: only $34.95 per year.
Additional subscriptions only $25.00 per year.
Name_____
Address_____
City/State/Zip_____
Amount enclosed $_____ Bill me_____
For additional gift subscriptions, send name and address on separate sheets of paper or call 1-800-336-0686

Mail this coupon to: The Village Voice Subscriptions, P.O. Box 1905, Marion, OH 43302. Rates and 'bill me' good in U.S. only. Canadian and foreign subscriptions $79.20 per year; must have payment with order. Please allow 4 to 6 weeks for delivery. D1CH50-3

☐ **No,** I don't want to subscribe to the Village Voice. Who needs your crummy little radical, left-wing editorials, you Commie Pinkos, with your mud-slinging stories on politics and the government, why don't you just leave well enough alone? Quite frankly, I'm sick and tired of worrying about the homeless and corruption and injustice, why don't you stop stirring up trouble, anyway... hey, you know, this is America, love it or leave it... and your "scathing" reports on abortion and drugs and censorship and animal research, nothing's ever good enough for you is it, you, you, radical lunatic subversive radicals! ...Besides, you don't have any T.V. listings.

☐ **YES,** I WANT TO BUY A ONE YEAR SUBSCRIPTION TO THE VILLAGE VOICE.

New York Metro Rate: $44.95 (NY, NJ & CT: Just 86c per copy)
National Rate: $47.95 (Just 92c per copy)

Name_____
Address_____
City/State/Zip_____
Amount enclosed $_____ Bill me_____
Charge Me: AmEx_____ M/C_____ VISA_____
Credit Card Number_____ Exp Date_____
Signature_____

the village VOICE

To order, call toll-free 1-800-336-0686 or mail this coupon to: The Village Voice Subscriptions, P.O. Box 1905, Marion, OH 43302. Rates good in U.S. only. Canadian and foreign subscriptions $79.20 per year; must have payment with order. Please allow 4 to 6 weeks for delivery. For address changes, call 1-800-347-6969

☐ **No,** I don't want to subscribe to the Village Voice. My skin crawls thinking about the kind of looks I'd get if my neighbors knew that I indulged in your "alternative publication". Are you people trying to ruin me? Gosh, I could lose everything. First the BMW goes down the pooper in the "crash" and now you want to rob me of what little standing I have left in society. Oh, you people think you're so high and mighty, parading around your self-righteous brand of downtown honesty, while people like me are forced to read your stinking paper in private. Go ahead. Destroy me. Strip me bare. Make me move back with my parents. Fine. I hope you people are really proud of yourselves.

☐ **YES,** I WANT TO BUY A ONE YEAR SUBSCRIPTION TO THE VILLAGE VOICE.

New York Metro Rate: $44.95 (NY, NJ & CT: Just 86c per copy)
National Rate: $47.95 (Just 92c per copy)

Name_____
Address_____
City/State/Zip_____
Amount enclosed $_____ Bill me_____
Charge Me: AmEx_____ M/C_____ VISA_____
Credit Card Number_____ Exp Date_____
Signature_____

the village VOICE

To order, call toll-free 1-800-336-0686 or mail this coupon to: The Village Voice Subscriptions, P.O. Box 1905, Marion, OH 43302. Rates good in U.S. only. Canadian and foreign subscriptions $79.20 per year; must have payment with order. Please allow 4 to 6 weeks for delivery. For address changes, call 1-800-347-6969

SITUATIONS WANTED

CHOREOGRAPHER.
☎ 5 6 7 8

SITUATIONS WANTED

Hark! I beseech thee, fore not a beggar nor vagrant I, But art now, and not by choosing, without haven of a guild. I beg of you; grant respite within your good premises.
ACTOR SEEKS RESTAURANT POSITION. ☎5802

SITUATIONS WANTED

I, right now, am at the current time presently in the throes of, or should I just simply say, am "involved" with an endeavor which is new to me and is, coincidentally, my first attempt, am basically now actively looking for, and over the course of the last several weeks, which by the way seemed more like several months, have made extensive inquiries about and the type of inquiries where you spend more time on the phone than doing other types of things that you wished you were really doing rather than making inquiries on the phone, but unfortunately not, as I'd originally had hoped for, with as much luck as that I had from the start desired, an appropriate, and fitting, according to my background, a position, at a particular firm, and or, agency or agencies, suited, in a fashion, to my particular skills and strengths and talents.   **COPY EDITOR** ☎ 8666

CONSUMER NEWSPAPER
600 LINES OR LESS:
CAMPAIGN

249
ART DIRECTOR
Sean Riley
WRITER
Tripp Westbrook
CLIENT
Johnston and
Wales University
AGENCY
The Martin Agency/
Richmond

250
ART DIRECTOR
Bryan Burlison
WRITER
Todd Tilford
PHOTOGRAPHER
Richard Reens
CLIENT
Harley-Davidson of Dallas
AGENCY
The Richards Group/Dallas

FINALLY A SCHOOL THAT ACCEPTS THE EXCUSE "MY DOG ATE MY HOMEWORK."

Everybody's got to eat, right? What better reason to begin a career than to satisfy a need that everyone has. Learn to become *a professional chef. Call today at (804) 853-3508 for more information on how to get your start. There's no excuse not to.*

JOHNSTON & WALES CULINARY UNIVERSITY

OUR STUDENTS ARE FLUENT IN FRENCH, ITALIAN AND THOUSAND ISLAND.

If this all sounds like greek to you, our culinary school can help. Find out how you can begin a career speaking a language *everyone understands. Food. Become a professional chef. Call (804) 853-3508 for more information on getting started in a great career.*

JOHNSTON & WALES CULINARY UNIVERSITY

BEGIN A CAREER WHERE THE ONLY THREAT TO JOB SECURITY IS WEIGHT WATCHERS.

Yes, they're a large and formidable group (but they're getting a little bit smaller every day). Don't let that discourage  *you from satisfying the rest. Become a professional chef. Call (804) 853-3508 for more information on getting started in a great career.*

JOHNSTON & WALES CULINARY UNIVERSITY

**CONSUMER NEWSPAPER
600 LINES OR LESS:
CAMPAIGN**

251
ART DIRECTOR
Lance Paull
WRITER
Nissen Ritter
CLIENT
Maternity Rack
AGENCY
Ritter & Paull/New York

252
ART DIRECTORS
*Dave Gardiner
Gary Greenberg*
WRITER
Court Crandall
ILLUSTRATOR
Arthur Matson
PHOTOGRAPHER
Jack Richmond
CLIENT
*Northeast Tractor Trailer
School*
AGENCY
*Rossin Greenberg Seronick/
Boston*

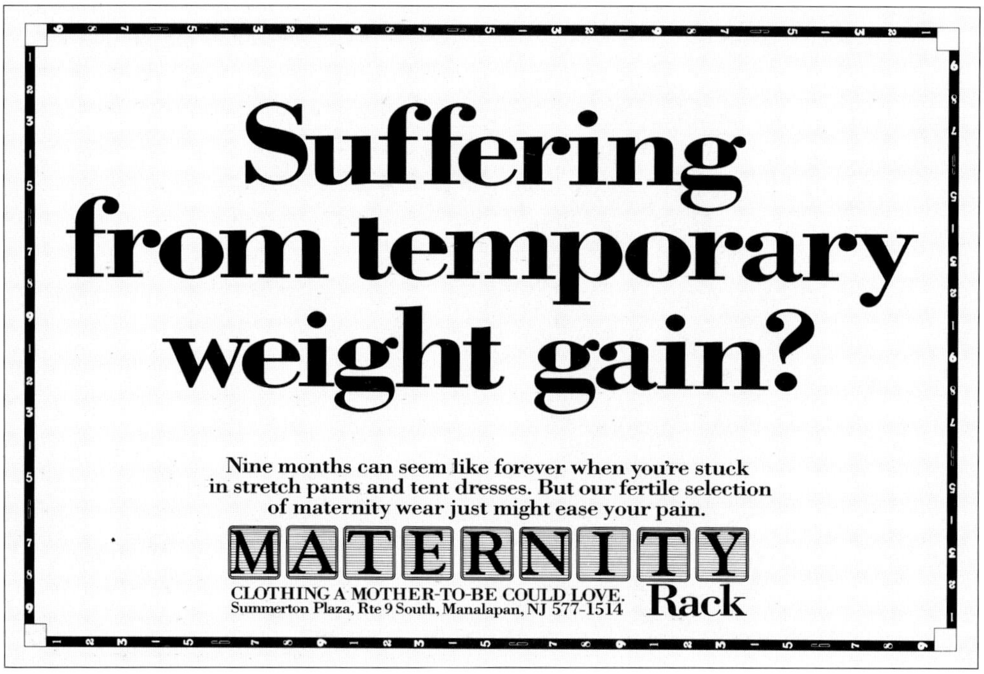

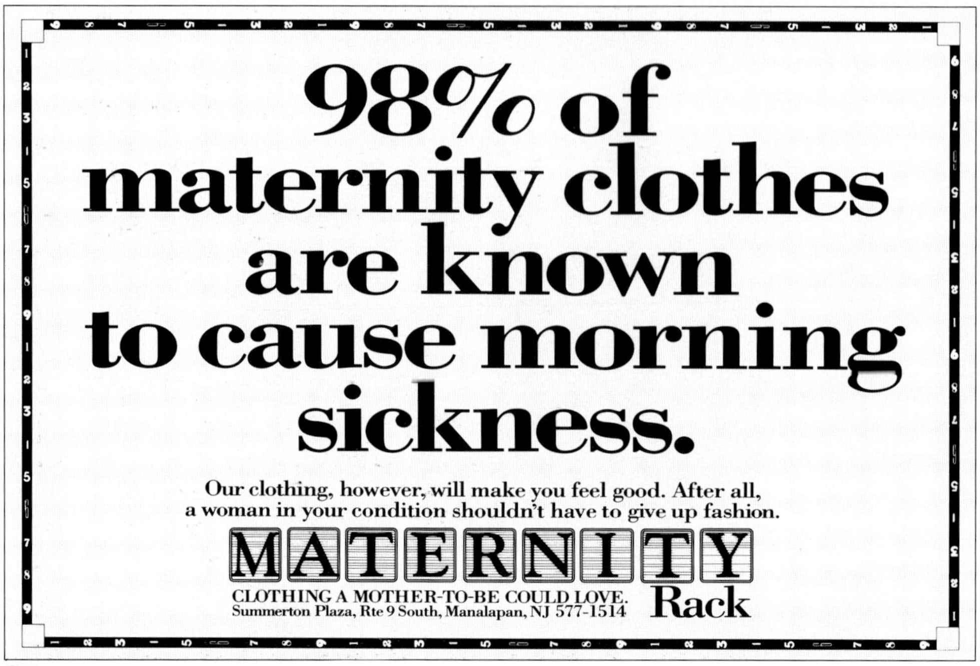

Suffering from temporary weight gain?

Nine months can seem like forever when you're stuck in stretch pants and tent dresses. But our fertile selection of maternity wear just might ease your pain.

MATERNITY Rack

CLOTHING A MOTHER-TO-BE COULD LOVE.
Summerton Plaza, Rte 9 South, Manalapan, NJ 577-1514

Our idea of the perfect figure is 36-54-36.

We think pregnant women deserve to wear clothes that are every bit as beautiful as they are. Come see us for a complete selection of maternity dresses, tops and bottoms that, for once, measures up.

MATERNITY Rack

CLOTHING A MOTHER-TO-BE COULD LOVE.
Summerton Plaza, Rte 9 South, Manalapan, NJ 577-1514

98% of maternity clothes are known to cause morning sickness.

Our clothing, however, will make you feel good. After all, a woman in your condition shouldn't have to give up fashion.

MATERNITY Rack

CLOTHING A MOTHER-TO-BE COULD LOVE.
Summerton Plaza, Rte 9 South, Manalapan, NJ 577-1514

251

At Northeast, we'll teach you all about driving an 18-wheeler on our private course, arrange interviews while you train and give lectures on just about everything but your bad habits. Call 1-800-255-8020. **Northeast Tractor Trailer School**

FINALLY, A CLASS WHERE YOU CAN CHEW GUM AND SMOKE CIGARETTES WITHOUT GETTING SENT TO THE PRINCIPAL'S OFFICE.

At Northeast, we'll teach you how to drive an 18-wheeler and we'll get you interviews while you train. So when graduation comes, you can hit the highway instead of the pavement. Call 1-800-255-8020. **Northeast Tractor Trailer School**

CONGRATULATIONS TO OUR RECENT GRADUATES.

Besides showing you everything from braking to parallel parking, we'll also plan interviews while you train. So you can get right out on the highway and tell everyone where to get off. Call 1-800-255-8020. **Northeast Tractor Trailer School**

WE'LL TEACH YOU ALL THE BASIC HAND SIGNALS.

Right turn.   *Left turn.*   *Up yours.*

CONSUMER NEWSPAPER
600 LINES OR LESS:
CAMPAIGN

253
ART DIRECTORS
Dana Edwards
Gary Greenberg
WRITERS
Peter Seronick
Dana Edwards
CLIENT
Waterstone's
AGENCY
*Rossin Greenberg Seronick/
Boston*

254
ART DIRECTOR
Sharon Mushahwar
WRITER
Dave Pullar
PHOTOGRAPHER
George Remington
CLIENT
Ristorante Barbarino's
AGENCY
Wyse Advertising/Cleveland

A bookstore
for people who know
Homer's <u>Odyssey</u>
isn't an episode
of The Simpsons.

WATERSTONE'S
BOOKSELLERS

One bookstore. 150,000 titles.

Boston · London · Edinburgh · Dublin
At the corner of Exeter and Newbury Streets, Boston.
Open daily until 11PM, Sunday Noon–9PM.

A bookstore
for people who crave the
written version of
The Three Musketeers.
Not the chocolate one.

WATERSTONE'S
BOOKSELLERS

One bookstore. 150,000 titles.

Boston · London · Edinburgh · Dublin
At the corner of Exeter and Newbury Streets, Boston.
Open daily until 11PM, Sunday Noon–9PM.

A bookstore
for people
who consider Spock
an expert on kids.
Not Klingons.

WATERSTONE'S
BOOKSELLERS

One bookstore. 150,000 titles.

Boston · London · Edinburgh · Dublin
At the corner of Exeter and Newbury Streets, Boston.
Open daily until 11PM, Sunday Noon–9PM.

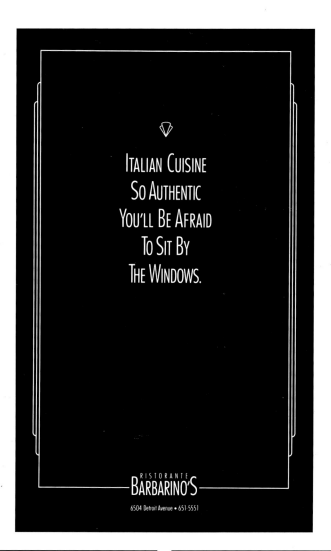

ITALIAN CUISINE
SO AUTHENTIC
YOU'LL BE AFRAID
TO SIT BY
THE WINDOWS.

RISTORANTE
BARBARINO'S

6504 Detroit Avenue • 651-5551

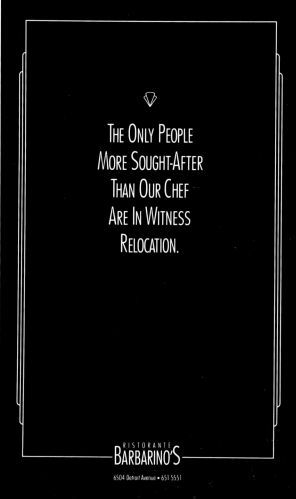

THE ONLY PEOPLE
MORE SOUGHT-AFTER
THAN OUR CHEF
ARE IN WITNESS
RELOCATION.

RISTORANTE
BARBARINO'S

6504 Detroit Avenue • 651-5551

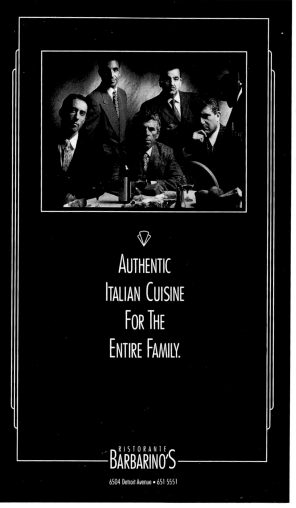

AUTHENTIC
ITALIAN CUISINE
FOR THE
ENTIRE FAMILY.

RISTORANTE
BARBARINO'S

6504 Detroit Avenue • 651-5551

Porsche wins 24 Hours of Daytona.

(And the Pope, of course, is Catholic.)

Once again, as usual, Porsche won the 24 Hours of Daytona sportscar race. In fact, we took three out of the first five places.

And while that certainly is a huge accomplishment, it isn't big news. Because in the last 23 races at the 24 Hours of Daytona we've run away with 18 overall victories. Even Hurley Haywood, one of the drivers of the winning Joest Blaupunkt Porsche 962C, broke the record last Sunday for the most major endurance driving victories in history.

Why do Porsches finish first so often? Because they last. And last and last. We were victorious in the first LeMans race we entered in 1951, and have ruled in the grueling world of endurance racing ever since. Our dynasty includes 17 overall wins at the 12 Hours of Sebring, 12 overall victories at LeMans, 27 World Championships, and more than 200 National and International Championships.

Which brings us to the important part of this ad. Considering that we use the same technology we develop in our race cars in our passenger cars, you can expect your Porsche to endure as long as our endurance cars. Just as sure as a bear... PORSCHE

255

There are 76
photographs
in this issue.

········

If we presume
each was shot
at a shutter
speed of 1/125th
of a second,
then you have
just seen the
combined total of
six-tenths of
a second in time.

········

It is quite a
world, isn't it?

········

To those of you
who saw it
so clearly,
for an instant,
well done.

256

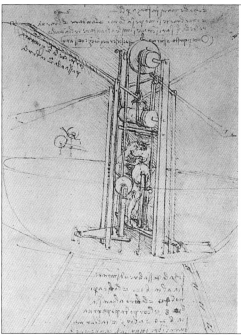

Florence, birthplace of air travel. It's taken 500 years to organise a direct flight.

No sooner did man walk upon the Earth than he began to dream of flying above it. A fantasy that was given form by Leonardo Da Vinci, almost five centuries ago. The Glider. The Helicopter. The Parachute. All were born on the drawing board of this Florentine Maestro. But, aeronautical visionary though he was, Leonardo could never have predicted the trials of reaching his native city by air. Ask any of the major international airlines to take you to Florence, and they will promptly take you to Pisa. A pleasant enough city, but a good hour or two's drive from the joys of the Uffizi. Thanks to Meridiana you'll soon be able to take a less roundabout route. Starting September 1st, Meridiana will fly you direct from London's Gatwick to Florence's Amerigo Vespucci Airport. And fly you there in style. Tourist passengers travel in Business Class comfort, while those in Electa Club enjoy facilities that put many a First Class in the shade. The spacious cabin has unique seats with winged headrests and the international menus are created by some of Italy's finest chefs. To learn more about Meridiana and its new scheduled service direct to Florence, call your travel agent. It's the ideal airline for those who don't have a leaning towards Pisa.

● **Meridiana**
Your Private Airline

257

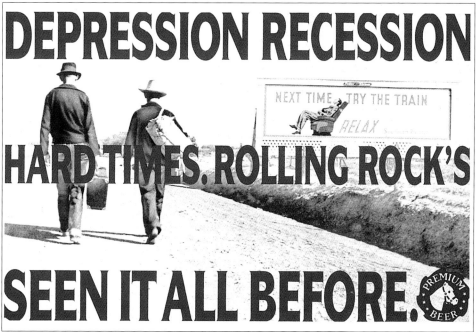

258

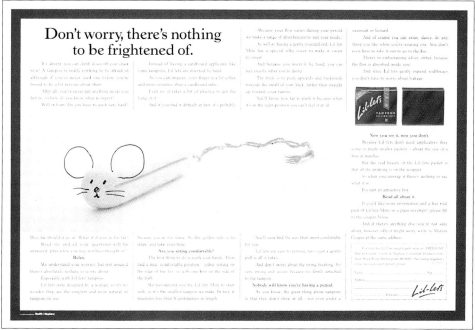

259

Kentucky has produced 2 Presidents, 4 Vice-Presidents, and one distinguished liquor cabinet member.

WILD TURKEY
101 proof, real Kentucky.

260

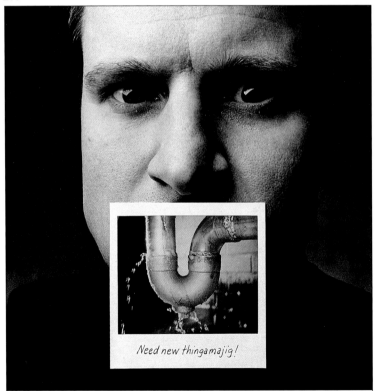

Need new thingamajig!

HOW TO SPEAK QUICKLY
WITHOUT SAYING A WORD.

It's a horrible feeling trying to describe something when you can't find the right words.

Most of the time "thingamabob" and "what-
chamacalit" just don't seem to cut it.

Well, the next time you need to explain some-

thing right away, take a Polaroid
Instant Picture. It'll save you de-
veloping a whole roll of film and
inventing a whole new vocabulary.
Enough said.

Polaroid.
DESCRIBE IT WITH POLAROID
INSTANT PHOTOGRAPHY.

261

THE QUESTION IS, WILL THERE BE ANY MONEY LEFT FOR DINNER?

IF IT'S ANY CONSOLATION, THE ARGO DINING TABLE WAS CRAFTED BY STUDIO NIKE FROM THE FINEST BLACK MARQUINA MARBLE IN VINCENZA, ITALY. AVAILABLE EXCLUSIVELY AT 362 OCEAN CENTRE, HARBOUR CITY, KOWLOON. TEL. 735 516. DESIGN**2000**

262

ISN'T IT AWFUL WHEN YOU SPEND A LOT OF MONEY AND NO ONE NOTICES?

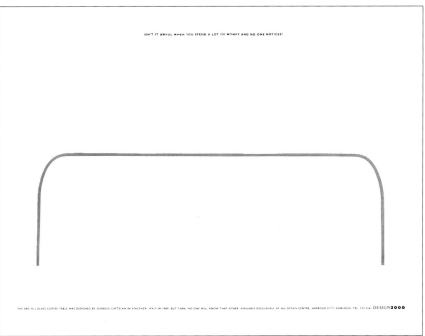

THE ABC ALL GLASS COFFEE TABLE WAS DESIGNED BY GIORGIO CATTELAN IN VINCENZA, ITALY IN 1989. BUT THEN, NO ONE WILL KNOW THAT EITHER. AVAILABLE EXCLUSIVELY AT 362 OCEAN CENTRE, HARBOUR CITY, KOWLOON. TEL. 735 516. DESIGN**2000**

263

CHUCK YEAGER. FIRST MAN TO BREAK THE SOUND BARRIER. OCTOBER, 1947.

WHO CARES WHO CAME SECOND?
The GLENLIVET
SCOTLAND'S FIRST MALT WHISKY.

AGED 12 YEARS.

264

**CONSUMER MAGAZINE
COLOR 1 PAGE OR SPREAD:
SINGLE**

265
ART DIRECTOR
David Ayriss
WRITER
Ron Saltmarsh
PHOTOGRAPHER
Robin Bartholik
CLIENT
O'Brien
AGENCY
*Borders Perrin & Norrander/
Seattle*

266
ART DIRECTOR
Gerard Stamp
WRITER
Loz Simpson
ILLUSTRATOR
Robin Heighway-Bury
CLIENT
H.J. Heinz
AGENCY
BSB Dorland/London

267
ART DIRECTOR
Brian Kroening
WRITER
Rob Wallace
PHOTOGRAPHER
Clint Clemens
CLIENT
Mercury Marine
AGENCY
*Campbell-Mithun-Esty/
Minneapolis*

268
ART DIRECTOR
Jim Keane
WRITER
Joe Nagy
PHOTOGRAPHER
Clint Clemens
CLIENT
Harley-Davidson
AGENCY
*Carmichael Lynch/
Minneapolis*

269
ART DIRECTOR
Jim Keane
WRITERS
*Joe Nagy
Dan Roettger*
PHOTOGRAPHER
Clint Clemens
CLIENT
Harley-Davidson
AGENCY
*Carmichael Lynch/
Minneapolis*

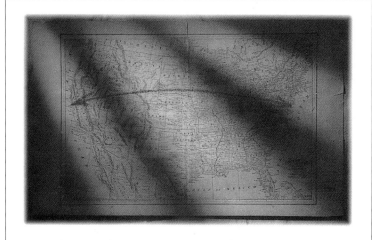

YOU NO LONGER HAVE TO LIVE ON THE EDGE TO SURF.

The thing about skiboarding is that it lets you live on the edge even if you're stuck in like, Iowa. Then again, if you really want to be out there, you need more than a piece of plywood. Meet the Apex by O'Brien. It starts with a new compression-molding technique O'Brien invented called Advanced Composite Reinforced Construction. What ACRC does is make the Apex lighter and thinner than other boards. While maintaining its strength. So it's more responsive and fast. You can rip off the wake, get air and do stunts MacGyver wouldn't touch. All without the fear of breaking the board or sub-marining the nose. Another cool thing is that the Apex has an adjustable tri-fin system which lets you customize the board to your own style. How far you go is up to you. But if you want to shred, you got to be on the edge. Even if you don't live there.

265

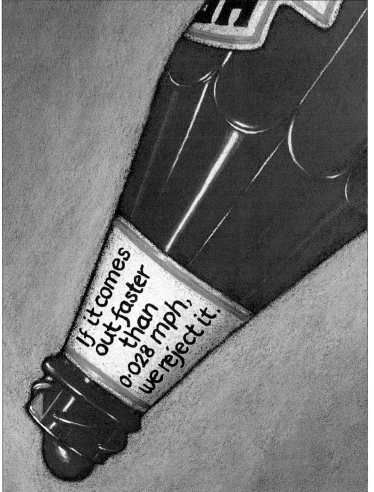

If it comes out faster than 0.028 mph, we reject it.

266

Our engineers have come up with a new way to melt glass.

In fact, they've come up with the hottest line of outboards ever built. Over the past six years, every Mercury has been totally redesigned, each bred from a line of racing champions. In the grueling 24 hours of Rouen endurance race in Rouen, France. Mercury powered the top seven finishers. That's an impressive record. But what's even more impressive is the fact that everything we learn on the proving grounds of racing goes into building a better engine for you. So if you're looking for a real feeling of power, just get your hands on any of our new Mercury outboards. Then get ready to melt some glass of your own.

 Set The Water On Fire

267

Ever look up and see a '59 Panhead ?

It's up there, sitting on its kickstand somewhere between dusk and dawn, and a Harley® rider has put it there. It's a dream, but not just any dream. For everyone who has ever had a Harley, it's real.

Because a Harley, any Harley, changes the way a person looks at things. It doesn't matter whether it's a '59 or a '91, whether the person is young or old, male or female. The effect is the same.

And there is no half-way. It gets into your blood, becoming not so much a possession as it is an obsession.

When you look at it that way, owning a Harley makes you part of a larger universe. You've bought into a tradition that was set down over 87 years ago. You've got a special view of the country that you can't get any other way.

Owning a Harley is also lots of little things. Like not being able to hide a grin when you see a police officer on one. Getting down on hands and knees to take a toothbrush to a cylinder's cooling fins. It's taking the long way to work. Seeing a kid's eyes light up at the end of a toy run. It's knowing that there are probably more Harley-Davidsons® in living rooms than any other make of motorcycle.

This is all something the average person cannot understand, and no explanation can ever bridge the gap. You're a Harley rider or you're not.

You get it or you don't. When you have a Harley, there's much more to it than just owning a motorcycle. Along with it comes something that is its own reward. It's the freedom to go places most people never go. The beauty of seeing things most people never see. The satisfaction of being Harley-Davidson, through and through.

 Through and Through.

268

It's not the town as much as the horse you rode in on.

Like a free-ranging Badlands spirit, it came and went.

And wherever it went, it brought a piece of Black Hills mystique from the town that gave it a name. The Harley-Davidson® Sturgis® And when it seemed to roll off into the distance for the last time, there were still those who awaited a time when it would return.

Now is that time. The Sturgis is back, looking for all the world as if it had never gone.

Long-time Harley® riders will recognize it immediately and yet not truly know it. Because there has never been another motorcycle, Harley-Davidson or otherwise, like the new Sturgis.

Beneath its black-as-sin paint lies new-from-the-ground-up technology.

It starts with the Dyna Glide™ chassis. While it looks to be a dead ringer for the one from the original Sturgis, this frame features a new two-point engine isolation mounting system.

Which makes it one of the best-riding Harleys ever. It's also one of the most finely detailed Harleys ever. For example, check out the new oil tank. Its location is not only convenient, it allows for shorter, more tucked-in oil lines for a cleaner look. Then there's the hidden exhaust crossover that fully exposes the 80 cubic inch Evolution® engine, finished in black. And like the original, the new Sturgis moves down the road with a final belt drive system that is clean, strong and quiet.

This is a motorcycle that will bring to any town the mystery of the country that inspired it and the town that named it.

A motorcycle bound by the script found next to its rider's knee. Sturgis. And just as the faithful have returned to the town every year, now at last, the motorcycle has been returned to the faithful.

 Through and Through.

269

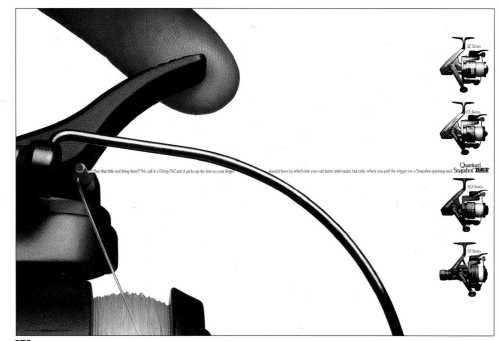

270

271

272

Most practical cars become impractical right about now.

This is not the time to find out your engine lacks horsepower. Here at Nissan, we believe that sort of discovery should be made at the drawing board. Or on a test track.

That's why our engineers equipped the Stanza GXE with a fuel-injected, 2.4 liter, 138-horsepower engine—a power plant most car companies might consider extravagant.

But sheer passing power isn't the GXE's only safety feature. You also have the option of anti-lock brakes. And, to improve handling and traction, we added front and rear stabilizer bars and a viscous limited-slip differential. Which, not coincidentally, also makes the driver's seat of the Stanza awfully fun to sit in.

After all, how practical can a car be if you never want to drive it?

The Stanza GXE with a fuel-injected, 2.4 liter, 138-horsepower engine. Anything less just wouldn't be sensible.

NISSAN Built for the Human Race.

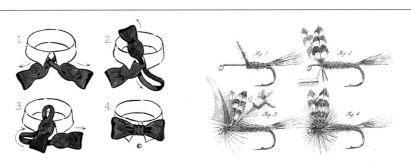

OUR PATHFINDER WILL GO WITH YOUR FAVORITE TIE.

NISSAN There are so many different things you want to do in life. Wouldn't it be nice if you could at least do them all in the same car? Well, that's the basic idea behind the Nissan Pathfinder 4x4.

With 153-hp and 180 ft./lbs. of torque, the Pathfinder is rugged enough to get you to those secluded little fishing holes that don't even show up on the map.

At the same time, it has a special five-link, coil spring rear suspension with unique two-way driver-adjustable shock absorbers. So when you're on your way to see La Traviata in a Pathfinder, you'll feel like you're riding in a luxurious sports sedan. Particularly when you have options like leather seating surfaces and a compact disc audio system.

There are all kinds of details you'd never expect a 4x4 to offer. Sound-reducing window seals, for example. Even a console designed to fit your cellular phone.

And while we're on the subject of 4x4s, Nissan encourages you to always treat off-road areas with care and respect. That's why we support Tread Lightly, a group that protects all the natural areas a Pathfinder can take you to.

We invite you to come in and find out all about the Nissan Pathfinder.

A tie, of course, is optional.

NISSAN. BUILT FOR THE HUMAN RACE.

The most fun you can have with your suit on.

The sport-tuned, multi-port fuel-injected V6, 160-horsepower Maxima SE. Think of it as a black leather jacket in a pinstripe world. Maxima. The 4-Door Sports Car. **NISSAN**

Built for the Human Race.

276

277

278

Counted as many as 500 graves along the North Platte. Sickness lasted usually but a day... and no man dared touch them.

– Oscar Hyde, May 2, 1850.

This wasn't the kind of cross-country trip we take nowadays, where you pile the kids in the mini-van and head off singing songs.

On this trip, there were no rest areas. No Holiday Inns. No Big Macs.

Just 2,000 miles of burning, freezing, scorched, drenched, dust-choked mountains and plains, separating Missouri from the land of paradise.

The land called Oregon.

Oregon wasn't yet a state in those days. Nor, for that matter, were Idaho or Wyoming or Nebraska or Kansas. All of which stood between the overland emigrants and their destination.

And yet, they came.

Almost 300,000 of them between 1840 and 1860, bound for Oregon and California. On a journey that took as much as six months to complete.

But forget, for a moment, the staggering distance.

the Trail, just outside the town of Baker City in Northeastern Oregon.

At a spot called Flagstaff Hill.

Here, the pioneers got their first glimpse of the lush beauty and promise that lay ahead.

And today, in that very same spot, the struggle and triumph of the pioneers is being brought to life like never before.

At a place called the National Historic Oregon Trail Interpretive Center. A very official-sounding name for a very human-feeling place.

Here, you'll find one of the most extensive re-creations of life on the Trail ever attempted.

You'll walk in the pioneers' actual wagon ruts, carved for eternity into the Powder Valley. You'll read from their diaries. You'll meet people living as they did 150 years ago.

And you'll feel what the pioneers felt, as the sights and sounds of the overland journey come to life all around you, through powerful interactive exhibits.

The center opens this spring. We hope you'll plan a trip to Oregon and visit.

WHEN THE PIONEERS REACHED FLAGSTAFF HILL THEY THOUGHT THEY'D DIED AND GONE TO HEAVEN. OF COURSE, MANY OF THEM HAD.

Forget the wilderness and weather.

Forget the absence of anything even remotely resembling a Denny's.

And consider the enormous hardships the pioneers faced on top of all that:

The men, women and children who made this trek covered every mile of it on foot – walking beside their weary oxen, horses and even milk cows as they pulled overburdened wagons.

They saw their prize possessions and precious supplies tossed by the wayside to lighten the load.

They persevered through cholera epidemics that reached epic proportions. And thievery under the cover of night.

To build fires for cooking, they gathered stray branches and twigs.

When they ran out of twigs they used old wagon parts.

And when they ran out of wagon parts they used buffalo chips.

(They rarely ran out of buffalo chips.)

In the early years, rivers like the Snake, the Sweetwater, the North Platte and the Big Blue had to be forded midstream – without bridges or ferries or any guarantee of making it across alive.

And if the disease, weather, thieves or rivers didn't kill you, a disastrous wagon accident or the deadly combination of greenhorns and guns just might.

Which brings us to The Big Question: Why would these people risk their lives, their health and, more importantly, their families to make this incredible journey?

Well, the answer lies near the end of

OREGON TRAIL INTERPRETIVE CENTER

Because once you share the pioneers' lives and dreams – once you stand on Flagstaff Hill and gaze off toward the Blue Mountains – you, too, will understand why they risked even death to make this miraculous journey.

For more information or to plan a trip to Oregon, call 1-800-547-7842.

How would you rate tonight's performance?

Over the years your vision may start to go. But your teeth don't have to.

How's that for an eye opener? You can keep your teeth for life.

Take it from the toothpaste that, over the years, has helped prevent more cavities than any other toothpaste. Which could explain why Crest is recommended by more dentists and hygienists than any other toothpaste.

And even as you get older and less prone to cavities, brushing with Crest is still essential. For helping to keep your teeth free of decay. Which will help you keep your teeth, period.

So we're sorry if we've strained your eyes. But it's only to make an important point about your teeth.

Helping to ensure a lifetime of healthy teeth.

282

283

284

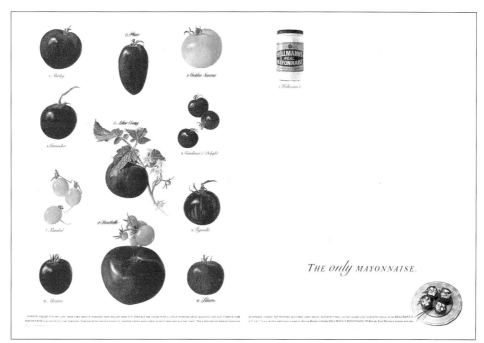

THE *only* MAYONNAISE.

285

There are feet that have never gotten the corner office. There are feet
that have never sat through a shareholder's meeting. There are feet that have
never had sushi for lunch. There are feet that have never seen the inside
of an Italian loafer. Dunham. They get the job done.

286

There are feet that will never meet the gas pedal of a Range Rover.
There are feet that will never see a condo in Aspen. There are feet that will
never winter in Palm Springs or Palm Beach or Palm anywhere.
Dunham. They get the job done.

287

288
ART DIRECTOR
John Doyle
WRITER
Ernie Schenck
PHOTOGRAPHER
Nadav Kander
CLIENT
The Dunham Company
AGENCY
Doyle Advertising/Boston

289
ART DIRECTOR
John Doyle
WRITER
Ernie Schenck
PHOTOGRAPHER
Nadav Kander
CLIENT
The Dunham Company
AGENCY
Doyle Advertising/Boston

290
ART DIRECTOR
Carol Henderson
WRITER
Doug de Grood
PHOTOGRAPHER
Kerry Peterson
CLIENT
Jim Beam Brands
AGENCY
*Fallon McElligott/
Minneapolis*

291
ART DIRECTOR
Houman Pirdavari
WRITER
Jarl Olsen
CLIENT
Penn Racquet Sports
AGENCY
*Fallon McElligott/
Minneapolis*

292
ART DIRECTOR
Dean Hanson
WRITER
Phil Hanft
PHOTOGRAPHER
Shawn Michienzi
CLIENT
*Ralston Purina/
Nature's Course*
AGENCY
*Fallon McElligott/
Minneapolis*

288

289

Double maturing does for Scotch
what earmuffs do for the bagpipes.

The Scotch whisky that's aged, blended, then aged again. Also available in 12, 21 & 30 year.
Whyte & Mackay® Scotch Whisky. Doubly matured for singular smoothness.

290

fiber

lawn care

uniformity

Our tennis balls have 75% fewer visible irregularities than our nearest competitor's!
(Are you still awake?) Penn tennis balls. You've seen one. You've seen them all.

291

Too many pesticides in your dog's food?

Our new, natural dog food uses whole grains certified grown without chemical pesticides. And only real chicken and real beef. And only the natural sweetness of molasses. All the good things.

No artificial preservatives. No artificial flavors. No artificial colors. No meat by-products.

None of that stuff. Nature's Course Brand Dog Food. Natural ingredients plus essential vitamins and minerals.

292

Plastic flowers in a Ming vase.
Curb feelers on a Jaguar.
Plato's Republic on cassette.

The Dalmore. Leave it alone.

293

Forget about cholesterol. It's your jeans that
have been cutting off your circulation.

PLEATED·RIDER

294

Larry Walters strapped 42 weather balloons to an aluminum lawn chair and soared to 16,000 feet before he shot out some of the balloons with a BB gun and crashed into a power line. He was spotted by both TWA and Delta airline pilots. Larry, appropriately, is wearing our moon dial watch. It costs about $50.

TIMEX

295

Boring things

flange

maturity

quality control

Harder to make but more fun to play with.
Penn tennis balls. You've seen one. You've seen them all.

296

New Whyte & Mackay Scotch.
As unexpected as a gust of wind up your kilt.

The only scotch that's aged, blended, then aged again. Also available in 12, 21 & 30 year.
Whyte & Mackay Scotch Whisky. Doubly-matured for singular smoothness.

297

298

299

It took a special drink to bring together men who hadn't bathed in two months.

For more than 300 years, sailors of Britain's Royal Navy were issued a daily ration of Pusser's Rum (a corruption of "Purser's Rum," referring to the ship's officer who dispensed the grog). Just since 1980 has this legendary rum been available commercially. It is, like the men who drank it, strong in character. Naturally, a rum as such is not for everyone. But rather, for a very small few. Known to those in the know as "The Pusser's Breed."

The romantic days of sail were anything but romantic. Especially in Britain's Royal Navy.

When a sailor went out to sea, he left civilization far behind. Gone were such luxuries as regular baths.

On the other hand, he did clean up on a rare treasure: our rum.

From as early as 1655, Royal Navy seamen were issued a daily ration of a half pint of rum by the ship's purser (corrupted to "pusser" by the men).

To a jack tar, "Pusser's Rum" was like a breath of fresh air. One swallow and suddenly his existence wasn't so stale after all. Even if his scent was.

The rum ration was so coveted, in fact, that it became currency under various names. Like: *Sippers*, just a little of your precious ration for somebody to sew on a button, or do a bit of washing. *Gulpers*, at least half of your tot for one of your friends to do a double shift. *See-ers offers*, the entire tot.

For this you'd be expected to pull a mate out of the sea. This glorious tradition went on for some 300 years.

Then, risking mutiny, the British Admiralty scrubbed the rum perk in 1970.

But today, that spirit is back.

In British Navy Pusser's Rum. A full, rich, dark, 95.5 proof luxury rum. The very same rum that was standard issue aboard Royal Navy ships. The only difference is, you no longer have to go to sea to get it; you need only chart a course to your local spirits merchant. Or to your favorite watering hole.

Like cognac, Pusser's is best enjoyed neat. For the purpose of mixing we offer an 80 proof Pusser's. A rum that, while lighter, still embodies the rich tradition that is Pusser's. Pick up a bottle and discover this tradition for yourself. Better yet, invite your mates. You'll come out smelling like a rose.

Pusser's Rum. The spirit of the British Royal Navy

PUSSER'S RUM

300

You always come back to the basics. JIM BEAM

302

These jeans were designed to give you more room in the knees and ankles.

With a side elastic waist, and absolutely nothing to pinch or bind you in the knees or ankles, these just might be the most comfortable pair of jeans you'll ever wear. 100% Pepper Wash cotton denim shorts. Nobody fits your body…or the way you live…better than Lee.

E L A S T I C · R I D E R · S H O R T

Lee

The brand that fits.

301

303

304

Jeans for life's little ups and downs.

*Lee jeans are designed to fit the natural curves of a woman's body. But most importantly, they're designed
to fit the natural curves of a woman's life. Nobody fits your body....or the way you live...better than Lee.*

E L A S T I C · R I D E R

The brand that fits.

305

306

Too many pesticides in your dog's food?

Our new, natural dog food uses whole grains certified grown without chemical pesticides.

And only real chicken and real beef. And only the natural sweetness of molasses. All the good things.

No artificial preservatives. No artificial flavors. No artificial colors. No meat by-products.

None of that stuff. Nature's Course Brand Dog Food.

Natural ingredients plus essential vitamins and minerals.

NATURE'S COURSE

307

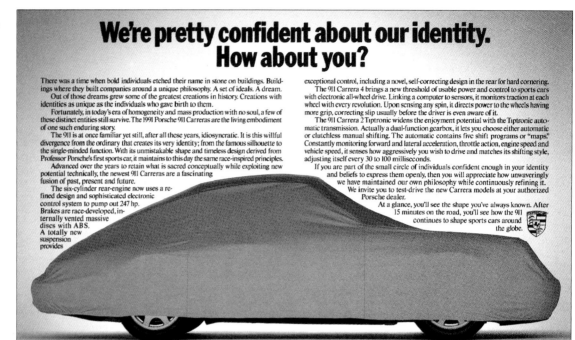

308

309

You can drop these hints this Christmas.
(They're made by Timex, after all.)

If they get the hint you might also want to mention that Timex watches range from just $14.95 to $79.95. Call 1-800-367-8463 for the retailer nearest you. And drop by soon.

TIMEX

310

312

After 4 years it's worth 92% of its original value. But don't worry, it'll probably go up.

Recent reports show a 1986 Porsche 911 to be worth over 92% of its original retail value. More astoundingly, a 1956 Porsche Speedster, originally under $3,000, has listed for $125,000. Of course, no one can promise what will happen to the value of any acquisition. But if you, like most, use past performance as a barometer, a 911 seems a very shrewd purchase indeed.

There is, simply, a small cadre of automobiles that qualify not just as joyous transportation, but collectable investments as well. Usually because of the very technology and craftsmanship that make them uniquely exciting. When Professor Porsche established his sports car philosophy with his first roadster in 1947, those were his parameters. Forward-thinking materials and engineering. Handcrafting in limited numbers. A design and personality wrought purely from function, not styling whims of the day. A design which would thus prove timeless.

In today's 911 Carreras, these same purebred principles live on. Still connected visibly to their past. Still reaching aggressively for the future.

The famous 911 silhouette continues. A shape directly evolved from Professor Porsche's original Type 356. A shape which has taken one more functional step forward, with aerodynamic integrated bumpers and side skirts. Retaining the concept of an air-cooled six in the rear, the powerplant now pours 247 hp to the drive wheels using race-inspired improvements and a sophisticated engine management system.

It is this sense of history, linked to constant advances, that creates much of the car's mystique and value.

As is true with any pioneering marque Porsche strives, through the 911, to prove what is possible, redefining the entire sports car category. The all-wheel drive 911 Carrera 4 makes the car's power more useable by continuously directing it to the wheels with the most grip, for a new threshold of adhesion and handling on all surfaces. And the 911 Carrera 2 Tiptronic offers an amazing automatic. One which continuously analyzes vehicle speed, engine speed, forward and lateral acceleration and throttle activity to determine how aggressively you wish to drive, then adjusts its shifting style. It also lets you switch over to clutchless manual shifting for full control.

A test-drive of the latest 911 Carreras at your authorized Porsche dealer will show just how we are sustaining a heritage of automotive benchmarks.

What will happen to the value of these cars in the future? All we can say is, we continue to fuse the purest principles of yesterday with the most advanced knowledge of today. Creating cars unlike anything else on the road.

Human appreciation for this never seems to wane. And history does, as you know, have a tendency to repeat itself.

The 1991 911 Carrera 2.

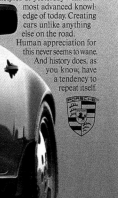

311

Willie Duberry,
age 121, was born five years
after the end of the Civil War.
His closest brush with death was
awhile ago—in the trenches in World
War I. He credits quitting smoking
and drinking with adding a few years
to his life. Then again, his sister
lived to 115. Willie is wearing our
Easy Reader® watch. It's easier
to see the numbers. It
costs about $35.

TIMEX

313

Fortunately, every day comes with an evening.

WINDSOR
CANADIAN
Supreme

314

There are some things in life that simply defy explanation to those who have not shared the experience. Such has always been our dilemma at Porsche.

In 1948, in the image of his own dream, Professor F. Porsche created a sports car so responsive and with such an individualistic personality it was almost alive; an extension of the driver's own thoughts and feelings; childlike in its unbridled spirit. For two generations we have sought to explain the sensation. And have always found ourselves saying, simply, you have to try it.

The 1991 Porsche 911 Carrera 4 is part of the current generation in this legendary, mystical family.

To test-drive the Carrera 4 is to discover a relationship between yourself and a car we can but feebly try to express here. Race-bred components are intricately matched to make it seem almost as if it were an extension of your own limbs.

It is this tactile sense of direct contact and control that has been the hallmark of every Porsche. Today, the Carrera 4 uses electronically controlled all-wheel drive to bring the feeling to an unprecedented peak.

Combining sensors and a sophisticated computer, the Carrera 4 monitors traction at each wheel with every revolution. Upon detecting any spin, within 25 thousandths of a second it directs power to the wheels having

more grip, correcting slip usually before the driver is even aware of it. Not only does it put more of the car's incredible potential to the ground, but it makes it more useable and predictable.

The all-wheel drive system works together with a new suspension, including a self-correcting design in the rear, to make cornering a startling display of synergy between car and driver.

Every facet of the car contributes to this character. Porsche engineers, for example, say the ideal brakes should make it feel as if you are squeezing the brake discs between your fingertips. Engage the massive, internally vented ABS disc brakes in the Carrera 4, and you'll sense time momentarily freeze as you are hauled to a rock-solid, straight-line standstill.

The fact is, it's ludicrous of us to try and explain the experience further. In over 40 years, we have yet to find a way to do so. All we can say is, if you are the type who looks for joy and stimulation where others see only one of life's necessities, you will no doubt visit your authorized Porsche dealer for a test-drive. Then we'll be able to talk.

The 1991 Porsche 911 Carrera 4

It's like children.
You can't understand until you've had one.

315

The body is guaranteed
for ten years.

The soul will last forever.

PORSCHE

316

Old cars go to scrap yards.
Old Porsches go to museums.

OUR FIRST PORSCHE: 1948 TYPE 356 ROADSTER.

PORSCHE

317

Self-propelled Hush Puppies.

With each step, raised areas on the bottom of our Bounce® shoe compress and cushion. As they spring back, they gently propel the foot forward. This technological innovation comes in men's and women's styles and is priced comparably with ordinary walking shoes. What more incentive do you need? For the retailer nearest you, call 1-800-6-HUSH PUP.

Hush Puppies
BOUNCE
makes walking easier.

The ultimate Porsche. (Isn't that redundant?)

Let us put it even more directly: The Porsche 911 Turbo is the Porsche of Porsches. A sportscar built not to the standards of a sportscar, but to the impossibly high standards of a race car.

A combination of 315 thoroughbred horses and massive ABS-fortified brakes not only propel it from 0 to 60 in a mere 4.25 seconds, but also stop it faster than any other production car in the world.* (Not surprisingly, it effortlessly defeated the world's other premier sportscars to win the inaugural IMSA Bridgestone Potenza Supercar Championship.)

Yet match that brawn to the dramatically-improved new transmission, steering, suspension, and creature comforts of the new generation of Carrera, and you have a beast that is remarkably well-mannered.

But we are becoming redundant. Test drive the new generation of 911 Turbo and you will agree it is not just the world's ultimate sportscar. It is the ultimate Porsche. **The Porsche 911 Turbo.**

Starting from "a clean sheet of paper" is fine. If you have nothing worth keeping.

You hear a lot of boasting these days about automotive engineers starting from scratch, with a clean sheet of paper. And, if it takes them three years to turn out a new car, that's what you get. The product of three years of thinking.

The new Porsche 968 is a result of quite the opposite philosophy. A new car which, by no accident, appears strikingly familiar. The product of over 40 years of fine tuning.

In 1948, Professor F. Porsche brought to life his dream car. Heralded then as, "The newest creation of one of history's most brilliant designers of sports and racing cars...a challenge to all designers," it began a legendary evolution.

Every day since, this band of idealistic engineers has practiced what they call "polishing the diamond." The 968 is the most current iteration of this timeless process.

Reaping the technological and performance harvest of 15 new patents, the 968 melds the Porsche essence with every last ounce of today's engineering potential. Imbued with unmistakable lines, it brings the classic family features forward with futuristic aerodynamics.

By introducing the racebred concept of "internal aerodynamics" to a production car, meticulous sculpting of chassis details now speeds air through the body and suspension, reducing drag and lift while cooling racing caliber components such as the massive, internally vented disc brakes with ABS.

From that first, handbuilt car, the visceral Porsche character, power and agility have historically set benchmarks for other cars of the era.

The 968 employs the patented new Porsche VarioCam™ to again set such standards. Continuously varying valve timing to burn fuel more precisely and thoroughly, torque is boosted to the highest of any 3 litre engine in the world, with instantaneous throttle response.

A stunning new catalytic converter with thin, rare metal inner walls increases airflow for still more power. Yet, resourcefully, the VarioCam and converter efficiency also lower emissions a dramatic 22%.*

Handling is heightened and refined as well. The famed transaxle platform with near perfect 50-50 weight balance is further buttressed for the added performance, yet detail changes have actually increased comfort.

If you were to drive an original Porsche 356, then climb behind the wheel of the new 968, the feelings and stimulations would be much the same. Merely enhanced, with ever more potential and a feeling of confidence to use it.

The bloodlines would be clearly intact.

It's the type of marque personality that has become regrettably rare today. Left behind in an age when cars reflected their creators. An age being kept alive at Porsche, and in the 968.

Call 1-800-252-4444 for more information or to arrange a personal viewing at your authorized Porsche dealer. A new Porsche doesn't come along every day. But then, when you start without compromise, you don't have to keep starting over.

Porsche 968: The next evolution.

There are some things that seem so right the way they are, it would be unnatural for them to change. Then again, no sooner do we believe something is sacrosanct than change comes along and shakes our notions apart. Such is the Porsche Tiptronic automatic transmission.

In fact, it has always been Porsche-like to do the unexpected. In 1947, when Professor F. Porsche created his first sports car, he ignored convention. The engine was placed in the rear. Lightweight materials employed. Styling foresook garish ostentation of the day for smooth, timeless aerodynamics. Porsche has spent the ensuing decades refining that original concept. Never changing for the sake of change, but never fearing to move ahead.

The truth is, the idea of a high performance automatic has always intrigued Professor Porsche. If you didn't have to let off the power and depress another pedal repeatedly, you could drive even harder and with greater concentration, right?

In keeping with the Porsche heritage, the answer was found on the racetrack. Working with drivers piloting our famed Type 962 racing cars, our engineers developed a clutchless electronic transmission that let them shift with just the flick of a lever, with no let-up in power. Championships followed.

To get an automatic for our sports cars, the remaining trick was to make the car "think." To sense when you want to shift. By combining the electronic concept with a sophisticated computer,

we created the Tiptronic: A dual-function gearbox that lets you choose either clutchless manual shifting, as in the racing 962, or full automatic operation.

As an automatic, the Tiptronic uses sensors to monitor forward and lateral acceleration; vehicle speed; engine speed; even how you are working the throttle. Then, seeing how aggressively you wish to drive, the car chooses the proper shifting style from five different "maps," adjusting every 30 to 100 milliseconds. In cases where a typical automatic would upshift, reducing control, the Tiptronic reads things such as hard cornering forces and prevents that upshift, just as you would when shifting yourself.

When you want to take over, slip the lever to the manual side. Then just "tip" it forward for upshifts and backward for downshifts. It's so quick that 8 out of 10 of our Porsche test-drivers had faster laps with the Tiptronic in manual mode than with a straight stick.

Of course, we know you're not going to believe all this until you see for yourself. Which is why we urge you to test-drive a 911 Carrera 2 Tiptronic at your authorized Porsche dealer.

Automobile Magazine named it Technology of the Year, saying, "Of all the good ideas that have popped up recently...Tiptronic...will have the most profound effect on future cars." There now. That doesn't sound like a certain hot spot is about to freeze over, does it?

The 1991 Porsche 911 Carrera 2 Tiptronic.

If you're one of those who thought you'd see an automatic in the 911 "when pigs fly," may we suggest you duck?

1956. 1965. 1969. 1972. 1975. 1985. 1988. 1991.

You always come back to the basics. Jim Beam

322

323

IF YOU DIDN'T WANT TO PUSH YOURSELF,
YOU WOULD'VE JOINED THE BASKETBALL TEAM.

THE FINALS®

FOR A FREE SWIMWEAR CATALOG, CALL 1-800-431-9111.

324

CLOTHES FOR PEOPLE WHO WARM UP FOR A MARATHON BY
SWIMMING 2.4 MILES AND BIKING 112.

THE FINALS®

FOR A FREE 1992 CATALOG OF OUR SWIMMING AND CROSS TRAINING WEAR
OR A DEALER NEAR YOU, CALL 1-800-431-9111.

325

THEY SAY MAN CAN SURVIVE FOR 5 DAYS WITHOUT WATER.
BUT NOT IF HE'S ON THE SWIM TEAM.

THE FINALS®

FOR A FREE 1992 CATALOG OR A DEALER NEAR YOU, CALL 1-800-431-9111.

326

CONSUMER MAGAZINE
COLOR 1 PAGE OR SPREAD:
SINGLE

327
ART DIRECTOR
Peter Holmes
WRITER
Peter Holmes
PHOTOGRAPHER
George Simhoni
CLIENT
Rubinet
AGENCY
Franklin Dallas/Toronto

328
ART DIRECTOR
Gary Goldsmith
WRITER
Dean Hacohen
CLIENT
US Magazine
AGENCY
Goldsmith/Jeffrey, New York

329
ART DIRECTOR
Gary Goldsmith
WRITER
Ty Montague
CLIENT
Everlast
AGENCY
Goldsmith/Jeffrey, New York

330
ART DIRECTOR
Noam Murro
WRITER
Dean Hacohen
CLIENT
Crain's New York Business
AGENCY
Goldsmith/Jeffrey, New York

Everyone knows the feeling.
There you are, half awake, enjoying the comfort of your usual morning shower. Suddenly, without warning, a blast of scalding hot water bursts out of the showerhead.
If you're one of those people who find this kind of thing exhilarating,

And as with all Rubinet faucets, the Temperature Balance Shower System is meticulously crafted to the most exacting standards.
Solid brass constructions are immersed in a vibrasonic bath. The parts are then polished to high lustre and vapour cleaned and dried. One

to three coats of epoxy are electrostatically applied and baked at 360° for up to forty minutes. The faucet is then hand-fit, examined for even the slightest imperfection and tested. It's also fully covered by Rubinet's unprecedented five-year warranty. A warranty which is the longest and

most comprehensive of its kind.
The Rubinet Temperature Balance Shower System.
A product built on the belief that violent shower scenes are best left in the movies.
For the authorized Rubinet dealer nearest you phone 1-800-461-5901.

RUBINET

The next time you're showering and the toilet flushes, here's something to consider other than murder.

don't bother to read any further.
If, on the other hand you're like the rest of us, you'll be pleased to note that there exists a product that will prevent it from ever happening again.
The Rubinet Temperature Balance Shower System is an advanced water pressure system which automatically balances water surges, constantly monitoring and equalizing water temperatures.
Just as importantly, it also controls water flow. So you'll never end up with creme rinse in your hair and no water to rinse it out.

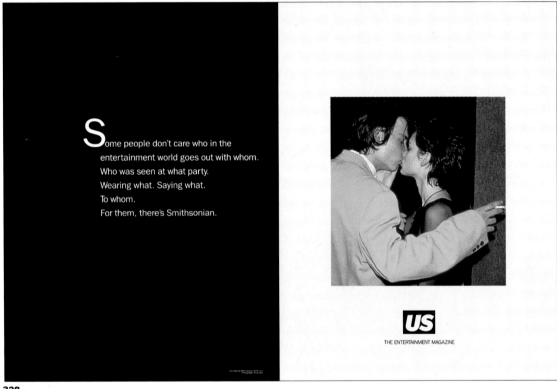

327

Some people don't care who in the entertainment world goes out with whom.
Who was seen at what party.
Wearing what. Saying what.
To whom.
For them, there's Smithsonian.

US
THE ENTERTAINMENT MAGAZINE

328

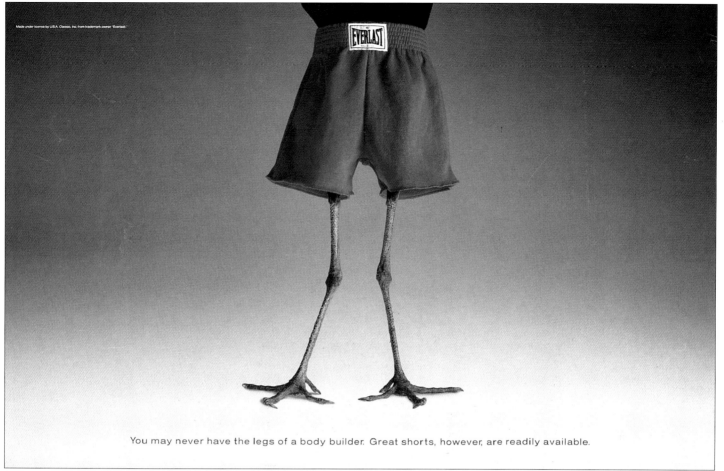

You may never have the legs of a body builder. Great shorts, however, are readily available.

329

What you don't know won't hurt you? The less you know the better? Ignorance is bliss? Good luck in New York.

CRAIN'S
NEW YORK BUSINESS

Call (800) 487-4871 to subscribe.

330

331

332

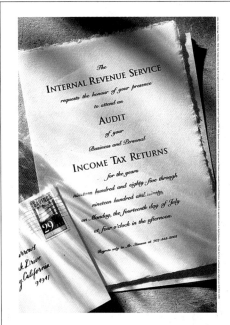

333

Private Drees had survived that random Scud attack on the Army barracks near Dhahran. "I caught my breath for a second and looked, and the whole building was gone," he continued. "My bunk was against the wall and it was gone. I reached back and pieces of my leg were missing. My right shoe was off. I tried to chase it around, and I couldn't."

THE
NEW YORKER
WHEN YOU READ IT, YOU'LL SEE.

For the past 50 years, we've taken great care to insure that you'll never mistake one for the other.

The Official Fast Food Choice Of The L.A. Kings.

There are three indispensable items for every Finnish fishing excursion: a fishing pole, a fishing buddy, and, of course, Finlandia. (As you might guess, one of these items may be a little more essential than the other two.)

Finlandia. Vodka From The Top Of The World.

336

337

Breathe easier underwater.

Relax.

A Range Rover is virtually dunk resistant.

Its anti-lock braking system is capable of stopping straight even on roads that bear a striking resemblance to small ponds.

And with the added traction of permanent 4-wheel drive, a Range Rover can grip the kind of rain-soaked pavement that sends ordinary luxury cars slip-

sliding away.

Of course, what makes a Range Rover and its owner even more comfortable during torrential downpours, Nordic

RANGE ROVER

blizzards, or whatever else the sky has to offer, are its abundant amenities.

Why not call 1-800-FINE 4WD for a dealer near you?

It's very rare that an investment of around $43,000 can make you feel quite this secure. Even in the midst of a blinding typhoon, you'll be at the helm of a rather seaworthy vehicle.

One designed to relieve a little of that cabin pressure.

Where do you suppose they keep the Range Rover?

A Range Rover is quite at home in weather that would keep other luxury cars, well, at home.

After all, with its permanent 4-wheel drive and powerful V-8 engine, you can plow through unplowed roads.

Tool along slushy streets.

Make it up sleet-covered hills.

And easily cope with conditions that would discourage a sled dog.

In fact, the Range Rover County even comes with an anti-lock braking system considered by many to be the most sophisticated one on four wheels.

RANGE ROVER

Which not only means you can drive with a reassuring amount of control.

You can stop with it too.

So why not call 1-800-FINE 4WD for the name of a dealer near you?

Granted, with Range Rovers starting at just under $39,000, it's not the sort of thing one should take lightly.

But then, neither is a ton of snow.

Introducing a mower for the man who has everything.

The trappings of success are nice. But they're difficult to trim around, especially with a conventional four-wheeled mower.

Now, John Deere offers you something revolutionary. Our highly maneuverable, three-wheeled front mower.

It's the residential version of our commercial front mower, which we originally designed for professional groundskeepers.

Both the 14-hp F510 and 17-hp F525 feature a low-profile mowing deck with a remarkable 7½-inch turning radius for close, easy trimming around and under typical backyard obstacles.

Mowing time is cut in half, because instead of having to cut first and trim second, you can just about do the whole

job in one clean pass.

And it's safe and easy to operate, thanks to our exclusive two-pedal control, which lets you shift into forward or reverse without taking your hands off the steering wheel. And on hillsides, with our patented Traction Assist System, you can transfer the weight of the mower deck to the

drive wheels, on-the-go, for greater traction and stability.

Ask your John Deere dealer to show you the other superior qualities of our three-wheeled front mower. Call 1-800-544-2122 for the one nearest you.

You'll spend less time working in your yard, and more time enjoying it.

NOTHING RUNS LIKE A DEERE.

YOU WILL NEVER forget this masterpiece. It tells the story of Bathsheba and King David. It was painted by REMBRANDT in 1654. ❀❀ A fateful detail is the letter from King David. It asks that Bathsheba meet him in secret. ❀ The consequences for her – already wed – can only be tragic. But there is an even more fateful detail, discovered only recently. It gives new meaning to the dark brooding poignancy of "BATHSHEBA." ❀✦❀✦❀✦❀ ❀ Look closely at the model's left breast. Can you see the dimpling? This detail, recorded unknowingly by Rembrandt, is advanced breast cancer. ❀ The model, *Hendrickje Stoffels*, died several years later. Almost certainly, experts now believe, of breast cancer. ❀ Hendrickje Stoffels was also Rembrandt's common-law wife and, within a year of the painting, mother of his daughter. (Indeed, could she have been pregnant as she posed?) ❀

A WOMAN'S BEST
PROTECTION IS
EARLY *DETECTION*.

These days, of course, almost everyone has heard of breast cancer. It is the most common cancer in Australian women. One in fifteen will develop this disease. ❀✦❀✦❀✦❀✦❀ ❀ These days, doctors can detect breast cancer long before it becomes

"Bathsheba with King David's Letter," Rembrandt 1654.

TO AN ART LOVER,
THIS IS A CLASSIC REMBRANDT.

even an unseen, unfelt lump. And long, long before it becomes the classic *"orange peel dimpling"* recorded by Rembrandt. ❀✦❀✦❀✦❀✦❀ ❀ It is this early detection of breast cancer that, for many women, can mean a complete cure. It can save your life, often without the need for a mastectomy. ❀✦❀✦❀✦❀ ❀ But how do you detect breast cancer long before it becomes a lump and early enough for it to be cured? By making sure that you have regular

TO A DOCTOR,
IT'S CLASSIC BREAST CANCER.

before a doctor can feel any abnormality in the breast. ❀✦❀✦❀✦❀ ❀ That is why modern treatment is often much simpler than the old days. Breast Health screening is essentially a programme to help confirm that a healthy woman has no obvious evidence of breast cancer. ❀✦❀✦❀ ❀ It can give you the reassurance that, as prevalent as the disease is, you are one of the vast majority who does not have it. (If you have any cause for concern you should see your local

Breast Health screenings. ❀✦❀✦❀ ❀ These breast X-rays, mammograms, are your best protection. They are able to find breast cancer one or two years

doctor immediately – you may be referred for a *full diagnostic testing*). ❀ ❀ If you are 50 and over, you should have a Breast Health screening every two years. If you are 40 and over and have not had a Breast Health screening you should have one now. If you are under 40 you are advised to have a Breast Health screening only if there is a history of breast cancer in mother or sister. Otherwise, wait until you have turned 40. ❀✦❀✦❀✦❀

BREAST HEALTH
SCREENINGS REBATE
FOR MBF MEMBERS.

Breast Health screenings are not covered by Medicare unless symptoms are present or unless there is that family history. ❀✦❀✦❀ ❀ MBF is determined to provide for its members what Medicare does not.❀ ❀ If you are 40 or over, see your local doctor for a referral. And if you are an MBF member you will be entitled to a rebate of up to $30. ❀✦ ❀ For more information on this initiative, telephone 0055 22 737. This recorded message gives you concise details. If you would like to discuss screening mammograms, or the MBF rebate plan, please call 008 030 630. ❀✦❀ **M✦F**

John Bevins MBT01402/1/L.

Medical Benefits Fund of Australia Limited. Incorporated in NSW. A non-profit, registered health benefits organisation.

John Bevins MBT01402/1/R

AT 30,000 FEET, FRANCE LOOKS A LOT LIKE DETROIT.

With an average cruising altitude of one foot, travelling through France by rail has its advantages. Not only does it offer magnificent views of the French countryside along the way, it whisks you directly to the heart of most cities at speeds up to 190 miles per hour.

It's also less expensive than you think. Especially when you have one of our France Railpasses.

The Superflexipass. For as little as $125, you can create your own rail pass with four to nine days of unlimited travel on any

train in France, including the TGV.

The Rail 'n Drive Pass. At $159, it offers four days of travel anywhere the trains go, with three days of car rental so you can go anywhere the trains don't. And you can add up to five more days of travel by train or car or both to your pass.

The Fly, Rail 'n Drive Pass. Just $229 puts you above the clouds to let you cover the most France in the least time. This add-on to the Rail and Drive Pass includes one day of unlimited travel

on Air Inter, the French domestic airline.

Passes like these and the original Eurailpasses are available for travel in and around other European countries where you'll find some of the world's most beautiful sights. None of which will remind you of Detroit. To learn more call 1-800-4-EURAIL.

France passes valid for one month.

Rail Europe

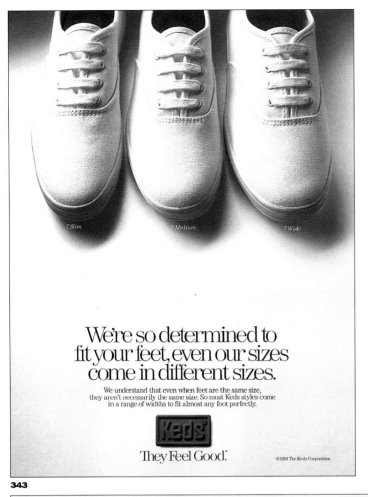

We're so determined to fit your feet, even our sizes come in different sizes.

We understand that even when feet are the same size, they aren't necessarily the same size. So most Keds styles come in a range of widths to fit almost any foot perfectly.

Keds®

They Feel Good.™

©1991 The Keds Corporation

343

Keds knows bows.

Keds' Essentials. They're a little dressy, lots of fun and make your feet feel good all day.

Keds®

They Feel Good.™

© 1992 The Keds Corporation

344

UNLIKE OTHER OUTER SPACE MOVIES, OURS WAS ACTUALLY FILMED ON LOCATION.

 OUTER SPACE MOVIES HAVE DEFINITELY COME A LONG WAY SINCE THE

FIRST EXTRATERRESTRIALS WERE CAPTURED ON CELLULOID. BUT WITH ALL DUE RESPECT TO HOLLYWOOD,

"THE DREAM IS ALIVE" CAPTURES SPACE TRAVEL BETTER THAN ANY SPECIAL EFFECTS CREW EVER WILL.

THAT'S BECAUSE INSTEAD OF BEING SHOT IN THE VAST RECESSES OF A STUDIO BACKLOT, "THE

DREAM IS ALIVE" WAS SHOT IN THE VAST RECESSES OF OUTER SPACE. TWO HUNDRED AND EIGHTY MILES

ABOVE THE EARTH, IN FACT, FROM THE FLIGHT DECK OF A REAL STARSHIP - NASA'S SPACE SHUTTLE.

YOU'LL JOIN THE SHUTTLE CREW AS THEY ORBIT THE EARTH ON A 2.7 MILLION MILE JOURNEY,

TAKING PART IN THE PRECISION MANEUVERS OF A SATELLITE RECOVERY. AND YOU'LL BE THERE TO

WITNESS THE HISTORIC FIRST WALK IN SPACE BY AN AMERICAN WOMAN. RIGHT FROM THE MOMENT

OF DISCOVERY'S THUNDEROUS BLAST OFF, YOU'VE GOT AN ASTRONAUT'S VIEW OF ALL THE ACTION.

BUT THE SPACE SHUTTLE ISN'T THE ONLY THING GETTING LAUNCHED HERE. "THE DREAM IS

ALIVE" IS BEING PRESENTED IN A SOPHISTICATED NEW FORMAT CALLED OMNIMAX. AN INNOVATIVE FILM

TECHNOLOGY THAT BOLDLY GOES WHERE NO FILM HAS GONE BEFORE.

WITH OMNIMAX, IMAGES OF ASTONISHING CLARITY ARE PROJECTED NOT ON A SCREEN, BUT

ON A GIANT DOME. AND IF YOU THINK THAT SEEMS UNCONVENTIONAL, LISTEN TO THIS: A SIX

CHANNEL AUDIO SYSTEM SURROUNDS YOU WITH 16,000 WATTS OF CRYSTAL CLEAR SOUND. CREATING

AN EXPERIENCE SO REALISTIC, YOU'LL BE WAITING FOR THE G-FORCES TO KICK IN.

VISIT THE NEW CHARLOTTE OBSERVER OMNIMAX THEATRE, LOCATED IN THE DISCOVERY PLACE

SCIENCE MUSEUM. AND BE SURE NOT TO MISS THE FILM "THE DREAM IS ALIVE" BECAUSE WHEN WE SAY

IT CAME FROM OUTER SPACE, IN THIS CASE, IT REALLY DID.

THE CHARLOTTE OBSERVER OMNIMAX AT DISCOVERY PLACE

"THE DREAM IS ALIVE" OPENING NOVEMBER 3.

345

CONSUMER MAGAZINE
COLOR 1 PAGE OR SPREAD:
SINGLE

346
ART DIRECTOR
Tom Routson
WRITER
Steve Skibba
PHOTOGRAPHER
Steve Murray
CLIENT
North Carolina Travel &
Tourism
AGENCY
Loeffler Ketchum Mountjoy/
Charlotte

347
ART DIRECTORS
Sean Ehringer
Michael Barti
WRITERS
Michael Barti
Sean Ehringer
PHOTOGRAPHERS
Bill Hatcher
Holly Stewart
CLIENT
The North Face
AGENCY
Mandelbaum Mooney Ashley/
San Francisco

348
ART DIRECTOR
Sean Ehringer
WRITERS
Michael Barti
Cathi Mooney
PHOTOGRAPHER
Holly Stewart
James L. Amos
CLIENT
The North Face
AGENCY
Mandelbaum Mooney Ashley/
San Francisco

349
ART DIRECTORS
Cathi Mooney
Michael Barti
WRITERS
Michael Barti
Cathi Mooney
PHOTOGRAPHER
Pete Stone
CLIENT
Gary Fisher Bicycle
AGENCY
Mandelbaum Mooney Ashley/
San Francisco

Here in North Carolina, autumn guests are given a colorful reception. One that could make you forget the mountains on our western border are known as the Blue Ridge. Brilliant reds. Lush auburns. Rich golds. The leaves on over a hundred species of

harvest festivals, held every year for as long as anyone can remember, and the glow of the setting sun on beaches inhabited not by high rise hotels, but by sea birds and shells. It's a land awash in local color. And as you wind your way through the state

WHEN WE ROLL OUT THE RED CARPET, IT'S 250 MILES LONG.

trees blend into miles and miles of crimson forests. Forests unchanged since the days when Daniel Boone first explored them. But then, you'll soon discover many things in North Carolina remain unchanged, as you do a little exploring of your own.

You'll see the firing of centuries-old pottery kilns. You'll see the vibrant panels of quilts, still stitched by patient hands instead of machines. You'll see the golden wares of our

Sir Walter Raleigh and the first English colonists called home, we think you'll find the term red carpet is very much appropriate. NORTH CAROLINA

You see, in North Carolina, hospitality is more than just a word. It's a way of life. So this fall, why not join us here, where the event of the season is the season itself. After all, nature will be going to some pretty great lengths to welcome you. And we will too.

346

[For a free color catalog including full details of our lifetime warranty and the location of your nearest North Face dealer call 1-800-654-1751.]

It's DAWN. You WAKE UP and start to roll out of bed. Then IT HITS YOU. The FLOOR IS three thousand feet DOWN.

Everybody's gotta sleep. ▪ Only for certain people it happens in some pretty interesting places. Like halfway up El Capitan's Salathé Wall. ▪ It's these people, however, who we keep foremost in our minds when designing The North Face gear. ▪ Not to mention those who may prefer extreme skiing down a 45-degree mountain face in Chamonix.

Or attempting to scale the south-southwest pillar of K2. Or maybe even rowing a boat from South America to Antarctica. ▪ At The North Face, we make a complete line of technical outerwear, clothing, tents, packs and sleeping bags built to overcome situations like these. ▪ Packs with zippers tested to withstand up to 300 pounds-per-inch of pull. Raingear made with waterproof, breathable Gore-Tex® **GORE-TEX** fabric. And tents whose fabric is meticulously cut along the grainline to insure tautness and proper shape. ▪ All guaranteed for a lifetime. ▪ So why do we go to such lengths to make our gear? ▪ Because out here it can make the difference between life and death. ▪ And we'd hate to lose a customer.

347

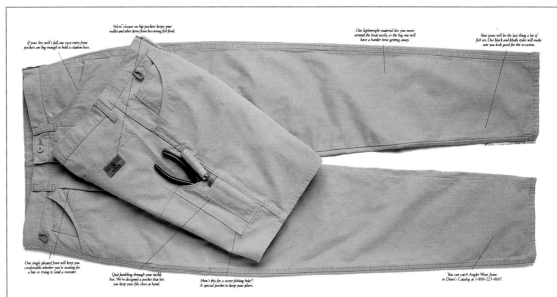

350

351

Designed under the auspices of MIT, not MTV.

One athletic shoe company pays pop stars millions to appear in its TV commercials.

Another company sponsors worldwide concert tours.

We at New Balance, however, prefer to direct our resources elsewhere:

Toward our shoes.

It's a philosophy that led us to recruit one of the world's leading specialists in composite materials, a professor at MIT, for our research team.

Which, in turn, led us to develop the M677, a performance shoe that supports the foot as well as it cushions it.

The M677's ENCAP midsole, with its Evathane heel plug, offers unprecedented energy dissipation. Its counter reinforcer provides maximum rearfoot stability. And its New Balance logo ensures a variety of widths, from B to 4E.

We've got nothing against Michael Jackson or Paula Abdul buying a pair. All we ask is that they run in them.

new balance
A more intelligent approach to building shoes.

352

What happens when a Product Development budget is six times greater than a Sales and Marketing budget.

The people in the product development department tend to discover things other athletic shoe companies don't.

Like Dymetrol, an exclusive DuPont support fabric that stretches with your foot—without losing its shape or creating stress points.

And XAR-1000, a carbon rubber outsole that road tests proved to be tougher than the treads on U.S. Army tanks.

And C-CAP Evathane, a compression resistant midsole that cushions your entire foot and disperses shock.

And CAD/CAM, a computer aided research, design and manufacturing system with absolutely no margin for human error.

Combined, all these discoveries enable New Balance to build shoes like the NBX M900.

An ideal combination of proper fit, cushioning, stability and durability; all in one of the lightest training shoes in the world.

And what about the people in sales and marketing? All they have to do is run a simple magazine ad telling people about it.

new balance
A more intelligent approach to building shoes.

353

Air bags, Hugo Mellander believes, are giving people a false sense of security.

Mellander is head safety engineer for Volvo in Sweden.

"I don't think people realize an air bag is designed to work in conjunction with a seat belt and only in frontal impacts," says Mellander. "Furthermore, frontal impacts account for only 36% of all accidents."

How will a car react the other 64% of the time? In side impacts (20% of all accidents)? In rear end collisions (7%)? Rollovers (12%)? Multiple impacts (17%)?

"These are questions people should be asking," says Mellander.

These are the questions the engineers of Volvo have been answering for over 60 years.

Volvo engineers pioneered crumple zones to absorb crash energy.

The 3 point self adjusting seat belt was invented by Nils Bohlin, a Volvo engineer.

Volvo began putting a steel reinforced passenger cage into all their cars not last year, or five years ago, but three decades ago.

"The increased focus on safety by the car industry and the public pleases us," says Mellander.

"Now that people have their eyes open to the importance of safety," he adds, "they should understand the differences between how car companies approach safety."

These differences have never been more evident than in the new 960.

A car that is years ahead of meeting government standards for side impact protection.

The first Volvo to have a 6-cylinder, 24-valve engine coupled with a sophisticated drivetrain adaptable to driving conditions.

A car that Mellander believes is the epitome of everything Volvo has ever learned about building automobiles.

"It is the ultimate proof that safety is not something you can just add on to a car, but rather has to be engineered in from the very beginning."

Drive safely.

VOLVO

AN AIR BAG IS ONLY AS GOOD AS THE CAR IT'S ATTACHED TO.

354

BOAT SHOES SHOULD BE JUDGED BY HOW THEY GO WITH A BLACK SKY. NOT A BLUE BLAZER.

Don't get us wrong. If you want to use our new boat shoes with the Interactive Grip System to fox-trot across the yacht club dance floor, that's your choice. We guarantee you and your blazer will look good, and we promise to accept your money.

Just be aware that we engineered these shoes so you could dance on a very different surface. The storm-blackened foredeck of a boat that's bucking like a rodeo bull.

On so wet and treacherous a playing field, one slip of the foot could be one slip too many. Preventing it is what the Interactive Grip System is all about.

As its name implies, the System starts where the foot interacts with the boat. At the sole. Our new design gives you such a profusion of siping (razor cuts for traction) that the number of leading edges exceeds the traction capacity of traditional boat soles by a good 50%. What's more, the edges are clustered in an exclusive quadrant cut pattern. (Competitors beware.

The Timberland® quadrant cut sole so outgrips standard wave cut soles it may cause mutiny at the yacht club.)

Part Two of the Interactive Grip System makes sure that your foot stays in the right place so the quadrant cut sole can do its work. Your foot is secured for proper balance and energy distribution by an Internal Fit System, a contoured sleeve that keeps your toes from jamming when the boat makes a violent lurch.

These brand new benchmarks for marine footwear aren't just high-tech, but true high performance for the 1990's. A new definition of authenticity that puts our imitators in an embarrassing place.

Overboard.

BOOTS, SHOES, CLOTHING,
WIND, WATER, EARTH AND SKY.

355

IF YOU WERE ANY MORE SUREFOOTED, YOU'D HAVE HOOVES.

Thinking of hiking boots? Think hooves and you won't go wrong.

Hooves are tough enough to endure the worst terrain. Yet their construction is so lightweight and comfortable they don't weigh you down.

(If they did, mountain goats would live in condos at sea level.)

This same combination of toughness and lightness is what puts the Timberland® Lightweight Hiker ahead of the pack in virtually every day-hiking environment imaginable.

Many boots out there are durable but heavy. Others are light but flimsy. Ours use classic Timberland rugged construction and advanced weight-saving technologies to reach a perfect balance of both.

For durability you have premium leathers whose seams are double-stitched at stress points. For lightness and comfort there are multi-density foam layers contoured to your foot and a removable dual-density footbed. Exclusive TrailGrip Plus™ soles are as feather light as they are heavy gripping.

Here at The Timberland Company people are so into hiking we make a boot for every trail situation. Our new multi-purpose TMT™ is for day-hiking, mountain biking and ridge running. Our all-leather

Backpacker is the best single choice for extended treks of one day or more. And our Waterproof Lightweight trail boot gives you specially-treated Timberland leather and a full Gore-Tex® bootie, the finest system anywhere for handling wet trail conditions.

Our aim is simple. To hike the standards of hiking.

BOOTS, SHOES, CLOTHING,
WIND, WATER, EARTH AND SKY.

356

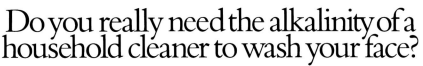

We never said it was a work of art.
We said it wouldn't leak.

357

Do you really need the alkalinity of a household cleaner to wash your face?

Dove

358

WHAT TO DRIVE WHEN YOU'RE THE ENGINE.

From aircraft to automobiles, a vehicle can only go as fast as the engine that propels it. In the case of cycling, the engine happens to be you.

Now if you are serious about this sport, you know that exploring the limits of your physiology requires the dedication of an Olympian and the devotion of a monk. So the last thing you want to do is waste the effort on an inefficient bicycle.

At Cannondale, our goal is to produce a bicycle that makes the most of your ability. That is why we spend nearly four hours hand-building each bicycle at our factory in Bedford, Pennsylvania. Doing what we feel must be done to create not just a good bicycle, but an exceptional one. To make our bicycle remarkably light and strong, we produce a hand-welded, heat-treated unibody frame of aircraft-quality aluminum. To heighten responsiveness and efficiency, we use large-diameter tubing. So, as you ride, the bicycle resists the normal twisting forces of pedaling. Hence, more energy goes to the rear wheel. And you suddenly discover how easy it is to go faster.

Alas, we can't give you any shortcuts to realizing your full potential. But we can offer you the perfect vehicle for getting there.

359

THERE ARE TIMES IT TAKES OUR BICYCLES FOUR HOURS TO GO 50 FEET.

Until it leaves our factory in Bedford, Pennsylvania, a Cannondale bicycle moves very slowly. Because here it takes nearly four hours to build each one by hand. And while we know hand-crafting is a time-consuming process, it's never been our aim to make lots of bicycles. Just the best bicycles.

To that end, we've always done what we believe to be right. Sometimes that meant doing things differently. Other times it meant doing things that had not been done before.

During the process of creating a Cannondale, we found that ultralight, aircraft-quality aluminum could make a bicycle fly, too. But aluminum alone is not the answer. It's what we do with it that yields a bicycle which not only moves you from place to place, but lets you enjoy getting there. To make our bicycle remarkably light and strong, we produce a hand-welded, heat-treated unibody frame. To heighten responsiveness and efficiency, we use large-diameter tubing. So, as you ride, the bicycle resists the normal twisting forces of pedaling. Hence, more energy goes to the rear wheel. And you suddenly discover how easy it is to go faster.

Which is why Cannondale refuses to cut corners. We know you can be quite passionate about riding extraordinary bicycles. Shouldn't we feel the same way about making them?

360

WE CREATED A SUSPENSION BIKE SO QUICK AND AGILE, WE HAD TO DESIGN A WHOLE NEW BRAKING SYSTEM TO STOP IT.

Mountains divide countries. Separate nations. Even after climates. But they are no longer an obstacle to those who possess the Cannondale E.S.T.

Short for Elevated Suspension Technology, the E.S.T. is a radical departure in bicycle design that lets you attack the most unsettling terrain as if it were paved.

The secret is the spring-supported, oil-dampened shock absorber. Once calibrated to your weight and the terrain, the E.S.T. soaks up all of the shock that's normally absorbed by you. And like a true suspension system, it holds the wheel to the road over bumps, ruts and rocks. So you can put less effort into controlling the bike, and more energy into something else. Going faster. In fact, the E.S.T. can increase your speed so dramatically, we had to devise a more efficient way to stop it. Force 40 braking. A cable routing system that increases stopping power by 40% over conventional cantilevers. And like every Cannondale, the E.S.T. is distinguished by its ultralight, hand-welded and heat-treated aluminum frame.

Maybe you can't move mountains. But with the Cannondale E.S.T., you can level them.

361

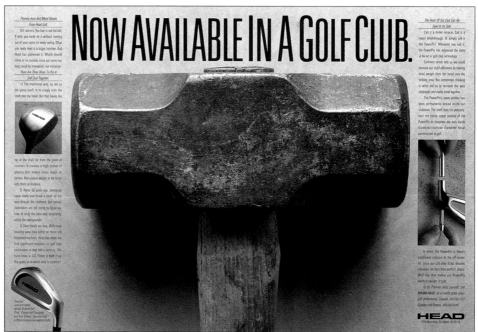

NOW AVAILABLE IN A GOLF CLUB.

362

CONSUMER MAGAZINE
COLOR 1 PAGE OR SPREAD:
SINGLE

366
ART DIRECTOR
Mark Arnold
WRITER
Chris Wigert
PHOTOGRAPHERS
Clint Clemens
Jon Bruton Studios
CLIENT
Ralston Purina
AGENCY
TBWA Kerlick Switzer/
St. Louis

367
ART DIRECTOR
Brian Burke
WRITER
Chris Wigert
PHOTOGRAPHER
Steve Umland
CLIENT
Fred Arbogast Company
AGENCY
TBWA Kerlick Switzer/
St. Louis

368
ART DIRECTORS
Marianne Besch
Sue Wiedorn
WRITER
Alan Levine
PHOTOGRAPHER
Steve Bronstein
CLIENT
Carillon Importers
AGENCY
TBWA /New York

THE BIRDS WON'T COME TO YOU.

So your dog had better have the energy to go get them. Reason enough to feed him Purina® brand HiPro Dog Food. The one with 29% more protein than regular dog food. And a whopping 1750 calories per pound.

366

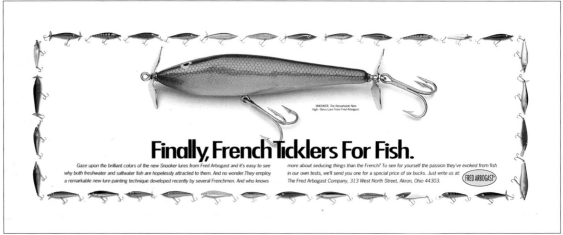

Finally, French Ticklers For Fish.

Gaze upon the brilliant colors of the new Snooker lures from Fred Arbogast and it's easy to see why both freshwater and saltwater fish are hopelessly attracted to them. And no wonder. They employ a remarkable new lure-painting technique developed recently by several Frenchmen. And who knows more about seducing things than the French? To see for yourself the passion they've evoked from fish in our own tests, we'll send you one for a special price of six bucks. Just write us at: The Fred Arbogast Company, 313 West North Street, Akron, Ohio 44303.

367

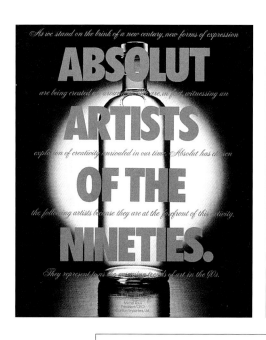

ABSOLUT GARCIA.

ABSOLUT SHIRE.

ABSOLUT WHITE.

ABSOLUT MICHELSON.

369

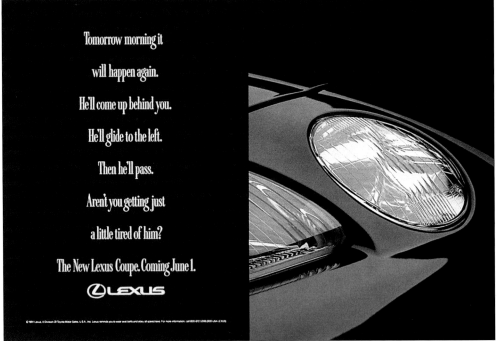

370

371

HOW HUMAN IS YOUR DOG?

Is this a smile?

What is he feeling here?

Does this mean he's sad?

Your dog is different from you. But he does belong to your family. So you need to feed him right. And that means feeding him Iams.

For over 40 years now we've been demonstrating the benefits of our meat-based diet in dogs like yours.

But you won't find Iams where you find your food. It's sold only at veterinary offices, pet stores, feed stores and other special places. *For a free sample, call 1-800-255-4738.*

PEOPLE SMILE WHEN THEY'RE HAPPY, FROWN WHEN THEY'RE SAD. DO DOGS?

Yes. And no. A dog's expression and body language is largely determined by how important he feels around other dogs or his owner.

Dogs are very concerned about their 'social rank'. Like humans, they love being a big shot and hate being ignored or reprimanded.

So when a dog looks like he's smiling (left-hand picture), it means he's happy and excited to see you. From experience he knows you're about to give him a giant hug.

The half-smile (middle picture) is his way of saying, "Hey, I've been a good dog...pet me...pay attention to me...Pleeease?"

As for what we'd call a frown (right-hand picture), it usually just means he's sleepy or bored.

IS HE A MEMBER OF YOUR FAMILY OR ARE YOU A MEMBER OF HIS?

Ready for a colossal misunderstanding? You get so attached to your dog, you come to think of

him as almost human.

Meanwhile he is thinking that you're a dog.

From his perspective you and your family are a prehistoric dog-pack which has taken

him into their den (i.e. your house).

This is why he likes to sleep on your bed—apart from the fact that it's warm, soft and dry. Every dog instinctively wants to sleep close to the leader of the pack and in your house, that's you.

So, treat your dog like one of the family. But if you want to understand him better, it helps to think like a dog.

YOU'RE CUTTING BACK ON MEAT. SHOULD YOUR DOG?

You've heard that people should eat less meat and more fruit, vegetables, fiber, and grains.

Maybe you think your dog should too. Judging by their labels, a lot of dog food manufacturers must think so.

Omnivores (that's us) digestive system takes nutrients from various foods

Carnivores (that's your dog) digestive system specializes in meat

But nothing could be further from the truth. Dogs are carnivores. They're supposed to eat meat. They thrive on meat.

Meat protein and fatty acids help your dog look and feel healthy. You can see what meat does for a dog by his thick and shiny coat.

(Dogs, by the way, never have problems with cholesterol. So they can eat more meat than we can.)

That's why dogs should eat Iams. It contains more meat protein than the leading supermarket dog food.

And since dogs naturally like meat, dogs will naturally like Iams.

So it's really very simple. If you're in the market for the best dog food, get out of the supermarket.

PUPPY FOOD
Iams Puppy Food
For the first year

CHUNKS
Iams Chunks
For the normal, active adult dog

MINI CHUNKS
Iams MiniChunks
The same nutrition, but in a smaller bite

LESS ACTIVE FOR DOGS
Iams Less Active for Dogs
For the overweight or under-exercised dog

IAMS
TREAT HIM LIKE A HUMAN, FEED HIM LIKE A DOG.

372

THE SLOWER THE HANDS, THE BETTER THE WATCH.

HANDS OF SWISS CRAFTSMEN TO MAKE CERTAIN THAT EACH WATCH IS PRECISION-MADE WITH THE FINEST MATERIALS - FROM OUR QUARTZ TUNING FORK MOVEMENT TO CUSTOM PAINTED DATE DIAL. IT'S THIS DEGREE OF DETAIL WHICH ALLOWS US TO OFFER OUR LIMITED 25 YEAR WARRANTY. AND TO ENSURE THAT WHEN AN

AFTER 116 YEARS, THE ENGINEERS AT BULOVA STILL BELIEVE A WATCH IS ONLY AS GOOD AS THE HANDS THAT GO INTO IT. SO TO CREATE THE NEW ACCUTRON COLLECTION, WE CALLED UPON THE HANDS OF OUR AMERICAN ARTISTS FOR A CLASSIC THREE TIERED DESIGN. THEN WE ENLISTED THE

ACCUTRON TIMEPIECE PASSES FROM OUR HANDS TO YOURS, ITS BEAUTY AND QUALITY WILL LAST FOR DECADES.

ACCUTRON
BULOVA

©1991 Bulova Corporation. Accutron® and the tuning fork symbol are registered trademarks of the Bulova Corporation. To learn more about our exclusive warranty, see your Accutron jeweler.

373

CALL OF THE REALLY REALLY WILD.

This is the Air Terra trail running shoe from Nike. Civilized, it ain't. It's got an outsole that's beveled like a mountain bike tire to take you over rocks and branches. It's got Nike-Air® in the heel for extra cushioning. It's even got a deflector shield under the forefoot so you won't bruise yourself on any bear or deer. Now put your tongue back in your mouth and go try on a pair.

374

375

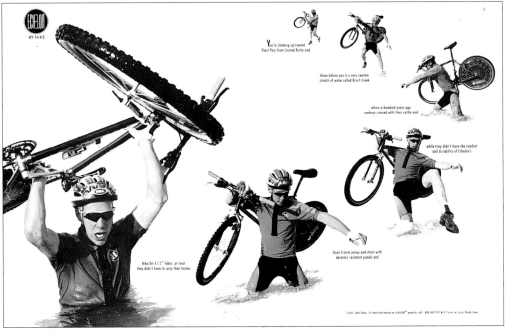

376

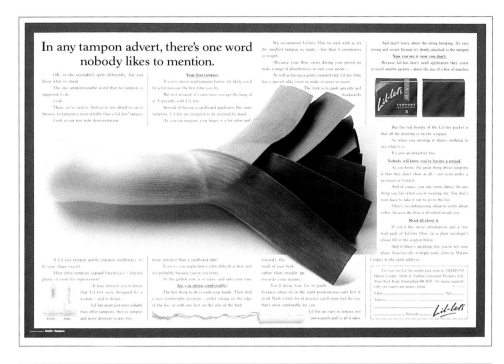

In any tampon advert, there's one word nobody likes to mention.

OK, so the vegetable's spelt differently, but you know what we mean.

The one unmentionable word that no tampon is supposed to do.

Leak.

There, we've said it. And we're not afraid to say it because no tampon is more reliable than a Lil-lets' tampon. Look at our test-tube demonstration.

Your first tampon.

If you've never used tampons before, it's likely you'll be a bit nervous the first time you try.

But rest assured, it's easy once you get the hang of it. Especially with Lil-lets.

Instead of having a cardboard applicator like some tampons, Lil-lets are designed to be inserted by hand.

As you can imagine, your finger is a lot softer and more sensitive than a cardboard tube.

Are you sitting comfortably?

The first thing to do is wash your hands. Then, find a nice comfortable position - either sitting on the edge of the loo, or with one foot on the side of the bath.

A Lil-lets tampon gently expands widthways, to fit your shape exactly.

Most other tampons expand lengthways - leaving plenty of room for improvement.

It may interest you to know that Lil-lets were designed by a woman - and it shows.

Lil-lets aren't just more reliable than other tampons, they're simpler and more discreet to use, too.

We recommend Lil-lets Mini to start with as it's the smallest tampon we make - less than 5 centimetres in length.

(Because your flow varies during your period, we make a range of absorbencies to suit your needs.)

As well as having a gently rounded end, Lil-lets Mini has a special silky cover to make it easier to insert.

The trick is to push upwards and backwards towards the small of your back, rather than straight up towards your tummy.

You'll know how far to push because when it's in the right position you can't feel it at all. With a little bit of practice you'll soon find the way that's most comfortable for you.

Lil-lets are easy to remove, too - just a gentle pull is all it takes.

And don't worry about the string breaking. It's very strong and secure because it's firmly attached to the tampon.

Now you see it, now you don't.

Because Lil-lets don't need applicators they come in much smaller packets - about the size of a box of matches.

But the real beauty of the Lil-lets packet is that all the printing is on the wrapper.

So when you unwrap it there's nothing to say what it is.

It's just an attractive box.

Nobody will know you're having a period.

As you know, the great thing about tampons is that they don't show at all - not even under a swimsuit or leotard.

And of course, you can swim, dance, do anything you like when you're wearing one. You don't even have to take it out to go to the loo.

There's no embarrassing odour to worry about either, because the flow is absorbed inside you.

Read all about it.

If you'd like more information and a free trial pack of Lil-lets Mini (in a plain envelope) please fill in the coupon below.

And if there's anything else you're not sure about, however silly it might seem, write to Marion Cooper at the same address.

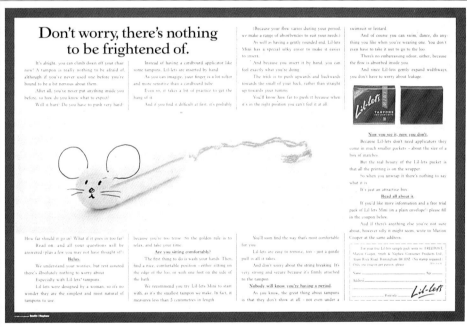

Don't worry, there's nothing to be frightened of.

It's alright, you can climb down off your chair now! A tampon is really nothing to be afraid of, although if you've never used one before you're bound to be a bit nervous about them.

After all, you've never put anything inside you before, so how do you know what to expect?

Will it hurt? Do you have to push very hard?

How far should it go in? What if it goes in too far?

Read on, and all your questions will be answered (plus a few you may not have thought of).

Relax.

We understand your worries, but rest assured there's absolutely nothing to worry about.

Especially with Lil-lets' tampons.

Lil-lets were designed by a woman, so it's no wonder they are the simplest and most natural of tampons to use.

Instead of having a cardboard applicator like some tampons, Lil-lets are inserted by hand.

As you can imagine, your finger is a lot softer and more sensitive than a cardboard tube.

Even so, it takes a bit of practice to get the hang of it.

And if you find it difficult at first, it's probably because you're too tense. So the golden rule is to relax, and take your time.

Are you sitting comfortably?

The first thing to do is wash your hands. Then, find a nice, comfortable position - either sitting on the edge of the loo, or with one foot on the side of the bath.

We recommend you try Lil-lets Mini to start with, as it's the smallest tampon we make. In fact, it measures less than 5 centimetres in length.

(Because your flow varies during your period, we make a range of absorbencies to suit your needs.)

As well as having a gently rounded end, Lil-lets Mini has a special silky cover to make it easier to insert.

And because you insert it by hand, you can feel exactly what you're doing.

The trick is to push upwards and backwards towards the small of your back, rather than straight up towards your tummy.

You'll know how far to push because when it's in the right position you can't feel it at all.

swimsuit or leotard.

And of course you can swim, dance, do anything you like when you're wearing one. You don't even have to take it out to go to the loo.

There's no embarrassing odour, either, because the flow is absorbed inside you.

And once Lil-lets gently expand widthways, you don't have to worry about leakage.

Now you see it, now you don't.

Because Lil-lets don't need applicators they come in much smaller packets - about the size of a box of matches.

But the real beauty of the Lil-lets packet is that all the printing is on the wrapper.

So when you unwrap it there's nothing to say what it is.

It's just an attractive box.

Read all about it.

If you'd like more information and a free trial pack of Lil-lets Mini (in a plain envelope) please fill in the coupon below.

And if there's anything else you're not sure about, however silly it might seem, write to Marion Cooper at the same address.

You'll soon find the way that's most comfortable for you.

Lil-lets are easy to remove, too - just a gentle pull is all it takes.

And don't worry about the string breaking. It's very strong and secure because it's firmly attached to the tampon.

Nobody will know you're having a period.

As you know, the great thing about tampons is that they don't show at all - not even under a

---

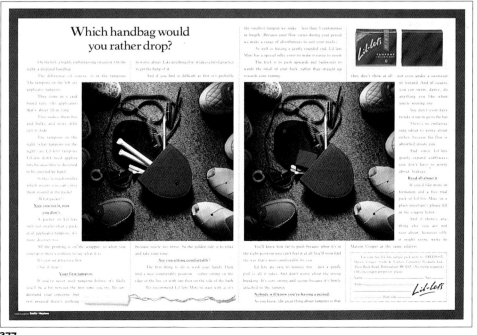

Which handbag would you rather drop?

On the left, a highly embarrassing situation. On the right, a dropped handbag.

The difference, of course, is in the tampons. The tampons on the left are applicator tampons.

They come in a cardboard tube - the applicator - that's about 15cm long.

This makes them big and bulky and more difficult to hide.

The tampons on the right (what tampons on the right) are Lil-lets' tampons. Lil-lets don't need applicators because they're designed to be inserted by hand.

So they're much smaller which means you can carry them around in the packet.

What packet?

Now you see it, now you don't.

A packet of Lil-lets isn't just smaller than a packet of applicator tampons, it's more discreet too.

All the printing is on the wrapper, so when you unwrap it there's nothing to say what it is.

It's just an attractive box.

Your first tampon.

If you've never used tampons before, it's likely you'll be a bit nervous the first time you try. We understand your concerns, but rest assured there's nothing

the smallest tampon we make - less than 5 centimetres in length. (Because your flow varies during your period we make a range of absorbencies to suit your needs.)

As well as having a gently rounded end, Lil-lets Mini has a special silky cover to make it easier to insert.

The trick is to push upwards and backwards towards the small of your back, rather than straight up towards your tummy.

And if you find it difficult at first it's probably

Because you're too tense. So the golden rule is to relax and take your time.

Are you sitting comfortably?

The first thing to do is wash your hands. Then, find a nice comfortable position - either sitting on the edge of the loo, or with one foot on the side of the bath.

We recommend Lil-lets Mini to start with as it's

You'll know how far to push because when it's in the right position you can't feel it at all. You'll soon find the way that's most comfortable for you.

Lil-lets are easy to remove, too - just a gentle pull is all it takes. And don't worry about the string breaking. It's very strong and secure because it's firmly attached to the tampon.

Nobody will know you're having a period.

As you know, the great thing about tampons is that

they don't show at all - not even under a swimsuit or leotard. And of course, you can swim, dance, do anything you like when you're wearing one.

You don't even have to take it out to go to the loo.

There's no embarrassing odour to worry about either, because the flow is absorbed inside you.

And since Lil-lets greatly expand widthways, you don't have to worry about leakage.

Read all about it.

If you'd like more information and a free trial pack of Lil-lets Mini (in a plain envelope) please fill in the coupon below.

And if there's anything else you are not sure about, however silly it might seem, write to Marion Cooper at the same address.

CONSUMER MAGAZINE
COLOR 1 PAGE OR SPREAD:
CAMPAIGN

378
ART DIRECTORS
Peter Gibb
Kit Marr
WRITER
Alfredo Marcantonio
PHOTOGRAPH
Stock
CLIENT
Meridiana
AGENCY
Abbott Mead Vickers. BBDO/
London

379
ART DIRECTORS
Steve Stone
Kirk Souder
WRITERS
David Fowler
Tony Gomes
Steve Biegel
PHOTOGRAPHERS
Peter Drake
Gary Hush
Jane Connors
CLIENT
Nikon
AGENCY
Ammirati & Puris/New York

Remember the romantic days when aircraft seats had wings? Well, they're back.

If other airlines are to be believed, this is Florence.

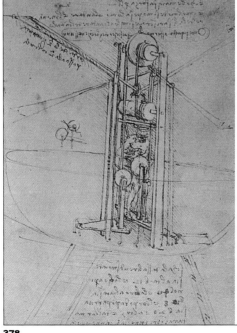

Florence, birthplace of air travel. It's taken 500 years to organise a direct flight.

Advertisement 1

Did Peter Drake pause to adjust focus, exposure or fill-flash on the N6006? In Times Square? Are you kidding?

The Nikon N6006 is exactly the SLR to clamp on the handlebars of your bike and take for a ride through Times Square at night in twenty-degree weather.

Oh. That's not high on *your* list of things to do?

Our apologies. Ex-bike messenger and amateur photographer Peter Drake thought it might be great fun dodging all those taxis and potholes, cable release in hand. He thought it might make an interesting picture.

We think he was at least half right.

Perhaps his daring self-portrait will serve as graphic evidence that the N6006 is a simple, fast SLR that's up for serious fun. It's the one a professional photographer would take on vacation. The one to have when your hands are busy or your mind is on something else.

Survival, for instance.

It autofocuses quickly and accurately in light as dim as a single candle, using a focusing sensor much like the one in the professional F4s.

You control almost all its functions with a simple multi-button keypad and a command dial that's next to your thumb.

It has a Spot Meter, Center-Weighted Meter, and Nikon's Matrix Metering, an exclusive system that reacts instantly to fast moving action and changing light. It sizes up a picture much like you would. If you had time.

The N6006 has a powerful built-in flash with wide 28mm coverage, and a guide number of 43 at ISO 100.

In the case of Peter Drake, it automatically selected the proper flash illumination for his face while letting the ambient light shine through in the background.

Also, the sense of motion in the shot came about through Rear Curtain Synchronization, one of the creative flash techniques that the N6006 performs automatically.

There's Focus Tracking, too, which keeps moving subjects such as freight trains and mules in focus for you. You can auto-bracket up to five shots in 1/3-stop increments.

You can choose from twenty auto-focus Nikkor lenses, the ones we're so particular about that we make our own glass and design our own coatings.

You can use almost every Nikkor lens made since 1977, because the N6006 still has the legendary mounting system we invented.

Thirty years ago.

This camera is not a toy, in other words. It's a Nikon.

Nearly seven out of ten professionals who shoot with 35mm carry Nikons because it's their job. People like Peter Drake carry them because it's fun.

Maybe you'd carry an SLR more often if you had one that was more fun and less job.

Well, here it is.

Let the good times roll.

Manhattan by night riding a bike with a camera
—by—
Peter Drake, nut

The N6006: autofocusing, built-in fill-flash, interchangeable Nikkor lenses. Fun like a toy, but not one. Call 1-800-NIKON-35 for a free booklet.

Nikon

Advertisement 2

Nikon

There was something odd happening the other day in Hollywood Boulevard. This will not come as news to many of you.

In addition to fourteen robed cultists selling roses and a tour bus from Tupelo, Mississippi (all carrying maps to the stars' homes), a gentleman was seen traveling at 15 mph wearing half a pair of pants and holding a curious electronic device.

It was Gary Hush, on skates, carrying the Nikon N6006, participating in what many call just another day in Southern California.

Here, well, *normal* it all must have seemed.

Mr. Hush is a photo student and crack roller skater from the Art Center College of Design in Pasadena.

He was using the Nikon N6006 because it is a very sophisticated SLR that also happens to be easy to use. Mr. Hush, you see, is averse to slamming into parked cars or robed fanatics while fiddling with *f*/stops and shutter speeds.

Neither forgive. Unlike the N6006.

Because, you see, if you ever feel you are doing something wrong, you simply push two buttons and the camera will revert to totally automatic.

It autofocuses quickly and accurately in light as dim as a single candle, using a focusing sensor similar to the one in the professional Nikon F4s.

You control the N6006 with a multi-button keypad and a command dial next to your thumb.

It has Spot Metering, Center-Weighted Metering and Nikon's exclusive Matrix Metering, which can react instantly to rapidly changing light or fast action.

Look out! Man with a cane ahead!

Got him.

There's even a built-in flash with 28mm coverage, and a guide number of 43 at ISO 100. Mr. Hush brightened his lovely legs (and aren't we all glad he did) by powering up the flash one stop. He also adjusted exposure compensation on the camera minus 1/3 stops to retain sidewalk detail.

To create the sense of motion, he invoked a feature called Rear Curtain Synchronization, which, well, basically creates a blur behind a moving subject by firing the flash just before the shutter closes.

The N6006 also has the legendary mounting system we invented thirty years ago, so you can use nearly every Nikkor lens made since 1977, including more than twenty autofocus Nikkors. A Nikkor lens is a very exacting instrument made with our own glass and our own coatings.

They are the same lenses carried by nearly seven out of ten professional photographers who use 35mm. You will find them, and Nikon cameras, on the scene of elections, coups, riots, and all sorts of events that pop up on the front pages of newspapers and magazines all over the country.

The N6006, however, is the Nikon we highly recommend when your mind is on photography and your body is on something else.

Like vacation. Or safari. Or skates.

Look out! TV mom at one o'clock!

Got her.

See?

1/15 of a second of fame
—by—
Gary Hush, student

Gary Hush, full-time student, part-time skater, immortalized on Hollywood Blvd. by the Nikon N6006.

The N6006: autofocusing, built-in fill-flash, interchangeable Nikkor lenses. Fun like a toy, but not one. Call 1-800-NIKON-35 for a free booklet.

Advertisement 3

Nuclear Slinky
—by—
Jane Connors, waitress

Pick up a Nikon N6006 and strange things can happen.

By pressing a button you can make a Ferris wheel look like a Slinky.

Ask Jane Connors, waitress in a Greenwich Village restaurant, fumble-fingers with a camera.

One night at an amusement park, after winning a few stuffed alligators and plucking at a beehive of cotton candy, Jane pointed her Nikon N6006 at a Ferris wheel spinning in motion, held her breath, crossed her fingers, then told her boyfriend to duck. Then she shot.

Bang. Art.

Was it luck?

Nope.

Divine intervention?

No. Again.

The camera?

You pressed it.

The Nikon N6006 is the serious SLR camera that's easy to experiment with and have fun.

It focuses automatically or manually in light as dim as a single candle. It selects the proper exposure automatically, or lets you do it. There's a Spot Meter, a Center-Weighted Meter, and a Matrix Meter, an exclusive system that reacts instantly when light conditions change unexpectedly, as in the case of fast-moving action.

In the case of "Nuclear Slinky" Jane used a feature called Slow Curtain Flash Sync, a fancy name for a simple function that automatically fires the camera's built-in flash even when you're making a time exposure.

It turns neon into nuclear, in other words.

Jane shot with a 28-70mm autofocus zoom lens. You can choose from nearly twenty interchangeable autofocus Nikkor lenses, the same Nikon lenses used by seven out of ten professional photographers who shoot with 35mm cameras.

To make operating easy, almost all the functions on the N6006 are controlled by a convenient dial next to your thumb, and a simple multi-button keypad.

An LCD readout clearly shows you exactly what you're doing.

Or exactly what the camera's doing. We won't get into semantics.

It has a built-in motor that advances the film fast and rewinds automatically. It even selects the correct film speed.

So what do you do?

You aim.

And shoot.

Weird, isn't it?

Jane Connors, waitress by night, amateur photographer by day, turned a Ferris wheel into a Slinky with a Nikon N6006.

The N6006: built-in fill-flash, autofocus, interchangeable Nikkor lenses. Call 1-800-NIKON-35 for a free booklet.

Nikon

Consumer Magazine
Color 1 Page or Spread:
Campaign

380
Art Director
Kirk Souder
Writers
David Fowler
Steve Biegel
Tony Gomes
Photographers
Robert Ammirati
Doug Whyte
Client
Nikon
Agency
Ammirati & Puris/New York

381
Art Director
Tan Shen Guan
Writer
Stuart D'Rozario
Photographer
Jonathan Brade
Client
Design 2000 Furniture Store
Agency
The Ball Partnership/
Hong Kong

At 186,000 miles per second,

it races through space,

· · · · · · · ·

finds a soldier in Iraq or

a pitcher in Yankee Stadium

· · · · · · ·

then lands on a circular

piece of glass the size

of a silver dollar.

· · · · · · · ·

To those of you who saw

it coming, and reacted

so brilliantly, well done.

Nikon.
We take the world's
greatest pictures.

There are 76
photographs
in this issue.

· · · · · · ·

If we presume
each was shot
at a shutter
speed of 1/125th
of a second,
then you have
just seen the
combined total of
six-tenths of
a second in time.

· · · · ·

It is quite a
world, isn't it?

· · · · ·

To those of you
who saw it
so clearly,
for an instant,
well done.

Nikon.
We take the world's
greatest pictures.

-sunflower-

This year,

more than 150 student

photographers

found light

and room to grow

· · · · · · ·

during the New Views

contest and seminars.

· · · · · · · ·

It's one of

the many educational

events we sponsor

to help ensure a world

full of incredible

things

to look at.

Nikon.
We take the world's
greatest pictures.

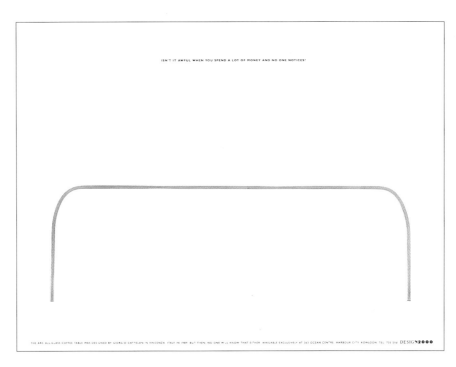

ISN'T IT AWFUL WHEN YOU SPEND A LOT OF MONEY AND NO ONE NOTICES?

THE ARC ALL-GLASS COFFEE TABLE WAS DESIGNED BY GIORGIO CATTELAN IN VINCENZA, ITALY IN 1989. BUT THEN, NO ONE WILL KNOW THAT EITHER. AVAILABLE EXCLUSIVELY AT 263 OCEAN CENTRE, HARBOUR CITY, KOWLOON. TEL. 735 5161 DESIGN**2000**

WHO KNOWS, ONE DAY YOU MAY GET TO VISIT SOMEBODY WHO OWNS ONE.

PERHAPS IT'S NONE OF YOUR BUSINESS, BUT THE CHESTERFIELD SOFA WAS DESIGNED BY THE EARL OF CHESTERFIELD IN ENGLAND, 1773. AVAILABLE EXCLUSIVELY AT 263 OCEAN CENTRE, HARBOUR CITY, KOWLOON. TEL. 735 5161 DESIGN**2000**

THE QUESTION IS, WILL THERE BE ANY MONEY LEFT FOR DINNER?

IF IT'S ANY CONSOLATION, THE ARGO DINING TABLE WAS CRAFTED BY STUDIO NIKE FROM THE FINEST BLACK MARQUINA MARBLE IN VINCENZA, ITALY. AVAILABLE EXCLUSIVELY AT 263 OCEAN CENTRE, HARBOUR CITY, KOWLOON. TEL. 735 5161 DESIGN**2000**

CONSUMER MAGAZINE
COLOR 1 PAGE OR SPREAD:
CAMPAIGN

382
ART DIRECTOR
Russell Ramsay
WRITER
John O'Keeffe
PHOTOGRAPHER
Andreas Heumann
CLIENT
K Shoes
AGENCY
Bartle Bogle Hegarty/London

383
ART DIRECTORS
Rooney Carruthers
Mike Wells
WRITERS
Larry Barker
Tom Hudson
PHOTOGRAPHER
Dave Stewart
CLIENT
Sony
AGENCY
Bartle Bogle Hegarty/London

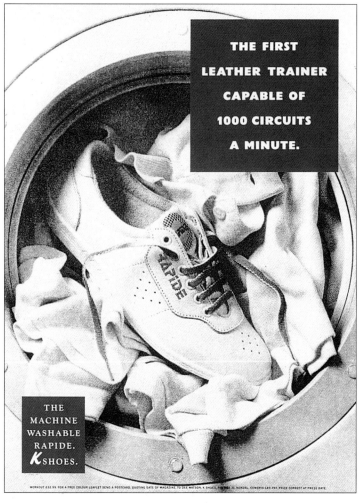

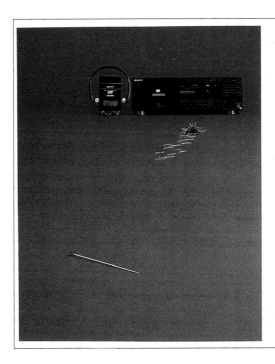

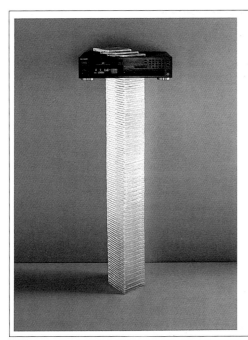

A REMINDER THAT EVOLUTION IS STILL JUST A THEORY.

They say all things must change. They say progress is an irresistible force. Evidently they haven't dined at Murray's. ◆ *At Murray's we partake of change sparingly. Since 1946, we've persisted in believing that dinner should be something more than a biological exercise. It should be one of*

life's purest, most unencumbered joys. ◆ *Here you'll find food designed to delight your senses, not assault them. Whether you choose our sumptuous Silver Butter Knife Steak, our exquisitely simple fish, or anything in between.* ◆ *You'll find decor as elegant as the cuisine. A staff more intent on serving you than on being your friend. And live musicians who do for your ears what our chef does for your palate.* ◆ *Does all this mean we're a bit old-fashioned? Well, we certainly hope so.* ◆ *Join us for dinner. You'll find that the more things change, the more Murray's stays the same.*

26 SOUTH SIXTH STREET **Murray's** MINNEAPOLIS, 339-0909

© 1991 MURRAY'S

IF THERE ISN'T TIME FOR A CIVILIZED LUNCH IN THE 1990s, HAVE ONE IN THE 1940s.

When did lunch come to be viewed as a necessary evil, as merely another daily task? ◆ *It's an interesting question. And, at Murray's, quite irrelevant.* ◆ *At Murray's we still serve lunch as if we meant it—just as we've been doing since 1946. And we've gotten pretty good at it.* ◆ *We've*

learned that civilized surroundings can lower the blood pressure. That a gracious staff can make an hour's break feel like two. And that it is, indeed, possible to dine at lunch. ◆ *But these are the 1990s. We know; we've checked. So if you feel compelled to move quickly, so will we. And if a life-affirming meal of steak, chicken or fish sounds ambitious, we'll whip you up a sandwich that more than competes with anyone's.* ◆ *Next time you're rushing out to lunch, try Murray's instead.* ◆ *We can't stop the world. But you'll be amazed at how we can slow it down.*

26 SOUTH SIXTH STREET **Murray's** MINNEAPOLIS, 339-0909

© 1991 MURRAY'S

REMEMBER WHEN YOU COULD DINE SPLENDIDLY FOR $11.95? IT WAS LAST NIGHT BETWEEN FOUR AND SIX.

There are those who natter endlessly about the good old days. And there are those who simply take an early dinner at Murray's. ◆ *Every evening between four and six, we cast the present to the wind and set out our Downtowner Menu.* ◆ *With prices from $11.95 to $15.95, the Downtowner is an unabashed exercise in nostalgia. And, by the way, in self-indulgence.* ◆ *Whether you indulge in shrimp and scallops, prime rib, chicken, or whatever, you'll also enjoy a cocktail, a bread basket, a crisp salad, and your choice of potato or vegetable.* ◆ *And it's all presented in the style we've been accustomed to since 1946: quietly elegant, supremely attentive, somehow almost magical.* ◆ *What's that? It seems early for dinner? Well, perhaps. But you'll have the whole evening to reminisce about the meal.* ◆ *And a lifetime to reminisce about the evening.*

26 SOUTH SIXTH STREET **Murray's** MINNEAPOLIS, 339-0909

© 1991 MURRAY'S

If it comes out faster than 0·028 mph, we reject it.

The only artificial preservative we use is the one you have to open.

Before it can become a Heinz bean, every raw bean is tested by a light beam.

**CONSUMER MAGAZINE
COLOR 1 PAGE OR SPREAD:
CAMPAIGN**

386
ART DIRECTORS
Paul Shearer
Richard Flintham
WRITERS
Rob Jack
Andy McLeod
PHOTOGRAPHER
Terence Donovan
ILLUSTRATOR
Malcolm Fowler
CLIENT
Windsor Healthcare
AGENCY
*Butterfield Day Devito
Hockney/London*

387
ART DIRECTOR
Joe Staluppi
WRITER
Yoni Mozeson
CLIENT
Crest
AGENCY
*D'Arcy Masius Benton &
Bowles/New York*

CHILDREN ALWAYS WANT TO LOOK OLDER THAN THEY ARE. IF YOU'RE NOT CAREFUL, THEY WILL.

WILL TWO WEEKS IN THE SUN ADD TWO YEARS TO YOUR SKIN?

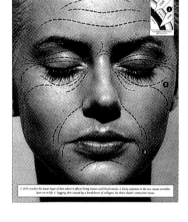

WHY DOES THE SKIN ON YOUR BOTTOM STAY YOUNGER THAN THE SKIN ON YOUR FACE?

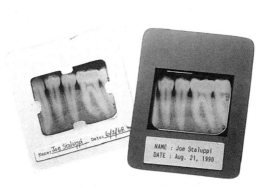

NAME : Joe Staluppi
DATE : Aug. 21, 1990

Name: Joe Staluppi Date: 6/2/68

With Crest you could look
as good at 40 as you did at 18.

It's like a fountain of youth for your teeth. And all you have to do is floss, go for regular checkups and brush with Crest.

True we can't guarantee results like this. But then again, we are a toothpaste that, over the years, has helped prevent more cavities than any other toothpaste.

Not to mention the fact that Crest is recommended by more dentists and hygienists than any other brand.

So don't leave your good looks to chance. Protect your teeth by brushing with Crest.

Because sometimes it takes more than being photogenic to look good in pictures.

Helping to ensure a lifetime of healthy teeth.

These should be part of your
permanent collection.

All 32.
All your life.
After all, we are the toothpaste that, over the years, has helped prevent more cavities and decay than any other. Which could explain why Crest is recommended by more dentists and hygienists than any other toothpaste.

And even as you get older and less prone to cavities, brushing with Crest is still essential. Because by helping to keep your teeth free of decay, we help keep every one of these precious objects where they belong. In your mouth.

So protect your teeth with Crest. Because, like any valuables, there's nothing like the original.

Helping to ensure a lifetime of healthy teeth.

Over the years your eyes may start to go. But your teeth don't have to.

How's that for an eye opener? You can keep your teeth for life.

Take it from the toothpaste that, over the years, has helped prevent more cavities than any other toothpaste. Which could explain why Crest is recommended by more dentists and hygienists than any other toothpaste.

And even as you get older and less prone to cavities, brushing with Crest is still essential. For helping to keep your teeth free of decay. Which will help you keep your teeth, period.

So we're sorry if we've strained your eyes. But it's only to make an important point about your teeth.

Helping to ensure a lifetime of healthy teeth.

CONSUMER MAGAZINE
COLOR 1 PAGE OR SPREAD:
CAMPAIGN

388
ART DIRECTOR
John Doyle
WRITER
Ernie Schenck
PHOTOGRAPHER
Nadav Kander
CLIENT
The Dunham Company
AGENCY
Doyle Advertising/Boston

389
ART DIRECTOR
Carol Henderson
WRITER
Luke Sullivan
CLIENT
Horst Salons
AGENCY
*Fallon McElligott/
Minneapolis*

There are feet that don't care what a Bentley Turbo is going for these days. There are feet that could care less what the Nasdaq is doing. There are feet that wouldn't know an espresso machine if they tripped over one. Dunham. They get the job done.

There are feet that have never gotten the corner office. There are feet that have never sat through a shareholder's meeting. There are feet that have never had sushi for lunch. There are feet that have never seen the inside of an Italian loafer. Dunham. They get the job done.

There are feet that will never meet the gas pedal of a Range Rover. There are feet that will never see a condo in Aspen. There are feet that will never winter in Palm Springs or Palm Beach or Palm anywhere. Dunham. They get the job done.

Make your ex-husband wish he weren't.

HORST
SALONS

Downtown ≈ Minnetonka ≈ Edina ≈ Roseville ≈ Uptown

Look so good, people will think you're shallow.

HORST
SALONS

Downtown ≈ Minnetonka ≈ Edina ≈ Roseville ≈ Uptown

Where the women you hate have their hair done.

HORST
SALONS

Downtown ≈ Minnetonka ≈ Edina ≈ Roseville ≈ Uptown

If we'd known then what we know now, it would have had an automatic.

There is a time for everything. A time for change. Sadly, however, the automotive world often institutes change for the sake of change. A practice we at Porsche have always defied.

At Porsche, we change only to advance. Since Professor F. Porsche created his first concept of the perfect sports car in 1947, our philosophy has been to gradually refine that initial set of ideals. At our research center in Weissach, one of the most advanced engineering think-tanks on the globe, we challenge the laws of physics every day. Uncovering new possibilities. But none go into a Porsche until they are practical additions to a thoroughbred sports car. They wait, on the shelf. Being tested and developed further. The saying at Weissach is that the shelves there are very, very deep.

Such is the case with our new Tiptronic automatic transmission, introduced on our 911 Carrera 2 Tiptronic. An automatic is nothing new. An automatic that can do total justice to Porsche performance is. Now, the time has come. And, typical of Porsche, it came through racing.

Think about it. If you were going to design the perfect high-performance car today, from scratch, you wouldn't require the driver to let off the power and depress an extra pedal 5 times on the way to top gear, would you? Think of the lost time and concentration.

So, when racing drivers piloting our Type 962 race cars asked for a better way, we developed a special transmission for them that allowed electronic clutchless shifting. No let-up in power. No loss of speed. The results were measured in championships.

For our sports cars, we then took the concept even further. And turned it into the dual-function Tiptronic transmission which allows either full automatic, or clutchless manual shifting.

As an automatic, it's nothing short of incredible. Electronic sensors continuously measure vehicle speed, engine speed, forward and lateral acceleration, even the way in which you're working the throttle. Based on these inputs, the car decides how aggressively you wish to drive and then chooses the proper shifting style from among five different "maps," adjusting itself every 30 to 100 milliseconds.

If you want total control, slip the lever to the manual side. Then just "tip" the shifter forward for upshifts or backward for downshifts. Without letting off the power. In track tests, 8 of 10 of our Porsche test-drivers had faster laps with the Tiptronic in manual than with a straight stick. (It's so advanced that if you mistakenly shift so as to over-rev the engine, the computer will hold the command until it's safe to implement.)

Automobile Magazine named it Technology of the Year, saying, "Of all the good ideas that have popped up recently...Tiptronic...will have the most profound effect on future cars." See the future for yourself, with a test-drive of the 911 Carrera 2 Tiptronic at your authorized Porsche dealer. And other Tiptronic models soon.

When asked which Porsche car is his favorite, Professor Porsche simply replies, "We haven't built it yet." Maybe not, but we're getting there.

It would seem, in the last year or two, that some astounding things are happening. And while we wouldn't presume to place our new Tiptronic automatic transmission on the same level of import as the crumbling of the Berlin Wall, the news does seem to leave people somewhat stunned.

An automatic in the world's classic performance sports car?

The simple fact is, automatics have always been a good idea. After all, if you don't have to let up on the power, and depress another pedal, you should be able to drive even harder, right? Professor Porsche has long believed this, and has long led the search for a true high performance version of this concept.

That was the idea when our Type 962 racing car teams developed a clutchless transmission they could shift with a simple flick of a lever. The result was a flurry of championships.

Still, the race drivers had to shift. The car couldn't sense what they wanted to do. For our sports cars, we solved that by combining the gearbox with a sophisticated computer. The result was the Tiptronic; a transmission that lets the driver choose between clutchless manual shifting like the racing 962, or a full automatic that actually "thinks."

In automatic mode, while you watch the road the Tiptronic watches you. Electronic sensors monitor forward and lateral acceleration; engine speed; vehicle speed; even the way

you are working the throttle. The car determines how aggressively you wish to drive, then chooses the proper shifting style from among five different "maps," adjusting continuously every 30 to 100 milliseconds.

Go into a hard turn with a typical automatic and let off the throttle, and the car will upshift, reducing your control. The Tiptronic reads the aggressive cornering forces and prevents such an upshift. The same choice you would make if you were shifting.

When you want to take over, slip the shifter through a channel to the manual side. Then just "tip," the shifter forward for upshifts and backward for downshifts. You needn't pause or let off the power. In fact, 8 of 10 of our Porsche test-drivers had faster laps with the Tiptronic in manual mode than they had with a straight stick.

A test-drive is so convincing that over 40% of all Carrera 2 Cabriolets now being bought are Tiptronics. Of course, only your own test-drive at an authorized Porsche dealer can actually prove to you how stunning this new concept is. Suffice it to say that Automobile Magazine named it Technology of the Year, saying, "Of all the good ideas that have popped up recently...Tiptronic...will have the most profound effect on future cars."

A Porsche having a profound effect on the future. Well, at least you know some things aren't going to change.

The 1991 Porsche 911 Carrera 2 Tiptronic.

The fall of Communism?
Broccoli banned in the White House?
A Porsche 911 with an automatic?

There are some things that seem so right the way they are, it would be unnatural for them to change. Then again, no sooner do we believe something is sacrosanct than change comes along and shakes our notions apart. Such is the Porsche Tiptronic automatic transmission.

In fact, it has always been Porsche-like to do the unexpected. In 1947, when Professor F. Porsche created his first sports car, he ignored convention. The engine was placed in the rear. Lightweight materials employed. Styling forsook garish ostentation of the day for smooth, timeless aerodynamics. Porsche has spent the ensuing decades refining that original concept. Never changing for the sake of change, but never fearing to move ahead.

The truth is, the idea of a high performance automatic has always intrigued Professor Porsche. If you didn't have to let off the power and depress another pedal repeatedly, you could drive even harder and with greater concentration, right?

In keeping with the Porsche heritage, the answer was found on the racetrack. Working with drivers piloting our famed Type 962 racing cars, our engineers developed a clutchless electronic transmission that let them shift with just the flick of a lever, with no let-up in power. Championships followed.

To get an automatic for our sports cars, the remaining trick was to make the car "think." To sense when you want to shift. By combining the electronic concept with a sophisticated computer,

we created the Tiptronic: A dual-function gearbox that lets you choose either clutchless manual shifting, as in the racing 962, or full automatic operation.

As an automatic, the Tiptronic uses sensors to monitor forward and lateral acceleration; vehicle speed; engine speed; even how you are working the throttle. Then, seeing how aggressively you wish to drive, the car chooses the proper shifting style from five different "maps," adjusting every 30 to 100 milliseconds. In cases where a typical automatic would upshift, reducing control, the Tiptronic reads things such as hard cornering forces and prevents that upshift, just as you would when shifting yourself.

When you want to take over, slip the lever to the manual side. Then just "tip" it forward for upshifts and backward for downshifts. It's so quick that 8 out of 10 of our Porsche test-drivers had faster laps with the Tiptronic in manual mode than with a straight stick.

Of course, we know you're not going to believe all this until you see for yourself. Which is why we urge you to test-drive a 911 Carrera 2 Tiptronic at your authorized Porsche dealer.

Automobile Magazine named it Technology of the Year, saying, "Of all the good ideas that have popped up recently...Tiptronic...will have the most profound effect on future cars." There now. That doesn't sound like a certain hot spot is about to freeze over, does it?

The 1991 Porsche 911 Carrera 2 Tiptronic.

If you're one of those who thought you'd see an automatic in the 911 "when pigs fly," may we suggest you duck?

Louisa Murray
was eating a sandwich
when a bowling ball fell off
a ledge three stories above and
hit her in the head. Doctors gave
her a one in a million chance, but
months later she graduated from
college. The ball did leave "a little
dent" in her head. Louisa is wearing a striking Timex women's
fashion watch. It costs
about $50.

TIMEX

Larry Walters
strapped 42 weather bal-
loons to an aluminum lawn
chair and soared to 16,000 feet
before he shot out some of the balloons with a BB gun and crashed into
a power line. He was spotted by
both TWA and Delta airline pilots.
Larry, appropriately, is wearing our moon dial watch.
It costs about $50.

TIMEX

DeAndra
Anrig was flying a kite in
a park near an airport when an
approaching plane snagged the
cord. She was lifted 10 feet and carried 200 feet before she dropped
to the ground. The cord broke one
of the plane's propellers. DeAndra
is wearing a Gizmoz® watch
for kids. They're very lightweight. They cost
about $25.

TIMEX

We're pretty confident about our identity.
How about you?

There was a time when bold individuals etched their name in stone on buildings. Buildings where they built companies around a unique philosophy. A set of ideals. A dream.

Out of those dreams grew some of the greatest creations in history. Creations with identities as unique as the individuals who gave birth to them.

Fortunately, in today's era of homogeneity and mass production with no soul, a few of these distinct entities still survive. The 1991 Porsche 911 Carreras are the living embodiment of one such enduring story.

The 911 is at once familiar yet still, after all these years, idiosyncratic. It is this willful divergence from the ordinary that creates its very identity; from the famous silhouette to the single-minded function. With its unmistakable shape and timeless design derived from Professor Porsche's first sports car, it maintains to this day the same race-inspired principles.

Advanced over the years to retain what is sacred conceptually while exploiting new potential technically, the newest 911 Carreras are a fascinating fusion of past, present and future.

The six-cylinder rear-engine now uses a re-fined design and sophisticated electronic control system to pump out 247 hp. Brakes are race-developed, internally vented massive discs with ABS. A totally new suspension provides

exceptional control, including a novel, self-correcting design in the rear for hard cornering.

The 911 Carrera 4 brings a new threshold of usable power and control to sports cars with electronic all-wheel drive. Linking a computer to sensors, it monitors traction at each wheel with every revolution. Upon sensing any spin, it directs power to the wheels having more grip, correcting slip usually before the driver is even aware of it.

The 911 Carrera 2 Tiptronic widens the enjoyment potential with the Tiptronic automatic transmission. Actually a dual-function gearbox, it lets you choose either automatic or clutchless manual shifting. The automatic contains five shift programs or "maps." Constantly monitoring forward and lateral acceleration, throttle action, engine speed and vehicle speed, it senses how aggressively you wish to drive and matches its shifting style, adjusting itself every 30 to 100 milliseconds.

If you are part of the small circle of individuals confident enough in your identity and beliefs to express them openly, then you will appreciate how unwaveringly we have maintained our own philosophy while continuously refining it. We invite you to test-drive the new Carrera models at your authorized Porsche dealer.

At a glance, you'll see the shape you've always known. After 15 minutes on the road, you'll see how the 911 continues to shape sports cars around the globe.

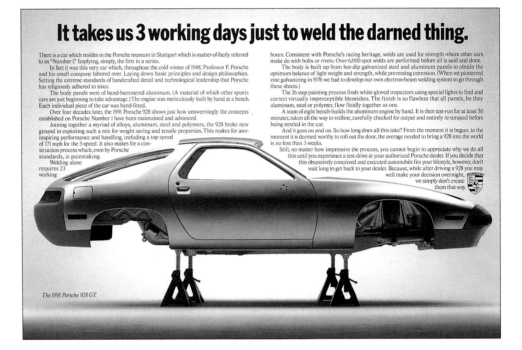

It takes us 3 working days just to weld the darned thing.

There is a car which resides in the Porsche museum in Stuttgart which is matter-of-factly referred to as "Number 1." Implying, simply, the first in a series.

In fact it was this very car which, throughout the cold winter of 1948, Professor F. Porsche and his small company labored over. Laying down basic principles and design philosophies. Setting the extreme standards of handcrafted detail and technological leadership that Porsche has religiously adhered to since.

The body panels were of hand-hammered aluminum. (A material of which other sports cars are just beginning to take advantage.) The engine was meticulously built by hand at a bench. Each individual piece of the car was hand-fitted.

Over four decades later, the 1991 Porsche 928 shows just how unswervingly the concepts established on Porsche Number 1 have been maintained and advanced.

Joining together a myriad of alloys, aluminum, steel and polymers, the 928 broke new ground in exploiting such a mix for weight saving and tensile properties. This makes for awe-inspiring performance and handling, including a top speed of 171 mph for the 5-speed. It also makes for a construction process which, even by Porsche standards, is painstaking.

Welding alone requires 23 working

hours. Consistent with Porsche's racing heritage, welds are used for strength where other cars make do with bolts or rivets. Over 6,000 spot welds are performed before all is said and done.

The body is built up from hot-dip galvanized steel and aluminum panels to obtain the optimum balance of light weight and strength, while preventing corrosion. (When we pioneered zinc galvanizing in 1976 we had to develop our own electron-beam welding system to go through these sheets.)

The 26 step painting process finds white-gloved inspectors using special lights to find and correct virtually imperceptible blemishes. The finish is so flawless that all panels, be they aluminum, steel or polymer, flow fluidly together as one.

A team of eight bench-builds the aluminum engine by hand. It is then test-run for at least 30 minutes, taken all the way to redline, carefully checked for output and entirely re-torqued before being nestled in the car.

And it goes on and on. So how long does all this take? From the moment it is begun, to the moment it is deemed worthy to roll out the door, the average needed to bring a 928 into the world is no less than 3 weeks.

Still, no matter how impressive the process, you cannot begin to appreciate why we do all this until you experience a test-drive at your authorized Porsche dealer. If you decide that this obsessively conceived and executed automobile fits your lifestyle, however, don't wait long to get back to your dealer. Because, while after driving a 928 you may well make your decision overnight, we simply don't create them that way.

The 1991 Porsche 928 GT.

It's there. Every line, every technical component, every single aspect of this car is part of an evolution begun with a small roadster hand-built two generations ago.

With that car, Professor F. Porsche not only built an automobile; he constructed a philosophy of the perfect sports car. Simple, fluid shape with a steeply sloping hood and fender lines that make the driver feel in direct contact with the road. A high power-to-weight ratio coupled with carefully matched, beefy racing components, for rapid acceleration and incredible control. (Early Porsches earned a reputation for vanquishing race cars with much larger displacement simply because of their amazing handling.)

This philosophy has grown and matured, one step at a time, with each Porsche since. Which is why today's 944S2 Cabriolet is such a clear and striking descendent of its ancestors. An integral part of a living heritage.

Following Porsche's racing lineage, the 944 was actually born to race; created for the famed, grueling 24-hours of Le Mans in 1981.

When it became a production model the following year, racing componentry came along. This is another hallmark of Porsche: Most so-called sports cars start with sedan parts and fortify them. We start with racing cars and make them street-worthy. Which is why so many Porsches are raced as is, right off the showroom floor, only adding

required safety gear. "Try that with most sports cars," says a longtime test-driver/engineer, "and you'll be smoking the brakes after 2 laps."

Today's Cabriolet is the latest variation on this theme. The transaxle design, a key 944 element since its introduction, provides near-perfect 50-50 weight balance front to rear. Handling is so precise, power so controllable, it set a benchmark others have sought to emulate for nearly a decade. Pressure cast alloy wheels house huge 4-piston disc brakes with ABS, a standard on every Porsche. (When we pioneered ABS in our racing cars years ago, our drivers initially resisted. But in no time, they were begging for it on their personal cars.)

Engine design, choices of alloys, engine cooling, all grow directly from our racing program which has continued uninterrupted from that first car; retaining the original concept, moving it forward unceasingly. At Porsche, it is called "polishing the diamond."

Of course, there are some things that must never change, one being the handcrafting Professor Porsche initiated. The four-layer cabriolet top, for example, is hand-stitched then hand assembled for an individualized fit on each and every car.

Test-drive a 1991 944 S2 Cabriolet at your authorized Porsche dealer, and you'll experience very much the same sensations early Porsche customers thrilled to decades ago. All that has changed is the level of capability and potential. In that sense, you'll experience things they never had the opportunity to enjoy. You might call it the best of both eras. We simply call it the next step.

The 1991 Porsche 944S2 Cabriolet

Find the 1956 Porsche in this picture.

Catsup on chateaubriand.
An ATM in The Parthenon.
Citizen Kane, colorized.

The Dalmore. Leave it alone.

A full-bodied single Highland malt Scotch whisky. Aged 12 years in oak and sherry casks. The only malt made with the coveted waters of the river Alness.

Nachos with caviar.
Aluminum siding on the Taj Mahal.
Tube socks with a tuxedo.

The Dalmore. Leave it alone.

A full-bodied single Highland malt Scotch whisky. Aged 12 years in oak and sherry casks. The only malt made with the coveted waters of the river Alness.

Plastic flowers in a Ming vase.
Curb feelers on a Jaguar.
Plato's Republic on cassette.

The Dalmore. Leave it alone.

A full-bodied single Highland malt Scotch whisky. Aged 12 years in oak and sherry casks. The only malt made with the coveted waters of the river Alness.

394
ART DIRECTOR
Carol Henderson
WRITER
Doug de Grood
PHOTOGRAPHERS
Jim Arndt
Rick Dublin
Shawn Michienzi
CLIENT
Jim Beam Brands
AGENCY
*Fallon McElligott/
Minneapolis*

395
ART DIRECTOR
Michael Fazende
WRITER
Bill Miller
PHOTOGRAPHER
Michael Johnson
CLIENT
The Lee Company
AGENCY
*Fallon McElligott/
Minneapolis*

We don't think wearing jeans should raise
your voice an octave.

Lee jeans are cut to fit your body, not to cut off your circulation. For a relaxed fit, try Lee Easy Riders. They're cut looser in the thighs and lower at the waist for a more comfortable fit. Or choose from three other great fits. Trim. Regular. Or baggy. Nobody fits your body...or the way you live...better than Lee.

E A S Y · R I D E R S

The brand that fits.

How many fashion trends can you think of
that are over 100 years old?

Unlike last year's hemlines, Lee jeans are not in one year and out the next. They're a fashion classic, year after year. Dress them up. Or dress them down. Nobody fits your body...or the way you live...better than Lee.

E A S Y · R I D E R

The brand that fits.

These jeans were designed to give you more
room in the knees and ankles.

With a side elastic waist, and absolutely nothing to pinch or bind you in the knees or ankles, these just might be the most comfortable pair of jeans you'll ever wear. 100% Pepper Wash cotton denim shorts. Nobody fits your body...or the way you live...better than Lee.

E L A S T I C · R I D E R · S H O R T

The brand that fits.

Consumer Magazine
Color 1 Page or Spread:
Campaign

396
ART DIRECTOR
Bob Barrie
WRITER
Jarl Olsen
PHOTOGRAPHER
Rick Dublin
CLIENT
Hush Puppies Shoes
AGENCY
Fallon McElligott/
Minneapolis

397
ART DIRECTOR
Michael Fazende
WRITER
Bill Miller
PHOTOGRAPHER
Michael Johnson
CLIENT
The Lee Company
AGENCY
Fallon McElligott/
Minneaplis

Self-propelled Hush Puppies.

Top Secret Hush Puppies.

Springy Hush Puppies.

Forget about cholesterol. It's your jeans that
have been cutting off your circulation.

*Lee Pleated Riders are cut to fit your body, not to cut off your circulation. They hug your curves. They lay flat across
your tummy. They fit any occasion, casual to dressy. Nobody fits your body...or the way you live...better than Lee.*

P L E A T E D · R I D E R

The brand that fits.

Our jeans fit your genes.

*Lee Relaxed Rider jeans are designed to fit the natural curves of a woman's body. But most importantly, they're
designed to fit the natural curves of a woman's life. Nobody fits your body...or the way you live...better than Lee.*

R E L A X E D · R I D E R

The brand that fits.

Jeans for life's little ups and downs.

*Lee jeans are designed to fit the natural curves of a woman's body. But most importantly, they're designed
to fit the natural curves of a woman's life. Nobody fits your body...or the way you live...better than Lee.*

E L A S T I C · R I D E R

The brand that fits.

**CONSUMER MAGAZINE
COLOR 1 PAGE OR SPREAD:
CAMPAIGN**

398
ART DIRECTOR
Houman Pirdavari
WRITER
Bruce Bildsten
PHOTOGRAPHER
Hiro
CLIENT
Timex Corporation
AGENCY
*Fallon McElligott/
Minneapolis*

399
ART DIRECTORS
*Bob Barrie
Bob Brihn*
WRITER
Bruce Bildsten
PHOTOGRAPHERS
*Jeff Zwart
Vic Huber*
CLIENT
Porsche Cars North America
AGENCY
*Fallon McElligott/
Minneapolis*

It's made like a Stradivarius.
But it sounds better.

Racecars are not built on conventional assembly lines. Tolerances are too exact. Demands too great. Goals too lofty.

And such is the case with the Porsche 911 Turbo. Meticulously handcrafted in extremely limited numbers, the new generation Turbo is not an automobile built to the standards of a street car, but to the dramatically higher standards of a race car.

The result? Perhaps *Automobile Magazine*'s description of the aural sensation of driving the Turbo says it best: "Soon the growl becomes a roar, then a thunder, and finally an inferno."

And it is an impressive instrument, indeed, that creates all that beautiful music. A turbocharged and inter-cooled boxer six that churns out 315 horsepower, 332 pounds of torque, and 0 to 60 times in a mere 4.25 seconds.

Thankfully, all those horses are harnessed by massive four-piston, cross-drilled brakes that give the Turbo the shortest stopping distance of any production car in the world. And dramatically-improved suspension, steering and shifting in the new generation of 911 Turbo make it surprisingly easy to drive.

You can now experience this astonishing automobile at your local Porsche dealer. We assure you, it is one performance you will never forget.

The Porsche 911 Turbo.

Look at it this way,
it's either an expensive sportscar
or a very reasonable racecar.

The new generation Porsche 911 Turbo is not an automobile built to the standards of a mere street car, but to the impossibly high standards of a race car.

From its immensely-powerful 315-horsepower turbocharged Porsche boxer six engine, to its massive ABS-fortified four-piston disc brakes, it is not just the world's ultimate sportscar. It is the ultimate Porsche.

The result? An automobile capable of accelerating from zero to sixty in a mere 4.25 seconds, and able to stop shorter than any production car in the world. Which is why a showroom stock version of the new 911 Turbo so handily defeated the world's reigning supercars to win the inaugural IMSA Bridgestone Potenza Supercar Championship.

True, that extra ten percent that separates the truly exceptional in this world from the merely good doesn't come easily. Or cheaply. But after one test drive, we're confident you'll agree, it's worth every penny.

The Porsche 911 Turbo.

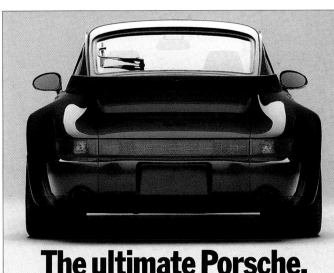

The ultimate Porsche.
(Isn't that redundant?)

Let us put it even more directly: The Porsche 911 Turbo is the Porsche of Porsches. A sportscar built not to the standards of a sportscar, but to the impossibly high standards of a race car.

A combination of 315 thoroughbred horses and massive ABS-fortified brakes not only propel it from 0 to 60 in a mere 4.25 seconds, but also stop it faster than any other production car in the world. (Not surprisingly, it effortlessly defeated the world's other premier sportscars to win the inaugural IMSA Bridgestone Potenza Supercar Championship.)

Yet match that brawn to the dramatically-improved new transmission, steering, suspension, and creature comforts of the new generation of Carrera, and you have a beast that is remarkably well-mannered.

But we are becoming redundant. Test drive the new generation of 911 Turbo and you will agree it is not just the world's ultimate sportscar. It is the ultimate Porsche. **The Porsche 911 Turbo.**

CONSUMER MAGAZINE COLOR 1 PAGE OR SPREAD: CAMPAIGN

400
ART DIRECTOR
Houman Pirdavari
WRITER
Jarl Olsen
CLIENT
Penn Racquet Sports
AGENCY
Fallon McElligott/ Minneapolis

401
ART DIRECTOR
Bob Barrie
WRITER
Jarl Olsen
ILLUSTRATOR
Bill Bruning
PHOTOGRAPHER
Rick Dublin
CLIENT
Jim Beam Brands
AGENCY
Fallon McElligott/ Minneapolis

Boring things

fiber

lawn care

uniformity

Our tennis balls have 75% fewer visible irregularities than our nearest competitor's! (Are you still awake?) Penn tennis balls. You've seen one. You've seen them all.

Boring things

funnel

Ed

integrity

The exciting news is that our nearest competitor lets balls with many more visible irregularities leave their factory. (Well, it excited *us*.) Penn tennis balls. You've seen one. You've seen them all.

Boring things

meat loaf

hygiene

consistency

If you crave variety, buy our nearest competitor's balls—you'll see four times as many irregularities. Penn tennis balls. You've seen one. You've seen them all.

You always come back to the basics. JIM BEAM

You always come back to the basics. JIM BEAM

You always come back to the basics. JIM BEAM

CONSUMER MAGAZINE
COLOR 1 PAGE OR SPREAD:
CAMPAIGN

402
ART DIRECTORS
Bryan Buckley
Frank Todaro
Hank Perlman
Martin Canellakis
WRITERS
Bryan Buckley
Frank Todaro
Hank Perlman
Martin Canellakis
CLIENT
The Finals
AGENCY
Frankfurt Gips Balkind/
New York

403
ART DIRECTOR
Rich Silverstein
WRITER
Dave O'Hare
PHOTOGRAPHERS
Terry Heffernan
Gordon Edwardes
CLIENT
Specialized Bicycle
Components
AGENCY
Goodby Berlin & Silverstein/
San Francisco

402

EVEN BEFORE THEY START A RACE, THEY'RE ALREADY 4.68 SECONDS AHEAD.

At a feather-like 8.5 ounces, our new Air Force™ II is the most aerodynamic hardshell helmet ever made, nearly 5 seconds faster than anything tested.* (That's a savings of 50 seconds over 40 km for those of you reaching for a calculator.) It's also incredibly comfortable, meets stringent ANSI/Snell test guidelines, and it ventilates like a hurricane. And while we're on the subject of cool, check out the way the Air Force II looks. It may very well be the first helmet ever designed to appeal to your sense of vanity. And that's something important to keep in mind, especially when you're the subject of as many first place photos as the guys over there on the left.

SPECIALIZED.

IF WINNING ISN'T EVERYTHING THEN WE SURE SCREWED UP WHEN WE DESIGNED THIS TIRE.

Because over the last five years, Ground Control™ tires have won more races than any other tire. Why? Well besides the obvious fact that the riders who use them are the best there are, Ground Control tires were the first to use our exclusive "working edge" tread pattern, giving the rider an obscenely large contact area, which in turn creates more traction and helps eliminate wash outs. And while a lot of other tires are designed to do little more than look cool, there is nothing cool about eating it in the corners. Nor is there anything particularly fun about discovering you're riding the wrong tire on the wrong terrain. Which is why there's a Ground Control tire for virtually every surface on the face of the earth. Or as one rider on the circuit put it, "You can win with a broken frame, a broken rim, even a broken bone, but you can't win on a crummy tire." Amen.

SPECIALIZED.

THE M2 TEAM EDITION IS SO LIGHT, SO FAST AND SO EXPENSIVE, WE'RE ONLY MAKING FIVE HUNDRED.

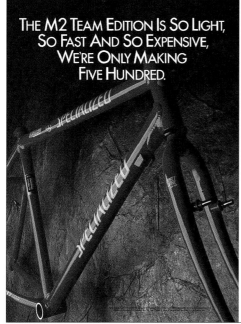

AND FIVE OF THEM ARE GOING TO THESE GUYS.

Technically speaking, it's called metal matrix composite, an advanced alloy of aluminum oxide particles and aluminum, used mainly to build stuff like the space shuttle. But that was before we called up Duralcan USA, the people who make metal matrix composite, and asked if we could do something really cool with it: build a bike. The result is the one and only M2™. Stiffer than titanium, stronger than steel, lighter and more fatigue resistant than chromium. What Bicycling magazine calls one of the year's nine hottest bikes. "Awesome" is how Mountain & City Biking

describes it. "climbs like some kind of crazed goat." A very rare goat we might add. Or at least the M2 Team Edition framesets are, the same frame Team Specialized will be riding this season's available now in very limited quantities. And if you don't score one, don't worry, our production Stumpjumper® M2 is going to be around for a long time. Now keep in mind you're going to fork out a bit more for an M2. But as the editor of Mountain Bike Action pointed out, "This bike is a veritable hot rod." And well, hot rods cost more than ordinary cars. They go faster too.

SPECIALIZED.

CONSUMER MAGAZINE
COLOR 1 PAGE OR SPREAD:
CAMPAIGN

404
ART DIRECTOR
Sean Ehringer
WRITERS
Michael Barti
Jenny Noble
Cathi Mooney
PHOTOGRAPHERS
Bill Hatcher
Chris Noble
Holly Stewart
James L. Amos
CLIENT
The North Face
AGENCY
Mandelbaum Mooney Ashley/
San Francisco

405
ART DIRECTOR
Margaret McGovern
WRITER
Paul Silverman
PHOTOGRAPHERS
John Holt Studios
Stock
CLIENT
The Timberland Company
AGENCY
Mullen/Wenham, MA

5:48 p.m. Trekking through the Southern Alps, New Zealand.

[For a free color catalog including full details of our lifetime warranty and the location of your nearest North Face dealer call 1-800-654-1751.]

Your RENT is LATE, your GOLDFISH is probably DEAD and you think you've LEFT the IRON ON.
YOU couldn't CARE LESS.

You're checking out a view that makes an Ansel Adams print look like a snapshot from one of those disposable cameras. But maybe the best part is you're 8,000 miles from the nearest Winnebago. For over twenty years, outdoor gear from The North Face has been helping people go places where people weren't supposed to go. Like scaling the 5.14a "Scarface" route at Smith Rock, Oregon. Or circling the base of Everest on skis. Which may be why The North Face has been the choice of practically every major expedition of the past two decades. And like them, you can expect every article of clothing, every tent, pack and sleeping bag we make to be guaranteed for life. Because, for us, it has always come down to one thing: making clothing and equipment whose performance you can take for granted. So you can concentrate on why you're out there in the first place.

[For a free color catalog including full details of our lifetime warranty and the location of your nearest North Face dealer call 1-800-654-1751.]

ALTHOUGH it's one of the MOST remote PEAKS IN ALASKA, several PEOPLE HAVE managed to CLIMB IT.
YOU, however, are the FIRST person to JUMP OFF IT.

You're looking down a 45-degree wall of packed powder and jagged granite. It's twenty below zero. But your palms are sweating. This isn't just some adrenaline junkie's idea of a good time. It's a test of North Face gear. For over twenty years, we've dedicated ourselves to making technical outerwear, clothing, tents, sleeping bags and packs that perform flawlessly under the most extreme conditions. Which means we spend a lot of time listening to the people whose lives may depend on it. Case in point: our Steep Tech™ skiwear. Extreme skier Scot Schmidt designed its technical innovations. Like three front zippers and pit zips under each arm for ventilation. Pockets and zippers designed so that they are still accessible while wearing a pack. And virtually indestructible CORDURA® panels at friction points. As with all The North Face products, it's guaranteed for life. Now, we'll admit that all this makes our gear more expensive than most. But then, you wouldn't buy a cheap parachute, would you?

[For a free color catalog including full details of our lifetime warranty and the location of your nearest North Face dealer call 1-800-654-1751.]

It's DAWN. You WAKE UP and start to roll out of bed. Then IT HITS YOU. The FLOOR IS three thousand feet DOWN.

Everybody's gotta sleep. Only for certain people it happens in some pretty interesting places. Like halfway up El Capitan's Salathé Wall. It's these people, however, who we keep fore-most in our minds when designing The North Face gear. Not to mention those who may prefer extreme skiing down a 45-degree mountain face in Chamonix.

Or attempting to scale the south-southwest pillar of K2. Or maybe even rowing a boat from South America to Antarctica. At The North Face, we make a complete line of technical outerwear, clothing, tents, packs and sleeping bags built to overcome situations like these. Packs with zippers tested to withstand up to 300 pounds-per-inch of pull. Raingear made with waterproof, breathable Gore-Tex® fabric. And tents whose fabric is meticulously cut along the grainline to insure tautness and proper shape. All guaranteed for a lifetime. So why do we go to such lengths to make our gear? Because out here it can make the difference between life and death. And we'd hate to lose a customer.

CONSUMER MAGAZINE
COLOR 1 PAGE OR SPREAD:
CAMPAIGN

406
ART DIRECTOR
Woody Kay
WRITER
Steve Bautista
PHOTOGRAPHER
Gregory Heisler
CLIENT
Cannondale Corporation
AGENCY
*Pagano Schenck & Kay/
Providence*

407
ART DIRECTOR
Tom Rosenfield
WRITERS
*Chuck McBride
Ken Lewis*
PHOTOGRAPHER
Rick Rusing
CLIENT
Lexus
AGENCY
*Team One Advertising/
El Segundo*

THERE ARE TIMES IT TAKES OUR BICYCLES FOUR HOURS TO GO 50 FEET.

Until it leaves our factory in Bedford, Pennsylvania, a Cannondale bicycle moves very slowly. Because here it takes nearly four hours to build each one by hand. And while we know hand-crafting is a time-consuming process, it's never been our aim to make lots of bicycles. Just the best bicycles.

To that end, we've always done what we believe to be right. Sometimes that meant doing things differently. Other times it meant doing things that had not been done before.

During the process of creating a Cannondale, we found that ultralight, aircraft-quality aluminum could make a bicycle fly, too. But aluminum alone is not the answer. It's what we do with it that yields a bicycle which not only moves you from place to place, but lets you enjoy getting there. To make our bicycle remarkably light and strong, we produce a hand-welded, heat-treated unibody frame. To heighten responsiveness and efficiency, we use large-diameter tubing. So, as you ride, the bicycle resists the normal twisting forces of pedaling. Hence, more energy goes to the rear wheel. And you suddenly discover how easy it is to go faster.

Which is why Cannondale refuses to cut corners. We know you can be quite passionate about riding extraordinary bicycles. Shouldn't we feel the same way about making them?

WHAT TO DRIVE WHEN YOU'RE THE ENGINE.

From aircraft to automobiles, a vehicle can only go as fast as the engine that propels it. In the case of cycling, the engine happens to be you.

Now if you are serious about this sport, you know that exploring the limits of your physiology requires the dedication of an Olympian and the devotion of a monk. So the last thing you want to do is waste the effort on an inefficient bicycle.

At Cannondale, our goal is to produce a bicycle that makes the most of your ability. That is why we spend nearly four hours hand-building each bicycle at our factory in Bedford, Pennsylvania. Doing what we feel must be done to create not just a good bicycle, but an exceptional one. To make our bicycle remarkably light and strong, we produce a hand-welded, heat-treated unibody frame of aircraft-quality aluminum. To heighten responsiveness and efficiency, we use large-diameter tubing. So, as you ride, the bicycle resists the normal twisting forces of pedaling. Hence, more energy goes to the rear wheel. And you suddenly discover how easy it is to go faster.

Alas, we can't give you any shortcuts to realizing your full potential. But we can offer you the perfect vehicle for getting there.

WE CREATED A SUSPENSION BIKE SO QUICK AND AGILE, WE HAD TO DESIGN A WHOLE NEW BRAKING SYSTEM TO STOP IT.

Mountains divide countries. Separate nations. Even alter climates. But they are no longer an obstacle to those who possess the Cannondale E.S.T.

Short for Elevated Suspension Technology, the E.S.T. is a radical departure in bicycle design that lets you attack the most unsettling terrain as if it were paved.

The secret is the spring-supported, oil-dampened shock absorber. Once calibrated to your weight and the terrain, the E.S.T. soaks up all of the shock that's normally absorbed by you. And like a true suspension system, it holds the wheel to the road over bumps, ruts and rocks. So you can put less effort into controlling the bike, and more energy into something else. Going faster. In fact, the E.S.T. can increase your speed so dramatically, we had to devise a more efficient way to stop it. Force 40 braking. A cable routing system that increases stopping power by 40% over conventional cantilevers. And like every Cannondale, the E.S.T. is distinguished by its ultralight, hand-welded and heat-treated aluminum frame.

Maybe you can't move mountains. But with the Cannondale E.S.T., you can level them.

Only Your Milk Should Be Homogenized.

Sadly, many of the new cars you see today have the tendency to resemble one another. It's as if those recent penchant for computer designs has stunted individuality and left everything the exact same flavor.

Vanilla.

Not so with the Lexus SC 400. In fact, during the entire developmental process, the organic shape was never committed to conventional two-dimensional drawings. Instead, only three-dimensional clay sculptures were used to constantly accentuate the graceful contours.

Like the exterior, the interior, too, is without a hard edge. The dash wraps around the cockpit, elegantly trimmed in Bird's-Eye Maple. Even the leather seats, with special concave backs and an automatic walk-in device, offer something rarely seen in a sport coupe. A back seat that can actually be used as a back seat.

All of which sounds quite civilized compared to what lies directly in front of you. A 250-horsepower, 32-valve, V8 engine that, with a hushed growl, accelerates from 0 to 60 in 6.9 seconds.

Of course to help hold this power in check, sophisticated anti-lock disc brakes and a driver's-side airbag SRS are responsibly provided.

No, the Lexus SC 400 is definitely not your common car. It is, however, the prescribed cure for one.

So Much For Traveling Incognito.

Take just one glance across the spectrum of new cars on the road today and it isn't hard to predict where your eyes will stop.

The Lexus SC 400.

As you can tell from the photo above, the unique design greatly contributes to this magnetism. What may not be so obvious, however, is the beauty that lies beneath the skin.

Such as a Four Cam 32-valve V8 powerplant that places 250 horsepower at your beck and call. Or the classic independent double-wishbone suspension that, in turn, is coupled to a technically advanced anti-lock disc brake system.

Sounds a lot like a muscle car, doesn't it. Yet the Lexus Coupe is far from being muscle-bound.

The leather seats, for example, conform to you, rather than the other way around. The climate control system will automatically maintain the cabin temperature to keep everything from your toes to your nose in complete comfort. And to accommodate your ears, a high-output, seven-speaker audio system surrounds you with sound few concert halls can duplicate.

Why know all this?

Because once you drive the Lexus Coupe, you must be prepared to answer a lot of questions. Autographs, mind you, are optional.

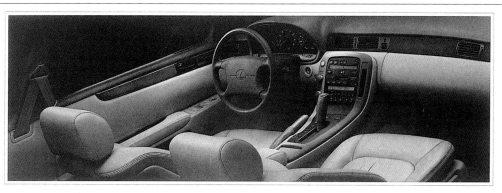

If You Weren't Spoiled As A Child, Here's A Second Chance.

Perhaps you got a chemistry set instead of a pony on your birthday. Or had to share a room through those crucial formative years.

Take heart. You can now own an automobile that gives you just what you want.

The Lexus Coupe. Its smooth, flowing lines can turn even the most stubborn heads. And the 32-valve V8 engine can turn those heads very quickly indeed.

There's also a racing-inspired suspension system to help straighten curves.

But, performance isn't the only focus. The Coupe is, after all, a Lexus.

The seats are studies in advanced ergonomics wrapped in supple leather. The trim is fine Bird's-Eye Maple. Even your ears are indulged; there is a seven-speaker Nakamichi sound system that brings your favorite CDs remarkably to life.

In fact, the Coupe pampers you as few automobiles can. And it has a lot more horsepower than a pony.

STATISTICS AND SIZES AND MEASUREMENTS DO NOT MAKE UP A WOMAN. THEY DO NOT DESCRIBE HER FRUSTRATIONS OR HER VICTORIES, HER EFFORTS OR HER INTENTS. BUT THEY DO MAKE UP THE TOOLS SHE USES TO COMPLETE HERSELF, WHICH IS WHY NIKE DESIGNED THE AIR ELITE ULTRA IN A SPECIFIC WAY, IN A WAY TO CUSHION YOUR FOOT AS IT LANDS, TO PROTECT YOUR FOOT FROM IMPACT AND TO SUPPORT YOUR FOOT WITH EACH AEROBIC MOVE YOU MAKE. BECAUSE STATISTICS MAY LIE WHEN IT COMES TO WOMEN, BUT THEY ARE VERY IMPORTANT WHEN IT COMES TO SHOES.

A WOMAN IS OFTEN MEASURED BY THE THINGS SHE CANNOT CONTROL. SHE IS MEASURED BY THE WAY HER BODY CURVES OR DOESN'T CURVE, BY WHERE SHE IS FLAT OR STRAIGHT OR ROUND. SHE IS MEASURED BY 36-24-36 AND INCHES AND AGES AND NUMBERS, BY ALL THE OUTSIDE THINGS THAT DON'T EVER ADD UP TO WHO SHE IS ON THE INSIDE. AND SO IF A WOMAN IS TO BE MEASURED, LET HER BE MEASURED BY THE THINGS SHE CAN CONTROL, BY WHO SHE IS AND WHO SHE IS TRYING TO BECOME. BECAUSE, AS EVERY WOMAN KNOWS, MEASUREMENTS ARE ONLY STATISTICS. AND STATISTICS LIE.

THIS IS A PICTURE OF A 40-YEAR OLD WOMAN. OR PERHAPS JUST A PICTURE OF THE WAY A 40 YEAR OLD WOMAN FEELS. SHE IS A WOMAN WHO DOES NOT FEEL HER AGE, OR THINK HER AGE, OR ACT HOWEVER IT IS HER AGE IS SUPPOSED TO ACT. IF AGES ARE TO BE BELIEVED, WE GROW OLD FROM THE MOMENT WE ARE BORN. IF AGES ARE TO BE BELIEVED, WE STOP BEFORE EXPERIENCE TEACHES US TO START. IF YOU BELIEVE YOUR AGE, YOU MIGHT NOT CLIMB WHATEVER HILLS YOU ARE SUPPOSEDLY OVER. IF YOU BELIEVE 25 OR 30 OR 48 OR 62, YOU MIGHT BELIEVE IT IS TIME TO STOP WHEN YOU ARE REALLY JUST BEGINNING TO GO.

IF YOU ARE LUCKY, YOU LEARN TO WALK FROM ALMOST THE MOMENT YOU ARE BORN. IF YOU ARE LUCKY, YOU HAVE FEET AND YOU USE THEM, AND IF YOU ARE SMART YOU HAVE SHOES TO MOVE YOU ALONG. SHOES LIKE THE AIR PROGRESS FROM NIKE. SHOES WITH THE SUPERIOR CUSHIONING OF NIKE-AIR. SHOES THAT ARE COMFORTABLE, SHOES THAT ACTUALLY FIT. IF YOU ARE LUCKY, YOU WALK AS LONG AS YOU CAN, AS WELL AS YOU CAN. FOR AS FAR AS YOU WANT TO GO. AND THEN IF ANYONE SAYS YOU'RE OVER THE HILL, YOU CAN TELL THEM YOU WALKED EVERY STEP OF THE WAY.

YOU DO NOT HAVE TO BE YOUR MOTHER UNLESS SHE IS WHO YOU WANT TO BE. YOU DO NOT HAVE TO BE YOUR MOTHER'S MOTHER, OR YOUR MOTHER'S MOTHER'S MOTHER, OR EVEN YOUR GRANDMOTHER'S MOTHER ON YOUR FATHER'S SIDE. YOU MAY INHERIT THEIR CHINS OR THEIR HIPS OR THEIR EYES, BUT YOU ARE NOT DESTINED TO BECOME THE WOMEN WHO CAME BEFORE YOU, YOU ARE NOT DESTINED TO LIVE THEIR LIVES. SO IF YOU INHERIT SOMETHING, INHERIT THEIR STRENGTH. IF YOU INHERIT SOMETHING, INHERIT THEIR RESILIENCE. BECAUSE THE ONLY PERSON YOU ARE DESTINED TO BECOME IS THE PERSON YOU DECIDE TO BE.

THE BODY YOU HAVE IS THE BODY YOU INHERITED, BUT YOU MUST DECIDE WHAT TO DO WITH IT. YOU MUST DECIDE IF YOU WANT STRENGTH, DECIDE IF YOU WANT AGILITY. YOU MUST DECIDE IF YOU WANT ABSOLUTELY EVERYTHING THAT COMES FROM CROSS-TRAINING, AND ABSOLUTELY ONE SHOE TO DO IT IN. BECAUSE THE NIKE CROSS-TRAINER LOW HAS INHERITED ITS OWN SET OF STRENGTHS, ITS OWN KIND OF RESILIENCE. IT HAS ALSO INHERITED A GOOD DEAL OF CUSHIONING, STABILITY, AND TRUE, INTELLIGENT FIT. SO THANK YOUR MOTHER FOR WHAT YOU HAPPENED TO BE BORN WITH. BUT THANK YOURSELF FOR WHAT YOU ACTUALLY DO WITH IT.

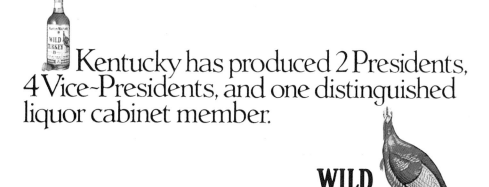

Kentucky has produced 2 Presidents, 4 Vice-Presidents, and one distinguished liquor cabinet member.

WILD TURKEY

101 proof, real Kentucky.

Official Pace Car Of The Winter Carnival.

We're proud to sponsor the Saint Paul Winter Carnival's Grande Day Parade. On Sat., Jan. 25 at 12:50. Come on down. And make sure you park on the even side. Or is it odd? **The St.Paul** COMPANIES

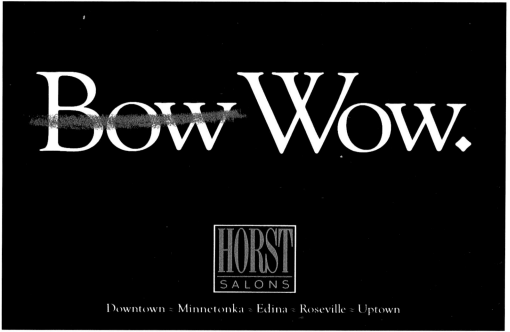

Bow Wow.

HORST
SALONS

Downtown ≈ Minnetonka ≈ Edina ≈ Roseville ≈ Uptown

We can even make the Yellow Pages look whiter.

Kayne & Sussman, Dentists, P.A.
318 Clifton Avenue, Clifton, N.J. 07011
Dentistry for children and adults for over 40 years / Hours by appointment only

Matthew S. Kayne, DMD
777-1230

Steven J. Tuckman, DMD
779-1086

414

Top desk publishing.

The Economist

415

The Economist

416

"Send cash, grain and a subscription to The Economist."

Boris.

417

418

419

420
ART DIRECTOR
Martin Galton
WRITER
Will Awdry
PHOTOGRAPH
Stock
CLIENT
Seagram
AGENCY
Bartle Bogle Hegarty/London

421
ART DIRECTOR
Jeremy Carr
WRITER
Jeremy Craigen
PHOTOGRAPHER
Robert Dowling
CLIENT
New Zealand Lamb
AGENCY
*BMP DDB Needham
Worldwide/London*

422
ART DIRECTOR
Frank Haggerty
WRITER
Kerry Casey
PHOTOGRAPHER
*Marvy! Advertising
Photography*
CLIENT
Normark
AGENCY
*Carmichael Lynch/
Minneapolis*

423
ART DIRECTORS
*Pam Cunningham
Dennis Mickaelian
Gail San Filippo*
WRITER
Hillary Jordan
PHOTOGRAPHER
Paul Gersten
CLIENT
Foster Farms
AGENCY
Chiat/Day/Mojo, Venice

424
ART DIRECTOR
Jerry Gentile
WRITER
Rob Feakins
CLIENT
Quaker State Minit Lube
AGENCY
Chiat/Day/Mojo, Venice

425
ART DIRECTOR
Lynn Kendrick
WRITER
David Shane
PHOTOGRAPHER
Russell Porcas
CLIENT
Neutrogena
AGENCY
Chiat/Day/Mojo, London

420

Each New Zealand lamb has up to 4 acres all to itself.

421

422

Legally fresh.   Morally fresh.

423

424

425

426
ART DIRECTOR
Cabell Harris
WRITER
Dion Hughes
PHOTOGRAPHER
Rick Dublin
CLIENT
NYNEX Information Resources
AGENCY
Chiat/Day/Mojo, New York

427
ART DIRECTOR
Cabell Harris
WRITER
Dion Hughes
PHOTOGRAPHER
Rick Dublin
CLIENT
NYNEX Information Resources
AGENCY
Chiat/Day/Mojo, New York

428
ART DIRECTOR
Christopher Cole
WRITER
Carl Pfirman
PHOTOGRAPH
Minneapolis Institute of Art
CLIENT
Minneapolis Institute of Art
AGENCY
Chuck Ruhr Advertising/ Minneapolis

429
ART DIRECTOR
Kenny Sink
WRITER
Tom McLoughlin
CLIENT
Borgess Medical Center
AGENCY
Earle Palmer Brown/ Kalamazoo

426

427

SEE THE EMPEROR'S CLOTHES.

IMPERIAL SILKS · MINNEAPOLIS INSTITUTE OF ARTS

428

429

430
ART DIRECTOR
Steve Cardon
WRITER
Bryan DeYoung
CLIENT
Reagan Outdoor
AGENCY
Evans/Salt Lake

431
ART DIRECTOR
Bob Brihn
WRITER
Mike Lescarbeau
PHOTOGRAPHER
Joe Lampe
CLIENT
Star Tribune
AGENCY
*Fallon McElligott/
Minneapolis*

432
ART DIRECTOR
Bob Brihn
WRITER
Mike Lescarbeau
PHOTOGRAPHER
Joe Lampe
CLIENT
Star Tribune
AGENCY
*Fallon McElligott/
Minneapolis*

433
ART DIRECTOR
Carol Henderson
WRITER
Luke Sullivan
CLIENT
Horst Salons
AGENCY
*Fallon McElligott/
Minneapolis*

434
ART DIRECTOR
Carol Henderson
WRITER
Doug de Grood
PHOTOGRAPHER
Kerry Peterson
CLIENT
Star Tribune
AGENCY
*Fallon McElligott/
Minneapolis*

435
ART DIRECTOR
Tom Lichtenheld
WRITER
John Stingley
PHOTOGRAPHERS
Craig Perman
Dave Jordano
CLIENT
Jim Beam Brands
AGENCY
*Fallon McElligott/
Minneapolis*

430

"HEY, CHECK OUT THE ADJECTIVES ON HER."

With our new voice mail system, the Star Tribune is making it easy to meet exactly the kind of people you'd like to. Call 673-9015 for sincere, honest, outgoing, friendly details today.

"Get Acquainted" in the **Star Tribune**

431

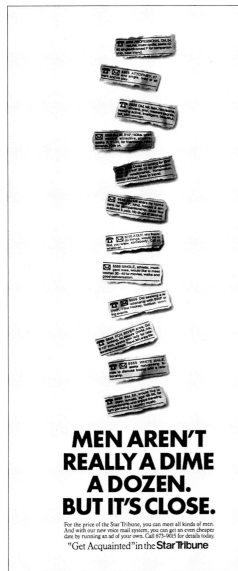

MEN AREN'T
REALLY A DIME
A DOZEN.
BUT IT'S CLOSE.

For the price of the Star Tribune, you can meet all kinds of men.
And with our new voice mail system, you can get an even cheaper
date by running an ad of your own. Call 673-9015 for details today.

"Get Acquainted" in the **Star Tribune**

432

Fortunately, every day
comes with an evening.

WINDSOR CANADIAN *Supreme*

435

Look so good, people will
think you're shallow.

HORST SALONS

433

GUESS WHCH SCTN OF THE
PPER HS BN REDSGND?

The new, easier-to-use Star Tribune classifieds. **Star Tribune**

NAEGELE

434

436
ART DIRECTOR
Carol Henderson
WRITER
Luke Sullivan
CLIENT
Horst Salons
AGENCY
*Fallon McElligott/
Minneapolis*

437
ART DIRECTOR
Bob Brihn
WRITER
Doug de Grood
CLIENT
Star Tribune
AGENCY
*Fallon McElligott/
Minneapolis*

438
ART DIRECTOR
Carol Henderson
WRITER
Luke Sullivan
CLIENT
Horst Salons
AGENCY
*Fallon McElligott/
Minneapolis*

439
ART DIRECTOR
Bob Brihn
WRITER
Mike Lescarbeau
PHOTOGRAPHER
Joe Lampe
CLIENT
Star Tribune
AGENCY
*Fallon McElligott/
Minneapolis*

440
ART DIRECTOR
Sal DeVito
WRITER
Sal DeVito
CLIENT
Daffy's
AGENCY
Follis DeVito Verdi/New York

436

437

Don't you hate it when this happens?

HORST
SALONS

438

WHEN A GUY ANSWERS YOUR PERSONALS AD, AT LEAST YOU KNOW HE CAN READ.

Looking for a well read person? Advertise to the readers of the Star Tribune. With a readership of over one million, we'll help you reach the people who share your interests. And your vocabulary. Call 673-9015 for details today.

"Get Acquainted" in the **Star Tribune**

439

WHAT 80% OFF ACTUALLY LOOKS LIKE.

Designer clothes 40-80% off.
DAFFY'S

GANNETT OUTDOOR

440

441
ART DIRECTORS
Abi Aron
Tom Gianfagna
Rob Carducci
Sal DeVito
WRITERS
Sal DeVito
Rob Carducci
Tom Gianfagna
Abi Aron
PHOTOGRAPHER
Cailor/Resnick
CLIENT
Solgar
AGENCY
Follis DeVito Verdi/New York

442
ART DIRECTORS
Rob Carducci
Abi Aron
Sal DeVito
Tom Gianfagna
WRITERS
Sal DeVito
Tom Gianfagna
Abi Aron
Rob Carducci
PHOTOGRAPHER
Cailor/Resnick
CLIENT
Solgar
AGENCY
Follis DeVito Verdi/New York

443
ART DIRECTOR
Walter Whitman
WRITER
Jeff Tobin
ILLUSTRATOR
Stan Watts
CLIENT
Farmers Insurance Group of Companies
AGENCY
Foote Cone & Belding/ Los Angeles

444
ART DIRECTOR
John Vitro
WRITER
John Robertson
PHOTOGRAPHER
Chris Wimpey
CLIENT
Union Tribune Publishing
AGENCY
Franklin & Associates/ San Diego

445
ART DIRECTOR
John Vitro
WRITER
John Robertson
PHOTOGRAPHER
Chris Wimpey
CLIENT
Union Tribune Publishing
AGENCY
Franklin & Associates/ San Diego

446
ART DIRECTOR
John Vitro
WRITER
John Robertson
PHOTOGRAPHER
Chris Wimpey
CLIENT
Union Tribune Publishing
AGENCY
Franklin & Associates/ San Diego

441

442

443

444

445

446

447
ART DIRECTOR
Michael Wilde
WRITER
Jim Noble
CLIENT
The Red and White Fleet
AGENCY
*Goldberg Moser O'Neill/
San Francisco*

448
ART DIRECTOR
Michael Wilde
WRITER
Jim Noble
CLIENT
The Red and White Fleet
AGENCY
*Goldberg Moser O'Neill/
San Francisco*

449
ART DIRECTOR
Michael Wilde
WRITER
Jim Noble
CLIENT
The Red and White Fleet
AGENCY
*Goldberg Moser O'Neill/
San Francisco*

450
ART DIRECTOR
Gary Goldsmith
WRITER
Ty Montague
PHOTOGRAPHER
Steve Hellerstein
CLIENT
Everlast
AGENCY
Goldsmith/Jeffrey, New York

451
ART DIRECTOR
Gary Goldsmith
WRITER
Ty Montague
PHOTOGRAPHER
Steve Hellerstein
CLIENT
Everlast
AGENCY
Goldsmith/Jeffrey, New York

452
ART DIRECTOR
Jeff Jahn
WRITER
Glen Wachowiak
CLIENT
*Metropolitan Transit
Commission*
AGENCY
*Kauffman Stewart
Advertising/Minneapolis*

453
ART DIRECTOR
Steve Dunn
WRITER
Tim Delaney
CLIENT
The Guardian
AGENCY
Leagas Delaney/London

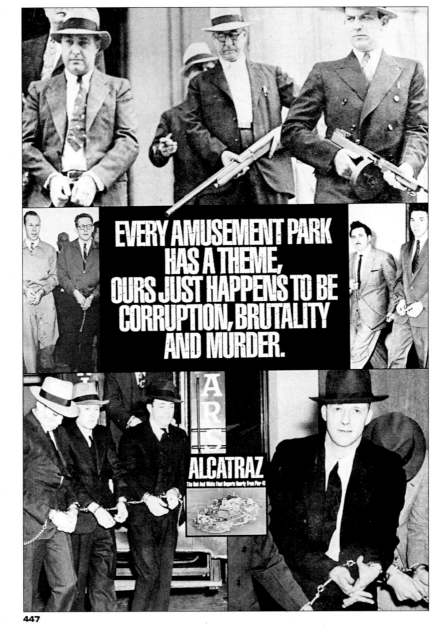

EVERY AMUSEMENT PARK HAS A THEME, OURS JUST HAPPENS TO BE CORRUPTION, BRUTALITY AND MURDER.

ALCATRAZ

447

VISIT THE ORIGINAL HARD ROCK CAFE.

ALCATRAZ

448

IT MADE SING SING LOOK LIKE BORA BORA.

ALCATRAZ

449

This is not one of those scented ads. Good thing.

Everlast Activewear is available at Department, Sporting Goods and Specialty Stores.

450

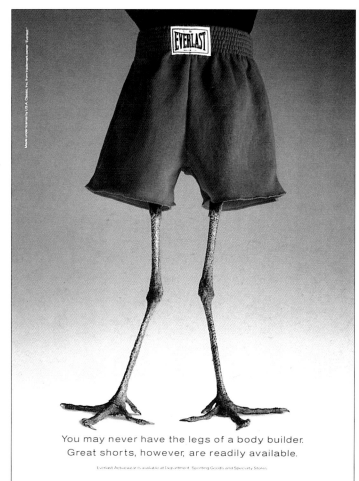

You may never have the legs of a body builder.
Great shorts, however, are readily available.

Everlast Activewear is available at Department, Sporting Goods and Specialty Stores.

451

Going To Work?
Misery Loves Company.

MINNESOTA RIDESHARE 349-RIDE

452

It's my Party and I'll lie if I want to.

Every day throughout the conference season one newspaper will make sure the truth will out.
The **Guardian**

453

454
ART DIRECTOR
Chris Poulin
WRITER
Phil Calvit
CLIENT
*NYNEX Mobile
Communications*
AGENCY
*Leonard Monahan Lubars &
Kelly/Providence*

455
ART DIRECTOR
David Ayriss
WRITER
Scott Vincent
PHOTOGRAPHER
*Ross Display & Skywalker
Industries*
CLIENT
Museum of Flight
AGENCY
*Livingston & Company/
Seattle*

456
ART DIRECTOR
David Ayriss
WRITER
Scott Vincent
PHOTOGRAPHER
Bruce Wolfe
CLIENT
Museum of Flight
AGENCY
*Livingston & Company/
Seattle*

457
ART DIRECTOR
Jim Mountjoy
WRITER
Ed Jones
CLIENT
North Carolina Zoo
AGENCY
*Loeffler Ketchum Mountjoy/
Charlotte*

458
ART DIRECTOR
Rod Waskett
WRITER
Adrian Holmes
ILLUSTRATORS
*Rod Waskett
Simon Warden
Jasvir Garcha*
CLIENT
Zoo Operations
AGENCY
Lowe Howard-Spink/London

454

455

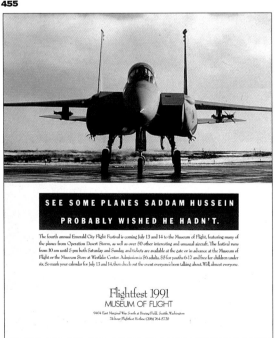

456

457

When we built the North Carolina Zoo, this is what we used for a roof.

462

463

458

464

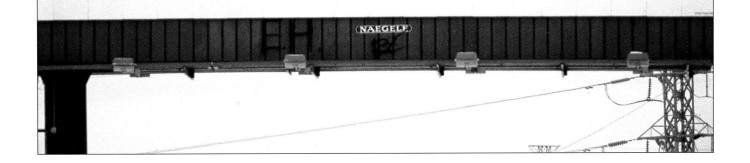

466
ART DIRECTOR
Bob Brihn
WRITER
Mike Lescarbeau
PHOTOGRAPHER
Joe Lampe
CLIENT
Star Tribune
AGENCY
Fallon McElligott/
Minneapolis

467
ART DIRECTOR
Carol Henderson
WRITER
Luke Sullivan
CLIENT
Horst Salons
AGENCY
Fallon McElligott/
Minneapolis

"HEY, CHECK OUT THE ADJECTIVES ON HER."

With our new voice mail system, the Star Tribune is making it easy to meet exactly the kind of people you'd like to. Call 673-9015 for sincere, honest, outgoing, friendly details today.

"Get Acquainted" in the **Star Tribune**

WHEN A GUY ANSWERS YOUR PERSONALS AD, AT LEAST YOU KNOW HE CAN READ.

Looking for a well read person? Advertise to the readers of the Star Tribune. With a readership of over one million, we'll help you reach the people who share your interests. And your vocabulary. Call 673-9015 for details today.

"Get Acquainted" in the **Star Tribune**

NEED A LAWYER?

With our new voice mail system, the Star Tribune is making it easy to meet exactly the kind of people you'd like to. Call 673-9015 for details today.

"Get Acquainted" in the **Star Tribune**

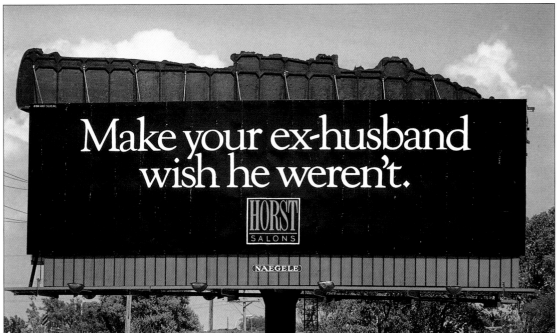

468
ART DIRECTORS
Tom Gianfagna
Rob Carducci
Abi Aron
Sal DeVito
WRITERS
Sal DeVito
Abi Aron
Rob Carducci
Tom Gianfagna
CLIENT
Solgar
AGENCY
Follis DeVito Verdi/New York

469
ART DIRECTOR
John Vitro
WRITER
John Robertson
PHOTOGRAPHER
Chris Wimpey
CLIENT
Union Tribune Publishing
AGENCY
Franklin & Associates/
San Diego

468

470
ART DIRECTOR
Gary Goldsmith
WRITER
Ty Montague
PHOTOGRAPHER
Steve Hellerstein
CLIENT
Everlast
AGENCY
Goldsmith/Jeffrey, New York

471
ART DIRECTORS
Nick Cohen
Taras Wayner
WRITERS
Ty Montague
Nick Cohen
PHOTOGRAPHERS
Ilan Rubin
Stock
CLIENT
*Tiny Mythic Theatre
Company*
AGENCY
*Mad Dogs & Englishmen/
New York*

This is not one of those scented ads. Good thing.

Who needs to see another celebrity jock?

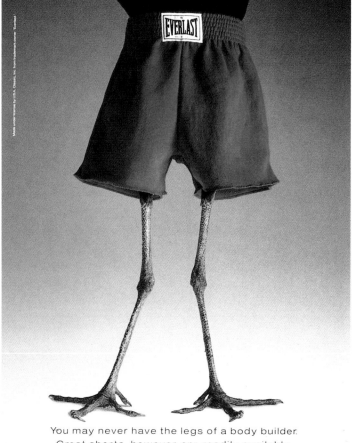

You may never have the legs of a body builder.
Great shorts, however, are readily available.

470

Our latest production deals with...well...you know.

Frankenstein. The Musical. Feb 22-Mar 10. Ohio Theatre.

$80   **$65**

**TINY MYTHIC
THEATRE CO.**
Presents
THE AMERICAN LIVING ROOM
27 different pieces by
27 different directors.
Every Saturday, 8 PM
July 13th-August 31st
at the Ohio Theatre.
66 Wooster St. Soho
New York City.
Call (212) 274-9807

$30   **$5**

You're part of a Resistance unit. Your mission is to help sabotage an enemy tank division. As the tanks and soldiers come into firing range you suddenly realise they're using innocent men, women and children as human shields. You know you should shoot.

What do you do?

Find out what a Polish Resistance fighter did by listening to his recording of an attack on an SS Panzer Division in 1944. It's just one of the thousands of exhibits at the Imperial War Museum.

The Imperial War Museum. Part of your family's history.
MUSEUM Open daily 10am to 6pm. Walking distance from Lambeth North and Elephant & Castle Tube Stations. Telephone (071) 416 5000.

You object to war. You've never hit anyone in your life. If you don't enlist, you know your family will be subjected to abuse from neighbours and school friends. Women will give you white feathers and your workmates will shun you. You could even be sent to prison.

What do you do?

Mr Brookes' postcard shows how Conscientious Objectors were treated during the First World War. It's just one of the thousands of exhibits at the Imperial War Museum.

The Imperial War Museum. Part of your family's history.
MUSEUM Open daily 10am to 6pm. Walking distance from Lambeth North and Elephant & Castle Tube Stations. Telephone (071) 416 5000.

It's midnight. You're among a party of men preparing for a surprise attack on the enemy trenches. Silently you crawl forward – any noise and you risk being wiped out by their machine guns. To your horror, a live grenade accidentally slips and falls to the ground. You have five seconds before it explodes.

What do you do?

Find out what Second Lieutenant Edward F. Baxter did that helped earn him the Victoria Cross in 1916. It's just one of the thousands of exhibits at the Imperial War Museum.

The Imperial War Museum. Part of your family's history.
MUSEUM Open daily 10am to 6pm. Walking distance from Lambeth North and Elephant & Castle Tube Stations. Telephone (071) 416 5000.

THE FIRST CONDOM SPECIALLY DESIGNED FOR SHOPKEEPERS.

Introducing Le Condom, the world's first discreetly packaged condom. Its stylish design won't look out of place whoever stocks it and wherever it's displayed.

More importantly it takes the embarrassment out of buying and selling what today is a vital consumer product.

18-24 year olds are already discovering the secret of Le Condom thanks to a stylish TV campaign now running on Scottish Television.

To discover the secret for themselves, shopkeepers should telephone free on 0800 24 32 26 now for wholesale and Cash and Carry stockists.

BX INTERNATIONAL HEALTHCARE LIMITED, BX HOUSE, THE DELTA CENTRE, GEMINI CRESCENT, DUNDEE TECHNOLOGY PARK, DUNDEE DD2 1SW. TELEPHONE: 0382 561286.

473

We set this ad in 6-point type because that's what advertising people expect from lawyers. But Steve Bergerson isn't just another lawyer. He's an advertising lawyer with ad agency experience. He enjoys a good headline and 12-point body copy as much as you do. So if you need a legal opinion about an ad, call Steve at 612-347-7043. We promise, your ad won't be reduced to this.

Fredrikson & Byron, P.A., 1100 International Centre, 900 Second Avenue South, Minneapolis, MN 55402-3397   ©1991

475

474

IF THE CONCEPTUAL POSSIBILITIES OF THIS PHOTO ELUDE YOU, PERHAPS YOU WOULD LIKE TO CONSIDER THE EXCITING FIELD OF ACCOUNT MANAGEMENT. IT'S BRIMMING WITH OPPORTUNITY FOR THOSE DILIGENT SOULS WHO, WHILE LACKING IN A CERTAIN QUALITY OF IMAGINATION, POSSESS A STUNNING KNACK FOR DETAIL. TO DISCUSS YOUR NEXT, AND UNDOUBTEDLY BRIGHTER, CAREER, CONTACT MICHAEL PAGE MARKETING, SPECIALIST RECRUITMENT CONSULTANTS, 12 GREEN ST., LEEDS LS1 5RU (0532) 424067. IF, ON THE OTHER HAND, YOU APPRECIATE THE CREATIVE OPPORTUNITY OF CONCEPTUAL PHOTOS, YOU MAY RECEIVE A SAMPLE IBID PORTFOLIO BY CALLING 071 370 0089 (U.K.); 49 89 349 306 (GERMANY); OR 312 733 8000 (NORTH AMERICA).

476

You shouldn't have to wait 18 years to get an accurate paternity test.

You can wait a few years for an accurate paternity test. Or you can consult Memorial Blood Center of Minneapolis.

Memorial Blood Center is the most experienced testing facility in the Midwest. And experience is vital because paternity test results are not simply "yes or no." They're complicated, and require skillful interpretation.

That's why all of our laboratory personnel have paternity testing experience, along with degrees in medical technology or a related science.

So the next time you have a paternity case, don't wait.

Consult the experts at Memorial Blood Center. Call (612) 871-3300, ext. 239 for more information today. **Memorial Blood Center**

477

How to raise the odds of winning your next paternity case.

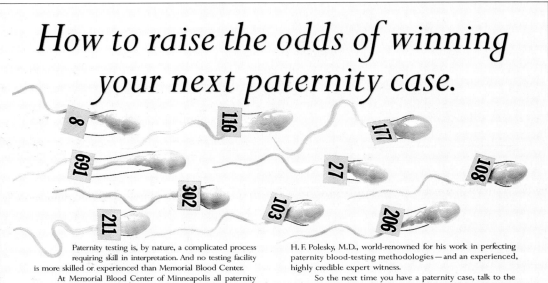

Paternity testing is, by nature, a complicated process requiring skill in interpretation. And no testing facility is more skilled or experienced than Memorial Blood Center.

At Memorial Blood Center of Minneapolis all paternity testing is performed by experienced, certified laboratory personnel with degrees in medical technology or related science. And all test results include a review and letter of explanation from

H. F. Polesky, M.D., world-renowned for his work in perfecting paternity blood-testing methodologies—and an experienced, highly credible expert witness.

So the next time you have a paternity case, talk to the people who have more blood testing experience over more years than any laboratory in the Midwest. Call (612) 871-3300, ext. 239 for more information today. **Memorial Blood Center**

478

On the Alaskan tundra at 50° below zero, the object isn't just to keep your toes from freezing.

It's to keep them from freezing off.

The boot in this ad is a custom-built, professional class, high technology adaptation of a traditional Eskimo mukluk. It is the only waterproof, breathable cold weather footwear system of its kind. And if you want to see it in action you'll have to visit the Timberland testing lab, a trip you might not want to make unless you plan to dress like a Polar bear. Our testing lab, you see, happens to be the Iditarod trail, a 1,049 mile stretch of blizzard-whipped tundra between Anchorage and Nome. There, champion Iditarod mushers have helped us develop this prototype mukluk as they trained for the coldest, most grueling race on earth.

Using a layering system consisting of an outer boot made of Gore-Tex² fabric and Thinsulate® insulation, combined with a specially designed inner boot of wool and polypropylene, the mukluk

gives the mushers all-in-one protection for the 100 temperature changes they inevitably encounter.

To develop a sole that would remain flexible even at the worst Arctic temperatures, the Timberland team worked closely with Vibram². The effort produced a specially-designed sole, unique in its sub-zero suppleness and its ability to shed ice and snow without losing traction.

All of which may not be necessary for normal winter conditions in New York, Chicago — or wherever you may be.

But we thought you'd like to know the stuff of which Timberland — and all its products — are made.

Timberland 🌳
Boots, shoes, clothing, wind, water, earth and sky.

479

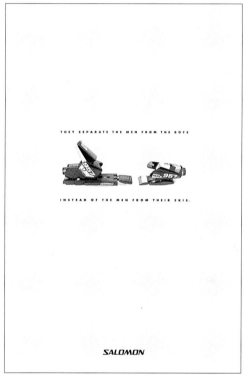

THEY SEPARATE THE MEN FROM THE BOYS

INSTEAD OF THE MEN FROM THEIR SKIS.

SALOMON

480

Just this once, we'd like to give our vehicles the image they deserve.

Of course you won't see any of our drivers making deliveries in anything like this. You will however notice the speed at which our ground service works.

Quite simply, UPS offers the fastest scheduled ground delivery serving the forty-eight states today. In fact, of the ten million packages we deliver each day, four million are overnight ground deliveries. And when you couple that with our well proven record for on-time

reliability, you can rest assured that your packages will consistently arrive at the time they are scheduled to arrive. All within the legal speed limits.

So why ship with anyone else but UPS. After all, with 64,000 vehicles on the road and eighty-four years of experience, it's no wonder our service is what some people might call up to speed. We run the tightest ship in the shipping business.

481

One click, and it will change people's minds.

"How do I work this #!@$%⚡ thing!" All across America, people are crying out. Tired of those impossible-to-understand gizmos and gadgets. Okay, enough already.

"Our strategy helps address consumer demands." We're changing people's minds with a complete line of Home Theatre™ products, such as big screen televisions and VCRs that are so incredibly simple everyone and his dog can figure them out. Take our Simple Touch™ remote. Six buttons. That's it. No Ph.D. required. We're taking all that technological stuff and making it easy. We're also making things easier for you by providing all kinds of valuable sales training. Not to mention strong marketing support. Interactive video displays that make your store more fun. Exciting new point-of-purchase materials. National promotions, like the "Name *that* pup!" contest. Easy-to-read instruction manuals. And advertising dollars. Lots of them. You see, we want to help *you* help your customers understand today's technology. And we want to do it better than anyone else in the business. It's as simple as that.

"Let's kick butt."

Changing Entertainment. Again.™ RCA

482

AFTER SEEING OUR WORK THE BURNETT CREATIVE REVIEW BOARD DUBBED IT "PROVOCATIVE, OUTRAGEOUS, AND NASTY." WE MUST BE DOING SOMETHING RIGHT.

SEE FOR YOURSELF. CALL DARYL TRAVIS FOR A COPY OF OUR AGENCY'S LATEST REEL.

ARIAN, LOWE & TRAVIS
833 WEST CHICAGO AVENUE CHICAGO ILLINOIS 60622 (312)243-3500

483

How to get paid before the Novocaine wears off.

Pardon us if we've struck a nerve. But for a dentist, the gap between services rendered and payment received can sometimes be positively excruciating.

With Visa,® though, it won't hurt a bit. When your patients pay with Visa, you get paid quickly. We don't need to tell you what that can do for your cash flow.

Or, for that matter, what it can do for the administrative burden of billing and collection.

Furthermore, a recent study indicates that of the 100 million Americans who carry the Visa card, a clear majority view it as an appropriate way to pay dental expenses. And why not? Visa lets

them defer the bill for up to a month, and it might even allow them to extend their payments over time.

Given all that, one might even speculate that the Visa card could encourage your patients to visit you on a more regular and timely basis.

For a free kit—including customized office signage, pre-authorization forms to streamline the payment process, and educational materials for your staff— give us a call at (800) VISA-311.

Your patients will thank you. Though they may be a bit numb when they do it. © Visa U.S.A. Inc. 1991.

484

Just a reminder that a bad picture can ruin a beautiful room.

A television does more than just entertain your guests. It also says a lot about your hotel. Unfortunately, if the picture is snowy, blurry or fuzzy, it's not saying anything nice. That's why you should put a Mitsubishi TV in your rooms. Like the 35" Stereo Digital Monitor/Receiver with Diamond Vision® for optimum contrast and color performance. It has a picture so incredibly clear your guests just might want to spend their entire visit inside, ordering room service and watching pay-per-view movies. Could happen. So if your hotel's image is important to you, just remember that Mitsubishi makes a full line of televisions, from 13" to 70". After all, you want your guests to make reservations. Not have them. ▲**MITSUBISHI**
TECHNICALLY, ANYTHING IS POSSIBLE®

© 1991 Mitsubishi Electronics America, Inc. For more information call (714) 229-6535. Model featured: CS-3535R.

485

Sales.   **Marketing.**

486

487
ART DIRECTOR
John Doyle
WRITER
Ernie Schenck
PHOTOGRAPHER
Nadav Kander
CLIENT
The Dunham Company
AGENCY
Doyle Advertising/Boston

488
ART DIRECTORS
John Doyle
Dale Edmondson
WRITER
Jonathan Plazonna
CLIENT
Chelsea Pictures
AGENCY
Doyle Advertising/Boston

489
ART DIRECTOR
John Doyle
WRITER
Ernie Schenck
PHOTOGRAPHER
Nadav Kander
CLIENT
The Dunham Company
AGENCY
Doyle Advertising/Boston

490
ART DIRECTOR
John Doyle
WRITER
Ernie Schenck
PHOTOGRAPHER
Nadav Kander
CLIENT
The Dunham Company
AGENCY
Doyle Advertising/Boston

491
ART DIRECTOR
John Doyle
WRITER
Ernie Schenck
PHOTOGRAPHER
Nadav Kander
CLIENT
The Dunham Company
AGENCY
Doyle Advertising/Boston

492
ART DIRECTOR
Bob Barrie
WRITER
Mike Gibbs
PHOTOGRAPHER
Rick Dublin
CLIENT
Continental Bank
AGENCY
*Fallon McElligott/
Minneapolis*

There are feet that have never seen a David Hockney. There are feet that have never walked the streets of Cannes. There are feet unfamiliar with beluga at midnight. Dunham. They get the job done.

487

488

There are feet that don't care what a Bentley Turbo is going for these days. There are feet that could care less what the Nasdaq is doing. There are feet that wouldn't know an espresso machine if they tripped over one. Dunham. They get the job done.

489

There are feet that will never meet the gas pedal of a Range Rover. There are feet that will never see a condo in Aspen. There are feet that will never winter in Palm Springs or Palm Beach or Palm anywhere. Dunham. They get the job done.

490

There are feet that have never gotten the corner office. There are feet that have never sat through a shareholder's meeting. There are feet that have never had sushi for lunch. There are feet that have never seen the inside of an Italian loafer. Dunham. They get the job done.

491

Capital is getting harder and harder to find.
(Perhaps you're just looking in the wrong places.)

Investors are cautious. Lenders are wary. Expectations are high. And you're on your hands and knees. Obviously, trying to secure capital these days can be a rather humbling experience.

Unless, of course, you know just where to look. Like we do at Continental Bank. To find capital we'll scrutinize options like commercial paper. Medium-term notes. Private placements. Acquisition financing. Asset securitization. Lease advisory. Mezzanine financing. Private equity. Mergers and acquisition advisory. Structured debt. And even, dare we say, a few couches.

Now look here: At a time when other banks were retrenching, external capital raised for Continental customers was up by more than 40%. In fact, we raised 15 billion dollars worth of capital last year.

Rest assured, the fine-toothed comb we use to find capital is finer than most. (Continental Bank has always stood tall as a recognized leader in the placement of straight debt, asset-backed commercial paper and securitized products.)

You see, over the last five years, we've found and hired a number of veteran corporate finance specialists, veritable capital sniffing bloodhounds, that make our expertise all the more expert. Ironically, many are former employees from some of our major competitors.

Working hand in hand with experienced relationship managers, they form a braintrust to assess each client's business. Then, and only then, can they create the customized capital financing tools each particular situation calls for. Finally, to bring things full circle as it were, we can quickly locate the investors needed to complete our deals. Our capabilities are worldwide and we're quite adept at arranging transactions with terms of overnight to 30 years or longer. If you need to find some capital before you completely lose it, contact your Continental relationship manager today. We'll leave no stone—or cushion—unturned. **Continental Bank**
A new approach to business.

492

493

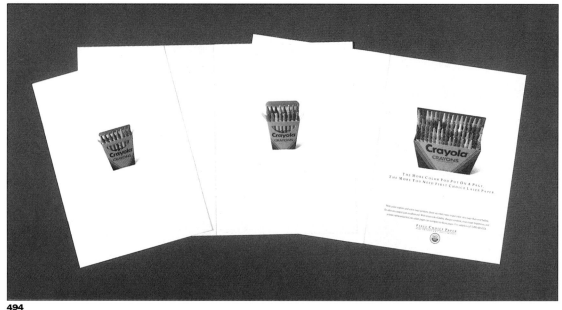

494

495

Lee. The #1 jean of girls, 4 to 13.

More pre-teen girls doll up in our jeans than in any other brand. And now that we've cut our wholesale prices up and down our entire line, the margin potential means a bigger cut for you. **Lee**

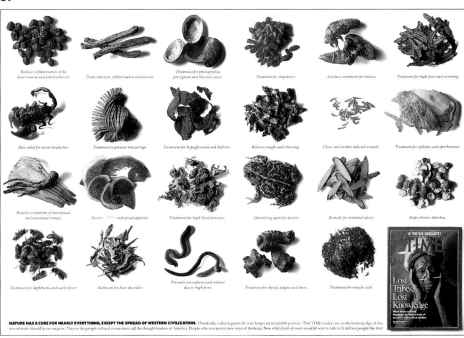

Petrochemicals might be fine for making Barbie dolls. But when it comes to cosmetics, we think it's time to stop playing around. ❦ Our mission at Aveda is to eliminate petrochemicals from beauty products entirely. Whenever possible, we use natural alternatives. ❦

Your face isn't made out of plastic. Why use cosmetics that are?

To that end, our researchers are constantly sourcing natural ingredients from around the world. ❦ From freshly harvested flowers and plants, we distill pure essential oils. Processing these essential oils does not pollute our environment or deplete it of a non-renewable resource. We think that's better for our planet. And ultimately, better for you. ❦ This spring, Aveda introduces colour cosmetics that combine the cool, softness of pink with the warm, burnished beauty of the summer desert. Aveda's *Summer Solstice* collection includes blushes, eye shadows, eye pencils, lip pencils and fresh-scented lipsticks. ❦ The full line of Aveda cosmetics, including the *Summer Solstice* collection, is sold only in fine salons by licensed professionals. ❦ Call, toll free, 1-800-328-0849 for the Aveda salon nearest you. Or visit the Aveda Esthetique in New York City or in Los Angeles (opening soon in The Beverly Center).

AVEDA
THE ART AND SCIENCE OF
PURE FLOWER AND PLANT ESSENCES

NATURE HAS A CURE FOR NEARLY EVERYTHING, EXCEPT THE SPREAD OF WESTERN CIVILIZATION. Thankfully, cultural genocide is no longer an acceptable practice. That TIME readers are on the leading edge of this new attitude should be no surprise. They're the people cultural researchers call the thought leaders of America. People who are open to new ways of thinking. Now, what client of yours wouldn't want to talk to 24 million people like that?

499

500

501

Our new price margins are the widest things we've offered since 1972.

We've lowered our wholesale prices on our entire line of Lee jeans. Which means, of course, more margin potential and more profit for you. We think it's something everyone in the retail establishment will dig, man.

502

Self-propelled Hush Puppies.

503

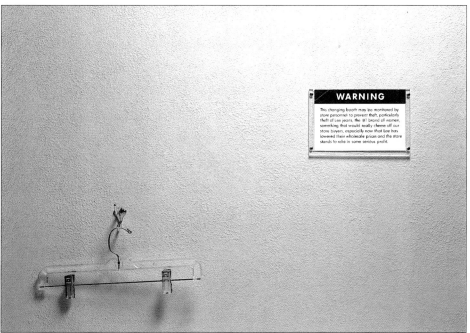

504

LOOKS LIKE THE PERFECT SPOT FOR ONE OF OUR BENCHES.

PLACE A WOODEN BENCH FROM LFI IN ANY GIVEN ENVIRONMENT AND AN AMAZING TRANSFORMATION HAPPENS. THAT SPACE SUDDENLY BECOMES MORE INVITING. IT ALSO GROWS MORE BEAUTIFUL. UNDERSTANDABLY. OUR NEW KENWORTHY COLLECTION FEATURES DESIGNS THAT ARE TASTEFUL...AS WELL AS UNIQUE. STURDILY CRAFTED TO ENSURE THAT YOU'LL BE ABLE TO SIT ON YOUR INVESTMENT FOR SOME TIME TO COME. CALL 1-800-521-2546 TO RECEIVE OUR COMPLETE KENWORTHY LINE BROCHURE. THAT IS. IF YOU HAVEN'T FALLEN FOR THEM ALREADY. **LFI/Landscape Forms** Lfi

505

At 95% cotton, the biggest threat to our Superweight sweatshirt isn't from the competition.

Lee's 11 oz., 95/5 Superweight Cotton Cross Grain sweatshirt will make the other guys get out their antiperspirant.
Comfort. Breathability. A generous cut. Rib inserts. Shrinkage control. And outstanding printability. This sweatshirt has it all.
Add to this the fact that Lee casualwear is highly recognized, preferred and trusted by consumers, and it's clear there really is no competition. To learn more, call toll free 1-800-735-5250. Or better yet, pick up the phone, and bug your Lee wholesaler today. Lee
The brand that fits.

BOLL WEEVIL

506

Perhaps there really is *a place* where you can *hear yourself think.*

*I*t seems the more efficient our offices become, the harder it is to get any real work done there. The big idea, the breakthrough, the clearing of the air, require an entirely different kind of environment. One of solitude and peace.

Places like The Outing Lodge at Pine Point, Stout's Lodge and the Seven Pines Lodge. Places as different from your standard movable-wall-and-formica-table "modern"

conference center as Aspen is from Akron.

Here you can get enormous amounts of work done without ever feeling like you're really working. And if that just sounds like wishful thinking to you, ask executives from Shell Oil and 3M who've already experienced it.

The Outing Lodge at Pine Point is a grand Georgian country home in the English tradition, surrounded by a 350-acre forest. Originally built in 1858, painstakingly restored, and appointed with fine period antiques, it is both elegant and warm.

The Seven Pines Lodge was originally built in 1903 by Minneapolis grain baron Charles Lewis. Nestled next to a natural trout stream and surrounded by a 100-acre forest, it has hosted such adventurous souls as Presidents Calvin Coolidge and Teddy Roosevelt. It is a rustic hand-hewn log structure with its original Stickley furniture, American Indian art and Oriental rugs, as well as world-renowned fly fishing.

Stout's Lodge was built by Chicago lumber tycoon Frank D. Stout at the turn of the century for what was then an astounding $1.5 million. Situated on its own island in a northern Wisconsin lake, this vast lodge was modeled after an Adirondack Camp with four-inch-thick plank floors and hand-carved beams from Germany.

At all properties the gourmet cuisine is superb, the attention to detail fanatical, the service impeccable, and the staff incredibly accommodating and personable. And, yes, we must admit that carefully hidden from sight we do have the requisite fax machines, computers and audio-visual equipment.

We are currently taking reservations, as well as offering limited corporate memberships. For more information you can simply call us at 439-9742. You'll be amazed at how much easier it is to think when you can hear those precious thoughts trickling through your head.

Stout's Lodge   The Outing Lodge   Seven Pines Lodge

It's where the other half *works.*

507

A pager you can wear with your pants off.

Until now, pagers had some serious mechanical problems. They were too big. Too ugly. Too easy to lose.

Wouldn't it make more sense to make a pager more the size and shape of, say, a wrist watch?

Introducing the Tracer® wrist watch pager, a reliable Timex quartz watch with a state-of-the-art Motorola pager built in. It is one of the smallest, lightest, most subtle pagers you can buy. Yet it has sophisticated features like six-message memory, time-page, priority signaling and auto turn-off.

Why choose paging in this age of cellular

phones, FAX machines and computer mail? Because a pager is still the most practical communication tool of all. It's simple. It's utterly reliable. And the service costs a mere fraction of cellular phone service: less than $10 a month.

Yet the Tracer by Timex costs about the same as a pager you wear on your belt.

Pick a Tracer up at a store near you and one phone call will start your service. For more information and your nearest retailer call 1-800-367-8463.

The Tracer wrist watch pager. It's the only thing you need to wear.

The Timex Tracer® Wrist Watch Pager
Ⓜ MOTOROLA®

508

LOOKS LIKE THE PERFECT SPOT FOR ONE OF OUR NEW CHAIRS.

INTRODUCING A NEW LINE OF STACKING CHAIRS FROM LFI. THEY'RE TASTEFUL, ELEGANT AND EASY TO HANDLE. EVERYTHING STACKING CHAIRS USUALLY AREN'T. CHOOSE FROM TWO DISTINCT DESIGNS, VERONA AND FIRENZE, IN A VARIETY OF EASY-TO-MAINTAIN MATERIALS, INCLUDING WIRE GRID AND PERFORATED METAL, WOOD, TOO. ALL METAL PARTS ARE FINISHED WITH OUR EXCLUSIVE PANGARD II POWDER-COAT FINISH FOR UNSURPASSED CHIP AND RUST RESISTANCE. TO RECEIVE OUR COMPLETE BROCHURE, CALL 800-521-2546. **LFI/Landscape Forms** ⌐┘

509

510

511

63.1% Of Our Subscribers Are In Top Management. 32.1% Are In Middle Management. The Other 4.8% Like The Pictures.

If you want to reach for the top you should know that 95.2% of our subscribers are in management positions. (When probed, they too admitted to liking the pictures.) Call 312-649-5370 for ad space.

If you've ever had a beer right at our brewery you would discover what experts on the subject have known all along — beer tastes better when it's fresh. When beer is exposed to this notorious threesome, it begins to lose its freshness and the worse it tastes.

But here at Coors, we're extremely protective of our beers. From the mountains to the marketplace, no other brewer goes to the lengths we do to make sure your customers get a fresh, great tasting beer time after time.

Heat is a very serious threat to beer. Amazingly, most breweries intentionally heat their beer after it's bottled or canned. This is called "pasteurization." Which is just a nice way of saying that it's run through a 140° hot water bath. This process kills any live bacteria or yeast. Unfortunately, it does nothing for the taste.

Coors, on the other hand, has used a sterile brewing process since 1959. Which means we don't have to pasteurize. Our beers are continuously chilled, and have been for thirty-three years.

And we're still the only brewery that safeguards our beer with cold packaging, shipping, and storage. Which means from the time it's brewed, all the way to your shelves, Coors, Coors Light, Coors Extra Gold and Coors Dry are continuously protected from the heat.

We're also unrelenting in our fight against beer's other enemies: light and age.

When beer is exposed to the sun or any other kind of light, it begins to deteriorate. So we put our beer in extremely dark, brown bottles.

It astounds us certain brewers put their beer in clear bottles.

And unlike wine, beer doesn't taste better when it's aged. Instead of improving, it starts to naturally break down. To fight this effect and ensure freshness, we pull our beer from the shelves a full two weeks before any of our major competitors.

All this adds up to our exclusive brewery-fresh taste in every can, bottle, party ball, and keg of Coors. And considering the demand for fresh products these days, stocking Coors adds up to more profits for you.

NEXT TO PROHIBITION, THESE ARE A BEER'S WORST ENEMIES.

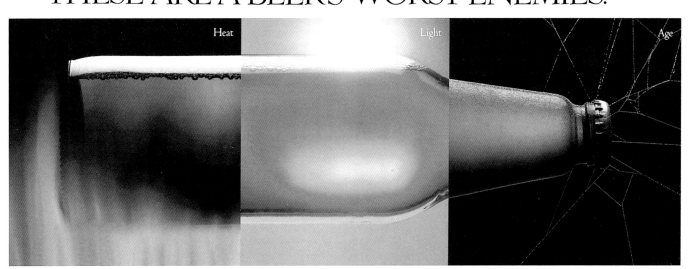

Heat Light Age

A Fresh Approach To Beer.

TRADE COLOR 1 PAGE OR SPREAD: SINGLE

514
ART DIRECTOR
Gary Goldsmith
WRITER
Ty Montague
PHOTOGRAPHER
Steve Hellerstein
CLIENT
Everlast
AGENCY
Goldsmith/Jeffrey, New York

515
ART DIRECTOR
Noam Murro
WRITER
Dean Hacohen
CLIENT
Crain's New York Business
AGENCY
Goldsmith/Jeffrey, New York

516
ART DIRECTOR
Noam Murro
WRITER
Dean Hacohen
CLIENT
Crain's New York Business
AGENCY
Goldsmith/Jeffrey, New York

517
ART DIRECTORS
Henriette Lienke
Noam Murro
WRITER
Dean Hacohen
CLIENT
Crain's New York Business
AGENCY
Goldsmith/Jeffrey, New York

Who needs to see another celebrity jock?

514

What you don't know won't hurt you? The less you know the better? Ignorance is bliss? Good luck in New York.

CRAIN'S
NEW YORK BUSINESS
Call (800) 487-4871 to subscribe.

515

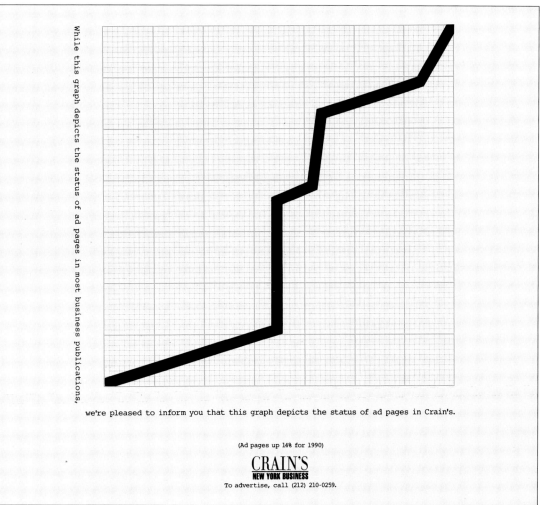

LAST YEAR, READERS OF US AND *Rolling Stone* PLUGGED IN OVER 3.8 BILLION DOLLARS WORTH OF NEW TV'S, VCR'S AND STEREOS. OUR SINCEREST APOLOGIES TO THE NEIGHBORS.

Advertisers who buy matching space in both US and Rolling Stone will receive a 15% discount in both publications. For details call Mr. Leslie Zeifman at (212) 484-1495.

518

THE INSTANT FILM DESIGNED FOR FAMILY PICNICS, BIRTHDAY PARTIES AND BAR MITZVAHS IS NOW BEING USED FOR, WELL, WE'RE NOT EXACTLY SURE WHAT IT'S BEING USED FOR.

Polaroid

519

WE SPEND 30 YEARS DESIGNING THE CRISPEST, CLEAREST, SHARPEST INSTANT COLOR FILM IN THE WORLD. AND THIS, THIS IS THE THANKS WE GET.

Polaroid

520

Millions are unemployed, Fascists are overrunning Europe, and *The Times* of London is using a new typeface.

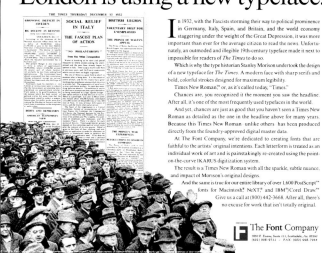

In 1932, with the Fascists storming their way to political prominence in Germany, Italy, Spain, and Britain, and the world economy staggering under the weight of the Great Depression, it was more important than ever for the average citizen to read the news. Unfortunately, an outmoded and illegible 19th-century typeface made it next to impossible for readers of *The Times* to do so.

Which is why the type historian Stanley Morison undertook the design of a new typeface for *The Times.* A modern face with sharp serifs and bold, colorful strokes designed for maximum legibility.

Times New Roman™ or, as it's called today, "Times."

Chances are, you recognized it the moment you saw the headline. After all, it's one of the most frequently used typefaces in the world.

And yet, chances are just as good that you haven't seen a Times New Roman as detailed as the one in the headline above for many years. Because this Times New Roman–unlike others–has been produced directly from the foundry-approved digital master data.

At The Font Company, we're dedicated to creating fonts that are faithful to the artists' original intentions. Each letterform is treated as an individual work of art and is painstakingly re-created using the point-on-the-curve IKARUS digitization system.

The result is a Times New Roman with all the sparkle, subtle nuance, and impact of Morison's original designs.

And the same is true for our entire library of over 1,600 PostScript™ fonts for Macintosh,® NeXT,® and IBM®/Corel Draw™

Give us a call at (800) 442-3668. After all, there's no excuse for work that isn't totally original.

F The Font Company
7850 E. Evans, Suite 111, Scottsdale, Az. 85260 (602) 998-9711 · FAX (602) 998-7964

9 out of 10 kids will walk through it. The 10th will sit in it.

Keds® premium True Wash® leather sneakers are tough enough to stand up to your washer and dryer. They come in lots of styles, colors, widths and are extra cushiony. So they're great for walking. Or sitting, as the case may be.

They Feel Good.®

The $19 Cassette. (And It's Blank.)

Nineteen dollars?!? For that kind of money, it would have to be the best tape in the world.

It is.

Ask *Audio* magazine. After subjecting 88 different audio cassettes to every test imaginable, they found that the TDK MA-XG is not only the best of any metal tape. But the best of *any* tape. Period.

We were happy, but not surprised. A few years ago, we gave our engineers a clean sheet of paper and a mission: to create the world's best tape, with money as no object.

They came to us with a tape so advanced, we had to give it a manufacturer's suggested retail price of $19.

If you took the TDK MA-XG apart (you'd need some patience for this: it's held together by enough screws to open a hardware store), you'd see why.

It's not just a tape. It's a tank.

The shell is an unprecedented super-rigid five-piece

mechanism with an inner layer of fiberglass-reinforced plastic for strength, and a non-rigid plastic outer layer to reduce resonance. A precisely balanced system of internal sound stabilizer weights serves to reduce modulation noise even further.

All this technology surrounds a unique dual-layer metal tape that provides the highest output and lowest noise of any tape in TDK's history.

In other words, the ultimate digital-ready tape.

If you still can't bring yourself to spend the better part of your paycheck on the MA-XG, we have good news. Everything we've learned from making the best tape

More music. Less noise. Audio magazine rates the MA-XG the best tape in the world.

in the world has gone into our less outrageously priced tapes. Which may explain why *Audio* magazine's tests also revealed TDK not only has the best normal bias tape, but the best high bias tape (in lowest noise and widest dynamic range) in the world.

If, after hearing all this, you're still not using TDK, we have just one question.

How many times do you have to be told before you listen?

TDK
As Serious As You Can Get.

TRADE COLOR 1 PAGE OR
SPREAD: SINGLE

524
ART DIRECTOR
Margaret McGovern
WRITER
Paul Silverman
PHOTOGRAPHERS
John Holt Studios
Stock
CLIENT
The Timberland Company
AGENCY
Mullen/Wenham, MA

525
ART DIRECTOR
Margaret McGovern
WRITER
Paul Silverman
PHOTOGRAPHERS
John Holt Studios
Stock
CLIENT
The Timberland Company
AGENCY
Mullen/Wenham, MA

526
ART DIRECTORS
Jennifer Solow
Dallas Itzen
WRITERS
Dallas Itzen
Jennifer Solow
PHOTOGRAPHER
Cailor/Resnick
CLIENT
Owens-Corning Fiberglas
AGENCY
Ogilvy & Mather/New York

527
ART DIRECTOR
Jim Dearing
WRITER
Alan Bertozzi
PHOTOGRAPHER
Viktor Budnik
CLIENT
Microsoft Corporation
AGENCY
Ogilvy & Mather/Los Angeles

528
ART DIRECTOR
Rich Buceta
WRITER
Zak Mroueh
PHOTOGRAPHER
Michael Kohn
CLIENT
Nikon Canada
AGENCY
SMW Advertising/Toronto

529
ART DIRECTOR
Dean Stefanides
WRITER
Larry Hampel
PHOTOGRAPHER
Hing Norton
CLIENT
Fedders
AGENCY
Scali McCabe Sloves/
New York

524

525

526

The only thing we intentionally left out of the new Microsoft Flight Simulator.

With the new Microsoft® Flight Simulator® for the Apple® Macintosh® you get the thrill and excitement of real flight, without the heartburn.

You can take off for the wild blue yonder in a Cessna, a Lear Jet, a sailplane and even a Sopwith Camel. Or if you're really daring, test out your own theories of aerodynamics by designing and flying your own experimental aircraft.

And with more than 100 million square miles to fly over and 125 airports, you'll have lots of places to visit.

So if you want to know more about the new Microsoft Flight Simulator, call us at (800) 541-1261, Department T26. We'll feed you the information right over the phone.

The new Flight Simulator offers colorful 3-D graphics for more realism.

Microsoft
Making it all make sense™

527

The Nikon F-401x.
So Simple, You'll Actually Use It.

ODDLY ENOUGH, IT SEEMS A LOT OF

Why work weekends? Let two simple dials make your life easier.

SLR owners use their cameras for collecting dust. But if they had the incredible F-401x, they'd be collecting memories instead. That's because Nikon's innovative Optics and design engineering have, once again, put the world's greatest pictures within your reach. This time with an SLR so easy-to-use, you'll actually enjoy using it. Once-in-a-lifetime moments won't be spoiled by poor focusing, under exposure, bad lighting, or complicated controls. The F-401x's Predictive Autofocus won't allow it. Neither will Nikon's exclusive Matrix Metering.

The F-401x enables you to capture special moments like this with professional quality.

Get everybody in the picture with the Built-In wide angle Flash.

Or the Built-in Matrix Balanced Fill-Flash for that matter. You see, features like these will ensure your photographs are nothing less than spectacular. Yet despite all its fancy gizmos (if we had

Advanced features let you concentrate on your subject rather than your camera.

space, we'd tell you about them all), the F-401x doesn't require any fancy set up. No matter how complex the scene,

We thought of everything, so you don't have to.

you still just point-and-shoot. It's that simple. In other words, not knowing what an F-Stop is won't stop you from taking your camera out more often. And, most important of all, won't stop you from taking *great pictures* more often.

Nikon
We take the world's greatest pictures®

528

(ACTUAL SIZE)   (ALMOST ACTUAL SOUND)

INTRODUCING MICRO SONIC AIR CONDITIONERS. QUITE POSSIBLY THE SMALLEST, QUIETEST AIR CONDITIONERS EVER MADE. **MICRO SONIC**

529

The first time you see a window in The Architect Series," you fall in love on looks alone. In this particular case, that's not so dangerous.

Because underneath its classic architectural beauty is a window designed for a harsh and practical world.

No matter which style you choose, windows in The Architect

THE ARCHITECT SERIES. THE WINDOW WHOSE DESIGN WAS INFLUENCED BY CHRISTOPHER WREN, FRANK LLOYD WRIGHT AND OPEC.

Series can be made with Low E2 argon gas-filled insulated glass for state-of-the-art thermal efficiency. In a world where you often have to choose between form and function, isn't it nice to have it all?

For more information and the location of The Pella Window Store" nearest you, call 1-800-524-3700.

BUILT TO IMPOSSIBLY HIGH STANDARDS. OUR OWN."

Free full-color Pella idea booklet. Call 1-800-524-3700 toll free or mail in this coupon.

Name_____
Address_____
City_____ State_____
Zip_____ Phone_____
I plan to: ☐ build ☐ remodel ☐ replace
Mail to: Pella Windows and Doors, Dept. C00811, 100 Main Street, Pella, IA 50219. Also available throughout Canada, Japan and Australia. Coupon answered in 24 hours. © 1991 Rolscreen Company

530

THESE VENTS SUCK.

THESE VENTS BLOW.

OUR LATEST TECHNOLOGICAL ACHIEVEMENT.

Using Bernoulli's theorem of fluid dynamics, the SC incorporates Supercool Engineering" to force air over and around your head while you ride. Cool, huh?

If there's one thing that cyclists tell us they could use more of it's ventilation. To that end we've created the new Hammerhead SC." We made the external vents 300% bigger, added internal channels that suck air up over your temples, replaced the full headband with spot padding to let even more air in, and overall, streamlined the shape to make it more aerodynamic. The new Hammerhead SC. Because while a ride on a sunny day is nice, a heatstroke isn't.

For more information on Giro helmets, call 800-969-GIRO. The three-panel design is a trademark of Giro Sport Design, Inc., 1992.

531

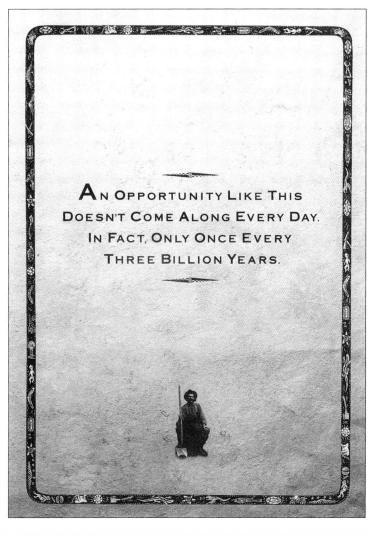

AN OPPORTUNITY LIKE THIS
DOESN'T COME ALONG EVERY DAY.
IN FACT, ONLY ONCE EVERY
THREE BILLION YEARS.

OUR MINE OFFICIALLY
OPENED FOR BUSINESS IN 1985,
THOUGH ACTUAL PRODUCTION BEGAN
AROUND 3,000,000,000 B.C.

It would still be a few billion years before dinosaurs roused about.

Yet 150 miles beneath the earth's surface, literally under the weight of the world, the first Champagne Diamonds™ were forming.

Pinned beneath a cataclysm of searing heat and tumultuous pressure, tightly bonded carbon atoms began to distort.

And then, something strange and wonderful happened.

Color.

A wash of rich golden color began to permeate the diamonds. And as adjoining carbon atoms feverishly stirred within the diamond's crystal lattice, the color magnified in intensity and warmth.

What resulted was a colorful array of natural, breathtaking Champagne Diamonds.

Still, the job of uncovering these rare treasures from their subterranean cradle would prove a task well beyond the primitive tools of the day.

In fact, it would require unequivocal acts of nature. Volcanic eruptions. Continental shifts. Fierce mood swings of an intemperate world. And finally, after a three-billion-year discord, these brilliant stones surfaced in the Kimberley Plateau of Western Australia, waiting for the next significant moment in an existence that for ages lay shrouded in secrecy.

That moment came in 1985, when we at the Argyle mine began making our precious Champagne Diamonds available to the rest of the world.

Some think, not a minute too soon.

1900 A.D.
500 A.D.
12 A.D.
47 B.C.
510 B.C.
1300 B.C.
8,000 B.C.
12,000 B.C.
25,000 B.C.
93,000 B.C.
4 Million B.C.
20 Million B.C.
900 Million B.C.
3 Billion B.C.

Cheap dog foods help keep the game population up for the rest of us.

533

Finally, French Ticklers For Fish.

534

While he was in the air,

4 babies were born,

527,004 couples kissed,

4,007,200 dogs barked,

the Snake River Canyon

grew smaller,

a cold front moved

through Mexico City,

all men named Bob sneezed,

2 crop circles were formed,

kangaroos worried,

and 29 feet 4 1/2 inches of Tokyo

blurred beneath his feet.

Nike and Foot Locker congratulate Mike Powell on breaking the world record in the long jump.

Actual Size

OK, so your child has already been blessed with your eyes, your nose, and your dazzling smile. How about tossing in a pair of Michael Jordan's shoes? Nike Baby Jordans look just like the real thing, but with the fit, flexibility and comfort every infant needs. With these shoes, you're going to have one bouncing baby on your hands.

WHAT CONSUMERS LOOK FOR IN A CROSS-TRAINING SHOE.

WHAT YOU LOOK FOR IN A CROSS-TRAINING SHOE.

←

Chiat Day Mojo liked my freelance work so much they fired me twice to get it.

In less than twelve months I've been fired twice by Chiat Day Mojo. And then been asked to freelance for them the very next day.

So if you'd like to see why Chiat Day Mojo thinks my freelance work is so good they'd fire me twice to get it, please telephone or fax me at the number below.

If nothing else, it makes a great story.

STEVE DODDS (02) 360 9064

538

Most animals are born able to walk. Others need help.

The soles on our Bounce· shoes have a soft middle for protection and a firm edge for stability. Some babies won't stand for anything less.  Hush Puppies· for Kids

© 1991 Hush Puppies· shoes is a registered trademark of Wolverine World Wide, Inc., Rockford, MI 49351

539

THE AD CLUB FIRED US, THE NAZIS SENT US HATE MAIL, AND YOU PROBABLY DON'T KNOW WE EXIST.

MAYBE IT'S TIME YOU DID. CALL DARYL TRAVIS
FOR A COPY OF OUR AGENCY'S LATEST REEL.

ARIAN, LOWE & TRAVIS
611 WEST CHICAGO AVENUE CHICAGO ILLINOIS 60622 (312) 243-3500

LAST MONTH WE GOT FOUR MINUTES ON NETWORK NEWS, AND A WOMAN IN OHIO SAID WE SHOULD HAVE OUR ARMS CHOPPED OFF.

SEE WHAT ALL THE FUSS IS ABOUT. CALL DARYL TRAVIS
FOR A COPY OF OUR AGENCY'S LATEST REEL.

ARIAN, LOWE & TRAVIS
611 WEST CHICAGO AVENUE CHICAGO ILLINOIS 60622 (312) 243-3500

AFTER SEEING OUR WORK THE BURNETT CREATIVE REVIEW BOARD DUBBED IT "PROVOCATIVE, OUTRAGEOUS, AND NASTY." WE MUST BE DOING SOMETHING RIGHT.

SEE FOR YOURSELF. CALL DARYL TRAVIS FOR
A COPY OF OUR AGENCY'S LATEST REEL.

ARIAN, LOWE & TRAVIS
611 WEST CHICAGO AVENUE CHICAGO ILLINOIS 60622 (312) 243-3500

THE LIGHTING EQUIPMENT
BRUCE BYERS USES IS SO OLD, IT ONLY
WORKS TWICE A DAY.

BRUCE BYERS PHOTOGRAPHY • 11 WEST 20TH ST • N.Y., N.Y. 10011 • 212-242-5846

APPARENTLY, BRUCE BYERS
CAN SAY "MAKE LOVE TO THE CAMERA"
IN AT LEAST SIX LANGUAGES.

BYERS PHOTOGRAPHY • 11 WEST 20TH ST • N.Y., N.Y. 10011 • 212-242-5846

THINK OF BRUCE BYERS
AS THE STUDIO PHOTOGRAPHER WITH A
20 TRILLION SQUARE FOOT STUDIO.

BRUCE BYERS • 11 WEST 20TH ST • NEW YORK, N.Y. 10011 • 212-242-5846

Trade Any Size B/W or Color: Campaign

543
ART DIRECTOR
John Doyle
WRITER
Ernie Schenck
PHOTOGRAPHER
Nadav Kander
CLIENT
The Dunham Company
AGENCY
Doyle Advertising/Boston

544
ART DIRECTOR
John Doyle
WRITER
Ernie Schenck
PHOTOGRAPHER
Nadav Kander
CLIENT
The Dunham Company
AGENCY
Doyle Advertising/Boston

There are feet that don't care what a Bentley Turbo is going for these days. There are feet that could care less what the Nasdaq is doing. There are feet that wouldn't know an espresso machine if they tripped over one. Dunham. They get the job done.

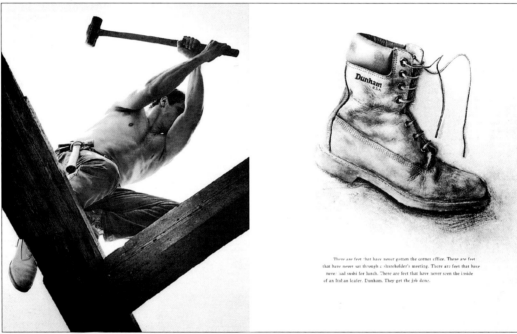

There are feet that have never gotten the corner office. There are feet that have never sat through a shareholder's meeting. There are feet that have never had sushi for lunch. There are feet that have never seen the inside of an Italian loafer. Dunham. They get the job done.

There are feet that will never meet the gas pedal of a Range Rover. There are feet that will never see a condo in Aspen. There are feet that will never winter in Palm Springs or Palm Beach or Palm anywhere. Dunham. They get the job done.

There are feet that have never seen a David Hockney. There are feet that have never walked the streets of Cannes. There are feet unfamiliar with lobster at midnight. Dunham. They get the job done.

There are feet that have never gotten the corner office. There are feet that have never sat through a shareholder's meeting. There are feet that have never had sushi for lunch. There are feet that have never seen the inside of an Italian loafer. Dunham. They get the job done.

There are feet that will never climb in the Andes. There are feet that will never photograph gorillas in the Congo. There are feet that will never catalog the native lichens of Northern Wales. Dunham. They get the job done.

544

TRADE ANY SIZE B/W OR COLOR: CAMPAIGN

545
ART DIRECTOR
Mark Johnson
WRITER
Bill Miller
ILLUSTRATOR
Michael David Brown
PHOTOGRAPHER
Kerry Peterson
CLIENT
Rolling Stone Magazine
AGENCY
*Fallon McElligott/
Minneapolis*

546
ART DIRECTOR
Bob Barrie
WRITER
Mike Gibbs
PHOTOGRAPHER
Rick Dublin
CLIENT
Continental Bank
AGENCY
*Fallon McElligott/
Minneapolis*

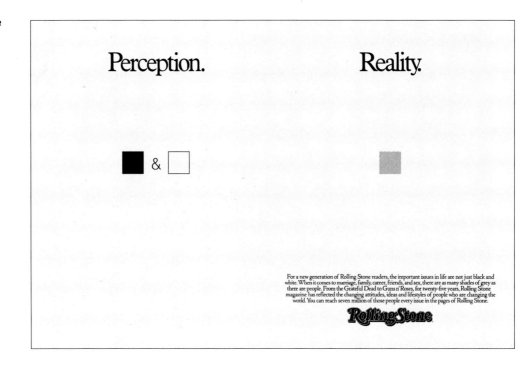

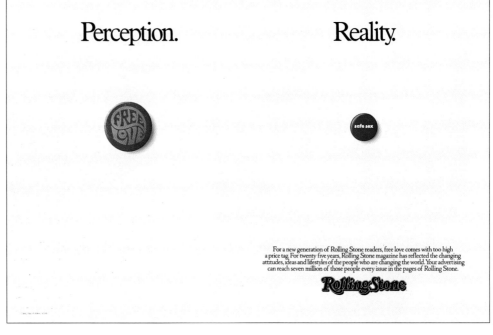

Shortly after mating, the black widow spider eats her mate.
Sadly, many business banking relationships don't last much longer.

Business banking, it seems, has long taken its cues from nature. You know, survival of the fittest. Natural selection. Cannibalism. Okay, wait a second. That last thing may occur in nature, but at Continental Bank, we prefer to share the future with our partners for a period of time that's just a wee bit shy of forever.

You see, more and more businesses are finding themselves caught in tangled webs of quick-fix financial quick fixes. Which all too often leads to a string of somewhat confusing, short-term, transaction-oriented acquaintances. The financial equal of a love-'em-and-leave-'em attitude.

So, to untangle the complexity of business banking, we encourage our customers to feed off us. (A sort of financial symbiosis, if you will.) And with all we have to offer, they're in for a long, satisfying feast. Through extensive consultation, our customers benefit from Continental's expertise in all aspects of financial risk management, corporate finance and treasury management. Through custom-designed solutions, our customers' problems meet with a quick, clean kill.

Through it all, moreover, our customers deal with relationship managers who are above reacting on instincts alone. Instead, they study, analyze and view each problem from every conceivable angle before using the tools needed to get the job done.

Perhaps that's why Continental can boast of so many steady client relationships that span not years, but decades. Chances are, the life span of your business banking relationships can last as long, too. Just call Continental Bank at (312) 828-5799. Who knows, to start things off, maybe we could have you...uh...that is...join you for lunch.

Burp.

Continental Bank
A new approach to business.

At Continental Bank, our business focus allows us to go beyond standard solutions.

It's likely you have very little use for cookie-cutter banking products. (Unless, of course, you happen to be in the cookie-cutter business.)

Why, then, do banks continue to insist on stamping out the same financial solutions for different financial problems? Well, while the exact answer escapes us, we have been sharp enough to take advantage of the situation and carve a new niche of our own: business banking pure and simple.

 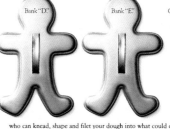

Bank "A." Bank "B." Bank "C." Bank "D." Bank "E." Continental Bank.

These days, Continental bankers are even more inventive. Our products even more sophisticated. And our ability to respond quickly, yet ever-so-prudently, has become polished and honed. Even to the point where we can draw on any of the expertise available throughout the bank without compromising expedience.

For example, we might couple lines of credit with commodity risk management solutions to create predictable revenue streams in volatile markets. Or we could combine asset securitization with a structured finance program to enhance your balance sheet. Or, we just might come up with something totally new for your business.

Which brings us to you. Will you settle for simple, run-of-the-mill, cookie-cutter answers and perhaps subsequently have your head bitten off? Or will you work with someone like Continental who can knead, shape and filet your dough into what could only be termed a financial thing of beauty? If the latter appeals to you, call a Continental banker at (312) 828-5799. You'll find that when it comes to customized business banking, we are indeed a cut above the rest.

Continental Bank
A new approach to business.

Capital is getting harder and harder to find.
(Perhaps you're just looking in the wrong places.)

Investors are cautious. Lenders are wary. Expectations are high. And you're on your hands and knees. Obviously, trying to secure capital these days can be a rather humbling experience.

Unless, of course, you know just where to look. Like we do at Continental Bank. To find capital we'll scrutinize options like commercial paper. Medium-term notes. Private placements. Acquisition financing. Asset securitization. Lease advisory. Mezzanine financing. Private equity. Mergers and acquisition advisory. Structured debt. And even, dare we say, a few couches.

Now look here: At a time when other banks were retrenching, external capital raised for Continental customers was up by more than 40%. In fact, we raised 15 billion dollars worth of capital last year.

Rest assured, the fine-toothed comb we use to find capital is finer than most. (Continental Bank has always stood tall as a recognized leader in the placement of straight debt, asset-backed commercial paper and securitized products.)

You see, over the last five years, we've found and hired a number of veteran corporate finance specialists, veritable capital sniffing bloodhounds, that make our expertise all the more expert. Ironically, many are former employees from some of our major competitors.

Working hand in hand with experienced relationship managers, they form a braintrust to assess each client's business. Then, and only then, can they create the customized capital financing tools each particular situation calls for. Finally, to bring things full circle as it were, we can quickly locate the investors needed to complete our deals. Our capabilities are worldwide and we're quite adept at arranging transactions with terms of overnight to 30 years or longer. If you need to find some capital before you completely lose it, contact your Continental relationship manager today. We'll leave no stone - or cushion - unturned.

Continental Bank
A new approach to business.

Most animals are born able to walk. Others need help.

The soles on our Bounce® shoes have a soft middle for protection and a firm edge for stability. Some babies won't stand for anything less.

Hush Puppies® for Kids

© 1991. Hush Puppies® shoes is a registered trademark of Wolverine World Wide, Inc., Rockford, MI 49351.

The only way these shoes could hurt is if kids put them on the wrong feet.

The soles of our Bounce® shoes not only have a firm edge for stability, but a soft center portion which absorbs shock and protects a child's tender heel. Available for toddlers in three comfortable styles. Use only as directed.

Hush Puppies® for Kids

© 1990. Hush Puppies® shoes is a registered trademark of Wolverine World Wide, Inc., Rockford, MI 49351.

Our new washable shoes. (They're under there, somewhere.)

If a kid gets these specially treated suede and canvas shoes dirty, you can throw them right in the washer. The shoes, that is. In five durable styles for spring and fall.

Hush Puppies® for Kids

© 1991. Hush Puppies® shoes is a registered trademark of Wolverine World Wide, Inc., Rockford, MI 49351.

547

IF YOU WANT A GREAT MODEL
CALL ELEANOR MOORE.

IF YOU WANT A ROCKET SCIENTIST
CALL NASA.

Eleanor Moore Agency, Inc.
612-827-3823

JUST HOW CONVINCING ARE OUR
CHARACTER ACTORS?

HERE'S FRANK PLAYING
A WOMAN ON THE BEACH.

Eleanor Moore Agency, Inc.
612-827-3823

THEY'VE WORKED WITH
ALL THE BIGGIES.

THEY DELIVER LINES
BRILLIANTLY.

JUST DON'T ASK THEM
WHO THE PRESIDENT IS.

Eleanor Moore Agency, Inc.
612-827-3823

TRADE ANY SIZE B/W OR
COLOR: CAMPAIGN

549
ART DIRECTOR
Bob Brihn
WRITER
Phil Hanft
PHOTOGRAPHER
Rick Dublin
CLIENT
Time, Inc.
AGENCY
Fallon McElligott/
Minneapolis

550
ART DIRECTOR
Gary Goldsmith
WRITER
Dean Hacohen
CLIENT
US Magazine
AGENCY
Goldsmith/Jeffrey, New York

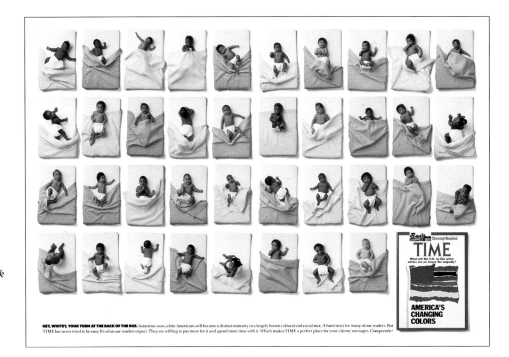

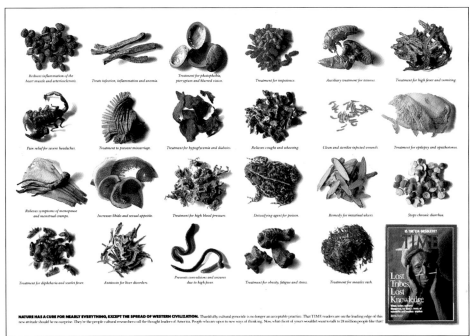

No. *Come on.* No. *Please.* No. *What's wrong?* Nothing. *Then come on.* No. *It'll be great.* No. *I know you want to.* No I don't. *Yes, you do.* No. *Well, I do.* Please stop it. *I know you'll like it.* No. *Come on.* I said no. *Do you love me?* I don't know. *I love you.* Please don't. *Why not?* I just don't want to. *I bought you dinner, didn't I?* Please stop. *Come on, just this once.* No. *But I need it.* Don't. *Come on.* No. *Please.* No. *What's wrong?* Nothing. *Then come on.* No. *It'll be great.* Please stop. *I know you need it too.* Don't. *Come on.* I said no. *But I love you.* Stop. *I gotta have it.* I don't want to. *Why not?* I just don't. *Are you frigid?* No. *You gotta loosen up.* Don't. *It'll be good.* No it won't. *Please.* Don't. *But I need it.* No. *I need it bad.* Stop it. *I know you want to.* No. Don't. *Come on.* No. *Please.* No. *What's wrong?* Nothing. *Then come on.* No. *It'll be great.* Stop. *Come on.* No. *I really need it.* Stop. *You have to.* Stop. *No, you stop.* No. *Take your clothes off.* No. Shut up and do it. Now.

WHEN THE MAN OF YOUR DREAMS BECOMES YOUR WORST NIGHTMARE. Date rape is one of those cover stories that over 24 million people couldn't ignore. In fact, it ignited a national debate. It's the kind of thing TIME does. Stories that engage the reader on a more personal level by addressing issues that touch their lives. Now, can your clients really afford to miss out on reader involvement and numbers like that?

549

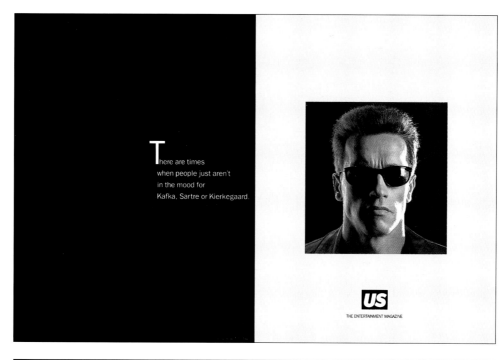

There are times
when people just aren't
in the mood for
Kafka, Sartre or Kierkegaard.

US
THE ENTERTAINMENT MAGAZINE

Some people don't care who in the
entertainment world goes out with whom
Who was seen at what party.
Wearing what. Saying what.
To whom.
For them, there's Smithsonian.

US
THE ENTERTAINMENT MAGAZINE

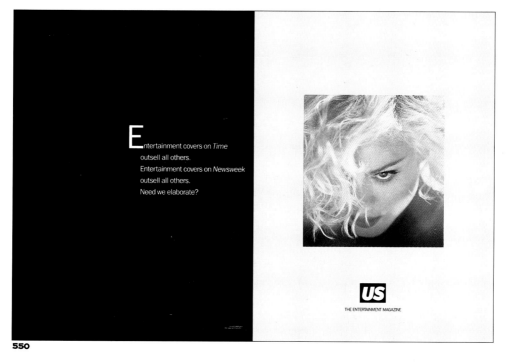

Entertainment covers on *Time*
outsell all others.
Entertainment covers on *Newsweek*
outsell all others.
Need we elaborate?

US
THE ENTERTAINMENT MAGAZINE

TRADE ANY SIZE B/W OR COLOR: CAMPAIGN

551
ART DIRECTOR
Gary Goldsmith
WRITER
Ty Montague
CLIENT
US/Rolling Stone
AGENCY
Goldsmith/Jeffrey, New York

552
ART DIRECTOR
Grant Richards
WRITER
Todd Tilford
PHOTOGRAPHER
Jim Olvera
CLIENT
Memorex
AGENCY
The Richards Group/Dallas

CONSIDERING THE NUMBER OF MOVIES READERS OF US AND Rolling Stone WENT TO LAST YEAR,
IT'S A WONDER THEY STILL HAD TIME TO SPEND OVER 3.8 BILLION ON CD'S, TAPES AND VIDEOS.

Advertisers who buy matching space in both US and Rolling Stone will receive a 15% discount in both publications. For details call Mr. Leslie Zeifman at (212) 484-1455.

LAST YEAR, THE READERS OF US AND Rolling Stone SPENT 734 MILLION DOLLARS
ON ENTERTAINMENT. AND THAT DOESN'T EVEN INCLUDE POPCORN.

Advertisers who buy matching space in both US and Rolling Stone will receive a 15% discount in both publications. For details call Mr. Leslie Zeifman at (212) 484-1455.

LAST YEAR, READERS OF US AND Rolling Stone PLUGGED IN OVER 3.8 BILLION DOLLARS WORTH
OF NEW TV'S, VCR'S AND STEREOS. OUR SINCEREST APOLOGIES TO THE NEIGHBORS.

Advertisers who buy matching space in both US and Rolling Stone will receive a 15% discount in both publications. For details call Mr. Leslie Zeifman at (212) 484-1455.

551

AFTER 20 YEARS OF PRODUCING THE BEST-SELLING CASSETTE,

WE REALIZED THAT WE DIDN'T HAVE ANYTHING TO PLAY IT ON.

PEOPLE HAVE ASKED "IS IT LIVE OR IS IT MEMOREX?" FOR 20 YEARS NOW.

OUR NEW LINE OF SPEAKERS AND SUBWOOFERS PROVIDES NO ANSWERS.

AFTER ASKING "IS IT LIVE OR IS IT MEMOREX?" FOR 20 YEARS,

WE FIGURED IT WAS ABOUT TIME FOR A NEW LINE.

553

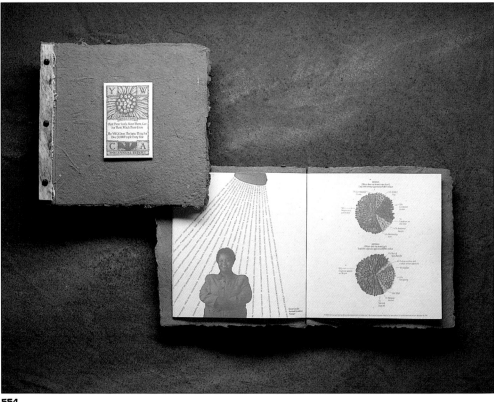

554

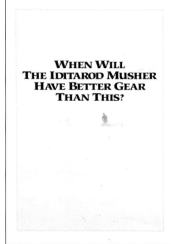

555

556

557

Kamora Coffee Liqueur
would like to introduce our
celebrity endorsers.

558

559

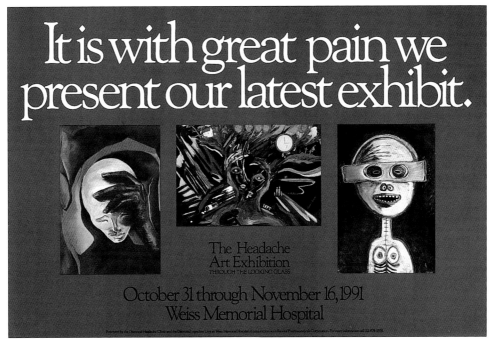

560

561

562

563
ART DIRECTOR
Bob Barrie
WRITER
Jarl Olsen
CLIENT
Jim Beam Brands
PHOTOGRAPHERS
Rick Dublin
Kerry Peterson
AGENCY
Fallon McElligott/
Minneapolis

564
ART DIRECTOR
Tom Lichtenheld
WRITER
Luke Sullivan
CLIENT
Fallon McElligott
AGENCY
Fallon McElligott/
Minneapolis

565
ART DIRECTOR
Tom Lichtenheld
WRITER
Luke Sullivan
CLIENT
Fallon McElligott
AGENCY
Fallon McElligott/
Minneapolis

566
ART DIRECTOR
Jay Deegan
WRITER
Lisa Garrone
CLIENT
Lisa Garrone

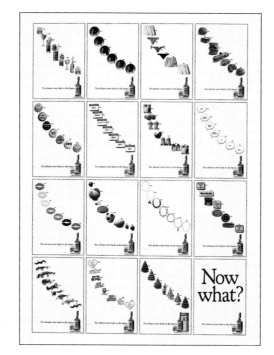

563

564

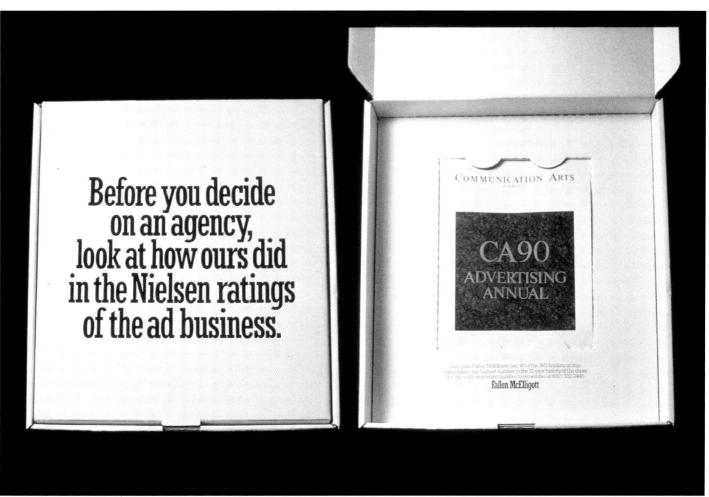

Before you decide on an agency, look at how ours did in the Nielsen ratings of the ad business.

COMMUNICATION ARTS

CA90 ADVERTISING ANNUAL

Fallon McElligott

I'M LOOKING FOR A NEW JOB
BECAUSE I'M NOT SATISFIED WITH THE WRITING
I DO AT MY CURRENT ONE.

WHILE YOU WERE OUT

For some reason, the position of Creative Assistant just hasn't fulfilled me. Oh sure, the challenge of answering three phones at once, or taking messages while filing at the same time is pretty exciting.

But you know, I was thinking of writing something else when I got into advertising. Like maybe a great ad here or there. Or an award-winning campaign or two.

So when I'm not speed-filing, I read advertising annuals. When I'm not typing other people's headlines, I write my own. And when I'm not learning to work office machinery, I take classes at the School of Visual Arts.

I'm determined to go on like this until I'm a copywriter. After all, how many phone messages receive One Show awards?

LISA GARRONE. 201·744·8233

567

568

After extensive research, we found our customers can't say a bad word about us.

Of course, most of them can't say a bad word about anything.

569

The Most Powerful Advertising Doesn't Run On TV.

It Runs On Diesel.

570

COME AND SEE HOW THE PRO'S PLAY.

THE NEW YORK ILLUSTRATORS SHOW AT MCCANN-ERICKSON

The School of Visual Concepts and McCann-Erickson/Seattle invite you to a private showing of the New York Society of Illustrators 1990-91 Traveling Exhibition on the evening of January 10, 1991, from 6 pm to 9 pm at the McCann-Erickson office, 1011 Western Avenue, Suite 600. Libations and hors d'oeuvres will be served. RSVP: 623-1560.

571

"Is this true or is it an ad, Dad?"

As this quote from "Advertising in America, The First 200 Years" painfully points out, the advertising business has a serious image problem.

It seems no one has much respect for us anymore. Consumers don't believe us. Clients have lost faith in us.

That's not the way it always was, though. There was a time in this business when client/agency relationships were based on trust.

In one another. And in advertising's ability to move people to act.

Ad agencies placed a priority on the business of making great ads over the business of making money.

And most advertising was based on well-thought-through strategies that could carry a brand for years.

It seems a lot of ad agencies have forgotten the principles upon which this business was founded, and indeed, flourished.

If you'd like to talk to one of those few ad agencies that have not, contact Chris Perry, Chairman, (216) 241-2141.

Meldrum & Fewsmith. Advertising. The way it was meant to be.

572

573

574

575

576

577

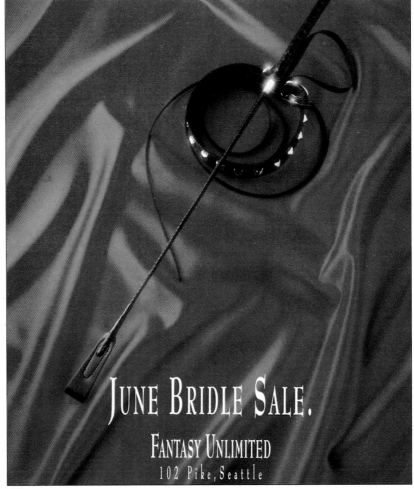

578

579

580

581

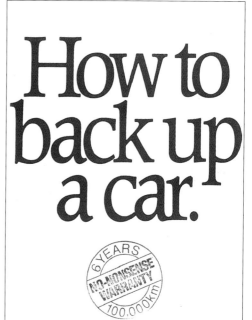

582

583
ART DIRECTOR
John Doyle
WRITER
Ernie Schenck
PHOTOGRAPHER
Nadav Kander
CLIENT
The Dunham Company
AGENCY
Doyle Advertising/Boston

584
ART DIRECTOR
Kenny Sink
WRITER
Dean Buckhorn
PHOTOGRAPHER
Larry Ketchum
CLIENT
Nautilus
AGENCY
*Earle Palmer Brown/
Bethesda*

585
ART DIRECTOR
Kenny Sink
WRITER
Jeff McElhaney
PHOTOGRAPHER
Dean Hawthorne
CLIENT
AFMC
AGENCY
*Earle Palmer Brown/
Bethesda*

586
ART DIRECTOR
Mark Johnson
WRITER
John Stingley
PHOTOGRAPHER
Jeff Zwart
CLIENT
Porsche Cars North America
AGENCY
*Fallon McElligott/
Minneapolis*

587
ART DIRECTOR
Mark Johnson
WRITER
John Stingley
PHOTOGRAPHER
Jeff Zwart
CLIENT
Porsche Cars North America
AGENCY
*Fallon McElligott/
Minneapolis*

There are feet that will never meet the gas pedal of a Range Rover. There are feet that will never see a condo in Aspen. There are feet that will never winter in Palm Springs or Palm Beach or Palm anywhere. Dunham. They get the job done.

583

WITH A LITTLE HELP THE SOUTH REALLY WILL RISE AGAIN.

NAUTILUS METAL DETECTORS

584

LEAVE IT TO NATURE TO DESIGN AN AIR FILTER THAT LOOKS AS GOOD AS IT WORKS.

Studies show that houseplants help rid the air of pollution. Another reason why plants are a breath of fresh air.

585

There are leaders and there are followers. Life is really quite simple, isn't it?

It's like children. You can't understand until you've had one.

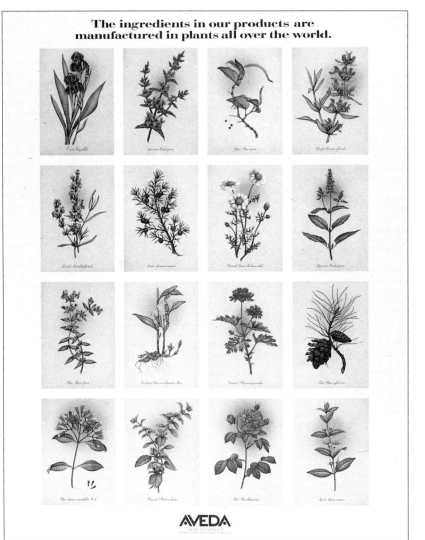

588

Official tennis ball of The Lipton Championships.

589

"YOU'RE GOING TO TAKE MY TEMPERATURE WHERE?"

It's safer and easier in the ear.

THERMOSCAN
INSTANT THERMOMETER

590

IT MADE SING SING LOOK LIKE BORA BORA.

ALCATRAZ

591

SOLITARY CONFINEMENT. BARBED WIRE FENCES. SHARK INFESTED WATERS. BRING THE IN-LAWS.

ALCATRAZ

592

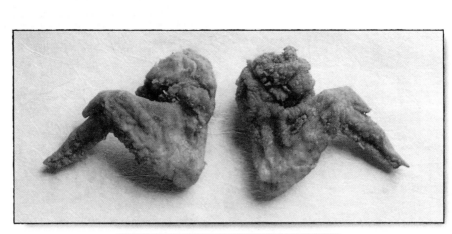

593

594

WE WROTE THE
BOOK ON FASHION.
UNFORTUNATELY,
IT ENDS WITH
CHAPTER 11.

At our going out of business sale you'll save
80% on European fashions. Au-revoir and Arrivederci.

the narragansett

595

The guy who did this poster is going as a Wieden & Kennedy art director.

596

Introduce your kids to a musician who's never made a video.

The Richmond Symphony

597

THINK OF IT AS A DO NOT DISTURB SIGN.

BERNIE'S TATTOOING

598

Even In The Bahamas, The Children Are Spoiled By Fast Food.

It's Better In The Bahamas.

599

If you were any more waterproof, you'd quack.

Why is a duck comfortable in a cold, wet marsh?

For the same reason a Timberland customer is comfortable in a cold, wet marsh.

Both creatures are protected by a total head-to-toe waterproofing system. Comfortable, sophisticated and natural. Quack if you want to read more.

The two systems have differences. But more important are the similarities, particularly the head-to-toe totality of the waterproofing. We know how bad a duck would feel if he couldn't be warm and dry above his webbed feet. So our repertoire includes outerwear as well as footwear. The only outerwear on earth that's as waterproven as a Timberland boot.

A microscope would show you why. Our outerwear and footwear have billions of pores scientifically sized to keep water out and let air in. This breathability is a special property of Gore-Tex® fabric, the miracle weave that allows perspiration to exit but won't let precipitation enter.

By selectively combining premium natural materials with Gore-Tex fabric, we've built a waterproof apparel system in which nothing is compromised. Good looks and performance are inseparable.

Let us give you the components that will allow you to put together such a system yourself.

On your feet, our rugged insulated field boots or lightweight hand-sewn shoes. Both use top Timberland leather and Gore-Tex fabric to keep your every step 100% waterproof, and both interface happily with our field coat, which uses Gore-Tex™ z-liner technology and the finest cottons to extend the same snug, dry comfort to the rest of your body.

It means this. Except for wings, no duck has better.

Timberland 🌳
*Boots, shoes, clothing,
wind, water, earth and sky.*

600

Where is it written that rain falls only on men?

We're about to let you in on a beauty secret. Timberland® leather. A kind of skin that does indeed resist moisture of the harshest form: rain, snow and sleet. Providing you head to toe protection that is so attractive you'll be proud to wear it on the sunniest days as well as the wettest.

Best of all, our leather is of such uncompromising quality that exposure to the elements only enhances its character. Proving skin truly can become more beautiful with age.

In the men's world, Timberland has long been known for a uniquely comfortable combination. The finest leathers available and the most effective waterproofing ever devised. But who is to say that rain falls only on men?

Every piece of footwear and clothing shown in this ad (as well as many that cannot be shown due to space limits) is the result of a painstaking manufacturing process involving four elements. The very best materials, hand craftsmanship, exquisite attention to detail and state-of-the-art waterproofing technology.

Each boot and shoe is crafted of leather whose every molecule has been silicone-waterproofed during the tanning process. In addition, some have inner booties of GoreTex® fabric, the miracle weave that lets perspiration exit but won't let precipitation enter.

The meticulously detailed field coat uses fine full grain leathers (more costly than split leather or suede).

A special tanning process gives our nubuck women's coats a soft, luxurious feel and flattering drape, while Timberland leather protection guarantees years of waterproof, stainproof comfort, even under extreme conditions.

Timberland. The skin you love to touch.

Timberland ®
Boots, shoes, clothing, wind, water, earth and sky.

601

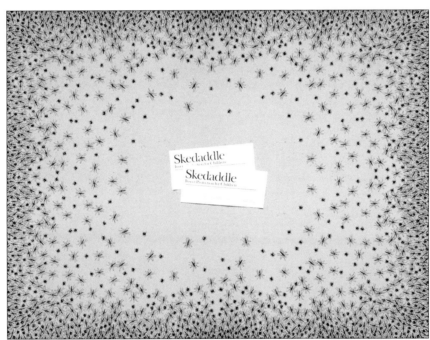

Skedaddle

602

We Are Currently Experiencing A Few Labor Pains.

Thanks for bearing with us. Once our new construction is complete, we'll all feel a whole lot better. In the meantime, watch your step.

Southampton
Memorial Hospital

603

COLLATERAL P.O.P.

604
ART DIRECTOR
Jeff Hopfer
WRITER
Todd Tilford
PHOTOGRAPHER
Richard Reens
CLIENT
Tabu Lingerie
AGENCY
The Richards Group/Dallas

605
ART DIRECTOR
Jeff Hopfer
WRITER
Todd Tilford
PHOTOGRAPHER
Richard Reens
CLIENT
Tabu Lingerie
AGENCY
The Richards Group/Dallas

606
ART DIRECTOR
Jeff Hopfer
WRITER
Todd Tilford
PHOTOGRAPHER
Richard Reens
CLIENT
Tabu Lingerie
AGENCY
The Richards Group/Dallas

607
ART DIRECTOR
Bryan Burlison
WRITER
Todd Tilford
PHOTOGRAPHER
Richard Reens
CLIENT
Harley-Davidson of Dallas
AGENCY
The Richards Group/Dallas

608
ART DIRECTOR
Brian Burke
WRITER
Eric Springer
PHOTOGRAPHER
Steve Umland
CLIENT
Fred Arbogast Company
AGENCY
*TBWA Kerlick Switzer/
St. Louis*

ACTUALLY, THERE IS ONE
KNOWN CURE FOR SNORING.

TABU
LINGERIE

604

REMEMBER, MEDICAL EXPERTS
RECOMMEND INCREASING YOUR HEARTRATE
AT LEAST THREE TIMES A WEEK.

TABU
LINGERIE

605

THE WAY TO A MAN'S HEART ISN'T
NECESSARILY THROUGH HIS STOMACH.

TABU
LINGERIE

606

NO ONE WILL EVER ACCUSE YOU OF
BEING DRESSED BY YOUR MOTHER.

HARLEY-DAVIDSON OF DALLAS 3914 S. SHILOH (214) 864-4647

607

To A Fish, This Is A Playboy Centerfold. FRED ARBOGAST

608

609

610

A Little Success Is Nice, But Don't Let It Go To Your Head.

Join us for our annual advertising awards show on December 12th at Windows On The River. And see if success can change your life, without changing your hat size.

The 1991 CSCA Awards Show

611

First, they stuff the parrot. Then it dies.

This is an infant parrot; a dead infant parrot.

It's one of the four million birds captured each year to supply European pet shops.

It was taken from its nest in Argentina by local traders.

Too young to feed itself, a mixture of maize and water was stuffed down its throat via a plastic squeezy bottle.

It choked to death and joined scores of other young birds in the trash can.

Its death was unremarkable. Three-quarters of the wild birds captured for the pet shop trade never make it into a cage.

They die in their thousands at every stage of their journey.

Recently the RSPCA commissioned the Environmental Investigation Agency (EIA) to prepare a report on the trade in wild and exotic birds.

Their findings reveal a trade that is as cruel as it is unnecessary.

In Senegal, they commonly use nets to trap the birds.

A decoy bird, its wing-tips hacked off with a machete, is left to flutter helplessly by the net. Its presence attracts the next cash crop.

Cynical dealers in Argentina are known to push a hot wire down a parrot's throat to puncture its gullet.

The bird will die a slow and painful death, but not before its new owner becomes attached to it and ready to buy a replacement.

What can you do?

The RSPCA and the EIA want a complete ban on the wild bird trade.

It's a sadistic business that's making some people very rich. (A pair of Hyacinth Macaws, for example, can sell for £25,000 in Europe.)

It is also making some people very angry.

Brazil, Bolivia and Paraguay have banned the trade in wild birds.

110 countries have signed a convention to limit the trade in endangered species.

But these initiatives aren't enough. Nothing less than a total ban will be effective.

Ruthless dealers find it easy to avoid the restrictions and licensing schemes.

We need to put our case to the European Commissioner for the Environment and we need your assistance.

Ring 0800 400 478 and we will send you a free action pack that shows you how to help in this campaign.

Do it soon.

If ever our feathered friends needed friendship, it's now.

ENVIRONMENTAL INVESTIGATION AGENCY   RSPCA

Ban the trade, save the birds.

612

WE'RE NOT ASKING FOR AN ARM AND A LEG.

ORGAN DONOR
In the hope that I help others live, I hereby make this anatomical gift, to take effect upon my death. My wishes are indicated on the back.

All we need is for you to sign an organ donor card. To get one, just call us at 599-7630.

Organ Donor Center of Hawaii

613

FINALLY, A PUBLIC SERVICE AD THAT'S NOT ASKING YOU TO DONATE MONEY.

ORGAN DONOR
In the hope that I help others live, I hereby make this anatomical gift, to take effect upon my death. My wishes are indicated on the back.

All we're asking is that you sign an organ donor card. To get one, call 599-7630. It's worth more than any amount of money.
Organ Donor Center of Hawaii

614

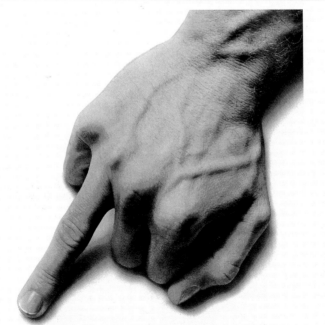

1. With your ring finger extended, rest your hand on a flat surface.
2. Press your hand down firmly.
3. Now try to lift your ring finger.
4. That's what it feels like to be paralyzed.
5. Now lift your whole hand and write a check.
6. That's what it feels like to give someone hope.

At the Miami Project, some of our scientists have proven what many thought impossible – adult human nerve cells *can* regenerate. Others are learning to repair nerve fibers that have lost their insulation at the point of injury. Your donation will bring us even closer to a cure. It all comes down to 500,000 Americans who can't move. Depending on the millions of us who can.

The Miami Project To Cure Paralysis
Send your tax-deductible contribution to: The Nick and Marc Buoniconti Fund, 1600 NW 10th Ave., R-48, Miami, FL 33136

615

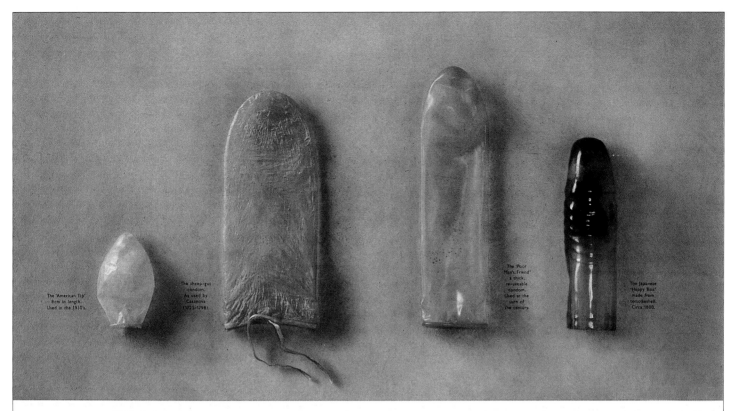

SEX HASN'T CHANGED MUCH OVER THE YEARS. FORTUNATELY CONDOMS HAVE.

There's nothing new about having to take precautions when making love. In the past, people contracting gonorrhoea risked becoming sterile. Before penicillin was invented, syphilis could kill. Nowadays of course, we have to protect ourselves from HIV.

Fortunately, modern condoms are stronger and safer than ever before. They're also a lot more sensitive. So if the world's greatest lover made do with sheep gut, surely you can use a condom.

HEALTH EDUCATION AUTHORITY

FOR MORE INFORMATION OR ADVICE ABOUT AIDS OR HIV PHONE THE FREE NATIONAL AIDS HELPLINE ON 0800 567 123. IT'S OPEN 24 HOURS A DAY AND IS COMPLETELY CONFIDENTIAL

Warning:
In
Minnesota
They Shoot
Drunk
Drivers.

In this state, if you're stopped for drunk driving you can be videotaped, providing evidence that can be used against you. So don't drink and drive, or you'll be shot on site.

MADD.

PUBLIC SERVICE NEWSPAPER OR MAGAZINE: SINGLE

618
ART DIRECTOR
Mark Robinson
WRITER
Mark Tweddell
PHOTOGRAPHER
John Claridge
CLIENT
The Royal British Legion
AGENCY
*Delaney Fletcher Slaymaker
Delaney & Bozell/London*

619
ART DIRECTOR
Mark Robinson
WRITER
Mark Tweddell
PHOTOGRAPHER
John Claridge
CLIENT
The Royal British Legion
AGENCY
*Delaney Fletcher Slaymaker
Delaney & Bozell/London*

620
ART DIRECTOR
Ty Harper
WRITER
Rob Schapiro
PHOTOGRAPH
Stock
CLIENT
Noah's Friends
AGENCY
*Earle Palmer Brown/
Richmond*

621
ART DIRECTORS
*Paul Asao
Lynne Scrimgeour*
WRITERS
*Dean Buckhorn
Sharyn Panagides*
PHOTOGRAPHER
Claude Vasquez
CLIENT
Goodwill
AGENCY
*Earle Palmer Brown/
Bethesda*

622
ART DIRECTORS
*Paul Asao
Lynn Scrimgeour*
WRITERS
*Dean Buckhorn
Sharyn Panagides*
PHOTOGRAPHER
Claude Vasquez
CLIENT
Goodwill
AGENCY
*Earle Palmer Brown/
Bethesda*

623
ART DIRECTOR
Dean Hanson
WRITER
Doug de Grood
PHOTOGRAPHER
Buck Holzemer
CLIENT
Children's Defense Fund
AGENCY
*Fallon McElligott/
Minneapolis*

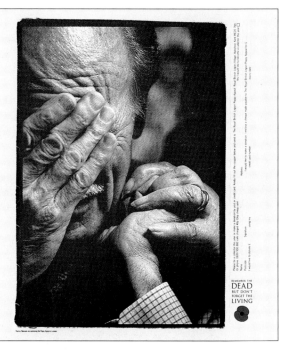
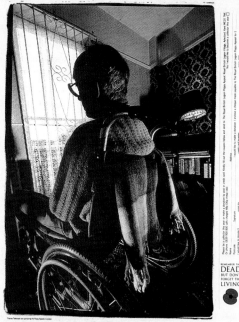

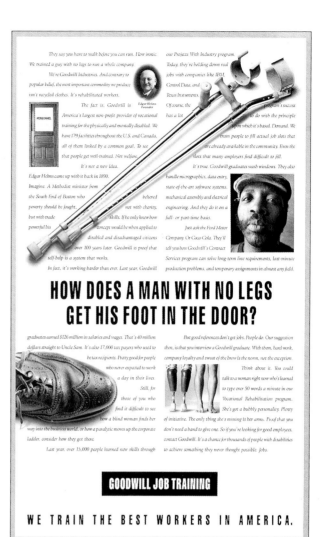

624

625

MORE FATHERS RUN AWAY FROM HOME THAN KIDS DO.

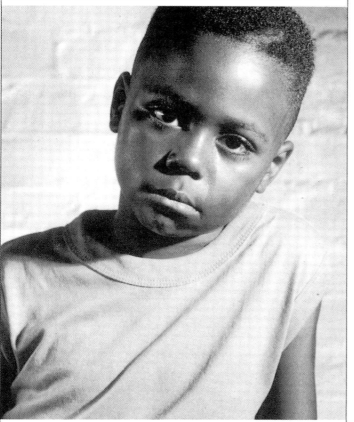

Families In Crisis. Children At Risk. The Hungry And Homeless. AIDS Crisis Fund. Health And Rehabilitation. The Elderly.

THE UNITED WAY OF METROPOLITAN ATLANTA.

626

On Tuesday, Bill Jackson died.

On Wednesday, he saved Lisa Kelly's life.

On August 28, 1990, Bill Jackson was tragically killed in an automobile accident. Several hours later, Lisa Kelly had an operation that saved her life—a liver transplant.

But what really saved Lisa's life was a decision that Bill Jackson had made and discussed with his family before his accident—the decision to become an organ donor.

Being a donor is easy. And although it won't increase your chance of dying, it just may increase someone else's chance to live.

For information about organ donation, call the New York Regional Transplant Program at 1-800-GIFT4NY.

NYCLT

NEW YORK CENTER FOR LIVER TRANSPLANTATION, INC.

627

DON'T TAKE YOUR TEETH FOR GRANTED.

628

GET PULLED OVER FOR DRUNK DRIVING AND YOU'D BETTER BE LOADED.

if the results of the test are positive, the violators can end up losing their licenses, and spend 24 hours in jail for a first time offense.

Attorney fees:	$4,500.00
Fines:	$850.00
Court fees:	$450.00
Drug and Alcohol evaluation:	$75.00
Alcohol and drug information school:	$100.00
Insurance:	$1,500.00
Alcohol and drug treatment:	$2,500.00
Lost wages:	$1,000.00
Towing:	$150.00
License reinstatement:	$50.00
TOTAL:	$11,275.00*

*Estimated cost for first time offense.

For about $10 you can ride home safely in a taxicab. You'll not only be saving yourself $11,265.00, you could also be saving someone's life.

MADD
Mothers Against Drunk Driving

629

Read this page.
Then you'll know as much
about drugs as the
average twelve year old.

**Partnership for a
Drug-Free America**

630

Introduce your nine
year old to drugs.

Nine years old isn't too young for kids to learn about drugs. The question is, who will teach them?
Show your kids this ad. Tell them about the dangers. Let them see what drugs and drug paraphernalia look like. Because if you don't, someone else will. **Partnership for a Drug-Free America**

HOW WOULD YOU LIKE IT IF SOME BOZO IN A 5000 POUND WHEELCHAIR PARKED RIGHT IN YOUR DRIVEWAY?

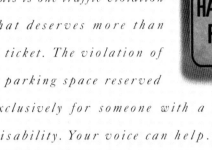

This is one traffic violation that deserves more than a ticket. The violation of a parking space reserved exclusively for someone with a disability. Your voice can help.

UNITED CEREBRAL PALSY NEEDS YOUR HELP NOW. 800-872-5827.

632

Could The Price Of Oil Be Any Higher?

The thick, dark sludge deposits its victims on shore. Black Necked Grebes, Great Crested Grebes, Socotra Cormorants, Caspian Terns.

Covered with oil, unable to swim or even stay afloat, the birds, among thousands overcome by the oil, struggle against all odds to stay alive.

Unfortunately, the scene is repeated over and over along Saudi Arabia's blackened coastline, where millions of native and migrating birds encounter the unexpected devastation of the Gulf.

Since the war's first oil spill, a team of rescue experts, veterinarians and volunteers have been working around the clock to save birds, turtles and marine animals.

In light of the destruction to the environment, it's an enormous task. But we're making progress. With your contribution we could do more. Every dollar helps us bring vets, water and food to the war's animal victims.

Please send the largest tax deductible contribution you can to WSPA, PO Box 190, Boston, MA 02130. Or call (617) 522-7000.

And help keep our oceans and wildlife alive.

World Society for the Protection of Animals

Thirty Years of Disaster Relief

633

Imagine forgetting the beginning of this sentence by the time you reach the end.

¶ At first, recent memories fade. Eventually, victims of Alzheimer's disease lose the ability to care for themselves. ¶ But they're not forgotten, thanks to the Alzheimer's Association of Puget Sound. We support and educate patients and families. Encourage favorable public policies. And contribute to research. ¶ Please call 1-800-848-7097 to find out how you can help. We're counting on you to remember. For those who can't.

ALZHEIMER'S
Someone to Stand By You.

The Alzheimer's Association of Puget Sound is a chapter of the national Alzheimer's Disease and Related Disorders Association, Inc. ©1991

634

PUBLIC SERVICE
NEWSPAPER OR
MAGAZINE: CAMPAIGN

635
ART DIRECTOR
Mark Robinson
WRITER
Mark Tweddell
PHOTOGRAPHER
John Claridge
CLIENT
The Royal British Legion
AGENCY
*Delaney Fletcher Slaymaker
Delaney & Bozell/London*

PUBLIC SERVICE:
OUTDOOR

636
ART DIRECTOR
Chris Hooper
WRITER
Scott Vincent
PHOTOGRAPHER
Steven Raber
CLIENT
United Way
AGENCY
Chiat/Day/Mojo, Venice

637
ART DIRECTOR
Share Reeves
WRITER
Helen Cho
PHOTOGRAPH
Library of Congress
CLIENT
The Feminist Majority
AGENCY
*Cho/Reeves Advertising,
Santa Monica*

638
ART DIRECTOR
Mark Freeman
WRITER
Kevin Endres
PHOTOGRAPHER
David Bailey
CLIENT
*Rape & Sexual Abuse Center
of Nashville*
AGENCY
*Earle Palmer Brown/
Nashville*

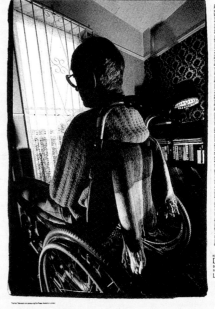

50 YEARS ON THERE ARE STILL PRISONERS OF WAR

RICHARD WENT OFF TO WAR IN 1950. HIS WIFE IS STILL WAITING FOR HIM TO RETURN

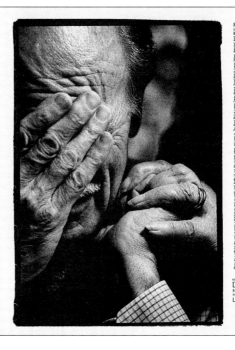

YOU CAN'T GO ANYWHERE IN VENICE WITHOUT SOMEBODY HITTING YOU UP FOR MONEY.

Pledge a day's salary to the United Way and Chiat/Day/Mojo will give you an extra vacation day. Because there are a lot of people out there who could use your help. And you could probably use the day off.

GIVE A DAY'S PAY. GET A DAY OFF.

636

IN THEIR EXPERT OPINION YOU DON'T NEED AN ABORTION.

If you don't make the call, they'll make it for you. Speak out for reproductive rights.

THE FEMINIST MAJORITY 213-651-0495

637

THERE'S A REASON SOME SEXUAL ABUSE VICTIMS DON'T REPORT THE CRIME.

They can't. And too often, children who can, don't. They're afraid of what might happen to a friend or family member. The Rape and Sexual Abuse Center of Nashville helps these children and their families. But we need people to volunteer. To help us treat, educate and prevent sexual abuse in our community. Call 259-9055. **RSAC**

638

639
ART DIRECTORS
Jeff Duncan
Jeff Olsen
WRITER
Bryan DeYoung
PHOTOGRAPH
United Way
CLIENT
United Way
AGENCY
Evans/Salt Lake

640
ART DIRECTOR
Dean Hanson
WRITER
Doug de Grood
PHOTOGRAPHER
Buck Holzemer
CLIENT
Children's Defense Fund
AGENCY
Fallon McElligott/
Minneapolis

641
ART DIRECTOR
Iain Allan
WRITER
Matthew Miller
PHOTOGRAPHER
Victor Albrow
CLIENT
The Scottish Office
Information Directorate
AGENCY
Faulds Advertising/
Edinburgh

642
ART DIRECTOR
Dom Farrell
WRITER
George Goetz
PHOTOGRAPHERS
Bruce Davidson
Magnum Photos
CLIENT
Good Samaritan Hospice
AGENCY
Ingalls Quinn & Johnson/
Boston

643
ART DIRECTOR
John Walker
WRITER
Jo Marshall
PHOTOGRAPHER
Rick Dublin
CLIENT
Model Cities Health Center
AGENCY
LaMaster Farmer Et Al/
Minneapolis

644
ART DIRECTOR
Jerry Torchia
WRITER
Tripp Westbrook
ILLUSTRATOR
Albrecht Durer
CLIENT
Amnesty International
AGENCY
The Martin Agency/
Richmond

IF WE CAN WALK PAST THIS, WHERE EXACTLY ARE WE GOING?

639

IF YOU REALLY WANT TO SEE HOW FAST HE CAN RUN, TELL HIM YOU'RE PREGNANT.

Become pregnant too soon and your whole life can get off track.

THE CHILDREN'S DEFENSE FUND.

640

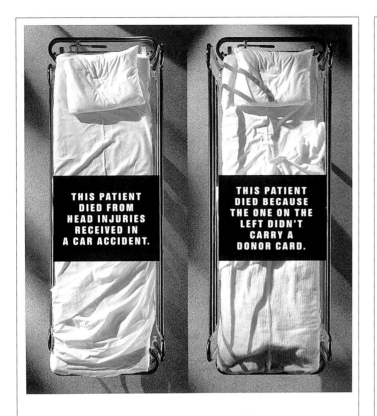

THIS PATIENT DIED FROM HEAD INJURIES RECEIVED IN A CAR ACCIDENT.

THIS PATIENT DIED BECAUSE THE ONE ON THE LEFT DIDN'T CARRY A DONOR CARD.

Donor Card
I would like to help someone to live after my death.

Please ask for your card here.

641

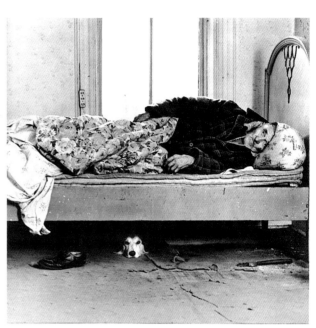

Nobody's visiting Charlie this weekend. Gee, Alzheimer's really does make people forget.

The Good Samaritan Hospice. Call 566-6242 to volunteer.

642

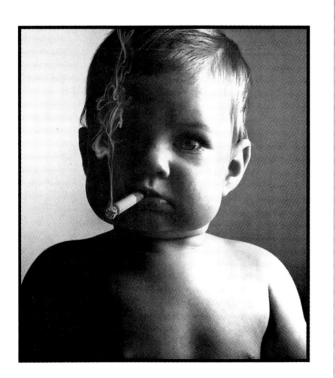

SMOKE WHEN YOU'RE PREGNANT, AND YOUR BABY SMOKES WITH YOU.

SMOKING CAN HAVE A VERY DANGEROUS EFFECT ON YOUR UNBORN CHILD. OUR FOCUS PROGRAM CAN BE HEALTHY FOR BOTH OF YOU.

MODEL CITIES HEALTH CENTER
Call 222-6029. We'll help you quit.

643

MAYBE THE DEATH PENALTY SHOULD HAVE BEEN ELIMINATED A LONG TIME AGO.

Every time the state kills it affects each one of us. Let's stop it. Call Amnesty International USA if you'd like to know how to help. **AMNESTY INTERNATIONAL USA.1-800-5SAMNESTY**

644

645
ART DIRECTOR
Jerry Torchia
WRITER
Tripp Westbrook
PHOTOGRAPH
Bettman Archives
CLIENT
Amnesty International
AGENCY
*The Martin Agency/
Richmond*

646
ART DIRECTOR
Ted Page
WRITER
Ted Page
CLIENT
*The Massachusetts Coalition
for the Homeless*
AGENCY
*Polaroid Visual
Communications*

647
ART DIRECTOR
Bernie Hogya
WRITER
Steve Saari
CLIENT
American Cancer Society
AGENCY
*Saari/Hogya Worldwide,
Sayreville, NJ*

648
ART DIRECTORS
*Peter Cohen
Leslie Sweet*
WRITERS
*Leslie Sweet
Peter Cohen*
CLIENT
Coalition for the Homeless
AGENCY
*StreetSmart Advertising/
New York*

649
ART DIRECTOR
Peter Cohen
WRITER
Amy Borkowsky
CLIENT
Coalition for the Homeless
AGENCY
*StreetSmart Advertising/
New York*

650
ART DIRECTOR
*Miriam Lisco
Katie O'Shea
Michael Stearns*
WRITER
Kevin Burrus
PHOTOGRAPHER
Harald Sund
CLIENT
A&A Printing
AGENCY
Walsh & Associates/Seattle

**ALL THOSE IN FAVOR OF THE
DEATH PENALTY, RAISE YOUR HAND.**

As we see it, the United States is in with some pretty unseemly company. Isn't it time we took a firm
stand against the death penalty? To find out what you can do, call us. **AMNESTY INTERNATIONAL USA, 1-800-55AMNESTY**

645

646

647

648

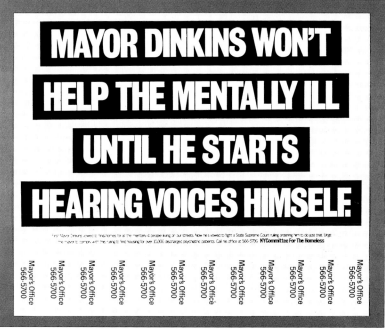

649

IMAGINE HAVING TO IMAGINE IT.

650

651
ART DIRECTOR
Kevin Kearns
WRITER
Jay Nelson
PHOTOGRAPHER
Marcus Halevi
AGENCY PRODUCER
Nancy Jordan
PRODUCTION COMPANIES
Editel
Sound Techniques
CLIENT
Free Romania Foundation
AGENCY
Arnold Fortuna Lane/Boston

652
ART DIRECTOR
Mark Robinson
WRITER
Mark Tweddell
AGENCY PRODUCER
Ruth Howard
PRODUCTION COMPANY
*The Boys Own Picture
Company*
DIRECTOR
Roger Lyons
CLIENT
The Royal British Legion
AGENCY
*Delaney Fletcher Slaymaker
Delaney & Bozell/London*

653
ART DIRECTOR
Sally Wagner
WRITER
Christopher Wilson
AGENCY PRODUCER
Anne Swarts
PRODUCTION COMPANY
Northwest Teleproductions
DIRECTOR
Brian Smith
CLIENT
*American Humane
Association*
AGENCY
Martin Williams/Minneapolis

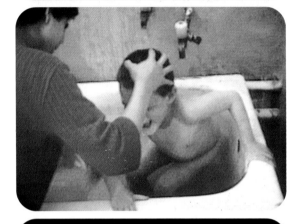

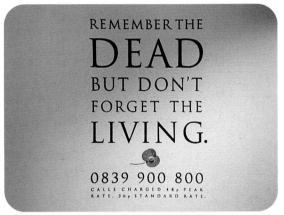

651
SUPER: IN ROMANIA, A LOT OF KIDS DON'T LIKE TO TAKE BATHS.
SUPER: THEY CRY WHEN THEY HAVE TO GO TO BED.
SUPER: THEY HATE BEING PUT IN A PLAYPEN.
ANNCR: There are thousands of unwanted children condemned to deficient institutions in Romania. The Free Romania Foundation is their only hope. Please help. Or even adopt. And give them back their childhood.
SUPER: FREE ROMANIA FOUNDATION. 617-876-3378.

652
(SFX: DEEP BREATH)
(SFX: MARCHING, A SERGEANT SHOUTING ORDERS TO HIS REGIMENT, MIX TO SCHOOLMASTER SHOUTING ORDERS, CHILDREN RUNNING)
(SFX: MACHINE GUN, MIX TO ROAD DRILL)
(SFX: SOUND OF DIVE BOMBER, MIX TO JET ENGINES OF 747)
ANNCR: Some people will never forget fighting for their country. Please don't forget them on Poppy Day. If you'd like to make a donation . . .
(SFX: COIN FALLING INTO TIN)
ANNCR: . . . call this number now.
SUPER: REMEMBER THE DEAD, BUT DON'T FORGET THE LIVING.
SUPER: BRITISH LEGION POPPY APPEAL.

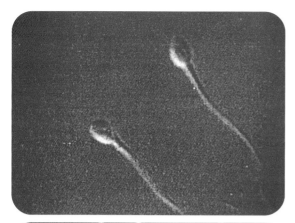

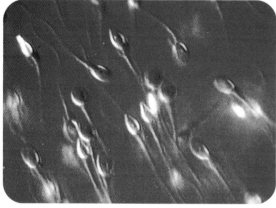

653

(SFX: CACOPHONY OF BARKING, HOWLING, YAPPING DOGS)

(MUSIC: "TRAVELOGUE")

(SFX: BARKING, HOWLING AND YAPPING CONTINUE)

SUPER: HELP CURB OVERPOPULATION. NEUTER
  YOUR DOG.

SUPER: AMERICAN HUMANE ASSOCIATION.
  1-800-227-4645.

Radio Finalists

654
WRITER
Doug Adkins
AGENCY PRODUCER
Adrienne Cummins
CLIENT
Valvoline Instant Oil Change
AGENCY
Bozell/Minneapolis

655
WRITER
April Winchell
AGENCY PRODUCER
Diane Hill
CLIENT
Nissan Motor Corporation
AGENCY
Chiat/Day/Mojo, Venice

656
WRITERS
Dion Hughes
John Crawford
Ian Hadley
Michael O'Brien
AGENCY PRODUCER
Lisa Horowitz
PRODUCTION COMPANY
John Crawford Radio
CLIENT
*NYNEX Information
Resources*
AGENCY
Chiat/Day/Mojo, New York

657
WRITER
Steve Dodds
AGENCY PRODUCER
Steve Dodds
PRODUCTION COMPANY
Street Remley Studios
CLIENT
Toyota
AGENCY
Chiat/Day/Mojo, Sydney

658
WRITER
Dion Hughes
AGENCY PRODUCER
Lisa Horowitz
PRODUCTION COMPANY
John Crawford Radio
CLIENT
*NYNEX Information
Resources*
AGENCY
Chiat/Day/Mojo, New York

659
WRITER
Steve Callen
AGENCY PRODUCER
Steve Callen
PRODUCTION COMPANY
Rivett's Recording Studio
CLIENT
Adelaide Zoo/Peat Soil
AGENCY
Young & Rubicam/Adelaide

660
WRITER
Mark Fenske
AGENCY PRODUCER
Shirley Radebaugh
PRODUCTION COMPANY
MacDonald Recording
CLIENT
Nike i.e.
AGENCY
Cole & Weber/Seattle

661
WRITER
Robert Woodiwiss
AGENCY PRODUCERS
Robert Woodiwiss
Michel Keidel
PRODUCTION COMPANY
Sound Images
CLIENT
WSTR-TV
AGENCY
Dektas & Eger/Cincinnati

654

CHARLES (BRITISH ACCENT): To demonstrate what a car with old antifreeze feels like in the winter, Nigel here is going to leap, naked, into this pool of ice water.

NIGEL (BRITISH ACCENT): No I'm not.

CHARLES: What do you mean, you're not?

NIGEL: I'm not going to jump into any pool naked.

CHARLES: Well then, keep your clothes on. But jump!

NIGEL: I won't.

CHARLES: What do you mean, you won't?

NIGEL: I've changed my mind. It's a stupid idea.

CHARLES: It's not! After I say all that business about how 'til March 7, you can get $7 off a Prestone cooling system flush at Valvoline Rapid Oil Change just by mentioning the extremely funny ad with the two witty British fellows, you jump into the water and emerge screaming terribly. It's funny, see.

NIGEL: Not for me it's not.

CHARLES: Then just throw something in to make a splash and scream as if you've jumped.

NIGEL: Throw in what?

CHARLES: I don' know, anything! Let's just get on with it while I'm still feeling funny! Here we go! To demonstrate what a car feels like . . . hey!

(SFX: HUGE SPLASH)

CHARLES: Aaaaaaaaaaaaaargh!!!

NIGEL: Oh fine! Then you steal my one line!

ANNCR: 'Til March 7, save $7 on a Prestone cooling system flush and get your Prestone $100 radiator guarantee. Valvoline Rapid Oil Change. People who know what they're doing.

656

MIKE: As they say, you can find anything in the NYNEX Yellow Pages and today under the heading "Genealogist," we found Dr. Ian Hadley.

IAN: Michael.

MIKE: Dr. Hadley, you trace family roots, I guess.

IAN: Yes, as a matter of fact, we traced your family roots as far back as the Battle of Hastings.

MIKE: What? That sounds pretty interesting.

IAN: Your ancestor Ethelred The Fleet, led the retreat from the battle to the forest.

MIKE: Probably just regrouping, I guess . . .

IAN: Spent the next 100 years living as vassals and indentured servants and they reappear interestingly at the time of the American Revolution.

MIKE: Oh.

IAN: Where the battle of Lexington was fought on their land.

MIKE: Minute men fighting for the young country . . .

IAN: Well, no, they had left a week earlier to disappear into the forest.

MIKE: To fight on as guerrillas.

IAN: Uh, that's speculation.

MIKE: I guess this is the family coat of arms?

IAN: Yes, this is your family crest.

MIKE: The mighty oak tree.

IAN: And if you look carefully you'll notice a small man cowering behind the mighty oak tree.

MIKE: Well, if it's out there, it's in your NYNEX Yellow Pages. We can't vouch for the accuracy of all these services . . .

IAN: And the Latin inscription, *Festina Ad Silva.*

MIKE: Why would anyone need another?

IAN: Or, "Make haste to the woods."

655

MAN: If I had a Nissan 4x4, I'd go to the mountains.

(SFX: HARMONICA, TRUCK SOUNDS)

MAN: Pack up my gear and drive those 153 horses over some nice, long, winding roads, find a spot in the middle of nowhere, and just go fishing. Yeah.

(SFX: BIRDS, RUSHING WATER)

MAN: Just sitting around . . . baiting the hook . . . not catching anything . . .

(SFX: CRICKETS, OWLS)

MAN: Wind up eating some stew that you mix with pond water and heat up in a can while you stir it with a stick. No. Okay, wait. If I had a Nissan 4x4, I'd go four-wheeling.

(SFX: ROCK GUITAR)

MAN: Yeah. Power that 180 foot-pounds of torque over some nasty trails, get out and climb a rock so high I can see everything. Trees . . . rivers . . . snakes . . . which are probably poisonous of course . . .

(SFX: SUBURBIA)

MAN: There's a lot to be said for just parking it in the driveway.

GIRL: Hey Steve, nice truck.

MAN: Yeah. That works.

ANNCR: The Nissan SE King Cab 4x4. The most powerful import brand V6 engine in its class.

Nissan. Built for the human race.

657

ENGINEER: Um, before we start, the advertising guys have had to take out a few things for legal reasons.

ANNCR: Well, read them out and I'll cross them off the script.

ENGINEER: Okay, delete line one where it says that the hot Toyota Corolla SX is faster than an F18 fighter.

ANNCR: Yeah, I wondered about that.

ENGINEER: Then the next bit, where it says this Hot Hatch is so hot it comes with a free date with Kim Basinger.

ANNCR: Shame, big selling point I thought.

ENGINEER: And they had a few problems with promising that the Corolla Hot Hatch can seat a whole football team in comfort.

ANNCR: Right.

ENGINEER: Then that whole section from "By Royal Command" to "You'll get an infectious disease if you don't buy one."

ANNCR: Including, um, "Guaranteed to increase your IQ by twenty points"?

ENGINEER: Just a sec', I'll check.

CLIENT: No, lose it.

ANNCR: It's lost.

ENGINEER: Right, what does that leave us with.

ANNCR: The 100kW Toyota Corolla SX. This Hot Hatch is really hot . . .

ENGINEER: Nothing else.

ANNCR: Just the usual music at the end.

(MUSIC: *OH WHAT A FEELING, COROLLA*)

658

MIKE: You know, it really is true you can find anything in the NYNEX Yellow Pages. For instance, today under "Entertainers," I found The Amazing Mr. Andy, and your ad says you're a man of a thousand voices.

ANDY (WEIRD VOICE): That's right, Michael.

MIKE: Hey, that's really funny. Who's it supposed to be?

ANDY: Whaddya mean? This is my real voice.

MIKE: Oh . . . uhhh . . . I'm sorry. I just thought . . .

ANDY: You find this amusing, pencil neck? You think I'm a clown.

MIKE: No, really, I ahhh . . .

ANDY (NORMAL VOICE): Just kidding, that was my big tough guy voice. Had you going though, didn't I?

MIKE: I, well, uh, what other voices do you do?

ANDY: Listen to this.

(SFX: THROAT CLEARING)

ANDY (BROOKLYN VOICE): Morning Andy. Can I borrow your hedge clippers?

MIKE: Gee, I can't seem to place that one.

ANDY: That's Jacky, my next door neighbor. You don't know Jacky?

MIKE: No.

ANDY: Aw, that's a shame. Sounds exactly like him.

MIKE: Oh, I bet it does.

ANDY: Okay, get this.

(SFX: THROAT CLEARING)

ANDY (SOUNDING LIKE MIKE): They say you can find anything in the NYNEX Yellow Pages.

MIKE: Now that would be . . .

ANDY: That's you, Mike. Yeah, even called your girlfriend this morning and proposed to her. I used your voice.

MIKE: What?

ANDY (AS MIKE): Well, there it is, more proof that if it's out there, it's in your NYNEX Yellow Pages.

MIKE: Boy, you have an awesome power, Andy. I hope you use it responsibly.

ANDY (AS MIKE): Why would anyone need another?

MIKE: Oooh, spooky.

659

(SFX: ANIMAL/JUNGLE SOUNDS THROUGHOUT)

ZOO KEEPER (SINGING):
Okay okay listen up all you animals
I'm the man they call your keeper
The one with all the demure
But I'm much, much more than just the
Guy that feeds ya
I also collect all your manure.

Every monkey, every peacock, every armadillo
Can help everybody's garden grow
If you keep on pooin'
Just keep doin'
That Zoo Poo that you do so well.

Green fingered gardeners try every potion
So let's give them our best
Let's all pass a motion
To keep on pooin'
All keep doin'
That Zoo Poo that you do so well.

$5.95's not too much to ask
When so much good can come
From such a simple task
It don't come from the horse's mouth
But if he's facin' north, it comes from the south.

So if you want a better zoo
And I know you all do
And gardeners too, really love our Zoo Poo.

Every poo, you do, helps you and the zoo
And everything'll be swell
Do that Zoo Poo that you do so well
Do that Zoo Poo that you do so well.

660

ANNCR: The woman who is leaving me wants to know what I've got to say about it. I say, you know, there's a road, Baby, and you gotta walk it. And it's a hard road. And it goes a long way. If I were you I'd get a pair of *i.e.* shoes with Nike Tensile Air to wear on that road cause you're going to need the cushioning of Tensile Air soles protecting your feet from the constant pounding of the cold cruel earth. 'Cause that road's gonna come to a fork where you gotta choose between two directions. And no matter which one you choose, Baby, it's still gonna be a road so you better have Nike Tensile Air soles to protect you from gravity's mean reality. 'Cause the goal is a place inside where you've never been. And every step is a new destination. . . . It wasn't much but it seemed more honorable than: BABYBABYBABYPLEASEDON'TLEAVEME. OHGOD. OHBABYPLEASE. Which is what I was thinking. *i.e.* casual shoes with Nike Tensile Air. From the ankles down, at least, life is solved.

661

ANNCR: John Wayne . . . as you've never seen him before. Well, okay, to be honest, maybe once before. Twice, tops. So, actually, it's . . . John Wayne . . . as you've rarely seen him before. Starring in "The Quiet Man." Though I'm also compelled to admit that he's really not quiet throughout the movie. Oh, there are moments when he's quiet, like while other actors are speaking or when he's fighting, but, truthfully, I'd have to say it's . . . John Wayne as you've rarely seen him before and with more or less the standard amount of dialogue starring in "The Quiet Man," tonight at 9:00 on Star 64. All part of Star 64's "Five Days of The Duke," which, strictly speaking, since this is Tuesday, and even though we did broadcast a Duke movie yesterday, we're technically down to four days. So . . . John Wayne as you've rarely seen him before and with more or less the standard amount of dialogue starring in "The Quiet Man," tonight at 9:00 on Star 64. All part of Star 64's remaining "Four Days of The Duke." See you tonight. Which is an entertainment cliché, not meant to be taken literally since it's impossible to see you through your TV set which is a receiver not a transmitter . . .

Consumer Radio:
Single

662
WRITER
Doug de Grood
AGENCY PRODUCER
Kathy Jydstrup
CLIENT
Star Tribune
AGENCY
Fallon McElligott/
Minneapolis

663
WRITER
Doug de Grood
AGENCY PRODUCER
Kathy Jydstrup
CLIENT
Star Tribune
AGENCY
Fallon McElligott/
Minneapolis

664
WRITER
Mike Lescarbeau
AGENCY PRODUCER
Kathy Jydstrup
CLIENT
Star Tribune
AGENCY
Fallon McElligott/
Minneapolis

665
WRITER
Daniel Russ
AGENCY PRODUCER
Greg Lane
CLIENT
Quality Bakers of America
AGENCY
GSD&M/Austin

666
WRITER
Dean Hacohen
CLIENT
Crain's New York Business
AGENCY
Goldsmith/Jeffrey, New York

667
WRITER
Dean Hacohen
CLIENT
Crain's New York Business
AGENCY
Goldsmith/Jeffrey, New York

668
WRITER
Jay Williams
AGENCY PRODUCER
Greg Roman
CLIENT
Museum of Fine Arts
AGENCY
Hill Holliday Connors
Cosmopulos/Boston

669
WRITER
John Barry
AGENCY PRODUCER
John Zwierzko
CLIENT
Southland Corporation/
7-Eleven
AGENCY
J. Walter Thompson/Chicago

662
(SFX: WRINKLING NEWSPAPER)
MAN 1: Rd Vlvt sfa mtchng chr.
MAN 2: Red velvet sofa with matching chair.
(SFX: WRINKLING NEWSPAPER)
MAN 1: Chmng aptmnt nat wdwrk.
MAN 2: Charming apartment with lots of
natural woodwork.
(SFX: WRINKLING NEWSPAPER)
MAN 1: Cckr Spnl exc bldlns. Shts.
MAN 2: Cocker Spaniel with excellent bloodlines.
Has shots.
ANNCR: The classifieds have a language all their own.
(SFX: WRINKLING NEWSPAPER)
MAN 1: Cnsle TV.
MAN 2: Console television.
ANNCR: And now it's easier than ever to learn.
Introducing the new Star Tribune classifieds, with an
improved design that makes it easier to read and
find things. Pick up a copy and start becoming more
fluent today.
(SFX: WRINKLING NEWSPAPER)
MAN 1: Bmpr pl tble. Brly usd.
MAN 2: Bumper pool table. Barely used.
ANNCR: The Star Tribune. Newspaper of the
Twin Cities.

664
ANNCR 1: I'm going to read you a description of a
house. Large Victorian home with old world charm
and huge basement workshop, plus extra tall
doorways. So. Can you imagine it pretty well? See
if this helps.
(MUSIC: "THE MUNSTERS" THEME)
ANNCR 1: That's right, it's *that* house. You get the
point. Until you actually see a home, you really
have no clue what it's like. And that's what gave us
a great idea for the Star Tribune's Thursday Real
Estate Section. Why not have right there above
every description of a home, you guessed it: the
title of a television theme song. How's this for a
nice suburban Colonial?
(MUSIC: "MY THREE SONS" THEME)
ANNCR 1: Or this one . . .
(MUSIC: "ANDY GRIFFITH" THEME)
ANNCR 1: . . . for a house in a rural setting. And we at
the Star Tribune got really excited about this. Then
we decided it was stupid and we should just
use pictures.
ANNCR 2: See The Real Estate Picture Classifieds, a
great, if painfully obvious idea, in tomorrow's
Star Tribune.

663
ANNCR: With the new, redesigned Star Tribune
classifieds, you can save about twenty seconds of
time finding what you're looking for.
(SFX: TICK, TOCK, TICK, TOCK . . .)
ANNCR: And you didn't think twenty seconds was a very
long time. The new, easier-to-use Star
Tribune classifieds.

665
ANNCR 1 (VERY COCKNEY BRITISHER): It seems that all you
good American folks are trying a new bread called
Sunbeam Lite. What's only 40 calories a slice as
opposed to 60 calories a slice for regular bread.
Frankly, we're concerned. The average American
bloke consumes ten slices of bread a week, then that
means in one year you would eat 10,400 fewer
calories. If you have to eat 3,000 fewer calories to
lose one pound, then by the end of the year, by
switching to Sunbeam Lite, you'd have lost four
pounds. By the time most of you retire, there's
gonna be nothing left of yous. I mean you'll all be a
bunch of bones walking around in suits that don't fit
anymore and all yer football players'll look like a
bunch of scarecrows and Halloween skeletons all
clattering and clacking about and that worries us
because you were our colonies and we fell sorta like
your older brothers and you always bring yer retired
tennis players to Wimbledon and besides Sunbeam
Lite is so delicious it's hard to turn down. So come
on, try Sunbeam Lite but don't go overboard,
America. I mean we think you Yanks look good
with a little meat on your bones.
Know what I mean?
ANNCR 2: Try delicious Sunbeam Lite Bread. Great
taste. Only 40 calories.

666

ANNCR: Just off the boardwalk in Coney Island, you'll find the New York Aquarium. There, in a tank in the main lobby, swims one of the smallest, yet most vicious predators the world has ever known: the red piranha. With its razor-sharp teeth, this bloodthirsty creature can attack, decimate and devour its unknowing prey in seconds. If you are an executive in the New York area, and feel you can stay safely ahead of your competitors without the information in Crain's New York Business, we strongly suggest you come down to the aquarium at feeding time for a demonstration.

667

ANNCR: At 79th Street and Central Park West stands The American Museum of Natural History. Inside, you'll find one of the most startling sights in all of New York: The Hall of Dinosaurs. A fascinating collection of what for thousands of years were the most powerful creatures on earth. However, due to continual changes in the environment, and an inability to adapt, these creatures quickly vanished. If you are a New York executive who does not feel it is absolutely necessary to read Crain's New York Business on a regular basis, we encourage you to visit this educational exhibit without delay.

668

ANNCR: So I'm looking for something to do this weekend, something a little different something a little out of the ordinary and this friend of mine who's a little out of the ordinary says I should catch the Robert Wilson exhibition at the Museum of Fine Arts says they've got a thing called "Memory of a Revolution" it's a room you go inside and there's six chairs and you sit down and about three feet in front of you there's these prison bars that go from the floor to the ceiling and behind the bars there's a huge elephant leg that goes from the floor to the ceiling and by now my eyebrows are starting to go from the floor to the ceiling and he says that cut into the elephant leg is a tiny cell that's lit up inside and sitting on a chair in the cell is an 80 year old man dressed like Napoleon and now I'm payin' real close attention to what he's sayin' and on this old man's lap he's holding a scale model of an opera stage and on the stage is a tiny soprano dressed in red and while you're looking at this they're piping Maria Callas singing "Medea" into the room and while all this is happening the dirt floor around the elephant foot is covered with rats fake rats but made to look so real it's hard to tell the difference and I said is that the whole exhibition and he said oh, no just one piece of it and I said, "Oh yeah, I gotta see this . . . "

ANNCR: Robert Wilson's Vision. With sounds and music by Hans Peter Kuhn. At The Museum of Fine Arts, February 6 through April 21. It's a . . . different way of looking at the world. Made possible by AT&T.

669

ANNCR 1: Ed Maroney, bumble bee trainer, tells us why he loves the new Caffeine Free Diet Coke Super Big Gulps at 7-Eleven.

(SFX: BUZZING OF BEES)

ED: Well, when you're training bees, *ow,* you get real, real thirsty, but you have to stay real, real calm. *Ow,* 'cause you don't want to upset the little rascals. *Ow,* they pick up on nervous energy. *Ow,* that's why I think the new Caffeine Free Diet Coke Super Big Gulps at 7-Eleven are a good thing. You see, *ow,* now I can have as many Caffeine Free Diet Coke Super Big Gulps as I want, without havin' to worry about getting stung.

(MUSIC: A BUZZING RENDITION OF "FLIGHT OF THE BUMBLE BEE")

ANNCR 1: Well, there you have it. Many people like Ed are finding it easy to appreciate the new Caffeine Free Diet Coke Super Big Gulps only at 7-Eleven. They're perfect for those who want to quench the ultimate thirst without the caffeine.

ED: *Ow.*

ANNCR 1: Uh, Ed, I thought you said you weren't getting stung?

ED: I'm not, but I can't let the bees know that. Otherwise they'd think they weren't doing a good job. *Ow,* I'd give 'em a complex, y'know. Performance anxiety thing. *Ow.*

ANNCR 1: 7-Eleven. The sign of the times.

ANNCR 2: If you're looking for extreme ice-cold refreshment, but don't want the caffeine, get a Caffeine Free Diet Coke Super Big Gulp. Now just 69¢. For a limited time, at participating 7-Eleven stores.

670
ANNCR 1: Today in Weekend Guardian we expose . . .
(SFX: SUBMACHINE GUN)
ANNCR 2: Today in Weekend Guardian we expose the outrageous . . .
(SFX: SUBMACHINE GUN)
ANNCR 3: Today in . . .
(SFX: SUBMACHINE GUN)
ANNCR 4 (VERY QUICKLY): Today in Weekend Guardian we expose the outrageous dealings of New York's new Mafia.
There done it, don't know what all the fuss was about . . .
(SFX: SUBMACHINE GUN)
ANNCR 5: The Mafia. The Guardian. Today.

671
ANNCR 1: The Metro Museum announces a giant clearance sale on all 18th and 19th century oil paintings. We must make way for 20th century models! Huge savings on all periods, schools and genres, from impressionism to expressionism, and much . . .
(SFX: RADIO TUNING/STATIC)
ANNCR 2: The Latimer Psychiatric Group is going nuts! Announcing incredible discounts on treatment of all psychiatric conditions. How can we do this? We must be crazy!!
(SFX: RADIO TUNING/STATIC)
ANNCR 3: Lately, everybody seems to be having a sale. But who would ever have thought Honda Civics would go on sale? Incredibly, your Honda dealer is holding a clearance sale on all Honda Civics. Hey, stranger things have happened, right?
(SFX: MORE TUNING)
ANNCR 4: Announcing sizzling summer savings on all legal services. Prices slashed on all civic and criminal cases. There's never been a better time to litigate!
(SFX: TUNING/STATIC)
ANNCR 3: The Scarcely Believable Honda Civic Clearance Sale. Ends September 2 at your Northern California Honda Dealer.

672
ANNCR 1: Haven't you always wanted your own F-14 Tomcat fighter? Well due to decreasing defense expenditures there's never been a better time to buy. We have too many planes.
ANNCR 2: Announcing Mrs. Flynn's House of Pianos Blowout Sale on all classical piano lessons. Beethoven, Mozart, Brahms. Prices slashed to the bone. If after three weeks you can't play your scales, I'll give you your daddy's money back. I'm Mrs. Flynn and I guarantee it.
ANNCR 3: Lately, everybody seems to be having a sale. But who would ever have thought Honda Civics would go on sale? Incredibly, your Honda dealer is holding a clearance sale on all Honda Civics. Heck, stranger things have happened, right?
ANNCR 4: A huge 40 percent discount on all university degrees. Bachelor of Arts, Master of Arts, Doctor of Philosophy.
ANNCR 3: The Scarcely Believable Honda Civic Clearance Sale. Ends soon at your Northern California Honda Dealer.

673
(SFX: TELEPHONE RINGS)
MAN: Hello.
CALLER: Oh. I'm sorry. I was looking for another number.
MAN: 976-EDEN?
CALLER: Well . . . yeah.
MAN: You got it.
CALLER: The flyer said to ask for Eve.
MAN: Yeah, well, she's not here. I can help you.
CALLER: Oh . . . no. That's okay, I'll just . . .
MAN: Hold on, hold on. Let me get the apple.
CALLER: The apple?
MAN: You ready? Here goes . . .
(SFX: CRUNCH)
CALLER: That's . . . you're eating an apple. That's the "little bit of paradise" you advertised?
MAN: Well, that's a "little bite of paradise." The printer made a mistake.
CALLER: I'm supposed to sit here and listen to you eat an apple?
MAN: Well, it is a Washington Apple . . .
(SFX: CRUNCH)
CALLER: Look, I'm not going to pay $3 a minute just to sit here while you . . .
MAN: Nice, big, Red Delicious Washington Apple.
(SFX: CRUNCH)
CALLER: . . . eat an apple. . . . It does sound good.
MAN: It is nice and crisp, you know.
CALLER: Sounds good . . .
MAN: Kinda sweet.
CALLER: Uh-huh.
MAN: Fresh.
CALLER: I shouldn't . . . this is silly . . .
(SFX: CRUNCH)
CALLER: What are you wearing?
MAN: Well, a flannel shirt and paisley ascot.
CALLER: Oh. Describe the apple again.
MAN: Mmmm-hmmm.
ANNCR: Washington Apple.
(SFX: CRUNCH)
ANNCR: They're as good as you've heard.

674

ANNCR: Everyone knows that Vice President Dan Quayle is the butt of more political jokes than anyone else. Everyone knows that Mr. Quayle once referred to the citizens of Pago Pago as "happy campers" living in "Pogo Pogo." Everyone knows that Mr. Quayle once told school kids to, "Dedicate yourself to your family, your school and yourself." Everyone knows that Mr. Quayle once said, "What a waste it is to lose one's mind. Or not to have a mind." Everyone knows that five of the last nine presidents were vice presidents . . . right? So maybe you'd better learn more about this vice president, beginning with the Washington Post's seven-part series on Dan Quayle. For six months, David Broder and Bob Woodward followed the vice president everywhere. What they uncovered is the man behind the cartoon. What they uncovered about Mr. Quayle and his wife Marilyn will surprise you. Read the Post on Quayle, starting this Sunday, January 5. Because today's caricature could be tomorrow's president.

675

ANNCR: There is a traffic accident every second in this country. There is an injury from a traffic accident every six seconds in this country. There is a death from a traffic accident every twelve minutes in this country. If you've never been involved in an automobile accident, and you think you're somehow safe, think again. According to the national average, you're going to have roughly seven accidents in your lifetime. There's not much you can do about it. Not much, perhaps, except find out how the car you're driving performs in an accident. Find out by watching "It Happens Every Second," a special 30 minute TV program sponsored by the makers of Volvo. This show features candid interviews wth the people who build cars, people who study them, and the people who drive them, people who know what they're like in the real world, not just the show room. Check your newspaper or TV guide for listings. And in the meantime, please drive safely.

676

ANNCR: Whenever a Volvo is in a severe accident in western Sweden, after the police get called, so does a man named Hans Noreen. Noreen is head of Volvo's accident investigation team. A group of engineers and researchers whose study of over 15,000 accidents has led to dozens of safety innovations. People who've seen the violence that can be created in an automobile accident. Who've seen the tragedy. Who have also seen how the construction of an automobile can many times protect the occupants of that automobile. How crumple zones and steel reinforced passenger cages can reduce the chances of fatality, even injury. This year with a new side impact protection system of 7 and 900 series cars, their work is once again validated. The work goes on though. Volvo will continue to analyze accidents as long as we can find ways to help people survive them. Drive safely.

677

ANNCR: The air bag has become one of the most heralded advances in the car industry. But there is a man in Sweden named Hugo Mellander who believes air bags are giving people a false sense of security. Mellander is head safety engineer for Volvo. He cites Swedish statistics that show frontal impacts, the only time an air bag activates, account for just 36 percent of total collisions. What happens the other 64 percent of the time, in roll-overs, rear end and side impacts? This is what people should be asking, Mellander stresses. This is what Volvo has been answering for over 60 years with crumple zones, reinforced passenger cages and now, in 7 and 900 series cars, a side impact protection system that puts Volvo years ahead of government requirements. The air bag is a great advance, Hugo Mellander believes, but an airbag, he warns, is only as good as the car it's attached to. Drive safely.

Consumer Radio:
Single

678
WRITERS
Colin Nimick
John Trainor
AGENCY PRODUCER
Lyn Woodcraft
PRODUCTION COMPANY
Mandy Wheeler Productions
CLIENT
Imperial War Museum
AGENCY
Ogilvy & Mather/London

Consumer Radio:
Campaign

679
WRITERS
David Shane
Steve Fong
AGENCY PRODUCERS
Lisa Horowitz
David Shane
PRODUCTION COMPANY
John Crawford Radio
CLIENT
Whitney's Yogurt
AGENCY
Chiat/Day/Mojo, New York

680
WRITERS
Fred Stesney
Lori Korchek
AGENCY PRODUCER
Rob Fassino
PRODUCTION COMPANY
Reel World
CLIENT
New York Newsday
AGENCY
Margeotes Fertitta & Weiss/
New York

681
WRITER
Max Turner
AGENCY PRODUCER
Sandy Douglas
PRODUCTION COMPANY
The Voice Plant
CLIENT
McWhirters Marketplace
AGENCY
McCann-Erickson/Brisbane

682
WRITER
Sharon Holcomb
AGENCY PRODUCER
Virginia Manion
CLIENT
The Pittsburgh Opera
AGENCY
Werner Chepelsky &
Partners/Philadelphia

678
(SFX: KETTLE WHISTLING)
ANNCR 1: Funny how the smallest thing can take you back. . . . The kettle whistles and suddenly shells are coming down. I'm crawling into a hole when a shell bursts, my pal's killed. I'm hurt . . . I can't feel my legs . . . I know I won't be fit for anything in this world now. I decide to kill myself by exploding a Mills bomb. Then I remember, the medical officer saying intoxicants are fatal for the wounded. So I get my bottle of rum from my haversack and drink the lot, what better way to finish myself off. Thing was I felt merry and bright instead . . . and I decided maybe it was still worth trying to save myself.
ANNCR 2: For Henry Russell the smallest thing can be a reminder. At the Imperial War Museum we don't glorify war, we just try to give you a better idea of what it was like, through exhibits like The Trench Experience. We're open 10:00 till 6:00 everyday. Nearest tube is Lambeth North. The Imperial War Museum. Part of your family's history.

679
ELLIOT: In all honesty, we're pretty happy with our current package design here at Whitney's Yogurt, Mr. Stavros.
STEPHAN (WITH VAGUELY EUROPEAN ACCENT): Stephan.
ELLIOT: Okay, Stephan, I appreciate you bringing by these rough sketches, but . . .
STEPHAN: Rough! Not rough, they're wildly primitive, they're powerful, strong.
ELLIOT: But this one here doesn't seem to have a lid of any kind.
STEPHAN: Well it doesn't have a hat or gloves either. What of it, Mr. Picky?
ELLIOT: Uh huh. So, how would it keep the yogurt fresh then?
STEPHAN: Well I suppose it doesn't. Big deal!
ELLIOT: You see Stephan, Whitney's Yogurt is known for being creamy and fresh, you know, quality ingredients, so naturally our container is . . .
STEPHAN: Old-fashioned.
ELLIOT: Uh, wait a minute . . .
STEPHAN: Boring.
ELLIOT: Actually, we at Whitney's were the first to use a foil seal under the lid.
STEPHAN: Well, you want me to do a little dance for you?! Foil is passé. And the color, oh, please.
ELLIOT: Well, the yellow color actually helps protect the yogurt.
STEPHAN: Well, I despise it.
ELLIOT: A lot of people . . .
STEPHAN: Yellow says caution, slow down. Look, magenta! It says, "Hello, I'm young, I'm alive . . .
ELLIOT: Uh huh.
STEPHAN: I'm full of the juices of life. I'm well-groomed!"
ELLIOT: Mr. Stavros!
ANNCR: All natural Whitney's Yogurt. It tastes better, 'cause we make it better.
STEPHAN: Give me those drawings!
ELLIOT: Uh . . .
STEPHAN: You keep your emotions locked under that foil seal! Mr. Northern Climate, Ice-in-the-Veins!

680

(MUSIC: JAZZ)

ANNCR: Mind your own business. It's New York's unwritten law. A law broken by New York Newsday's columnists every day. Because sometimes, to find the truth, you have to do more than cover a story. You have to uncover it. Like Ellis Henican's subway column. He's New York's only subway reporter. Going deep into the tunnels to find out where your $1.15 disappeared to. Or Sydney Schanberg. He won a Pulitzer prize reporting the war in Cambodia. Now, he's patrolling the jungle of New York City politics. And the moral of the story usually comes from Pulitzer prize winner, Murray Kempton. Because, if it isn't fair, it isn't right. And if it isn't right, Murray writes about it. Now nobody asked them to butt in, but, in New York, speech is one of the few things that's free. That means they're entitled to their opinions. And you're entitled to their opinions, too. New York Newsday. Truth, justice, and the comics.

681

GUITARIST (SINGING):
Two hours parking is for free
Yeah, it's where I'm gonna be
McWhirters Marketplace, you see
Is open till half past. . . . five.

682

(MUSIC: DR. FALKE'S SOLO THROUGHOUT)

ANNCR: You're listening to a highly respected physician who was stranded at a costume party. Had to walk home in broad daylight dressed as a bat. And now is planning to get even.

(MUSIC: THE MELISMA PART OF FALKE'S SOLO)

ANNCR: It gets a little complicated.

(MUSIC: THE "HA, HA, HA" PART OF FALKE'S SOLO)

ANNCR: But it's all in good fun. Of course, there's only one way to tell if his practical joke comes off without a hitch. And that's to come to Die Fliedermaus March 16, 19, 22, and 24 at the Benedum. For tickets, call 281-0912.

(MUSIC: DR. FALKE REACHES A CRESCENDO)

ANNCR: And see who gets the last laugh.
The Pittsburgh Opera. Tito Capobianco, General Director.

TV Finalists

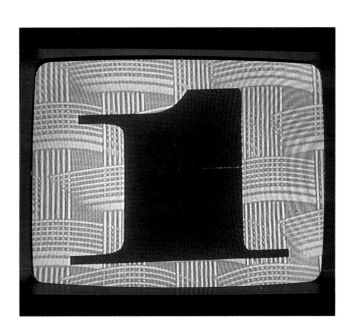

683
ART DIRECTOR
Matt Haligman
WRITERS
Kirk Citron
Jeff Atlas
AGENCY PRODUCER
Ara Haligman
PRODUCTION COMPANY
Pytka Productions
DIRECTOR
Joe Pytka
CLIENT
The Gap
AGENCY
Atlas Citron Haligman &
Bedecarre/San Francisco

684
ART DIRECTOR
Don Schneider
WRITER
Lee Garfinkel
AGENCY PRODUCER
David Frankel
Lisa Steinman
PRODUCTION COMPANY
Pytka Productions
DIRECTOR
Joe Pytka
CLIENT
Pepsi Cola
AGENCY
BBDO/New York

685
ART DIRECTOR
Ron Taylor
WRITERS
Michael Patti
Bill Bruce
Ted Sann
Al Merrin
AGENCY PRODUCER
Regina Ebel
PRODUCTION COMPANY
Pytka Productions
DIRECTOR
Joe Pytka
CLIENT
Pepsi Cola
AGENCY
BBDO/New York

686
ART DIRECTOR
Steve Sweitzer
WRITER
Dick Sittig
AGENCY PRODUCER
Andrew Chinich
PRODUCTION COMPANY
Mont Blanc
DIRECTOR
Didier LaFond
CLIENT
Reebok
AGENCY
Chiat/Day/Mojo, New York

683
(MUSIC: "MOODY'S MOOD FOR LOVE" BY KING PLEASURE)

684
(MUSIC: THROUGHOUT)
KID 1: Is that a great new Pepsi can or what!!
ANNCR: Introducing a whole new way to look at Pepsi
and Diet Pepsi.
SUPER: NEW LOOK. SAME GREAT TASTE. COMING
SOON TO YOUR AREA.
KID 2: It's beautiful.

PATRICK DE GAYARDON

685

RAY (SINGING): *Uh-huh you got the right one baby.*
  You know I just love this new Diet Pepsi song but
  do you think it's caught on yet?
CROWD (SINGING): *Uh-huh, uh-huh, you got the right one
  baby! Uh-huh, uh-huh, Diet Pepsi.*
AFRICAN TRIBE (SINGING): *Uh-huh, uh-huh, uh-huh,
  uh-huh.*
MAN: If it's irresistibly sippable . . .
COWBOY (SINGING): *Uncontestably tasteable and
  eminently wonderful . . .*
ENGLISH WAITER: You got the right one baby.
GOSPEL CHOIR (SINGING): *You got the right one baby.*
GEISHA GIRLS (SINGING): *Uh-huh, uh-huh, you got the
  right one baby.*
MONKS (CHANTING): *Uh-huh, uh-huh, uh-huh, uh-huh.*
STADIUM CROWD (SINGING): *Uh-huh, uh-huh, uh-huh,
  uh-huh, uh-huh.*
CROWD (SINGING): *Uh-huh*
RAY: Do you think it's caught on yet!? Naaah!
(RAYLETTES LAUGH)

686

(SFX: HIGH ALTITUDE WINDS)
PATRICK: I wear the Pump Reebok cross trainer because
  I like a secure fit.
(MUSIC: SURFER THROUGHOUT)
ANNCR: Life is short.
ANNCR: Play hard.
ANNCR: Reebok.
(SFX: AIR COMING OUT OF SHOES)

CONSUMER TELEVISION
OVER :30 (:45/ :60/ :90)
SINGLE

687
ART DIRECTOR
Gary Horner
WRITER
John O'Donnell
AGENCY PRODUCER
Mark Andrews
PRODUCTION COMPANY
Tony Kaye Films
DIRECTOR
Tony Kaye
CLIENT
Tower of London
AGENCY
*Collett Dickenson & Pearce/
London*

688
ART DIRECTOR
Brian Aldrich
WRITER
Bruce Adlhoch
AGENCY PRODUCER
John Tripp
PRODUCTION COMPANY
Coppos Films
DIRECTOR
Mark Coppos
CLIENT
*G. Heileman Brewing
Company*
AGENCY
*Della Femina McNamee/
New York*

689
ART DIRECTOR
Eric McClellan
WRITER
Paul Goldman
AGENCY PRODUCER
Randy Cohen
PRODUCTION COMPANY
James Frame Enterprises
DIRECTORS
*Paul Goldman
Eric McClellan*
CLIENT
IKEA
AGENCY
Deutsch/New York

690
ART DIRECTOR
Mark Lees
WRITERS
*Scott Brunsdon
Mark Lees*
AGENCY PRODUCER
Nick Thomson
PRODUCTION COMPANY
Great Southern Films
DIRECTOR
Peter Schmidt
CLIENT
TNT Couriers
AGENCY
Foote Cone & Belding/Sydney

687
EDMUND:
To the Tower of London I was borne, the year
of 1510.
By Traitors Gate I came in.
And will not go out again.
And I can tell of deeds blacker than a raven's wing.
Of princes in their prime snuffed out.
Of Lady Jane, Guy Fawkes and Anne Boleyn.
Where now I tread, I tread on ancient bones.
Where history brimful with blood, spilled and
seeped into the stones.
ANNCR: Visit the Tower of London. It's alive
with history.

688
SUPER: CENTRAL POINT, OREGON 1887.
SHELL GAME PLAYER: Hear you got a new piano player . . .
CARD PLAYER: Hope he's better than the last one . . .
ANNCR: Over a hundred years ago, good entertainment
was as rare as a good beer . . .
BAR PATRON: Ain't never had this before . . .
ANNCR: 'Til a man named Henry Weinhard made the
West's first true premium beer . . .
BARTENDER: It's Henry Weinhard's . . .
ANNCR: Brewed in the traditional manner . . . and
served in finer establishments.
CARD PLAYER: Word is, he played up in Tumwater . . .
ANNCR: Henry Weinhard made finding a good
beer easier . . .
BARTENDER: Gentlemen . . . Tex Velvet!
TEX: Thank you, thank you . . . you are beautiful!
ANNCR: Good entertainment, however, was still a long
ways off.
TEX (SINGING): *She'll be comin' round the mountain
when she comes . . .*
C'mon you know the words . . . *She'll be comin'
round that big ol' mountain when she comes . . .
She'll be comin' round that mountain . . .*

689

TWO OLDER GENTLEMEN: There are three things to see in
   Hicksville, the Gregory Museum, the famous Golden
   Doors, and starting tomorrow, the IKEA store.
   Welcome to Hicksville. Welcome to Hicksville.
   Welcome to Hicksville.

WOMAN: I'd like to welcome all you IKEA shoppers.

TWO OLDER LADIES: Welcome to Hicksville, the friendly town.

OLDER GENTLEMEN: And this is IKEA.

PRIEST: I understand that the grand opening of IKEA is
   going to be like Mardi Gras. This is a wonderful
   occasion for Hicksville.

HAIRDRESSER: I think that IKEA opening will be real exciting.

OLDER LADIES: I think the grand opening of IKEA will
   be wonderful.

MANAGER: Welcome to Hicksville, I am Toma the store
   manager of IKEA Hicksville. Hope to see you
   tomorrow for the grand opening.

CHEFS: Hi, we're the IKEA chefs. Come to the grand opening
   early tomorrow morning. We'll be serving swedish
   meatballs, lingonberries, cold salads, and salmon.

TAILOR: For the IKEA colors for the grand opening, I
   have a special tie and cummerbund. It's a blue and
   yellow tie cummerbund.

FIREMAN: Hi, I'm Joe Defanzo. I'm captain of the Hicksville
   Fire Department. The chief's office and myself went to
   IKEA and found everything to be up to par.

OLDER LADIES: And the one nice thing about the
   Broadway mall is that they have sufficient parking.
   A lot of places you go and you can't park. They
   have ample parking.

SUPER: GRAND OPENING. TOMORROW 9 AM
   HICKSVILLE. LIE EXIT 41S.

690

COURIER: I think that might be for me.
   Jump in.

CAMERAMAN: Okay.

COURIER: Last thing I want to do is get stuck in
   traffic . . . take a bit of a short cut.
   Where do I go?

RECEPTIONIST: Third floor next building.

COURIER: Wait a minute.
   You right?

CAMERAMAN: Yep.

GUARD: Down the corridor.

COURIER: Mark?

OPERATOR: No it's the other bloke's turn.

ANNCR: TNT Air Couriers. More planes, no excuses.

OPERATOR: Thanks.

691
ART DIRECTOR
Chris Dewey
WRITER
Jeff Glover
AGENCY PRODUCER
Norman Zuppicich
PRODUCTION COMPANY
Window Productions
DIRECTOR
Ray Lawrence
CLIENT
Pacific Access
AGENCY
George Patterson/Melbourne

692
ART DIRECTOR
Chris Chaffin
WRITER
Greg Wilson
AGENCY PRODUCER
Carey S. Crosby
PRODUCTION COMPANY
Dektor/Higgins & Associates
DIRECTOR
Leslie Dektor
CLIENT
Tele-Communications
AGENCY
*Hal Riney & Partners/
San Francisco*

693
ART DIRECTOR
Chris Chaffin
WRITER
Greg Wilson
AGENCY PRODUCER
Carey S. Crosby
PRODUCTION COMPANY
Dektor/Higgins & Associates
DIRECTOR
Leslie Dektor
CLIENT
Tele-Communications
AGENCY
*Hal Riney & Partners/
San Francisco*

694
ART DIRECTOR
Richard Crispo
WRITER
Jeanette Tyson
AGENCY PRODUCER
Lesley Crews
PRODUCTION COMPANY
Dektor/Higgins & Associates
DIRECTOR
Leslie Dektor
CLIENT
Saturn Corporation
AGENCY
*Hal Riney & Partners/
San Francisco*

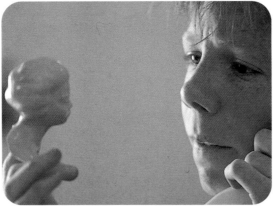

691
BOY: It's a pink lady and she hasn't got any clothes on
and she's sort of leaning back on the pole . . .
It's a pink lady, yes, yeah she hasn't got any clothes
on and she's leaning back on this pole which is
the lamp . . .
It was sort of like a pink lady and she had all these
drapes coming down . . .

692
KARL: So, learn anything today?
SON: I don't know.
ANNCR: Karl Vogel is a plumber . . . in the town of
Carrollton, Georgia.
SON: We learned about The Wall coming down.
ANNCR: A town where TCI recently introduced cable
television to the high school, so the kids could learn
more about the world and how it's changing.
SON: How come you never talked about it?
KARL: It was a long time ago.
SON: Germany's becoming this new paradigm.
KARL: What is that about a pair of dimes?
Pair of dimes?
ANNCR: At first, Karl didn't understand what cable
television had to do with education . . .
SON: Paradigm . . . it's like a new . . . a new way of
doing things.
ANNCR: But the world has changed a little, hasn't it?
SON: Dad, I've been thinkin' . . .
ANNCR: And chances are if you happened to ask Karl
Vogel today . . .
SON: I think maybe I might want to go to college.
ANNCR: He'd say it's changed for the better.
SON: Do ya think that'd be okay? Dad?
KARL: Yeah . . . yeah, I think maybe . . . I think maybe
that would be okay.
SUPER: TCI OFFERS FREE CABLE TO MORE THAN 5000
SCHOOLS, INCLUDING CARROLLTON HIGH.
SUPER: TCI. WE'RE TAKING TELEVSION
INTO TOMORROW.

693

RADIO ANNCR: It's Wednesday, January 16, and here is the morning report . . .

ANNCR: For Harland Edwards . . . it was a day he'll never forget. At breakfast, he ordered his toast burnt . . .

HARLAND: And burn the toast.

ANNCR: Just like he's been ordering for years. Only this time . . . it came back burnt. Over at Leo's . . .

HARLAND: I never win, Leo, I never win.

ANNCR: He took his daily shot at getting rich. And for the first time . . .

LEO: Harland!

ANNCR: Won. At least a little. But if you ask Harland what he remembers most about January 16 . . .

RADIO ANNCR: The liberation of Kuwait has begun.

ANNCR: He'll tell you it's what he did once he'd heard that war had started.

ARNETT: If you are still with us you can hear the bombs now, they are hitting the center of the city . . .

CNN NEWS ANCHOR: Operation Desert Storm.

ANNCR: Harland, like almost all of America, sat down in front of the television.

SHAW: The most violent day . . .

ANNCR: Was it right? He didn't know. All he knew was that for better or worse, the world was now changed forever.

CNN ANNCR: . . . put on our gas masks . . .

ANNCR: Not to mention, our way of learning about it.

SUPER: TCI IS THE LARGEST FINANCIAL SUPPORTER OF CNN.

SHAW: A night none of us, none of us will ever forget.

SUPER: TCI. WE'RE TAKING TELEVISION INTO TOMORROW.

694

ANNCR: My first car didn't even have a seat belt. Of course, I drove a tank, and I guess there weren't so many places to go. That's all changed. Except it seems when people talk about safety, they're still talking size. Now we knew the Saturn would be a small car, but we always thought it should behave, safety-wise, well, bigger than it looks. So for all the ugly head-ons we had with concrete walls, our space-frame had more crashes with computers. And we used dummies so sophisticated, they were almost human. Which inspired more changes. And patents. Imagine, having the option of anti-lock brakes on a car this size. We've done all this to put a safer car on the road for less than $10,000.

ANNCR: Because the way we see it, if you can't afford certain luxuries, well, that's life. But if you have to spend $40,000 to feel safe . . . that's scary.

SUPER: A DIFFERENT KIND OF COMPANY.
A DIFFERENT KIND OF CAR.

SUPER: SATURN.

695
ART DIRECTOR
Norman Icke
WRITER
Bob Stanners
AGENCY PRODUCER
David Manson
PRODUCTION COMPANY
H.L.A.
DIRECTOR
Gerrard De Thame
CLIENT
Barclay's Bank
AGENCY
Leo Burnett/London

696
ART DIRECTOR
Tony Miceli
WRITER
Cheryl Berman
AGENCY PRODUCER
Bob Harley
PRODUCTION COMPANY
Sandbank & Partners
DIRECTOR
Stan Scofield
CLIENT
McDonald's
AGENCY
*Leo Burnett Company/
Chicago*

697
ART DIRECTOR
Charles Inge
WRITER
Jane Garland
AGENCY PRODUCER
Sue Braley
PRODUCTION COMPANY
BFCS
DIRECTOR
Michael Seresin
CLIENT
Whitbread & Company
AGENCY
Lowe Howard-Spink/London

698
ART DIRECTOR
Alan Waldie
WRITER
Mark Wnek
AGENCY PRODUCER
Sarah Horry
PRODUCTION COMPANY
Paul Weiland Film Company
DIRECTOR
Paul Weiland
CLIENT
Whitbread & Company
AGENCY
Lowe Howard-Spink/London

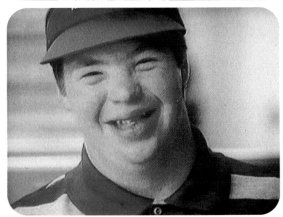

695
(MUSIC: THROUGHOUT)
SUPER: A TRUE STORY RECREATED WITH ACTORS.
SUPER: GOOD FRIDAY 1991 NORTHERN FRANCE.
SUPER: HOURS EARLIER. MIDHURST, SUSSEX.
ANNCR: Sergeant Stan Jackson's last minute decision to
attend his unit's anniversary reunion was only made
possible by Barclays on the spot help. It was an
occasion he will never forget. Barclays. When it
matters most.
SUPER: YOU'RE BETTER OFF TALKING TO BARCLAYS

696
MIKE: Hi. My name is Mike. This is a story about me
and my friends. That's my mom. She's a wonderful
mother. And my dad. He's a wonderful dude.
That's my teacher. She is the best.
TEACHER: Mike is very . . .
MIKE: Brilliant.
TEACHER: Outspoken.
MIKE: That's my friend Tracy. I think she's beautiful.
Come on. Let's take a ride to McDonald's. There's
my friends. You know, me and James are best pals.
We are a great team. The pie is up. Perfect. Ever
since I was a little baby, people are always tryin' to
help me. So now I love to say, welcome to
McDonald's, may I help you.

697

(MUSIC: "LA FORZA DEL DESTINO" BY VERDI)

PAINTER (IN FRENCH): Hello, I was wondering would you accept my painting in return for a beer.

BARMAN (IN FRENCH): It's pretty but . . . oh alright.

PAINTER (IN FRENCH): Thank you.

SUPER: STELLA ARTOIS. REASSURINGLY EXPENSIVE.

698

(MUSIC: GUITAR STRUMMING)

SINGER (SINGING): *Woke up this morning and the sun smiled down on me.*

Sun smiled on me? That ain't the blues.

WIFE: Oh honey, that's cute.

SINGER (SINGING): *Woe . . . woe, woe, woe the boat happily down the stream.*

Damn that ain't the blues either.

WIFE: What is this lipstick doing on your collar?

SINGER: Honey, that ain't no lipstick.

WIFE: Honey or nothing!

SINGER: I was shaving.

WIFE: You're lying!

REPO MAN: We're repossessing your car.

(SFX: THUNDERCLAP)

WIFE: And I ain't never coming back!

(MUSIC: GUITAR, HARMONICA)

SINGER (SINGING): *Sadness is my first name, last name is Misery, I lost my woman and the rain is coming down . . . oh . . . yer.*

SUPER: HEINEKEN REFRESHES THE PARTS OTHER BEERS CANNOT REACH.

699
ART DIRECTOR
John Danza
WRITER
Paul Wolfe
AGENCY PRODUCER
Sherry Bloom
PRODUCTION COMPANY
Danza Productions
DIRECTOR
John Danza, Jr.
CLIENT
MCI Telecommunications
AGENCY
*Messner Vetere Berger Carey
Schmetterer/New York*

700
ART DIRECTOR
Jim Scalfone
WRITER
Ron Berger
AGENCY PRODUCER
Jill Gordon
CLIENT
MCI Telecommunications
AGENCY
*Messner Vetere Berger Carey
Schmetterer/New York*

701
ART DIRECTOR
Barry Vetere
WRITER
Ron Berger
AGENCY PRODUCER
Trish O'Reilly
PRODUCTION COMPANY
Danza Productions
DIRECTOR
John Danza, Jr.
CLIENT
MCI Telecommunications
AGENCY
*Messner Vetere Berger Carey
Schmetterer/New York*

702
ART DIRECTOR
Anthony Easton
WRITER
Adam Keane
AGENCY PRODUCER
Arnold Pearce
PRODUCTION COMPANY
Tony Kaye Films
DIRECTOR
Tony Kaye
CLIENT
Le Creuset
AGENCY
Saatchi & Saatchi/London

699
ANNCR: When Jordan was born, my mother was thrilled
we'd named him after my dad. But she hasn't seen
him yet. Oregon's 3000 miles away. I know she
doesn't call as often as she'd like. She's kind of
frugal and all and she has this thing about calling
collect. So I'm thinking about this and one day I'm
ordering some stuff from a catalog . . . I'm dialing
this 800 number and it hits me: If I had an 800
number my mother could call me anytime free of
charge too. Then I thought: Why can't people have
800 numbers? I guess I wasn't the only one asking
that question. They started the service in November.
I sent my mother one of the first personal 800 cards
MCI printed along with a note that said: For
cuteness and love call toll free now. . . .
Ask for Jordan.
SUPER: MCI. 1-800-695-4555.

700
ANNCR: This is a commercial about a love affair. A love
affair between all of us and a game. A game we
grew up watching and playing and talking about.
How many of your phone conversations even today
begin with, did you see the game last night, why did
he pinch hit in the eighth inning, that guy was out
by a mile, even before you say hello. It's with that
feeling in mind that MCI has created Friends &
Family. Now every time MCI customers call another
customer on their Friends & Family list they save an
extra 20 percent. Over a season, that could mean a
savings of hundreds of dollars to those customers.
Enough to do the only thing we love more than
talking about baseball, and that's go to a few
more games.
SUPER: MCI FRIENDS AND FAMILY. 1-800-444-LIST.

701

MIKE: Hello.

OPERATOR: Mr. O'Reilly, this is the MCI Operator. I have a call for you from New York.

TRISH: Hi Uncle Mike.

MIKE: Trish?

TRISH: I have a little surprise for you.

OPERATOR: Mrs. O'Reilly, I have a call for you from New York and San Diego.

(SFX: PHONE RINGS)

MAN: Hello.

OPERATOR: A call from the United States for Seamus O'Reilly.

MAN: I'll try to find him.

GRANDFATHER: He's in Ireland.

MEG: This is Meg O'Reilly.

COP: Sarge line one.

SRGT. O'REILLY: O'Reilly.

GRANDMOTHER: You still chasing the bad guys, Sean?

DAD: Who is it?

KID: It's everybody.

MEG: I can't believe this.

SEAMUS: Hello?

SEAN: Seamus?

SEAMUS: Who's this?

SEAN: Happy New Year Seamus.

SEAMUS: Sean!

ALL: (SINGING "AULD LANG SYNE")

SUPER: MCI. NEWER. DIFFERENT. BETTER. CALL 1-800-444-REUNION.

702

(MUSIC: THE FRENCH NATIONAL ANTHEM "LA MARSEILLAISE")

WORKERS: We are great cooks.

703
ART DIRECTOR
Larry Frey
WRITER
Geoff McGann
AGENCY PRODUCER
Derek Ruddy
PRODUCTION COMPANY
Limelight Productions
DIRECTOR
Alex Proyas
CLIENT
Nike
AGENCY
Wieden & Kennedy/Portland

704
ART DIRECTOR
Larry Frey
WRITER
Jerry Cronin
AGENCY PRODUCER
John Adams
PRODUCTION COMPANY
M & Co.
DIRECTORS
Joe Pytka
Larry Frey
Doug Zimmerman
Tibor Kalman
CLIENT
Subaru of America
AGENCY
Wieden & Kennedy/Portland

705
ART DIRECTOR
Ron Brown
WRITER
David Abbott
AGENCY PRODUCER
Frank Lieberman
PRODUCTION COMPANY
Sedelmaier Film Productions
DIRECTOR
Joe Sedelmaier
CLIENT
Comet
AGENCY
*Abbott Mead Vickers. BBDO/
London*

706
ART DIRECTOR
Kirk Souder
WRITER
Tony Gomes
AGENCY PRODUCER
Jack McWalters
CLIENT
Aetna Life & Casualty
AGENCY
Ammirati & Puris/New York

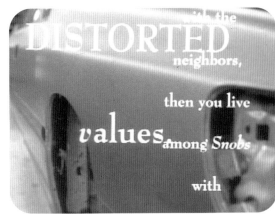

703
(MUSIC: "TWILIGHT ZONE" STYLE)
TOMMY DAVIDSON: Forget the limits of ordinary
 basketball shoes. You've entered the weightless
 environment of . . . the Nike Flight Dimension.
 Examine if you will . . . Scottie Pippen . . . about to
 discover . . . the power of his Nike Air Flight
 Shoes . . . by way of a time warp.
(MUSIC: TWANGY 50'S STYLE)
(MUSIC: 90'S STYLE)
TOMMY: And so the laws of ordinary basketball are
 rewritten . . . in the higher court of . . .
(MUSIC: "TWILIGHT ZONE" STYLE)
TOMMY: The Flight Dimension
(MUSIC: 90'S STYLE)
COACH: Son, you could make hundreds of dollars
 a year in professional basketball.

704
(MUSIC: THROUGHOUT)
ANNCR: A car is a car. And its sole reason for existence
 is to get you from point A to point B. And back
 again. It won't make you handsome. Or prettier.
 Or younger. And if it improves your standing with
 the neighbors, then you live among snobs with
 distorted values. A car is steel, electronics, rubber,
 plastic and glass. A machine. And in choosing one
 the questions should be: How long will it last? How
 well will it do the job? Could I get a comparable
 one for less? And do I like the way this machine
 feels and looks? And in the end, with an absence of
 marketing glamour about the automobile: May the
 best machine win.
SUPER: SUBARU. WHAT TO DRIVE.

COMET

YOU KNOW WHERE TO COME.

The nursery.
The braces.
The college
education.

Funded
by their
Aetna
life policy.

Now that's
life insurance.

705

(MUSIC: THROUGHOUT)

WIFE: According to this, we spend a third of our lives sleeping. Twenty percent eating. Fifteen percent on unsuccessful shopping trips. And three percent making love.

ANNCR: At Comet, we can't sort out all of life's priorities, but with big brands, stocked in depth, at low, low prices, we do our best to make every shopping trip a successful trip.

SUPER: COMET. YOU KNOW WHERE TO COME.

706

(SFX: DELIVERY ROOM SOUNDS)

DOCTOR: Here comes the baby. . . . Push . . . so we can get the baby's head out . . .

NURSE: Give a good push now . . .

DOCTOR: A little more . . . a little more. . . . Give it a good push now.

NURSE: Breathe through your nose.

DOCTOR: Stay like that . . .

MOTHER: Oh, it's a beautiful baby . . .

DOCTOR: Here we go . . .

MOTHER: I can't believe it.

DOCTOR: Look at that . . . it's a little girl!

(SFX: GENTLE SLAP ON BABY'S BEHIND)

(SFX: BABY STARTS CRYING)

707
ART DIRECTOR
Paul Jervis
WRITER
Charlie Breen
AGENCY PRODUCERS
Robin Dobson
Lynne Lyons
Gary Walker
PRODUCTION COMPANY
Boss Films
DIRECTOR
Brian Loftus
CLIENT
North American Philips
AGENCY
*Backer Spielvogel Bates/
New York*

708
ART DIRECTOR
Pat McGuinness
WRITER
Jim Houck
AGENCY PRODUCER
Laura Citron
DIRECTOR
Mark Story
CLIENT
Louisiana Lottery
AGENCY
Bauerlein/Atlanta

709
ART DIRECTOR
David Harner
WRITER
David Johnson
AGENCY PRODUCER
Tony Frere
PRODUCTION COMPANY
Pytka Productions
DIRECTOR
Joe Pytka
CLIENT
DuPont
AGENCY
BBDO/New York

710
ART DIRECTORS
Rick Midler
Mike Campbell
WRITER
Mark Abellera
AGENCY PRODUCER
Linda Kligman
PRODUCTION COMPANY
Pfeifer Lopes Productions
DIRECTOR
Rob Lopes
CLIENT
HBO
AGENCY
BBDO/New York

707
SPOKESMAN 1: This is a commercial for this ingenious personal portable CD player from Magnavox, the inventors of CD technology. It gives you incredible stereo sound and . . .
SPOKESMAN 2: I'm sorry, actually this is a commercial for this intelligent Magnavox 13-inch TV that has a built-in VCR that you can . . .
SPOKESMAN 3: I'm sorry. This is really a commercial for the brilliant Magnavox 52-inch TV with 100 Watt Dolby surround sound and . . .
SPOKESMAN 4: I'm sorry. This is really a commercial for this clever little 8mm EasyCam that weighs less than two pounds and . . .
SPOKESMAN 5: I'm sorry . . . wrong again. . . . This is supposed to be a commercial for this Magnavox 386 Notebook computer . . .
SPOKESMAN 4: Hang on. I haven't finished.
SPOKESMAN 5: I'm sorry. You have!
ANNCR: The ingenious products from Magnavox. They're smart. Very Smart.
SUPER: MAGNAVOX SMART. VERY SMART.

708
(SFX: HOSPITAL INTERCOM THROUGHOUT)
ANNCR: Introducing Mardi Gras, the new instant scratch game from the Louisiana Lottery. You could win up to $50,000, instantly.
MR. VANDERLIP: I won, I won, I won, I won! . . . Fifty, fifty . . . $50,000!
DOCTOR: Mr. Vanderlip, I'm afraid your mother-in-law will indeed require the surgery, and it's going to cost you $50,000.
MR. VANDERLIP: Doctor, I don't have that kind of money.
SUPER: LOUISIANA LOTTERY.

709

MOTHER: That's Mommy's little sweetheart.

(SFX: VROOM, VROOM)

(MUSIC: THROUGHOUT)

ANNCR: Now there's a new Stainmaster carpet that handles foot traffic like never before. New Stainmaster Xtra Life. It stays beautiful longer.

SUPER: ONLY FROM DUPONT.

710

ANNCR: George Foreman is hungry to fight again and only HBO's got him. See him step back into the ring to devour his next opponent. Coming soon. Live. Only on HBO.

GEORGE: I wanna fight so bad, I can taste it.

711
ART DIRECTOR
Terry Schneider
WRITER
Greg Eiden
AGENCY PRODUCER
Josh Reynolds
PRODUCTION COMPANY
Johns + Gorman Films
DIRECTOR
Gary Johns
CLIENT
Portland General Electric
AGENCY
*Borders Perrin & Norrander/
Portland*

712
ART DIRECTORS
*Gaynor Notman
Cab Richardson*
WRITER
Peter Smith
AGENCY PRODUCER
Angela Zabala
PRODUCTION COMPANY
Spots Films
DIRECTOR
Barry Myers
CLIENT
B&Q
AGENCY
BSB Dorland/London

713
ART DIRECTOR
Jim Keane
WRITER
Joe Nagy
AGENCY PRODUCER
Jack Steinmann
PRODUCTION COMPANY
James Production
DIRECTOR
Jim Lund
CLIENT
Zebco
AGENCY
*Carmichael Lynch/
Minneapolis*

714
ART DIRECTOR
Frank Haggerty
WRITER
Dan Roettger
AGENCY PRODUCER
Brynn Hausmann
PRODUCTION COMPANY
Lotter, Inc.
DIRECTOR
Jim Lotter
CLIENT
Skeeter
AGENCY
*Carmichael Lynch/
Minneapolis*

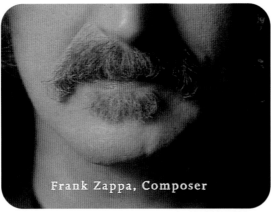

Frank Zappa, Composer

711
SUPER: FRANK ZAPPA, COMPOSER.
FRANK: Portland General Electric offered to pay me to
appear in this commercial. I told them, "I refuse to
sell your product." They said, "Great." "In fact," I
said," I will tell people to use less of it." And they
said, "Perfect."
SUPER: CURRENT THINKING ON ENERGY.
SUPER: PORTLAND GENERAL ELECTRIC.

712
(SFX: RESTAURANT)
(NOTE: TWIN & EARTH CABLE, 50 METRE REEL, £6.95 AT B&Q)
SUPER: 6242Y 1MM x 50M REEL (UP TO 14 AMPS) £6.95.
SUPER: B&Q.
ANNCR: B&Q. Prices so low you just have to
tell somebody.

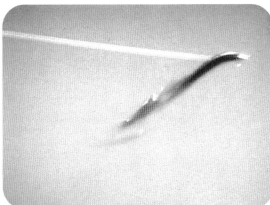

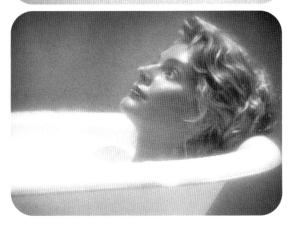

713

(MUSIC: SOFT, ELEGANT PIANO)
(SFX: WORM FLYING THROUGH AIR)
(SFX: PLOOP)
WOMAN: Larry, you weirdo.
SUPER: THE REEL YOU CAN'T WAIT TO CAST.
ANNCR: Zebco Bullet. The world's most castable reel.
SUPER: THE BULLET. ZEBCO.

714

WOMAN: You know, I love my husband. He's bright, witty, makes good money . . . and has the body of a man ten years his junior. In fact, he's everything a woman could want. Six months ago he bought a new Skeeter fishing boat. And if he'd ever drag his buns out of it and come home, I might introduce him to my new boyfriend Bob here.
ANNCR: Eat. Sleep. Fish.
SUPER: SKEETER.

CONSUMER TELEVISION
:30/ :25 SINGLE

715
ART DIRECTOR
Corey Stolberg
WRITER
Tom Witt
AGENCY PRODUCER
Helen Erb
PRODUCTION COMPANY
Werts Films
DIRECTOR
Bill Werts
CLIENT
Nissan Motor Corporation
AGENCY
Chiat/Day/Mojo, Venice

716
ART DIRECTOR
Dennis Mickaelian
WRITER
Bob Ancona
AGENCY PRODUCER
Richard O'Neill
PRODUCTION COMPANY
Limelight Productions
DIRECTOR
Alex Proyas
CLIENT
Nissan Motor Corporation
AGENCY
Chiat/Day/Mojo, Venice

717
ART DIRECTOR
Ian Potter
WRITER
Steve Rabosky
AGENCY PRODUCER
Nancy Sanders
PRODUCTION COMPANY
HSI
DIRECTOR
Ian Giles
CLIENT
McKesson Water Division
AGENCY
Chiat/Day/Mojo, Venice

718
ART DIRECTORS
Gail San Filippo
Craig Tanimoto
WRITER
Hillary Jordan
AGENCY PRODUCERS
Jennifer Golub
David Verhoef
PRODUCTION COMPANIES
RSA/USA
Fernbach/Robbins
DIRECTORS
Jake Scott
Alex Fernbach
CLIENT
TV Guide
AGENCY
Chiat/Day/Mojo, Venice

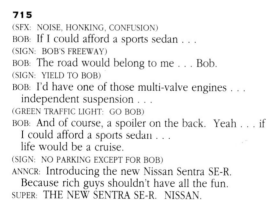

715
(SFX: NOISE, HONKING, CONFUSION)
BOB: If I could afford a sports sedan . . .
(SIGN: BOB'S FREEWAY)
BOB: The road would belong to me . . . Bob.
(SIGN: YIELD TO BOB)
BOB: I'd have one of those multi-valve engines . . .
  independent suspension . . .
(GREEN TRAFFIC LIGHT: GO BOB)
BOB: And of course, a spoiler on the back. Yeah . . . if
  I could afford a sports sedan . . .
  life would be a cruise.
(SIGN: NO PARKING EXCEPT FOR BOB)
ANNCR: Introducing the new Nissan Sentra SE-R.
  Because rich guys shouldn't have all the fun.
SUPER: THE NEW SENTRA SE-R. NISSAN.

716
STANZA DREAMER: Let me tell you my fantasy. I'm
  driving . . . with the stereo on. The sunroof's open.
  Just me and Michael . . . winding our way to this
  little . . . Bed 'n Breakfast in my Nissan Stanza.
  Oh, I know. As fantasies go, it sounds pretty tame.
  But . . . you should see my real life.
(SFX: DOMESTIC AND OFFICE CHAOS)
SUPER: NISSAN. THE NISSAN STANZA.

717

GUY: Great . . . next. Wonderful . . . next.
Good one . . . next. Perfect . . . next.
Fabulous . . . next. Oh, nice form . . . next.
ANNCR: Sparkletts. Guaranteed pure, drop after drop
after drop.
SUPER: SPARKLETTS. NOBODY LOVES WATER
LIKE WE DO.
GUY: Beautiful . . . next.

718

SUPER: S.K.U.M. SCREAMING AT THE TOP OF OUR
LUNGS. TANIMOTO RECORDS.
HEAVY METAL SINGER (SINGING): *We're coming, we're
coming. We're coming for your young. We're
coming, we're coming, screaming at the top of our
lungs! Screaming at the top of our lungs! Screaming
at the top of our lungs! Screaming,
screaming, screaming.*
ANNCR: Were you watching something like this when
the Beatles reappeared on the "Best of Ed Sullivan"?
SUPER: TV GUIDE. DON'T WATCH TV IN THE DARK.

719
ART DIRECTOR
Cabell Harris
WRITER
Dion Hughes
AGENCY PRODUCER
Andrew Chinich
PRODUCTION COMPANY
Pelorus Films
DIRECTOR
Lol Creme
CLIENT
NYNEX Information Resources
AGENCY
Chiat/Day/Mojo, New York

720
ART DIRECTOR
Bruce Hurwit
WRITER
Don Austen
AGENCY PRODUCER
Melanie Klein
PRODUCTION COMPANY
Steifel & Company
DIRECTOR
Jon Francis
CLIENT
Little Caesar Enterprises
AGENCY
Cliff Freeman & Partners/ New York

721
ART DIRECTOR
Steve Miller
WRITERS
Arthur Bijur
Don Austen
AGENCY PRODUCER
Anne Kurtzman
PRODUCTION COMPANY
Story Piccolo Guliner
DIRECTOR
Mark Story
CLIENT
Little Caesar Enterprises
AGENCY
Cliff Freeman & Partners/ New York

722
ART DIRECTOR
John Colquhoun
WRITERS
Cliff Freeman
Arthur Bijur
AGENCY PRODUCER
Lisa Connolly
PRODUCTION COMPANY
Firehouse Films
DIRECTOR
Peter Lauer
CLIENT
Cub Foods/Supermarkets
AGENCY
Cliff Freeman & Partners/ New York

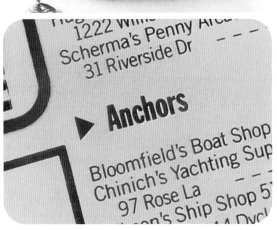

719
CAROL: I had a lovely meal, and that's the way it was. Over to you, Hal.
HAL: Thanks Carol. This weather will carry us through to the weekend. Joan?
JOAN: Thanks Hal. Great tie. Jim?
JIM: Joan. The paté was fabulous. Carol?
CAROL: Jim. We must do this again. Hal?
HAL: Carol. Sounds great. This just in, $455 plus tip. Joan?
JOAN: Hal. Jim?
JIM: Joan. Carol?
CAROL: Jim. Hal?
HAL: Carol.
ANNCR: If it's out there . . .
(NYNEX HEADING: "ANCHORS")
ANNCR: It's in here. The NYNEX Yellow Pages. Why would anyone need another.

720
(SFX: BANGING RATTLE, LOUD SQUIRT OF WATER GUN, CAT'S MEOW)
(SFX: CHEESE STRETCHING)
(SFX: HIGHCHAIR DRAGGING ON THE FLOOR)
(SFX: CARTOON ROCKET SOUND)
(SFX: BABY GIGGLES)
GRANDPA: Well . . . look who's here!
(SFX: CRASH OF HIGHCHAIR)
ANNCR: Little Caesars. Cheeser! Cheeser! Not one but two pizzas with extra cheese, up to four toppings, and free Crazy Bread for $8.98.
LITTLE CAESAR: Cheeser! Cheeser!

721

ANNCR: Recently these people walked out of Little
  Caesars with extra pepperoni and cheese . . .
  without paying for it.
(SFX: SPRAYING)
(SFX: WIPING)
ANNCR: Extra pepperoni.
(SFX: SPLATT)
(SFX: GUM STRETCHING)
ANNCR: Extra cheese.
(SFX: SUCTION NOISE)
ANNCR: Without paying for it.
ANNCR: It's Lotsa! Lotsa! Get extra pepperoni and extra
  cheese on two pizzas without paying extra.
(SFX: POLICE SIREN)
LITTLE CAESAR: Lotsa! Lotsa!
ANNCR: At $8.98, it's a steal!

722

ANNCR: Every week supermarkets send out fliers
  containing all their low priced items. If Cub Foods
  put all their low priced items in a flier it would be a
  somewhat . . . heftier proposition.
MASTER: Fetch the paper, Spot.
(SFX: DOG WHIMPERS)
(SFX: DOG GROWLS)
MASTER: Spot, is there a problem?
(SFX: DOG GROWLING)
(SFX: CAT LAUGHING)
ANNCR: Cub doesn't have fliers. All 25,000 of our items
  are already low-priced. See what food should
  cost . . . at Cub.

723
ART DIRECTOR
Mark Kuehn
WRITER
Patrick Pritchard
AGENCY PRODUCERS
Neil Casey
Patrick Pritchard
PRODUCTION COMPANY
Backyard Productions
DIRECTOR
Kevin Smith
CLIENT
Dremel
AGENCY
Cramer-Krasselt/Milwaukee

724
ART DIRECTOR
Tom Moyer
WRITER
Rick Rosenberg
AGENCY PRODUCER
Connie Myck
PRODUCTION COMPANY
Story Piccolo Guliner
DIRECTOR
Mark Story
CLIENT
GTE
AGENCY
DDB Needham/Los Angeles

725
ART DIRECTOR
David Angelo
WRITER
Paul Spencer
AGENCY PRODUCER
Eric Herrmann
PRODUCTION COMPANY
Coppos Films
DIRECTOR
Brent Thomas
CLIENT
New York State Lottery
AGENCY
DDB Needham
Worldwide/New York

726
ART DIRECTOR
David Leinwohl
WRITER
Marian Godwin
AGENCY PRODUCER
David Cohen
PRODUCTION COMPANY
Red Dog Films
DIRECTORS
Marc Chiat
Harry Prichett
CLIENT
A&W Brands
AGENCY
Della Femina McNamee/
New York

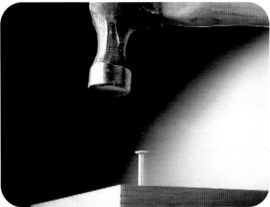

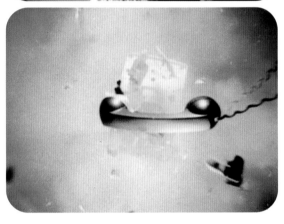

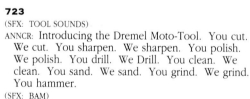

723
(SFX: TOOL SOUNDS)
ANNCR: Introducing the Dremel Moto-Tool. You cut.
We cut. You sharpen. We sharpen. You polish.
We polish. You drill. We Drill. You clean. We
clean. You sand. We sand. You grind. We grind.
You hammer.
(SFX: BAM)
ANNCR: Did I mention we cut? The Dremel Moto-Tool.
With more than 150 available accessories, why settle
for some two-bit Christmas gift?

724
MALE: When you rent a phone from GTE, and
something happens to it, we'll repair or replace it for
free. Under certain conditions.
ANNCR: This is not covered. This is covered. Not
covered. Covered. Not Covered. Covered.
MAN: Pull!
ANNCR: Definitely not covered. So why take chances.
Rent a phone from GTE.
SUPER: RENT A PHONE. 1-800-438-RENT. GTE.
THE POWER IS ON.

725

(MUSIC: OPERA)
(MUSIC: STOPS)
WOMAN: Thank you.
(MUSIC: CONTINUES)
ANNCR: New York Lotto. Hey, you never know.

726

DIRECTOR: Just pick up the glass and say, "When I want
   a diet soft drink nothing beats the smooth light
   vanilla taste of . . .
WOMAN: Quiet please.
DIRECTOR: A&W Diet Cream Soda and rich, creamy Diet
   A&W Root Beer with 100% NutraSweet."
MADGE: Got it.
DIRECTOR: Good.
MAN: Marker.
DIRECTOR: And action . . . cut! Just pick it up. Good.
MAN: Marker.
DIRECTOR: Let's try it again. Action. No . . . no . . . just
   pick it up.
MAN: Marker.
DIRECTOR: Action. No. No. No. Cut. No. No. No.
   No. Just pick it up. No. Will you just pick it up.
   No. No. No. Why do you keep doing that?
MADGE: I have no idea.
DIRECTOR: It's the taste that made A&W famous.

727
ART DIRECTOR
Eric McClellan
WRITER
Paul Goldman
AGENCY PRODUCER
Randy Cohen
PRODUCTION COMPANY
Concrete Productions
DIRECTOR
Mike Cerney
CLIENT
British Knights
AGENCY
Deutsch/New York

728
ART DIRECTOR
Wayne Gibson
WRITER
Dean Buckhorn
AGENCY PRODUCER
Robin Sherman
PRODUCTION COMPANY
Werts Films
DIRECTOR
Wayne Gibson
CLIENT
Captain D's
AGENCY
*Earle Palmer Brown/
Bethesda*

729
ART DIRECTOR
Kris Salzer
WRITER
Laurie Sinclair Fritts
AGENCY PRODUCER
Trish Murray
PRODUCTION COMPANY
Pinnacle Post
DIRECTOR
Alan Lawrence
CLIENT
JanSport
AGENCY
*Elgin Syferd/
DDB Needham, Seattle*

730
ART DIRECTORS
*Tim Ryan
Crafton Stagg*
WRITER
Rick Ender
AGENCY PRODUCER
Sara Cherry
PRODUCTION COMPANY
Johns + Gorman Films
DIRECTOR
Jeff Gorman
CLIENT
Honda Power Equipment
AGENCY
Fahlgren Martin/Atlanta

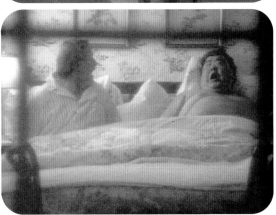

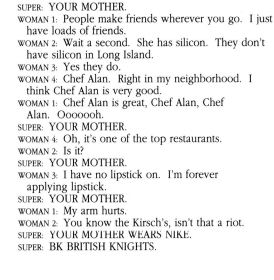

727
SUPER: YOUR MOTHER.
WOMAN 1: People make friends wherever you go. I just have loads of friends.
WOMAN 2: Wait a second. She has silicon. They don't have silicon in Long Island.
WOMAN 3: Yes they do.
WOMAN 4: Chef Alan. Right in my neighborhood. I think Chef Alan is very good.
WOMAN 1: Chef Alan is great, Chef Alan, Chef Alan. Ooooooh.
SUPER: YOUR MOTHER.
WOMAN 4: Oh, it's one of the top restaurants.
WOMAN 2: Is it?
SUPER: YOUR MOTHER.
WOMAN 3: I have no lipstick on. I'm forever applying lipstick.
SUPER: YOUR MOTHER.
WOMAN 1: My arm hurts.
WOMAN 2: You know the Kirsch's, isn't that a riot.
SUPER: YOUR MOTHER WEARS NIKE.
SUPER: BK BRITISH KNIGHTS.

728
ANNCR: To prove nothing can distract you from Captain D's Seafood Sampler, we've secretly replaced this man's family with three sumos. Let's watch . . .
GUY: Hi, honey . . . hey . . . Captain D's . . . great.
(SFX: KISS)
ANNCR: There go the three fried shrimp.
GUY: How was school, Tiger. Great, great.
ANNC: And the seafood crabcakes . . .
GUY: You gonna eat your fish?
SUMO 1: Grrwwl.
ANNCR: Close one!
GUY: Great Meal.
ANNCR: There you have it! Captain D's irresistible new Seafood Sampler . . . just $2.99* ($3.49).
SUMO 2 AND GUY (IN BED): AARGHHH!

729

SINGER 1: *Hey, life is not something to be taken lightly.*
SINGER 2: *You can't go out looking like that . . . just who do you think you are?*
SINGER 3: *When are you gonna grow up and get a real job?*
SINGER 1: *You don't even have an I.R.A.*
SINGER 2: *When are you gonna mow the lawn?*
SINGER 3: *Your hair's too long.*
SINGER 1: *The bills are late . . .*
SINGER 2: *Are late again.*
CHORUS: *Why can't you be more like Elliot????*
SINGER 3: *Show a little respect!*
SINGER 1: *Don't talk back!*
SINGER 2: *Get to work!*
SINGER 3: *To work, to work.*
CHORUS: *You can't always do what you want to do!!!*
SUPER: GET OUT WHILE YOU CAN. JANSPORT.

730

(MUSIC: JUNGLE MUSIC THROUGHOUT)
ANNCR: It has come to our attention that a lot of you don't know that Honda makes mowers and tractors, let alone such a wide selection.
SUPER: HONDA. NOTHING'S EASIER.

731
(MUSIC: "BOBBY'S GIRL")
ANNCR: It's been ten years since you graduated from high school. But you're still trying to get into the same old jeans. Maybe you should try a pair of Easy Rider Relaxed Fit jeans. From Lee. The brand that fits.

732
(SFX: CHEERING)
(SFX: CHEERING FADES)
SUPER: DON'T WORRY.
SUPER: WE'LL TELL YOU WHAT YOU MISSED TOMORROW.
SUPER: STAR TRIBUNE.
ANNCR: The Star Tribune. The newspaper of the Twin Cities.

733

(SFX: NEWS)

(MUSIC: SPANISH)

SUPER: DON'T WORRY.

SUPER: WE'LL TELL YOU WHAT YOU
MISSED TOMORROW.

SUPER: STAR TRIBUNE.

ANNCR: The Star Tribune. The newspaper of the Twin Cities.

734

WOMAN: Time for the 10:00 news.

SUPER: LATER.

SUPER: MUCH LATER

SUPER: A LOT LATER.

TV ANNCR: Well that's it . . . that's tonight's news.

SUPER: TOO LATE.

SUPER: DON'T WORRY.

SUPER: WE'LL TELL YOU WHAT YOU
MISSED TOMORROW.

SUPER: STAR TRIBUNE.

ANNCR: The Star Tribune. The newspaper of the Twin Cities.

735
ART DIRECTOR
Tom Lichtenheld
WRITER
Doug de Grood
AGENCY PRODUCER
Becky Fischer
PRODUCTION COMPANIES
Young & Company
Wilson-Griak
DIRECTORS
Eric Young
Buck Holzemer
CLIENT
Bringer's
AGENCY
Fallon McElligott/
Minneapolis

736
ART DIRECTOR
Jeff Eamer
WRITER
Michael O'Reilly
AGENCY PRODUCER
Pat Lyons
PRODUCTION COMPANY
Partners/Canaz
DIRECTORS
Doug Moshian
Hall Train
CLIENT
Fisons Consumer Health
AGENCY
Franklin Dallas/Toronto

737
ART DIRECTORS
Nick Park
Paul Cardwell
WRITERS
Paul Cardwell
Nick Park
AGENCY PRODUCERS
Samantha Payne
Debbie Turner
PRODUCTION COMPANY
Aardman Animations
DIRECTOR
Nick Park
CLIENT
Electricity Association Selse &
Consortium
AGENCY
GGK/London

738
ART DIRECTOR
David Page
WRITER
Dave O'Hare
AGENCY PRODUCER
Debbie King
PRODUCTION COMPANY
Johnson-Burnett Productions
DIRECTOR
Jeffrey Goodby
CLIENT
National Basketball
Association
AGENCY
Goodby Berlin & Silverstein/
San Francisco

735
SPOKESMAN: So, you've come home from work. What sounds better . . . the same old pizza? Or salad and lasagna from Bringer's? First, the pizza . . .
(SFX: AWFUL SOUNDS FROM TURNTABLE)
SPOKESMAN : A real meal from Bringer's has got to sound better.
SUPER: BRINGERS. 941-FOOD.
ANNCR: Bringer's. Real food delivered real fast.

736
(SFX: MAN COUGHS)
(SFX: MAN COUGHS)
SUPER: WANT A LONGER LASTING COUGH MEDICATION?
(SFX: MAN COUGHS)
SUPER: LASTS FOR 12 FULL HOURS.

737

MR. & MRS. PENGUIN: Ooh electric hob? Yes they are easy to clean, they just wipe over.
BABY PENGUIN 1: Dishwater.
MRS. PENGUIN: And it looks like new.
MR. PENGUIN: It looks good and err . . .
BABY PENGUIN 1: It's not like some of these other things, you know, that are just there to, you know, ooo! This looks pretty in my kitchen, you know, it's there to do its job, and . . .
BABY PENGUIN 2: It does it.
BABY PENGUIN 1: It does it.
MRS. PENGUIN: And it does it well.
MR. PENGUIN: And it does it efficiently.
MRS. PENGUIN: And it does it well. That's right.
MR. PENGUIN: Isn't that right Andrew?
BABY PENGUIN: Yes, Dad.
SUPER: COOK ELECTRIC.
ANNCR: For all your creature comforts. Cook Electric.

738

(MUSIC: WISTFUL PIANO THROUGHOUT)
SUPER: DOWN BY ONE.
SUPER: THREE SECONDS LEFT ON THE CLOCK.
SUPER: THE NBA.
ANNCR: I love this game.

739
ART DIRECTOR
David Page
WRITER
Dave O'Hare
AGENCY PRODUCER
Debbie King
PRODUCTION COMPANY
Johnson-Burnett Productions
DIRECTOR
Jeffrey Goodby
CLIENT
*National Basketball
Association*
AGENCY
*Goodby Berlin & Silverstein/
San Francisco*

740
ART DIRECTOR
Tracy Wong
WRITER
Steve Simpson
AGENCY PRODUCER
Betsy Flynn
PRODUCTION COMPANY
In-House
DIRECTORS
Tracy Wong
Steve Simpson
CLIENT
Chevys Mexican Restaurants
AGENCY
*Goodby Berlin & Silverstein/
San Francisco*

741
ART DIRECTOR
Tracy Wong
WRITER
Steve Simpson
AGENCY PRODUCER
Betsy Flynn
PRODUCTION COMPANY
In-House
DIRECTORS
Tracy Wong
Steve Simpson
CLIENT
Chevys Mexican Restaurants
AGENCY
*Goodby Berlin & Silverstein/
San Francisco*

742
ART DIRECTOR
Tracy Wong
WRITER
Steve Simpson
AGENCY PRODUCER
Betsy Flynn
PRODUCTION COMPANY
In-House
DIRECTORS
Tracy Wong
Steve Simpson
CLIENT
Chevys Mexican Restaurants
AGENCY
*Goodby Berlin & Silverstein/
San Francisco*

739
(MUSIC: FRENETIC ROCK 'N ROLL THROUGHOUT)
GUY IN LAUNDROMAT: I love this game!
LOCKER ROOM GUY: I really love this game.
SUPER: THE NBA.

740
(MUSIC: THROUGHOUT)
SUPER: THIS COMMERCIAL WAS MADE TODAY.
ANNCR: Yeah, we made this commercial today.
BOB 1: September 16.
TWO GUYS: Monday, September 16.
SUPER: FRESH TV.
ANNCR: We call this "Fresh TV."
SUPER: FRESH MEX
ANNCR: At Chevys we make our tortillas from scratch
   every day. And serve them up, still hot, within three
   minutes. We call this "Fresh Mex." Other
   restaurants don't do this.
STEVE: Okay, now which tortilla would you rather eat?
BOB 2: That one, right there.
ANNCR: So what are their tortillas good for?
BOB 1: Pull!
BOB 2: Pull!
ANNCR: Chevys. Fresh Mex.

741

(MUSIC: THROUGHOUT)

STEVE: Free lie detector test! One day only! Can you tell me today's date?

MAN: June 20.

ANNCR: This commercial was made today.

SUPER: FRESH TV.

ANNCR: We call this "Fresh TV."

SUPER: FRESH MEX.

ANNCR: At Chevys, our guacamole is made fresh every day. We call this "Fresh Mex." At Chevys, we make everything fresh every day. Hey, would we lie?

STEVE: Have you ever cheated at golf?

PRIEST: Yes, I have.

ANNCR: Chevys Fresh Mex.

STEVE: Do you usually cheat at golf?

PRIEST: No. Rarely.

742

(MUSIC: THROUGHOUT)

SUPER: THIS COMMERCIAL WAS MADE TODAY.

STEVE: Good morning!

ANNCR: To prove this commercial was made today, we'll resort to any method.

MAN: Are you joking? It's Wednesday.

SIGN: TRANSIT APPRECIATION DAY MAY 15.

MAN: May 15.

WOMAN: 1991.

MAN: It's payday.

SUPER: FRESH TV.

ANNCR: We call this "Fresh TV."

SUPER: FRESH MEX.

ANNCR: To prove Chevys guacamole was made today, we'll give you the pit from the avocado it was made from. We call this "Fresh Mex." At Chevys, we make everything fresh every day. Chevys. Fresh Mex. Proof . . . you want proof?

STEVE: Did you know the queen is coming?

MAN: Yeah, she's here. She's going to the baseball game!

ANNCR: Chevys. Fresh Mex.

STEVE: Hey, come back! You missed a spot.

743
ART DIRECTOR
Tracy Wong
WRITER
Steve Simpson
AGENCY PRODUCER
Ben Latimer
PRODUCTION COMPANY
In-House
DIRECTORS
Tracy Wong
Steve Simpson
CLIENT
Chevys Mexican Restaurants
AGENCY
Goodby Berlin & Silverstein/
San Francisco

744
ART DIRECTOR
Tracy Wong
WRITER
Steve Simpson
AGENCY PRODUCER
Betsy Flynn
PRODUCTION COMPANY
In-House
DIRECTORS
Tracy Wong
Steve Simpson
CLIENT
Chevys Mexican Restaurants
AGENCY
Goodby Berlin & Silverstein/
San Francisco

745
ART DIRECTOR
Tracy Wong
WRITER
Steve Simpson
AGENCY PRODUCER
Betsy Flynn
PRODUCTION COMPANY
In-House
DIRECTORS
Tracy Wong
Steve Simpson
CLIENT
Chevys Mexican Restaurants
AGENCY
Goodby Berlin & Silverstein/
San Francisco

746
ART DIRECTOR
Tracy Wong
WRITER
Steve Simpson
AGENCY PRODUCER
Betsy Flynn
PRODUCTION COMPANY
In-House
DIRECTORS
Tracy Wong
Steve Simpson
CLIENT
Chevys Mexican Restaurants
AGENCY
Goodby Berlin & Silverstein/
San Francisco

743
(MUSIC: THROUGHOUT)
SUPER: THIS COMMERCIAL WAS MADE TODAY.
ANNCR: Cowabunga! This commercial was made today.
PHONE: Hi! This is the surf report for June 27, 1991. High tide today . . .
SUPER: FRESH TV.
ANNCR: We call this "Totally Fresh TV."
SUPER: FRESH MEX.
ANNCR: Every day at Chevys, we serve up two or three fresh fish of the day. We call this "Totally Fresh Mex." At Chevys, we we make everything fresh every day. So come on in. But remember . . . no shirt, no shoes, no service.
SUPER: CHEVYS FRESH MEX.
ANNCR: Chevys. Totally Fresh Mex.
STEVE: Don't be alarmed . . . the shark is just curious.

744
(MUSIC: THROUGHOUT)
ANNCR: At Chevys, all of our servers undergo rigorous physical training. They have to. Because at Chevys they'll rush our fresh tortilla chips to your table, while they're still hot, within seconds. And with every basket of chips, they'll bring salsa that's made fresh every hour.
SUPER: FRESH MEX.
ANNCR: We call this "Fresh Mex." Like all good athletes, they make this look easy. Yeah. You try it sometime.
ANNCR: Chevys Fresh Mex.

745

(MUSIC: THROUGHOUT)

SUPER: THIS COMMERCIAL WAS MADE TODAY.

STEVE: Can you tell me today's date?

MAID: Today's May 14, 1991.

SUPER: FRESH TV.

ANNCR: We made this commercial from scratch this morning. We call this "Fresh TV."

SUPER: FRESH MEX.

ANNCR: At Chevys we made our tamales from scratch this morning. We call this "Fresh Mex." At Chevys we make everything fresh every day. So you won't see these tamales tomorrow. Or this commercial. What a shame, huh?

ANNCR: Chevys. Fresh Mex.

STEVE: Where'd you get those tricycles?

746

(MUSIC: THROUGHOUT)

SUPER: THIS COMMERCIAL WAS MADE TODAY.

STEVE: Hey, you guys! What's the fish today?

ANNCR: Every day, Chevys features a fresh commercial of the day.

RADIO: Thursday, May 23. Over.

SUPER: FRESH TV.

ANNCR: We call this "Fresh TV."

STEVE: Hey, where's our fish?

SUPER: FRESH MEX.

ANNCR: Every day, Chevys features a fresh fish of the day . . . or two, or three. We call this "Fresh Mex." But at 6 AM, our fish was still on the boat.

STEVE: Do I have to do this myself?

ANNCR: Which means it'll be a lot fresher than this commercial.

TRACY: You're nuts, man!

ANNCR: Chevys. Fresh Mex.

CONSUMER TELEVISION
:30/ :25 SINGLE

747
ART DIRECTOR
Rich Silverstein
WRITER
Jeffrey Goodby
AGENCY PRODUCER
Ben Latimer
PRODUCTION COMPANY
Debra Bassett Productions
DIRECTORS
Rich Silverstein
Jeffrey Goodby
CLIENT
Heinz Pet Products/
Skippy Premium Dog Food
AGENCY
Goodby Berlin & Silverstein/
San Francisco

748
ART DIRECTOR
Noam Murro
WRITER
Dean Hacohen
PRODUCTION COMPANY
HKM
DIRECTOR
Danny Boyle
CLIENT
Crain's New York Business
AGENCY
Goldsmith/Jeffrey, New York

749
ART DIRECTOR
Noam Murro
WRITER
Dean Hacohen
PRODUCTION COMPANY
HKM
DIRECTOR
Henry Sandbank
CLIENT
Crain's New York Business
AGENCY
Goldsmith/Jeffrey, New York

750
ART DIRECTOR
Christopher Dean
WRITER
Rocky Botts
AGENCY PRODUCER
Gary Streiner
PRODUCTION COMPANY
RSA/USA
DIRECTOR
Jake Scott
CLIENT
Saturn Corporation
AGENCY
Hal Riney & Partners/
San Francisco

748

747

INTERVIEWER: Your honor, may I approach the
bench, please?
Fellas, I know you're in the middle of a big
tournament and everything, but I just wanted
to cast your attention to the screen up there.
Which one of these leading dog foods looks the best
to you? We need a ruling almost immediately
if we can.
JUDGE: I prefer the chunky myself.
STUDENT: I think the squashed one.
BOWLER 1: That one.
INTERVIEWER: You picked the Skippy Premium. It just
plain looks better, doesn't it?
SUPER: IT JUST PLAIN LOOKS BETTER.
CLASS: It just plain looks better.
INTERVIEWER: In bowling terms, what would you call the
Skippy, there?
BOWLER 1: That's a strike. Definitely a strike.
BOWLER 2: A strike.
INTERVIEWER: A strike, huh?

748
(SFX: SNORING THROUGHOUT)
ANNCR: What you don't know won't hurt you.
Ignorance is bliss. The less you know, the better.
And you expect to survive in New York?
SUPER: NEW YORK'S ONLY BUSINESS NEWSPAPER.

Stegosaurus

Tyrannosaurus

749
(SFX: SLIDE PROJECTOR CHANGING SLIDES)
ANNCR: They lacked the necessities for survival . . . in a changing environment.
Just a reminder . . . to New York executives.
SUPER: NEW YORK'S ONLY BUSINESS NEWSPAPER.

750
(MUSIC: THROUGHOUT)
ANNCR: When it comes to meeting women, New York City resident Wendal Wilson has at least one thing going for him.
SUPER: THE SATURN COUPE.

751
ART DIRECTOR
Amy Nicholson
WRITERS
Glen Porter
Jeff Watzman
AGENCY PRODUCER
Amy Saunders
PRODUCTION COMPANY
Crossroads Films
DIRECTOR
Mark Pellington
CLIENT
Multimedia Entertainment
AGENCY
Kirshenbaum & Bond/
New York

752
ART DIRECTOR
Kevin Donovan
WRITERS
Todd Godwin
Marian Godwin
AGENCY PRODUCER
Camie Taylor
PRODUCTION COMPANY
Crossroads Films
DIRECTOR
Steve Eichelman
CLIENT
Luis Gomez
AGENCY
LHS & Used to B/New York

753
ART DIRECTOR
Mark Erwin
WRITER
Harold Einstein
AGENCY PRODUCERS
Ben Grylewicz
Shelley Predovich
PRODUCTION COMPANY
Industrial Light & Magic
DIRECTOR
Steve Beck
CLIENT
Acura Division of
American Honda
AGENCY
Ketchum Advertising/
Los Angeles

754
ART DIRECTORS
Cathi Mooney
Michael Barti
WRITERS
Michael Barti
Cathi Mooney
AGENCY PRODUCER
Tammy Smith-White
PRODUCTION COMPANY
Jon Francis Films
DIRECTOR
Jon Francis
CLIENT
Seagram Classics Wine
Company
AGENCY
Mandelbaum Mooney Ashley/
San Francisco

751
MAN: Men undress me with their eyes. I wax my long beautiful legs to make sure that they're smooth and silky. I look real nice in a bikini. Construction workers whistle at me all the time. The camera loves me.
SUPER: THINGS A FASHION MODEL WOULD SAY.
ANNCR: The $100,000 pyramid. Get a clue.

752
WOMAN: Now Skippy, be good while I'm gone.
(SFX: DOOR CLOSES)
(MUSIC: THROUGHOUT)
(SFX: APARTMENT BEING DESTROYED)
ANNCR: Just a reminder, 90 percent of all accidents occur in the home.
SUPER: LUIS GOMEZ. MASTER DOG TRAINER. 212-866-7836.

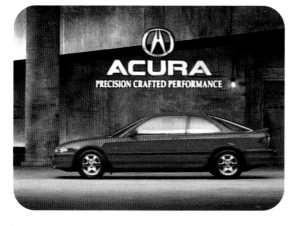

753

ANNCR: It has a dual overhead camshaft design . . . four valves per cylinder . . . and a responsive double-wishbone suspension. The Acura Integra. An idea that began with a Formula One race car . . . and has been evolving ever since.

ANNCR: Acura. Precision-crafted performance.

754

(MUSIC: FRENCH)

ANNCR: Recently, a strange thing happened in California's Napa Valley: the French moved in.

(MUSIC: FRENCH ARRANGEMENT OF SURFING MUSIC)

ANNCR: And among other things, they created a sparkling wine. One that combines the grapes of California's Napa Valley with the tradition of France's Champagne Mumm. Some California customs, however, remain.

FRENCHMAN: Have a nice day.

SUPER: MADE IN NAPA VALLEY IN THE FRENCH TRADITION.

ANNCR: Mumm Cuvee Napa.

755
ART DIRECTOR
Danny Boone
WRITER
Joe Alexander
AGENCY PRODUCER
Pam Campagnoli
PRODUCTION COMPANY
BES
CLIENT
The Richmond Symphony
AGENCY
*The Martin Agency/
Richmond*

756
ART DIRECTOR
Dean Noble
WRITER
David Wecal
AGENCY PRODUCER
Robyn Boardman
PRODUCTION COMPANY
Zuma Films
DIRECTOR
Doug Taub
CLIENT
Volvo Cars of North America
AGENCY
*Messner Vetere Berger Carey
Schmetterer/New York*

757
ART DIRECTORS
*Jim Scalfone
Barry Vetere*
WRITERS
*Evan Stark
Ron Berger*
AGENCY PRODUCER
Cristina Delouise
PRODUCTION COMPANY
Danza Productions
DIRECTOR
John Danza, Jr.
CLIENT
Volvo Cars of North America
AGENCY
*Messner Vetere Berger Carey
Schmetterer/New York*

758
ART DIRECTOR
John Danza
WRITER
Paul Wolfe
AGENCY PRODUCER
Sherry Bloom
PRODUCTION COMPANY
Danza Productions
DIRECTOR
John Danza, Jr.
CLIENT
MCI Telecommunications
AGENCY
*Messner Vetere Berger Carey
Schmetterer/New York*

755
(MUSIC: BRAHM'S "SYMPHONY NO. 1" THROUGHOUT)
ANNCR: Ludwig.
ANNCR: Giuseppe.
ANNCR: Frederic.
ANNCR: Giacomo.
ANNCR: Wolfgang.
ANNCR: Gomer.
ANNCR: Johann.
ANNCR: Franz.
ANNCR: Gomer?
SUPER: JIM NABORS, JANUARY 25.
SUPER: THE SYMPHONY ALL-STAR POPS.
    CALL 788-1212.

756
ANNCR: In many ways, it looks and feels like nothing
    we have ever built.
ANNCR: In many ways, it looks and feels like everything
    we've ever built.
SUPER: VOLVO. DRIVE SAFELY.

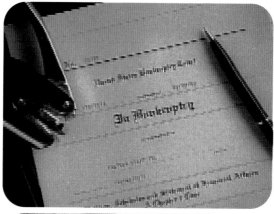

757

CHILD 1: My daddy loves me so much, he bought me a baseball glove.

CHILD 2: My daddy loves me so much, he bought me a baseball glove and a video game.

CHILD 3: My daddy loves me so much, he bought me a baseball glove and three video games.

LITTLE GIRL: My daddy loves me so much, he bought a Volvo.

SUPER: VOLVO. DRIVE SAFELY.

758

ANNCR: After the fire we declared bankruptcy. When we tried to start up again we called AT&T. They said, "Your company track record makes it impossible for us to do business at this time." So we called MCI. They said, "No problem, we'll work out a payment schedule you can handle." Now we're rolling again. Guess who calls? AT&T. I told them, "Your company track record makes it impossible for us to do business at this time."

SUPER: MCI. CALL 1-800-695-0505.

759
ART DIRECTOR
Simon Bowden
WRITER
Paul Wolfe
AGENCY PRODUCER
Felycia Sugarman
PRODUCTION COMPANY
Danza Productions
DIRECTOR
John Danza, Jr.
CLIENT
Nasdaq Stock Exchange
AGENCY
*Messner Vetere Berger Carey
Schmetterer/New York*

760
ART DIRECTOR
Tom McConnaughy
WRITERS
*Jim Schmidt
Robin Hawkins*
AGENCY PRODUCER
Carey Zeiser
CLIENT
*Illinois Institute of
Technology*
AGENCY
*McConnaughy Stein Schmidt
Brown/Chicago*

761
ART DIRECTOR
Guy Tom
WRITER
Tom Gabriel
AGENCY PRODUCER
Dianne Brown
PRODUCTION COMPANY
Johns & Gorman Films
DIRECTOR
Gary Johns
CLIENT
Aloha Airlines
AGENCY
*Milici Valenti Gabriel DDB
Needham/Honolulu*

762
ART DIRECTOR
Clive Yaxley
WRITER
Jerry Gallaher
AGENCY PRODUCER
Marshall Goodhew
PRODUCTION COMPANY
Annex Films
DIRECTOR
Ian Giles
CLIENT
Nestle
AGENCY
Ogilvy & Mather/London

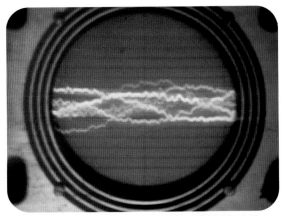

759
ANNCR: There will soon be a stock market that opens for business in the middle of the night. Who on earth would want to trade at this hour? Most of the earth, actually.

760
ANNCR: At this very moment, you're relying on two inventions from Illinois Institute of Technology. The vacuum tube responsible for TV's and radios, and recording tape for cassettes and video. Without these, rock and roll wouldn't be so big.
SUPER: MTV WOULDN'T EXIST.
SUPER: AND YOU'D BE DOING YOUR HOMEWORK RIGHT NOW.
SUPER: ILLINOIS INSTITUTE OF TECHNOLOGY. 312-567-3025.

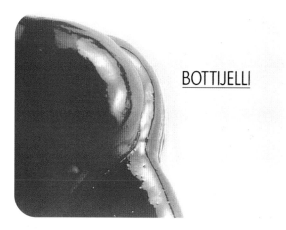

BOTTIJELLI

TOM AND JELLY

**IF IT'S NOT ROWNTREE'S JELLY
THROW A WOBBLY.**

761

ANNCR: Flight 18 is now arriving.
(SIGN: ON TIME)
ANNCR: Flight 52 to Kona will be delayed . . .
(SFX: FLIPPING SIGNS)
ANNCR: 52.
(SIGN: AGAIN?)
(SIGN: DELAYED)
ANNCR: Attention . . .
(SIGN: GATE CHANGE)
ANNCR: We have a gate change for Flight 52 . . .
(SIGN: WHAT?!)
ANNCR: 52.
(SIGN: DELAYED)
(SIGN: CANCELLED)
ANNCR: Update on Flight 52. Flight 52 has
   been cancelled.
(SIGN: NO WAY!)
(SIGN: AW. C'MON!)
(SIGN: I DON'T BELIEVE IT!)
(SIGN: GIVE ME A BREAK!)
(SIGN: *!?!#)
ANNCR: Next time, fly Aloha. The airline you haven't
   been waiting for.
SUPER: ALOHA AIRLINES.

762

SUPER: DAVID JELLAMY.
SUPER: DAVID JELLAMY'S JELLINGTONS.
SUPER: ROWNTREE'S.
SUPER: JELLY-FLOP.
SUPER: JUST AS JELLICIOUS IN POTS.
SUPER: BOTTIJELLI.
SUPER: ROWNTREE'S.
SUPER: TOM AND JELLY.
SUPER: TOM.
ANNCR: If it's not Rowntree's Jelly, throw a wobbly.

763
ART DIRECTOR
Nancy Miller Vonk
WRITER
Janet Kestin
AGENCY PRODUCER
Linda Gillies
PRODUCTION COMPANY
Circle Productions
DIRECTOR
Stephen Yeates
CLIENT
Lever Brothers
AGENCY
Ogilvy & Mather/Toronto

764
ART DIRECTOR
Anne Baylor
WRITER
Al Lowe
AGENCY PRODUCER
Will McDonald
PRODUCTION COMPANY
Red Dog Films
DIRECTOR
Marc Chiat
CLIENT
Blue Cross & Blue Shield of Rhode Island
AGENCY
Pagano Schenck & Kay/ Providence

765
ART DIRECTOR
Anne Baylor
WRITER
Al Lowe
AGENCY PRODUCER
Will McDonald
PRODUCTION COMPANY
Red Dog Films
DIRECTOR
Marc Chiat
CLIENT
Blue Cross & Blue Shield of Rhode Island
AGENCY
Pagano Schenck & Kay/ Providence

766
ART DIRECTOR
Keith Weinman
WRITER
Jack Fund
AGENCY PRODUCER
Gary Paticoff
PRODUCTION COMPANY
Dick James, Inc.
DIRECTOR
Dick James
CLIENT
American Honda Motor Company
AGENCY
Rubin Postaer and Associates/Santa Monica

763
(MUSIC: INSTRUMENTAL THROUGHOUT)
SUPER: LITMUS PAPER MEASURES ALKALINITY.
SUPER: THE DARKER, THE HARSHER.
SUPER: IVORY™.
SUPER: PALMOLIVE™.
SUPER: CUTICURA®.
SUPER: NEUTROGENA®.
SUPER: DOVE®.
SUPER: DOVE IS MILDEST.
SUPER: BAR NONE.

764
MAN: So there I am, on the operating table . . . and the anesthesiologist comes in and tells me to count backwards . . . you know . . . 100 . . . 99 . . . 98 . . . 97 . . .
ANNCR: There's nothing more boring than hearing about someone's operation. But at least with Healthmate, you won't have to hear how much it costs.
MAN: I wake up. I've got all these stiches. Lookit . . . 1 . . . 2 . . .
ANNCR: Healthmate. From Blue Cross and Blue Shield.

765

UNCLE ED: Yeah, yeah, just got back from my doctor . . . bet you can't guess what my cholesterol is . . .

YOUNG MAN: Bet I can't.

UNCLE ED: 184, Uh huh, uh huh.

YOUNG MAN: Good cholesterol, Uncle Ed.

UNCLE ED: And my blood pressure? 104 over 75.

YOUNG MAN: That's great.

ANNCR: At least with Healthmate from Blue Cross, there's one number you'll never have to hear about . . . the cost of a trip to the doctor's office.

UNCLE ED: I bet you can't guess how many sit-ups I do every morning.

YOUNG MAN: Ten.

UNCLE ED: Ten?! Look at me!

YOUNG MAN: Eleven?

UNCLE ED: Eleven?!

ANNCR: Healthmate. From Blue Cross and Blue Shield of Rhode Island.

766

(MUSIC: THROUGHOUT)

ANNCR: Instead of trying to give your car a personality, maybe you should try a car that already comes with one. The Civic Si from Honda.

SUPER: HONDA. THE CIVIC SI.

CONSUMER TELEVISION
:30/ :25 SINGLE

767
ART DIRECTOR
Jon Iles
WRITER
Paul Fishlock
AGENCY PRODUCER
Alison Moss
PRODUCTION COMPANY
The Film House
DIRECTOR
Derek Hughes
CLIENT
DHL International
AGENCY
Saatchi & Saatchi/Sydney

768
ART DIRECTOR
John Boone
WRITER
Ron Huey
AGENCY PRODUCER
Chris Anthony
PRODUCTION COMPANY
Lovinger Grasso Cohn & Associates
DIRECTOR
Michael Grasso
CLIENT
Lexus
AGENCY
Team One Advertising/ El Segundo

769
ART DIRECTOR
Lisa Gargano
WRITER
Betsy Hamilton
AGENCY PRODUCER
Francesca Cohn
PRODUCTION COMPANY
Johns + Gorman Films
DIRECTOR
Jeff Gorman
CLIENT
Lexus
AGENCY
Team One Advertising/ El Segundo

770
ART DIRECTOR
Murray Partridge
WRITER
Murray Partridge
AGENCY PRODUCER
Rachel Perry
PRODUCTION COMPANY
Spots Films
DIRECTOR
Theo Delaney
CLIENT
Jiffi Condoms
AGENCY
TBWA/Holmes Knight Ritchie, London

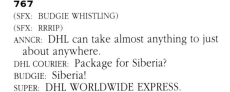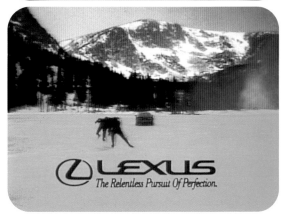

767
(SFX: BUDGIE WHISTLING)
(SFX: RRRIP)
ANNCR: DHL can take almost anything to just about anywhere.
DHL COURIER: Package for Siberia?
BUDGIE: Siberia!
SUPER: DHL WORLDWIDE EXPRESS.

768
(SFX: MYSTERIOUS AMBIENCE THROUGHOUT)
(SFX: TIRES SPINNING)
(SFX: ENGINE REVVING)
ANNCR: The traction control system of the Lexus LS 400 . . . helps reduce tire spin. Across rain, sleet, snow . . . or even an occasional patch of ice.
SUPER: LEXUS. THE RELENTLESS PURSUIT OF PERFECTION.

769

(SFX: NATURAL DESERT SOUNDS, WIND)
(MUSIC: SLOW, MUFFLED INDIAN DRUM BEAT COMING FROM CAR)
ANNCR: Just how realistic is the audio system in
 the Lexus LS 400?
SUPER: LEXUS. THE RELENTLESS PURSUIT
 OF PERFECTION.

770

(SFX: HOME MOVIE PROJECTOR)
SUPER: MR. AND MRS. MUSSOLINI, PARENTS OF
 BENITO MUSSOLINI.
SUPER: MR. AND MRS. AMIN, PARENTS OF IDI AMIN.
SUPER: MR. AND MRS. HITLER, PARENTS OF
 ADOLF HITLER.
SUPER: IF ONLY THEY'D USED A JIFFI CONDOM.

771
ART DIRECTORS
Rob Lawton
Ben Vergati
WRITERS
Ben Vergati
Poppy Sundeen
PHOTOGRAPHER
Phillip Thomas
AGENCY PRODUCER
Ben Vergati
PRODUCTION COMPANY
Bednarz Film
DIRECTOR
Jeff Bednarz
CLIENT
McCuistion Medical Center
AGENCY
Vergati Stevenson/Dallas

772
ART DIRECTOR
Michael Prieve
WRITER
Evelyn Monroe
AGENCY PRODUCER
Bill Davenport
PRODUCTION COMPANY
The A&R Group
DIRECTOR
Tarsem
CLIENT
Anne Klein
AGENCY
Wieden & Kennedy/Portland

773
ART DIRECTOR
Michael Prieve
WRITER
Evelyn Monroe
AGENCY PRODUCER
Bill Davenport
PRODUCTION COMPANY
The A&R Group
DIRECTOR
Tarsem
CLIENT
Anne Klein
AGENCY
Wieden & Kennedy/Portland

774
ART DIRECTOR
Michael Prieve
WRITER
Jim Riswold
AGENCY PRODUCER
Derek Ruddy
PRODUCTION COMPANY
Propaganda Films
DIRECTOR
Michael Bay
CLIENT
Nike
AGENCY
Wieden & Kennedy/Portland

771
ANNCR: There's only one thing worse than discovering a breast tumor on March 23: discovering it on June 23. Or some time in the fall. Next spring or summer. Or in a couple of years. The $50 mammogram screening. For more information, call the Women's Pavilion at McCuistion Regional Medical Center, (903) 737-1234.
SUPER: McCUISTION MEDICAL CENTER.
SUPER: (903) 737-1234.

EARLIER THIS EVENING, SALLY WAS WEARING AN IVORY AND BLACK

SHE WAS ALSO WEARING SILVER EARRINGS

MADE OF CAGE LOVE HEARTS.

772
(MUSIC: THROUGHOUT)
ANNCR: Earlier this evening, Sally was wearing an ivory & black buffalo check jacket over a black bodysuit. A black miniskirt. She was also wearing silver earrings. Made of caged love hearts.
ANNCR: A Line.
ANNCR: Anne Klein.

AND BLACK
RUBBERIZED
LEGGINGS
UNDER HER
WEDDING
DRESS.

SHE ALSO
HID A
LONG
BLACK
LEATHER
MOTORCYCLE
JACKET

IN THE
CHOIR
ROOM.

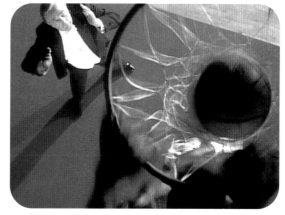

773

(MUSIC: THROUGHOUT)

ANNCR: Uncertain about her future, Pam wore a velour scoop-neck top. And black rubberized leggings under her wedding dress. She also hid a long black leather motorcycle jacket . . . in the choir room.

ANNCR: A Line.

ANNCR: Anne Klein.

774

ROBINSON: Today, we have a special visitor.

SUPER: FIRKUSNY.

ROBINSON: It's Rudolf Firkusny! He's going to play classical piano with Mr. Robinson.

(MUSIC: CLASSICAL)

ROBINSON: Geez! Mister Firkusny's a better piano player than Mr. Robinson, but Mr. Robinson can really cream him at basketball!

(MUSIC: HIP HOP)

ROBINSON: Foul!

ROBINSON: Yes!

SUPER: NIKE.

775
ART DIRECTOR
Michael Prieve
WRITER
Jim Riswold
AGENCY PRODUCER
Derek Ruddy
PRODUCTION COMPANY
Propaganda Films
DIRECTOR
Michael Bay
CLIENT
Nike
AGENCY
Wieden & Kennedy/Portland

776
ART DIRECTOR
David Kennedy
WRITER
Jim Riswold
AGENCY PRODUCERS
Elinor Shanklin
Susan Ashmore
PRODUCTION COMPANY
Colossal Pictures
DIRECTOR
Mike Smith
CLIENT
Nike
AGENCY
Wieden & Kennedy/Portland

777
ART DIRECTORS
Vince Engel
Bob Pullum
WRITER
Jerry Cronin
AGENCY PRODUCER
Ruth Richardson
PRODUCTION COMPANY
Modern Video
CLIENT
Subaru of America
AGENCY
Wieden & Kennedy/Portland

778
ART DIRECTOR
Rick McQuiston
WRITER
Bob Moore
AGENCY PRODUCER
Derek Ruddy
PRODUCTION COMPANY
Pytka Productions
DIRECTOR
Joe Pytka
CLIENT
Pacific First Bank
AGENCY
Wieden & Kennedy/Portland

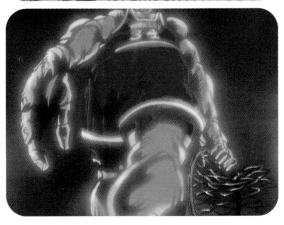

775
(MUSIC: CUTS IN AND OUT)
SUPER: MISTER ROBINSON'S NEIGHBORHOOD.
ROBINSON: It's Gary Payton. He's a good player . . .
SUPER: ROOKIE.
ROBINSON: But he's a rookie . . . and most rookies
aren't very smart. Gary, tell us what a rookie does?
PAYTON: A rookie waits on the veterans hand and foot.
He shines their shoes. He buys them lunch. He
carries their bags. He washes their cars.
ROBINSON : For a rookie . . . Gary's pretty smart.
You missed a spot.
SUPER: NIKE.

776
(MUSIC: THROUGHOUT)
BARKLEY: Pardon me, I'm sorry, excuse me.
SUPER: JUST DO IT. NIKE AIR.

777

(SFX: WIND AND BREATHING)
ANNCR: At ninety miles an hour . . .
  It's tough to ask for help.
SUPER: PLEASE SUPPORT THE U.S. SKI TEAM.
SUPER: 1-800-USA-4-SKI.
SUPER: SUBARU. THE OFFICIAL CAR OF THE U.S.
  SKI TEAM.

778

TEACHER: I remind you to use only a number
  two pencil . . .
SUPER: UNIVERSITY OF WASHINGTON $23,900.
TEACHER: And mark only in the space provided . . .
SUPER: OREGON STATE $37,100.
TEACHER: If you should decide to change a response . . .
SUPER: UNIVERSITY OF PUGET SOUND $62,800.
TEACHER: Erase the incorrect response thoroughly . . .
SUPER: YALE $90,100.
TEACHER: Stray marks may be counted as answers . . .
SUPER: GOOD LUCK.
TEACHER: You have 30 minutes for section one.
SUPER: PACIFIC FIRST BANK. WE FUND REALITY.

Consumer Television
:30/ :25 Single

779
ART DIRECTOR
Rick McQuiston
WRITER
Bob Moore
AGENCY PRODUCER
Derek Ruddy
PRODUCTION COMPANY
Pytka Productions
DIRECTOR
Joe Pytka
CLIENT
Pacific First Bank
AGENCY
Wieden & Kennedy/Portland

780
ART DIRECTOR
Rick McQuiston
WRITER
Bob Moore
AGENCY PRODUCER
Derek Ruddy
PRODUCTION COMPANY
Pytka Productions
DIRECTOR
Joe Pytka
CLIENT
Pacific First Bank
AGENCY
Wieden & Kennedy/Portland

781
ART DIRECTOR
Martin Schaus
WRITER
Tom O'Conner
AGENCY PRODUCER
Gary O'Riley
PRODUCTION COMPANY
August Productions
DIRECTOR
Larry August
CLIENT
Pic 'N Pay
AGENCY
*W.B. Doner & Company/
Southfield*

782
ART DIRECTORS
*John D'Asto
Tom Shortlidge*
WRITERS
*Peter McHugh
Mike Faems*
AGENCY PRODUCER
Peter McHugh
CLIENT
Adidas
AGENCY
Young & Rubicam/Chicago

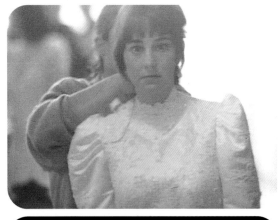

779
WOMAN: Now honey that's darling really, but trust me,
not the open back, it'll get all drafty.
SUPER: DRESS $960.
WOMAN: Try, uh, something a little more traditional.
Uh, that's so much better. Uh, you know, I've been
working on the guest list. I think we're going to
need a bigger chruch.
SUPER: CHURCH $590.
WOMAN: Oh, and by the way honey, you can leave the
dance music to me.
SUPER: RECEPTION $14,750.
WOMAN: I know this little string quartet, they're perfect.
Oh, I hope I don't fall completely apart
at the ceremony.
SUPER: ELOPING TO HAWAII $3,800.
WOMAN: Uh . . . it's going to be so beautiful.
SUPER: PACIFIC FIRST BANK. WE FUND REALITY.

780
(MUSIC: THROUGHOUT)
(SFX: VOICES THROUGHOUT)
SUPER: EAR PLUGS $1.90.
SUPER: SOMINEX $3.75.
SUPER: SHOTGUN $550.
SUPER: NEW HOUSE, NEW NEIGHBORS $144,800.
SUPER: SLEEP ON IT.
SUPER: PACIFIC FIRST BANK. WE FUND REALITY.

The essentials never change.

adidas
EQUIPMENT

781

ANNCR: Between now and September 3, Pic 'n Pay will give you $5 off any new pair of Reeboks when you trade in any old pair of athletic shoes. So bring those old sneakers into Pic 'n Pay. We'll take it from there. Get $5 off Reeboks when you bring in your old sneakers at Pic 'n Pay.
SUPER: PIC 'N PAY.

782

BOBBY KNIGHT: I do an interesting thing on the first day. I ask the kids, "How many of you had a coach you didn't like?" And every kid raises his hand. They want me to know that they don't like every coach and they don't buy every coach. And I say to them, "The first thing you gotta understand is that we don't like all you little bastards either." The expressions are great.
SUPER: THE ESSENTIALS NEVER CHANGE.
SUPER: ADIDAS EQUIPMENT.

Last year, drunk drivers cost Aetna policyholders more than $200 million.

So we've given 1102 video cameras to police departments.

Aetna.
A policy to do more.

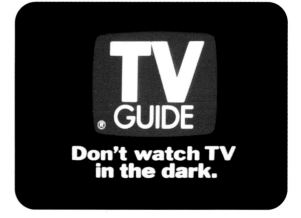

TV GUIDE
Don't watch TV in the dark.

783
(SFX: COP ARRESTING A DRUNK DRIVER)
COP: Sir, I want you to stand right here for me, okay? Go on, get your hands out of your pockets. Go ahead stand and face me. Put your heels and toes together. All the way together. All the way together. See my pen in front of your eyes? I want you to follow my pen with your eyes. Okay, turn around sir, go ahead turn around. Put your hands behind your back. You're under arrest for DWI, sir. Okay, we're going to have to go downtown for a saliva test, okay?

784
HOSTESS: To the novice, pleated pants can present a particularly pressing problem. But ladies, before you throw your hands up in despair, let's try this simple technique. Place the top of the iron at the top corner of the pleat closest to the zipper, like so. Then, pressing firmly but gently, stroke downwards . . . and hipping and hopping . . . never smushing open . . .
ANNCR: Were you watching something like this when Sam and Rebecca did it on Cheers?
SUPER: TV GUIDE. DON'T WATCH TV IN THE DARK.

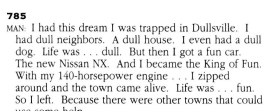

785

MAN: I had this dream I was trapped in Dullsville. I had dull neighbors. A dull house. I even had a dull dog. Life was . . . dull. But then I got a fun car. The new Nissan NX. And I became the King of Fun. With my 140-horsepower engine . . . I zipped around and the town came alive. Life was . . . fun. So I left. Because there were other towns that could use some help.
SUPER: AVAILABLE IN SELECTED MARKETS.
SUPER: NISSAN. THE NEW NX.

786

TEACHER: Number one?
KID: Uh, true?
TEACHER: False. Number two?
KID: Uh, false?
TEACHER: True. Number three?
KID: True?
TEACHER: False. Number four?
KID: 1492?
TEACHER: 1776.
ANNCR: Need a little luck? Come to Little Caesars and get Lucky Sevens. Two medium pizzas with seven toppings for only $7.77.
LITTLE CAESAR: Pizza! Pizza!

787
(MUSIC: THROUGHOUT)
SCROLL AT BOTTOM OF SCREEN: ATTENTION ALL GUYS. THIS IS A COMMERCIAL FOR BUGLE BOY'S NEW COLOR DENIMS. AT LEAST THAT'S WHAT WE TOLD BUGLE BOY. THEY WANTED TO SHOW A BUNCH OF MALE MODELS. WE SAID SHOWING NOTHING BUT BEAUTIFUL WOMEN WOULD WORK BETTER. SO IF THIS IS THE SORT OF THING YOU WANT TO SEE MORE OF, BUY SOME COLOR DENIMS. OTHERWISE BUGLE BOY WILL FORCE US TO PUT MEN IN THE COMMERCIALS. LIKE THIS. NONE OF US WANT THAT. DO WE?

788
(MUSIC: THROUGHOUT)
BUTLER: Admiral and Lady Billingsly, of Devonshire.
Lord and Lady Atherton of Sussex.
Sir Alfred and Lady Sheffield of Dunnsmar.
And Bob of Buffalo.
ANNCR: New York Lotto. Hey, you never know.

789
DENNIS: Hey, Kenny?
KEN: Yeah Dennis?
DENNIS: Listen I, I don't wanna whine but shouldn't this mark be over there just a little bit.
KEN: Uh, if you think so.
DENNIS: Uh, I really do think so . . . Gussy, big favor my man, can you slide that back around four inches?
GUS: Eh, no problem.
DENNIS: You are the grooviest!
KEN: Good call, Dennis.
DENNIS: Just trying to do my part boys. Thank you. Bye-bye.
KEN: Hey Gus? Just leave it.
SUPER: THE DENNIS MILLER SHOW. PREMIERING JANUARY 20.

790
(SFX: GAME ANNOUNCER, CROWD CHEERING)
(SFX: BABY CRYING)
(SFX: GAME ANNOUNCER, CROWD CHEERING)
(SFX: BABY CRYING)
(SFX: GAME ANNOUNCER, CROWD CHEERING)
(SFX: BABY CRYING)
(SFX: GAME ANNOUNCER, CROWD CHEERING)
(SFX: BABY CRYING)
TV ANNOUNCER: The game is over! You saw it here folks.
(SFX: MAN CRYING)
ANNOUNCER: The Star Tribune. The newspaper of the Twin Cities.

791
ART DIRECTOR
Mark Lees
WRITERS
Scott Brunsdon
Mark Lees
AGENCY PRODUCER
Nick Thomson
PRODUCTION COMPANY
Great Southern Films
DIRECTOR
Peter Schmidt
CLIENT
TNT Couriers
AGENCY
Foote Cone & Belding/Sydney

792
ART DIRECTOR
Scotti Larson
WRITER
Gene Payne
George Brumis
AGENCY PRODUCER
Royce Graham
PRODUCTION COMPANY
Video Wisconsin
DIRECTORS
Scotti Larson
Gene Payne
George Brumis
CLIENT
*Milwaukee World Festival/
Summerfest*
AGENCY
*Frankenberry Laughlin &
Constable/Milwaukee*

793
ART DIRECTOR
David Page
WRITER
Dave O'Hare
AGENCY PRODUCER
Debbie King
PRODUCTION COMPANY
Johnson-Burnett Productions
DIRECTOR
Jeffrey Goodby
CLIENT
*National Basketball
Association*
AGENCY
*Goodby Berlin & Silverstein/
San Francisco*

794
ART DIRECTOR
Rich Silverstein
WRITER
Jeffrey Goodby
AGENCY PRODUCER
Ben Latimer
PRODUCTION COMPANY
Debra Bassett Productions
DIRECTORS
Rich Silverstein
Jeffrey Goodby
CLIENT
*Heinz Pet Products/
Skippy Premium Dog Food*
AGENCY
*Goodby Berlin & Silverstein/
San Francisco*

791
RECEPTIONIST: Third floor, next building.
GUARD: Down the corridor.
COURIER: We're not going to make this. Wait a minute.
  You right?
CAMERAMAN: Yep.
ANNCR: TNT Air Couriers. More planes, no excuses.
COURIER: Mark . . .
OPERATOR: Hi.
COURIER: Got him.

792
(MUSIC: BEBOP)
ANNCR: There are over 2,000 acts scheduled to perform
  this year at Summerfest. This is not one of them.
(SFX: RESOUNDING DOOR SLAM)
(MUSIC: SUMMERFEST TRADEMARK)
SUPER: SUMMERFEST. THE GREATEST GIG ON THE
  GLOBE. MILWAUKEE'S LAKEFRONT,
  JUNE 27-JULY 7.

793

(MUSIC: JAZZ THROUGHOUT)
HERO: Ha! I love this game!
SUPER: THE NBA.

794

INTERVIEWER: I've got something that I believe to be pretty valuable. It's been in the family now for almost . . . a week. Just very quickly: Which one of these two leading dog foods looks more valuable to you?
APPRAISER: Very difficult to say without conducting some research.
INTERVIEWER: Is that right?
CHEF: This one.
WOMAN 1: That one.
INTERVIEWER: You think that one looks the best?
WOMAN 2: Definitely this one.
INTERVIEWER: You picked the Skippy Premium. It just plain looks better, doesn't it.
ASSISTANT: Sure, even on a fax.
INTERVIEWER: I wonder if something like this would increase in value over the years.
APPRAISER: I don't think it would particularly help the value in this case, probably rather the reverse.

795
(MUSIC: DIXIELAND JAZZ)
ANNCR: Feeling good about the people who sold him
his Saturn, Cut Bank, Montana rancher Jim Bishop
throws a barbecue.
SUPER: THE $7,995 SATURN SL.

796
ANNCR: Whenever a Volvo is in an accident in Sweden,
after the police get called, so does Hans Noreen,
head of Volvo's accident investigation team. People
whose findings helped Volvo develop the collapsible
steering wheel . . . front and rear energy absorbing
impact zones . . . and today, a side impact protection
system years ahead of government requirements.
Volvo will continue to analyze accidents as long as
we can find ways to help people survive them.
SUPER: VOLVO. DRIVE SAFELY.

797

WOMAN: Lately, I have been to the doctor nearly every other day. First, it was this neck problem. Then, I felt sort of . . . oh, queasy.

ANNCR: Even people who complain about their health can't complain about Healthmate. The plan that gives you the peace of mind you can only get with Blue Cross protection.

WOMAN: Then, there was this thing with my foot . . . let me get my shoe off . . .

ANNCR: Healthmate. From Blue Cross and Blue Shield.

798

(MUSIC: CUTS IN AND OUT)

SUPER: MISTER ROBINSON'S NEIGHBORHOOD.

ROBINSON (WHISPERS): Who could that be?

ROBINSON: It's Charles Barkley with today's word.

SUPER: FINED.

BARKLEY: Today's word is fined.

ROBINSON: Tell the boys and girls how you get fined, Charles.

BARKLEY: You can get fined for a lot of things. Like yelling, arguing, and bad-mouthing an official. But most of all . . . for fighting!

ROBINSON: Have you ever been fined, Charles?

BARKLEY: Never, ever. . . . No, no, no, no, no . . . No, no, no, no, no, no, no . . .

ROBINSON: Charles is a great player but he has a lousy memory.

SUPER: NIKE.

BARKELY: Never, ever. And that's my problem.

799
BOBBY KNIGHT: There's a lot of focus right now on
doing away with scholarships in basketball. Almost
600 kids are not going to, in the next four years,
have an opportunity to play basketball. I simply
look around for another way.
(SFX: HORN)
BOBBY: It's easy . . . we just simply charge the news
media people for attending games.
SUPER: THE ESSENTIALS NEVER CHANGE.
SUPER: ADIDAS EQUIPMENT.

800
(MUSIC: "ALFRED HITCHCOCK PRESENTS" THEME)
(SFX: BOOM, BOOM, BOOM . . .)
ENERGIZER ANNCR: Still going. Nothing outlasts the
Energizer. They keep going and going and going . . .

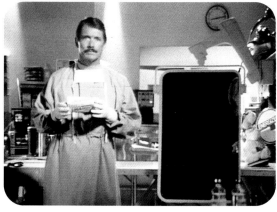

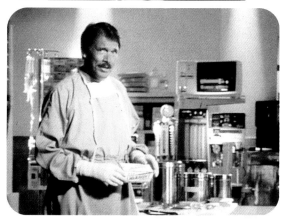

801

NURSE: Thank you, Doctor.

DOCTOR: I'm not a real doctor, but if I were, I'd recommend Ligamint for occasional muscle pain.

(SFX: BOOM, BOOM, BOOM . . .)

ENERGIZER ANNCR: Still going. Nothing outlasts the Energizer. They keep going and going and going . . .

802

(SFX: DOOR OPENING AND CLOSING)

ANNCR: Too many pesticides in your dog's food? There are no pesticides in new Nature's Course.

803
ART DIRECTOR
Dean Hanson
WRITER
Phil Hanft
AGENCY PRODUCER
Char Loving
PRODUCTION COMPANY
Coppos Films
DIRECTOR
Mark Coppos
CLIENT
*Ralston Purina/
Nature's Course*
AGENCY
*Fallon McElligott/
Minneapolis*

804
ART DIRECTOR
Bob Barrie
WRITER
Mike Gibbs
AGENCY PRODUCER
Becky Fischer
PRODUCTION COMPANY
Sandbank & Partners
DIRECTOR
Henry Sandbank
CLIENT
Continental Bank
AGENCY
*Fallon McElligott/
Minneapolis*

805
ART DIRECTORS
*Tom Gianfagna
Rob Carducci*
WRITERS
*Rob Carducci
Tom Gianfagna*
AGENCY PRODUCER
Teri Altman
DIRECTOR
Mark Story
CLIENT
Daffy's
AGENCY
Follis DeVito Verdi/New York

806
ART DIRECTORS
*Leslie Sweet
Dave Berger
Amy Borkowsky*
WRITERS
*Amy Borkowsky
Dave Berger
Leslie Sweet*
AGENCY PRODUCER
Robyn Boardman
DIRECTOR
Jim Perretti
CLIENT
South Street Seaport
AGENCY
Follis DeVito Verdi/New York

803
ANNCR: Too many artificial colors in your dog's food?
There are no artificial colors in new Nature's Course.

804
ANNCR: At Continental Bank, we try to get to you with
solutions before you realize you need them.
(SFX: THUNK)
SUPER: CONTINENTAL BANK. ANTICIPATING THE
NEEDS OF BUSINESS.

805

ANNCR: If you're paying $100 or more for a dress shirt . . . May we suggest a jacket to go with it?
SUPER: DESIGNER SHIRTS 40-70% OFF, EVERY DAY.
ANNCR: Daffy's. Clothes that will make you, not break you.

806

(SFX: LOCKS UNLOCKING)
ANNCR: Considering what New Yorkers have to go through just to leave their apartments, it's amazing that over 100,000 of them made it down here last weekend. The South Street Seaport. Where New Yorkers go to get away from New York.

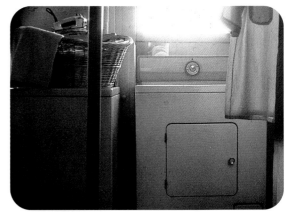

807
(MUSIC: THROUGHOUT)
SUPER: A REAL FLOWER.
SUPER: A FLOWER FRESH AIR FRESHENER.
(SFX: BUZZING)
SUPER: A STUPID BEE.
ANNCR: Flower Fresh. The air freshener that doesn't
   look like an air freshener.

808
(SFX: BANGING)
ANNCR: The idea of washable and dryable leather Keds
   sounds great. Except, of course, when they're in
   the dryer.
ANNCR: Keds. They feel good.

809

(MUSIC: THROUGHOUT)

ANNCR: In this car, you'll find a sophisticated handling
system that corners sharply and turns on a dime.

ANNCR: Introducing the Easy Turn Tracking System
from American Tourister.

SUPER: LUGGAGE THAT COOPERATES.

**CONSUMER TELEVISION
:20 AND UNDER SINGLE**

810
ART DIRECTOR
Charles Inge
WRITER
Simon Carbery
AGENCY PRODUCER
Charles Crisp
PRODUCTION COMPANY
Rose Hackney Productions
DIRECTOR
Graham Rose
CLIENT
Whitbread & Company
AGENCY
Lowe Howard-Spink/London

**CONSUMER TELEVISION
:20 AND UNDER CAMPAIGN**

811
ART DIRECTOR
Carolyn Tye McGeorge
WRITER
Rob Schapiro
AGENCY PRODUCER
Betsy Barnum
PRODUCTION COMPANY
Big Fish Films
DIRECTOR
Robert Latorre
CLIENT
St. Mary's Hospital
AGENCY
*Earle Palmer Brown/
Richmond*

812
ART DIRECTORS
*Dave Berger
Leslie Sweet
Amy Borkowsky
Sal DeVito*
WRITERS
*Dave Berger
Leslie Sweet
Amy Borkowsky
Sal DeVito*
AGENCY PRODUCER
Robyn Boardman
DIRECTOR
Jim Perretti
CLIENT
South Street Seaport
AGENCY
Follis DeVito Verdi/New York

810
(SFX: SOUND OF TV STATIC)
(SFX: SOUND OF TV)
SUPER: ONLY HEINEKEN CAN DO THIS.

811
(SFX: RUNNING WATER)
ANNCR: You'd be surprised where some children have
drowned. Very surprised. When your child is near
water, stay near your child.

812

(SFX: JACKHAMMER)

ANNCR: You'll be happy to hear that most of our construction was completed in 1825.
The South Street Seaport. Where New Yorkers go to get away from New York.

813
ART DIRECTOR
Jamie Colonna
WRITER
James Betts
AGENCY PRODUCER
Suzi Baldwin
PRODUCTION COMPANY
Ian Single Film Company
DIRECTOR
Ian Single
CLIENT
Whitbread Beer Company
AGENCY
Bartle Bogle Hegarty/London

814
ART DIRECTOR
Gary Goldsmith
WRITER
Dean Hacohen
DIRECTORS
Henry Sandbank
Steve Hellerstein
CLIENT
*NYNEX Business to
Business Yellow Pages*
AGENCY
Goldsmith/Jeffrey, New York

815
ART DIRECTORS
Sam Hurford
Gaia Pollini
WRITERS
Sam Hurford
John Weston
AGENCY PRODUCER
Adam Saywood
PRODUCTION COMPANY
Turk Derek Productions
DIRECTORS
Mike Derek
Howard Turk
CLIENT
The Guardian
AGENCY
*TBWA/Holmes Knight
Ritchie, London*

It has come to our attention that the

With Boddlette. Without Boddlette.

NYNEX Business to Business Yellow Pages
can barely withstand a year of use.

We're working on it.

813
ANNCR: Every yo-yo has its limitations . . . but not the
new, two-speed electronic Bo-Bo. Don't be a do-do,
get a Bo-Bo.
ANNCR: This is the revolutionary Boddlette. Simply
place in your wash and see the difference it makes.
The Boddlette. It guarantees a wobble-free wash.
ANNCR: This is the new Boddibath. Simply place in the
water and it'll give you an instant bubble bath. The
Boddibath. The most relaxing way to end your day.
ANNCR: Contrary to anything else you might
have heard . . .
(SFX: TREE FALLING)
ANNCR: . . . this is Boddingtons' Draughtflow . . .
thingy. As you can see, its purpose in life is to make
Boddingtons' canned draught bitter smooth and
creamy just like you get down the Pub. Only
Boddingtons has this draughtflow thingy.
SUPER: BODDINGTONS. THE CREAM OF MANCHESTER.
ANNCR: So don't fall for anything else.

814
SUPER: IT HAS COME TO OUR ATTENTION . . .
SUPER: THAT THE NYNEX BUSINESS TO BUSINESS
YELLOW PAGES . . .
SUPER: CAN BARELY WITHSTAND A YEAR OF USE.
(SFX: LOUD METAL CLANK)
SUPER: WE'RE WORKING ON IT.
SUPER: NYNEX BUSINESS TO BUSINESS YELLOW
PAGES. ALWAYS AT WORK.

*The***Newspaper of** *The***Year.**

815

INTERVIEWER: What do you think of The Guardian?
MR. ANGRY: Absolutely, utterly, revolting.
INTERVIEWER: Really.
MR. ANGRY: Crap.
INTERVIEWER: Why do you find it's like that?
MR. ANGRY: It misleads the people. It tells lies.
INTERVIEWER: Do you think so?
MR. ANGRY: Sure so.
INTERVIEWER: Er . . . anything else about it? I think that's pretty definitive really, isn't it. Would you ever read it?
MR. ANGRY: No, I wouldn't read it. It's drivel. It deceives the people. It's crap. I wouldn't give it house room. I'll tell you what I'd do with it . . .
INTERVIEWER: Bin it? Throw it away?
MR. ANGRY: No, I'd wipe my arse with it.
SUPER: THE GUARDIAN. THE NEWSPAPER OF THE YEAR.

College Competition

816

817

"**What can I say? I sent my son there.**"

Harry Jacobs, Chairman
The Martin Agency

"His book needed a little more refinement. To me the school is a rarity. It really prepares kids for entry level positions. Many students go on to do great things."

PORTFOLIO CENTER
SCHOOL FOR ADVERTISING PHOTOGRAPHY DESIGN AND ILLUSTRATION
RECOMMENDED BY THE PEOPLE YOU WANT TO WORK FOR. CALL 1.800.255.3169

818

IT HAS THE INTELLIGENCE OF A *3-YEAR-OLD CHILD*, AND IS JUST AS *VULNERABLE*.

HOW TO WIN FRIENDS AND INFLUENCE PEOPLE.

Save the planet. Touch someone's heart with a beautiful photograph. Persuade a family to buy a pet. Learn how to do it at Portfolio Center. Our graduates are some of the most influential junior creatives in the business. Art directors, copywriters, graphic designers, photographers, and illustrators. Agencies and studios clamor to hire them. Who needs friends when your book looks like this.

PORTFOLIO CENTER
125 BENNETT STREET ATLANTA, GA 30309 TELEPHONE 404.351.5055 TOLL FREE 1.800.255.3169

819

What's wrong with this ad?

It's got an intriguing headline, which got you into the body copy. And if you look down at the logo, you'll see that this is an ad for the Portfolio Center.

The Portfolio Center is a school for Art Direction, Copywriting, Graphic Design, Photography, and Illustration. And if you're really interested in analyzing – and doing – killer creative work, this is the place to be.

To find out more, fill out the coupon below. Or call 1-800-255-3169.

Oh, and if you've gotten this far, there's nothing wrong with this ad.

Please send me a Portfolio Center catalog. I am interested in:
( ) Photography ( ) Art Direction ( ) Copywriting
( ) Illustration ( ) Graphic Design
Name
Address
City/State_____ Zip Code
Phone

PORTFOLIO CENTER
123 Bennett St. Atlanta, Georgia 30309

820

We'll Let You Graduate After You Finish Just One Book.

But it's got to be outstanding. Because your book is what will get you a job. Whether it's in Art Direction, Copywriting, Photography, Graphic Design or Illustration. And the better your book is, the better your job will be. At the Portfolio Center, you'll learn what it takes to produce killer creative work. And you'll do it. In classes taught by award-winning professionals in whatever field you choose. After eight quarters here, you'll find you've learned a lot. You'll find you've finished your book. And you'll find a terrific job.

Please send me a Portfolio Center catalog. I am interested in:
( ) Photography ( ) Art Direction ( ) Copywriting
( ) Illustration ( ) Graphic Design
Name
Address
City/State_____ Zip Code
Phone

PORTFOLIO CENTER
123 Bennett St. Atlanta, Georgia 30309

821

822

823

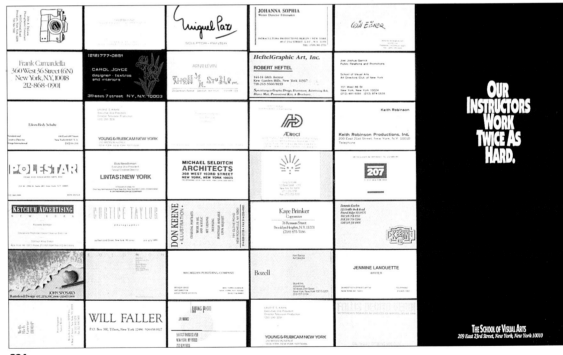

824

TO OTHER ART SCHOOLS,

THESE AWARD ANNUALS ARE TEXTBOOKS.

TO US, THEY'RE ALUMNI DIRECTORIES.

SCHOOL OF VISUAL ARTS

825

Marshall Arisman

Illustration Instructor
School of Visual Arts
Chair, MFA Program in Illustration,
School of Visual Arts

PUBLICATIONS:
Omni; The New York Times; Rolling Stone;
Nation; Time; Sports Illustrated;
Boston Globe; Playboy; Penthouse

AWARDS:
Society of Illustrators; Playboy Illustrator of the
Year; AIGA Political Advertisment Award;
Graphis; Print Casebook; Silver Medal, Society
of Illustrators; Gold Medal, Society of
Publication Designers

Sal DeVito

Advanced Advertising instructor
School of Visual Arts
Creative Director, Follis/DeVito/Verdi
Formerly, Creative Director, LHS&B
Vice President, Art Supervisor, Slater, Hanft,
Martin
Formerly, Wells, Rich, Greene, Inc.

AWARDS:
Gold Medal; The One Show

Milton Glaser

Graphic Design instructor
School of Visual Arts
President,Milton Glaser,Inc.; Co-Founder,
Push Pin Studios; Push Pin Graphic Magazine;
New York; Board Member, School of Visual
Arts, International Design Conference, Aspen,
Colorado; Member and former Vice-President,
AIGA

AWARDS:
Art Directors Club Hall of Fame; Fulbright
Scholarship; Honorary Fellow, Society of Arts,
England; Society of Illustrators Gold Medal

Work for them, before you graduate.

Develop working relationships with the top professionals in the field while you are still in school. There should be more to your education, than learning how to draw. Become
acquainted with the business as a whole. So when you graduate, you won't have to work toward becoming a professional. You'll be one.   **SCHOOL of VISUAL ARTS**

826

Convince your parents

this top-ranked university

costs $14,000 a year,

and you'll have $10,000 left

for spring break.

The University of Texas at Austin

Higher education without the higher bill.

827

Index

AGENCIES

AGENCY PRODUCERS

TYPOGRAPHERS

WRITERS